Mastering Blockchain

Distributed ledgers, decentralization and smart contracts explained

Imran Bashir

BIRMINGHAM - MUMBAI

Mastering Blockchain

First published: March 2017

Production reference: 1090317

Published by Packt Publishing Ltd.
Livery Place
35 Livery Street
Birmingham
B3 2PB, UK.
ISBN 978-1-78712-544-5

www.packtpub.com

Credits

Author

Imran Bashir

Reviewer

Daniel Kraft

Commissioning Editor

Veena Pagare

Acquisition Editor

Ajith Menon

Content Development Editors

Sumeet Sawant

Amrita Noronha

Technical Editor

Nilesh Sawakhande

Copy Editor

Laxmi Subramanian

Project Coordinator

Shweta H Birwatkar

Proofreader

Safis Editing

Indexer

Pratik Shirodkar

Graphics

Tania Dutta

Production Coordinator

Shraddha Falebhai

About the Author

Imran Bashir has a M.Sc. in Information Security from Royal Holloway, University of London, and has a background in software development, solution architecture, infrastructure management, and IT service management. He is also a member of **Institute of Electrical and Electronics Engineers (IEEE)** and **British Computer Society (BCS)**. Imran has sixteen years of experience in the public and financial sectors. He worked on large scale IT projects for public sector before moving to financial services industry. Since then he has worked in various technical roles for different financial companies in Europe's financial capital, London. He is currently working for an investment bank in London as Vice President in the technology department.

I would like to thank the talented team at Packt including Ajith Menon, Nilesh Sawakhande, Sumeet Sawant, and Tushar Gupta, who provided prompt guidance and very valuable feedback throughout this project. I am also extremely thankful to the reviewer, Daniel Kraft, who provided constructive and very useful feedback that helped tremendously to improve the material in this book.

I thank my wife and children for putting up with my all-night and weekend-long writing sessions.

Finally, I would like to thank my parents, whose blessings on me have made everything possible for me.

About the Reviewer

Daniel Kraft studied mathematics and physics, and holds a PhD in applied mathematics from the University of Graz in Austria. He has been involved in development with cryptocurrencies since 2013, has been the lead developer and chief scientist for both Namecoin and Huntercoin since 2014, and has published two research papers about cryptocurrency in peer-reviewed journals. He works as a software engineer and is a co-founder of Crypto Realities Ltd, a start-up that works on building decentralised multi-player game worlds with blockchain technology.

www.PacktPub.com

For support files and downloads related to your book, please visit www.PacktPub.com.

Did you know that Packt offers eBook versions of every book published, with PDF and ePub files available? You can upgrade to the eBook version at www.PacktPub.com and as a print book customer, you are entitled to a discount on the eBook copy. Get in touch with us at service@packtpub.com for more details.

At www.PacktPub.com, you can also read a collection of free technical articles, sign up for a range of free newsletters and receive exclusive discounts and offers on Packt books and eBooks.

https://www.packtpub.com/mapt

Get the most in-demand software skills with Mapt. Mapt gives you full access to all Packt books and video courses, as well as industry-leading tools to help you plan your personal development and advance your career.

Why subscribe?

- Fully searchable across every book published by Packt
- Copy and paste, print, and bookmark content
- On demand and accessible via a web browser

Customer Feedback

Thanks for purchasing this Packt book. At Packt, quality is at the heart of our editorial process. To help us improve, please leave us an honest review on this book's Amazon page at `http://www.amazon.in/dp/1787125440`.

If you'd like to join our team of regular reviewers, you can e-mail us at `customerreviews@packtpub.com`. We award our regular reviewers with free eBooks and videos in exchange for their valuable feedback. Help us be relentless in improving our products!

Table of Contents

Preface

This book has one goal: to provide a comprehensive introduction to the theoretical and practical aspects of blockchain technology. This book contains all the material that is required to fully understand blockchain technology. After reading this book, readers will be able to develop a deep understanding of inner workings of blockchain technology and will be able to develop blockchain applications. This book covers all topics relevant to blockchain technology, including cryptography, cryptocurrenices, Bitcoin, Ethereum, and various other platforms and tools used for blockchain development.

It is recommended that readers have a basic understanding of computer science and basic programming experience in order to benefit fully from this book. However, if that is not the case then still this book can be read easily, as relevant background material is provided where necessary.

What this book covers

Chapter 1, *Blockchain 101*, introduces the basic concepts of distributed computing on which blockchain technology is based. It also covers history, definitions, features, types, and benefits of blockchains along with consensus mechanisms that are at the core of blockchain technology.

Chapter 2, *Decentralization*, covers the concepts of decentralization and its relationship with blockchain technology. Various methods and platforms that can be used to decentralize a process or system have also been introduced.

Chapter 3, *Cryptography and Technical Foundations*, introduces the theoretical foundations cryptography, which is necessary to fully understand blockchain technology. Concepts such as public and private key cryptography, with practical examples, are included. Finally, an introduction to financial markets is also included as there are many interesting use cases for blockchain technology in the financial sector.

Chapter 4, *Bitcoin*, covers Bitcoin, the first and largest blockchain. It introduces technical concepts related to bitcoin cryptocurrency in detail.

Chapter 5, *Alternative Coins*, introduces alternative cryptocurrencies that were introduced after the invention of Bitcoin. It also presents examples of different altcoins, their properties, and how they have been developed and implemented.

Chapter 6, *Smart Contracts*, provides an in-depth discussion on smart contracts. Topics such as history, the definition of smart contracts, Ricardian contracts, Oracles, and the theoretical aspects of smart contracts are presented in this chapter.

Chapter 7, *Ethereum 101*, introduces the design and architecture of the Ethereum blockchain in detail. It covers various technical concepts related to the Ethereum blockchain that explains the underlying principles, features, and components of this platform in depth.

Chapter 8, *Ethereum Development*, provides a detailed practical introduction to development of decentralized applications and smart contracts using the Ethereum blockchain. An introduction to solidity and different relevant tools have also been included in this chapter.

Chapter 9, *Hyperledger*, presents a discussion about the hyperledger project from the Linux foundation, which includes different blockchain projects introduced by its members.

Chapter 10, *Alternative Blockchains*, introduces alternative blockchain solutions and platforms. It provides technical details and features of alternative blockchains.

Chapter 11, *Blockchain – Outside of Currencies*, provides a practical and detailed introduction to applications of blockchain technology in fields others than cryptocurrencies, including Internet of Things, government, media, and finance.

Chapter 12, *Scalability and Other Challenges*, is dedicated to a discussion of the challenges faced by blockchain technology and how to address them.

Chapter 13, *Current Landscape and What's Next*, is aimed at providing information about the current landscape, projects, and research efforts related to blockchain technology. Also, some predictions based on the current state of blockchain technology have also been made.

What you need for this book

All examples in this book have been developed on Ubuntu 16.04.1 LTS (Xenial). As such, it is recommended to use Ubuntu. However, any appropriate operating system, either Windows or Linux, can be used, but examples, especially those related to installation, may need to be changed accordingly.

Examples related to cryptography have been developed using the OpenSSL 1.0.2g 1 Mar 2016 command-line tool.

Ethereum solidity examples have been developed using Browser Solidity, available online at https://ethereum.github.io/browser-solidity/.

Ethereum's homestead release is used to develop Ethereum-related examples. At the time of writing, this is the latest version available and can be downloaded from `https://www.ethe` `reum.org/`.

Examples related to IoT have been developed using a Raspberry Pi kit by Vilros, but any latest model or kit can be used. Specifically, Raspberry Pi 3 Model B V 1.2 has been used to build a hardware example of IoT. Node.js V7.2.1 and npm V3.10.10 have been used to download related packages and run Node.js server for IoT examples.

The Truffle framework has been used in some examples of smart contract deployment, and is available at `http://truffleframework.com/`. Any latest version available via npm should be appropriate.

Who this book is for

This book is for anyone who wants to understand blockchain technology in depth. It can also be used as a reference by developers who are developing applications for blockchain. In addition, this book can also be used as a textbook for courses related to blockchain technology and cryptocurrencies. It can also be used as a learning resource for various examinations and certifications related to cryptocurrency and blockchain technology.

Conventions

In this book, you will find a number of text styles that distinguish between different kinds of information. Here are some examples of these styles and an explanation of their meaning.

Code words in text, database table names, folder names, filenames, file extensions, pathnames, dummy URLs, user input, and Twitter handles are shown as follows:

"This line of code simply uses console.log to print the coinbase by calling `web3.eth.coinbase` method."

A block of code is set as follows:

```
function difference(uint x) returns (uint y)
{
    z=x-5;
    y=z;
}
```

When we wish to draw your attention to a particular part of a code block, the relevant lines or items are set in bold:

```
function difference(uint x) returns (uint y)
{
    z=x-5;
    y=z;
}
```

Any command-line input or output is written as follows:

```
$ geth --datadir .ethereum/PrivateNet/ --networkid 786 --rpc --
rpccorsdomain 'http://192.168.0.17:9900'
```

New terms and **important words** are shown in bold. Words that you see on the screen, in menus or dialog boxes for example, appear in the text like this: "Clicking the **Next** button moves you to the next screen."

Warnings or important notes appear in a box like this.

Tips and tricks appear like this.

Reader feedback

Feedback from our readers is always welcome. Let us know what you think about this book-what you liked or disliked. Reader feedback is important for us as it helps us develop titles that you will really get the most out of. To send us general feedback, simply e-mail feedback@packtpub.com, and mention the book's title in the subject of your message. If there is a topic that you have expertise in and you are interested in either writing or contributing to a book, see our author guide at www.packtpub.com/authors.

Customer support

Now that you are the proud owner of a Packt book, we have a number of things to help you to get the most from your purchase.

Downloading the example code

You can download the example code files for this book from your account at `http://www.p acktpub.com`. If you purchased this book elsewhere, you can visit `http://www.packtpub.c om/support`and register to have the files e-mailed directly to you.

You can download the code files by following these steps:

1. Log in or register to our website using your e-mail address and password.
2. Hover the mouse pointer on the **SUPPORT** tab at the top.
3. Click on **Code Downloads & Errata**.
4. Enter the name of the book in the **Search** box.
5. Select the book for which you're looking to download the code files.
6. Choose from the drop-down menu where you purchased this book from.
7. Click on **Code Download**.

Once the file is downloaded, please make sure that you unzip or extract the folder using the latest version of:

- WinRAR / 7-Zip for Windows
- Zipeg / iZip / UnRarX for Mac
- 7-Zip / PeaZip for Linux

The code bundle for the book is also hosted on GitHub at `https://github.com/PacktPubl ishing/Mastering-Blockchain`. We also have other code bundles from our rich catalog of books and videos available at https://github.com/PacktPublishing/. Check them out!

Downloading the color images of this book

We also provide you with a PDF file that has color images of the screenshots/diagrams used in this book. The color images will help you better understand the changes in the output. You can download this file from `https://www.packtpub.com/sites/default/files/down loads/MasteringBlockchain_ColorImages.pdf`.

Errata

Although we have taken every care to ensure the accuracy of our content, mistakes do happen. If you find a mistake in one of our books-maybe a mistake in the text or the code-we would be grateful if you could report this to us. By doing so, you can save other readers from frustration and help us improve subsequent versions of this book. If you find any errata, please report them by visiting http://www.packtpub.com/submit-errata, selecting your book, clicking on the **Errata Submission Form** link, and entering the details of your errata. Once your errata are verified, your submission will be accepted and the errata will be uploaded to our website or added to any list of existing errata under the Errata section of that title.

To view the previously submitted errata, go to https://www.packtpub.com/books/content/support and enter the name of the book in the search field. The required information will appear under the **Errata** section.

Piracy

Piracy of copyrighted material on the Internet is an ongoing problem across all media. At Packt, we take the protection of our copyright and licenses very seriously. If you come across any illegal copies of our works in any form on the Internet, please provide us with the location address or website name immediately so that we can pursue a remedy.

Please contact us at copyright@packtpub.com with a link to the suspected pirated material.

We appreciate your help in protecting our authors and our ability to bring you valuable content.

Questions

If you have a problem with any aspect of this book, you can contact us at questions@packtpub.com, and we will do our best to address the problem.

1
Blockchain 101

It is very likely that anyone reading this book has already heard about blockchain and has some basic appreciation of its enormous potential.

With the invention of bitcoin in 2008 the world was introduced to a new concept that is now likely to revolutionize the whole of society. It's something that has promised to impact every industry including but not limited to finance, government, and media. Some describe it as a revolution whereas another school of thought says that it's going to be an evolution and it will take many years before any practical benefits from blockchain come to fruition. This is correct to some extent but in my opinion the revolution has already started; many big organizations all around the world are already writing proofs of concept using blockchain technology as its disruptive potential has now been fully recognized. However, some organizations are still at the preliminary exploration stage but are expected to progress more quickly as the technology is now becoming more mature. It is a technology that has an impact on current technologies too and possesses the ability to change them at a fundamental level.

According to Gartner's technology hype cycle graph shown below, the blockchain technology is currently at the *peak of inflated expectations* (as of July 2016) and is expected to be ready for mainstream adoption in 5 to 10 years:

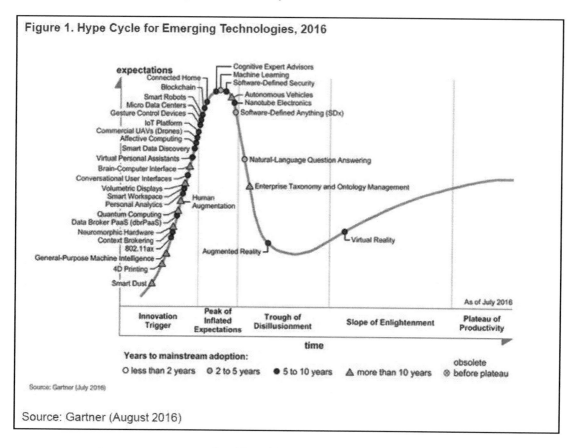

Gartner's hype cycle for emerging technologies

Interest in blockchain technology has soared in the last few years and, once disregarded by some as geek money from a cryptocurrency point of view or as something that was not really considered worthwhile, it is now being researched by the largest companies and organizations around the world with millions of dollars being spent in order to adopt and experiment with this technology. A simple trend search on Google reveals the scale of interest in the blockchain technology over the last few years:

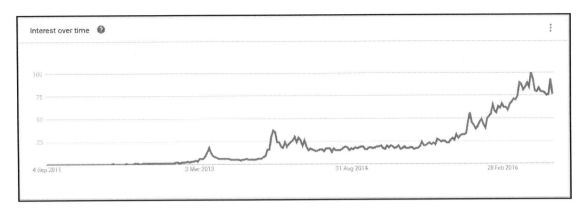

Google trends for blockchain

Various benefits of this technology are being envisaged such as decentralized trust, cost savings, transparency, and efficiency. However, there are various challenges too that are an area of active research such as scalability and privacy. Chapter 12, *Scalablity and Other Challenges* is dedicated to a discussion of the limitations and challenges of blockchain technology.

This chapter is an introduction to blockchain technology, its technical foundations, the theory behind it, and various technologies that have been combined together in order to build what is known today as blockchain.

In 2008 a groundbreaking paper *Bitcoin: A Peer-to-Peer Electronic Cash System* was written on the topic of peer-to-peer electronic cash under the pseudonym *Satoshi Nakamoto* and introduced the term *chain of blocks*. This term over the years has now evolved into the word blockchain.

In this chapter, first the theoretical foundations of distributed systems are described, then the precursors of bitcoin (with which blockchain technology was introduced) such as e-cash and hashcash, and then finally the blockchain technology is introduced. This is a logical way of understanding blockchain technology because the roots of blockchain are in distributed systems.

Distributed systems

Understanding distributed systems is essential in order to understand blockchain because basically blockchain at its core is a distributed system. More precisely it is a decentralized distributed system.

Distributed systems are a computing paradigm whereby two or more nodes work with each other in a coordinated fashion in order to achieve a common outcome and it's modeled in such a way that end users see it as a single logical platform.

A node can be defined as an individual player in a distributed system. All nodes are capable of sending and receiving messages to and from each other. Nodes can be honest, faulty, or malicious and have their own memory and processor. A node that can exhibit arbitrary behavior is also known as a Byzantine node. This arbitrary behavior can be intentionally malicious, which is detrimental to the operation of the network. Generally, any unexpected behavior of a node on the network can be categorized as Byzantine. This term arbitrarily encompasses any behavior that is unexpected or malicious:

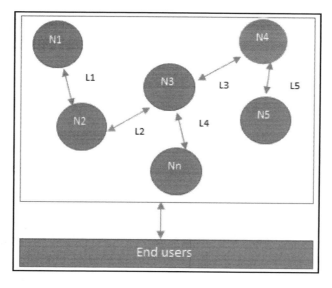

Design of a distributed system; N4 is a Byzantine node, L2 is broken or a slow network link

The main challenge in distributed system design is coordination between nodes and fault tolerance. Even if some of the nodes become faulty or network links break, the distributed system should tolerate this and should continue to work flawlessly in order to achieve the desired result. This has been an area of active research for many years and several algorithms and mechanisms has been proposed to overcome these issues.

Distributed systems are so challenging to design that a theorem known as the CAP theorem has been proved and states that a distributed system cannot have all much desired properties simultaneously. In the next section, a basic introduction to the CAP theorem will be provided.

CAP theorem

This is also known as Brewer's theorem, introduced originally by *Eric Brewer* as a conjecture in 1998; in 2002 it was proved as a theorem by *Seth Gilbert* and *Nancy Lynch*.

The theorem states that any distributed system cannot have Consistency, Availability, and Partition tolerance simultaneously:

- **Consistency** is a property that ensures that all nodes in a distributed system have a single latest copy of data
- **Availability** means that the system is up, accessible for use, and is accepting incoming requests and responding with data without any failures as and when required
- **Partition tolerance** ensures that if a group of nodes fails the distributed system still continues to operate correctly

It has been proven that a distributed system cannot have all the afore mentioned three properties at the same time. This is strange because somehow blockchain manages to achieve all these properties, or does it really? This will be explained later in the chapter where the CAP theorem in the context of blockchain is discussed.

In order to achieve fault tolerance, replication is used. This is a common and widely used method to achieve fault tolerance. Consistency is achieved using consensus algorithms to ensure that all nodes have the same copy of data. This is also called **state machine replication**. Blockchain is basically a method to achieve state machine replication.

In general there are two types of fault that a node can experience: where a faulty node has simply crashed and where the faulty node can exhibit malicious or inconsistent behavior arbitrarily. This is the type which is difficult to deal with since it can cause confusion due to misleading information.

Byzantine Generals problem

Before discussing consensus in distributed systems, events in history are presented that are precursors to the development of successful and practical consensus mechanisms.

In September 1962, *Paul Baran* introduced the idea of cryptographic signatures with his paper *On distributed communications networks*. This is the paper where the concept of decentralized networks was also introduced for the very first time. Then in 1982 a thought experiment was proposed by *Lamport et al.* whereby a group of army generals who are leading different parts of the Byzantine army are planning to attack or retreat from a city. The only way of communication between them is a messenger and they need to agree to attack at the same time in order to win. The issue is that one or more generals can be traitors and can communicate a misleading message. Therefore there is a need to find a viable mechanism that allows agreement between generals even in the presence of treacherous generals so that the attack can still take place at the same time. As an analogy with distributed systems, generals can be considered as nodes, traitors can be considered Byzantine (malicious) nodes, and the messenger can be thought of as a channel of communication between the generals.

This problem was solved in 1999 by *Castro* and *Liskov* who presented the **Practical Byzantine Fault Tolerance (PBFT)** algorithm. Later on in 2009, the first practical implementation was made with the invention of bitcoin where the **Proof of Work (PoW)** algorithm was developed as a mechanism to achieve consensus.

Consensus

Consensus is a process of agreement between distrusting nodes on a final state of data. In order to achieve consensus different algorithms can be used. It is easy to reach an agreement between two nodes (for example in client-server systems) but when multiple nodes are participating in a distributed system and they need to agree on a single value it becomes very difficult to achieve consensus. This concept of achieving consensus between multiple nodes is known as distributed consensus.

Consensus mechanisms

A consensus mechanism is a set of steps that are taken by all, or most, nodes in order to agree on a proposed state or value. For more than three decades this concept has been researched by computer scientists in the industry and Academia. Consensus mechanisms have recently come into the limelight and gained much popularity with the advent of bitcoin and blockchain.

There are various requirements which must be met in order to provide the desired results in a consensus mechanism. The following are their requirements with brief descriptions:

- **Agreement**: All honest nodes decide on the same value.
- **Termination**: All honest nodes terminate execution of the consensus process and eventually reach a decision.
- **Validity**: The value agreed upon by all honest nodes must be the same as the initial value proposed by at least one honest node.
- **Fault tolerant**: The consensus algorithm should be able to run in the presence of faulty or malicious nodes (Byzantine nodes).
- **Integrity**: This is a requirement where by no node makes the decision more than once. The nodes make decisions only once in a single consensus cycle.

Types of consensus mechanism

There are various types of consensus mechanism; some common types are described as follows:

- **Byzantine fault tolerance-based**: With no compute intensive operations such as partial hash inversion, this method relies on a simple scheme of nodes that are publishing signed messages. Eventually, when a certain number of messages are received, then an agreement is reached.
- **Leader-based consensus mechanisms**: This type of mechanism requires nodes to compete for the *leader-election lottery* and the node that wins it proposes a final value.

Many practical implementations have been proposed such as **Paxos**, the most famous protocol introduced by **Leslie Lamport** in 1989. In Paxos nodes are assigned various roles such as Proposer, Acceptor, and Learner. Nodes or processes are named replicas and consensus is achieved in the presence of faulty nodes by agreement among a majority of nodes.

Another alternative to Paxos is RAFT, which works by assigning any of three states, that is, Follower, Candidate, or Leader, to the nodes. A Leader is elected after a candidate node receives enough votes and all changes now have to go through the Leader, who commits the proposed changes once replication on the majority of follower nodes is completed.

More details about the theory of consensus mechanisms from a distributed system point of view is beyond the scope of this chapter. Later in this chapter, a full section is dedicated to the introduction of consensus protocols. Specific algorithms will be discussed in chapters dedicated to bitcoin and other blockchains later in this book.

The history of blockchain

Blockchain was introduced with the invention of bitcoin in 2008 and then with its practical implementation in 2009. For this chapter, it is sufficient to introduce bitcoin very briefly as there is a full chapter on bitcoin later on but it is also essential to refer to bitcoin because without it, the history of blockchain is not complete.

The concept of electronic cash or digital currency is not new. Since the 1980s, e-cash protocols have existed that are based on a model proposed by *David Chaum*.

Electronic cash

Just as understanding the concepts of distributed systems is necessary in order to understand blockchain technology, the idea of electronic cash is also essential to appreciate the first and astonishingly successful application of blockchain: the bitcoin, or broadly cryptocurrencies. Theoretical concepts in distributed systems such as consensus algorithms provided the basis of the practical implementation of Proof of Work algorithms in bitcoin; moreover, ideas from different electronic cash schemes also paved the way for the invention of cryptocurrencies, specifically bitcoin.

In this section, the reader will be introduced to the idea of electronic cash and then various other concepts that existed before cryptocurrencies that led to the development of bitcoin are presented.

The concept of electronic cash

Fundamental issues that need to be addressed in e-cash systems are accountability and anonymity. *David Chaum* addressed both of these issues in his seminal paper in 1984 by introducing two cryptographic operations, namely blind signatures and secret sharing. These terminologies and related concepts will be discussed in detail in Chapter 3, *Cryptography and Technical Foundations*. At the moment, it is sufficient to say that blind signatures allow signing a document without actually seeing it and secret sharing is a concept that allows the detection of using the same e-cash token twice (double spending).

After this other protocols emerged such as **Chaum, Fiat, and Naor** (CFN), e-cash schemes that introduced anonymity and double spending detection. Brand's e-cash is another system that improved on CFN, made it more efficient, and introduced the concept of security reduction to prove statements about the e-cash scheme. Security reduction is a technique used in cryptography to prove that a certain algorithm is secure by using another problem as a comparison. Put another way, a cryptographic security algorithm is as hard to break as some other hard problem; thus by comparison it can be deduced that the cryptographic security algorithm is secure too.

A different but relevant concept called **hashcash** was introduced by *Adam Back* in 1997 as a PoW system to control e-mail spam. The idea is quite simple: if legitimate users want to send e-mails then they are required to compute a hash as a proof that they have spent a reasonable amount of computing resources before sending the e-mail. Generating hashcash is a compute intensive process but does not inhibit a legitimate user from sending the e-mail because the usual number of e-mails required to be sent by a legitimate user is presumably quite low. On the other hand, if a spammer wants to send e-mails, usually thousands in number, then it becomes infeasible to compute hashcash for all e-mails, thus making the spamming effort expensive; as a result this mechanism can be used to thwart e-mail spamming. Hashcash takes a considerable amount of computing resources to compute but is easy and quick to verify. Verification is performed by the user who receives the e-mail. Hashcash is popularized by its use in the bitcoin mining process. This idea of using computational puzzles or pricing functions to prevent e-mail spam was introduced originally in 1992 by *Cynthia Dwork* and *Moni Naor*. Pricing function was the name given to the hard functions that are required to be computed before access to a resource can be granted. Later, *Adam Back* invented hashcash independently in 1997, which introduced the usage of computing hash functions as PoW.

In 1998 **b-money** was introduced by *Wei Dai* and proposed the idea of creating money via solving computational puzzles such as hashcash. It's based on a peer-to-peer network where each node maintains its own list of transactions.

Another similar idea by *Nick Szabo* called BitGold was introduced in 2005 and also proposed solving computational puzzles to mint digital currency. In 2005 *Hal Finney* introduced the concept of cryptographic currency by combining ideas from b-money and hashcash puzzles but it still relied on a centralized trusted authority.

There were multiple issues with the schemes described in infeasible preceding paragraphs. These problems range from no clear solution of disagreements between nodes to reliance on a central trusted third party and trusted timestamping.

In 2009 the first practical implementation of a cryptocurrency named bitcoin was introduced; for the very first time it solved the problem of distributed consensus in a trustless network. It uses public key cryptography with hashcash as PoW to provide a secure, controlled, and decentralized method of minting digital currency. The key innovation is the idea of an ordered list of blocks composed of transactions and cryptographically secured by the PoW mechanism. This will be explained in more detail in `Chapter 4`, *Bitcoin*.

Looking at all the aforementioned technologies and their history, it is easy to see how ideas and concepts from electronic cash schemes and distributed systems were combined together to invent bitcoin and what now is known as blockchain.

This can also be visualized with the help of the following diagram:

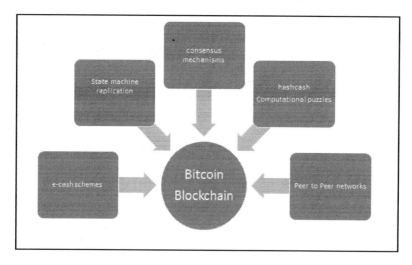

The various ideas that helped with the invention of bitcoin and blockchain

Introduction to blockchain

There are various definitions of blockchain; it depends on how you look at it. If you look at it from a business perspective it can be defined in that context, if you look at it from a technical perspective one can define it in view of that.

Blockchain at its core is a peer-to-peer distributed ledger that is cryptographically secure, append-only, immutable (extremely hard to change), and updateable only via consensus or agreement among peers.

Blockchain can be thought of as a layer of a distributed peer-to-peer network running on top of the Internet, as can be seen below in the diagram. It is analogous to SMTP, HTTP, or FTP running on top of TCP/IP. This is shown in the following diagram:

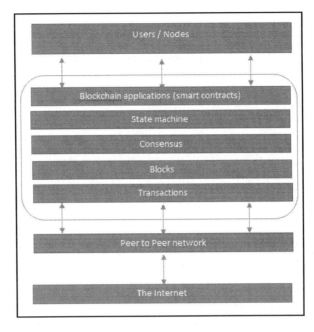

The network view of a blockchain

From a business point of view a blockchain can be defined as a platform whereby peers can exchange values using transactions without the need for a central trusted arbitrator. This is a powerful concept and once readers understand it they will realize the tsunamic potential of blockchain technology. This allows blockchain to be a decentralized consensus mechanism where no single authority is in charge of the database.

A block is simply a selection of transactions bundled together in order to organize them logically. It is made up of transactions and its size is variable depending on the type and design of the blockchain in use. A reference to a previous block is also included in the block unless it's a genesis block. A genesis block is the first block in the blockchain that was hardcoded at the time the blockchain was started. The structure of a block is also dependent on the type and design of a blockchain, but generally there are a few attributes that are essential to the functionality of a block, such as the block header, pointers to previous blocks, the time stamp, nonce, transaction counter, transactions, and other attributes.

This is shown in a simple block diagram as follows. This is a general depiction of a block; specific block structures relative to their blockchain technologies will be discussed later in the book with more in-depth technical details:

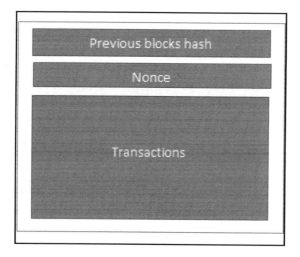

The structure of a block

Various technical definitions of blockchains

- Blockchain is a decentralized consensus mechanism. In a blockchain, all peers eventually come to an agreement regarding the state of a transaction.
- Blockchain is a distributed shared ledger. Blockchain can be considered a shared ledger of transactions. The transaction are ordered and grouped into blocks. Currently, the real-world model is based on private databases that each organization maintains whereas the distributed ledger can serve as a single source of truth for all member organizations that are using the blockchain.
- Blockchain is a data structure; it is basically a linked list that uses hash pointers instead of normal pointers. Hash pointers are used to point to the previous block.

The structure of a generic blockchain can be visualized with the help of the following diagram:

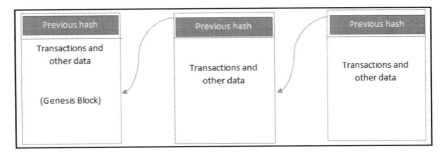

Generic structure of a blockchain

Generic elements of a blockchain

In this section, the generic elements of blockchain are presented. More precise elements will be discussed in the context of their respective blockchains in later chapters, for example, the Ethereum blockchain.

Addresses

Addresses are unique identifiers that are used in a transaction on the blockchain to denote senders and recipients. An address is usually a public key or derived from a public key. While addresses can be reused by the same user, addresses themselves are unique. In practice, however, a single user may not use the same address again and generate a new one for each transaction. This newly generated address will be unique. Bitcoin is in fact a pseudonymous system. End users are usually not directly identifiable but some research in de-anonymizing bitcoin users have shown that users can be identified successfully. As a good practice it is suggested that users generate a new address for each transaction in order to avoid linking transactions to the common owner, thus avoiding identification.

Transaction

A transaction is the fundamental unit of a blockchain. A transaction represents a transfer of value from one address to another.

Block

A block is composed of multiple transactions and some other elements such as the previous block hash (hash pointer), timestamp, and nonce.

Peer-to-peer network

As the name implies, this is a network topology whereby all peers can communicate with each other and send and receive messages.

Scripting or programming language

This element performs various operations on a transaction. Transaction scripts are predefined sets of commands for nodes to transfer tokens from one address to another and perform various other functions. Turing complete programming language is a desirable feature of blockchains; however, the security of such languages is a key question and an area of important and ongoing research.

Virtual machine

This is an extension of a transaction script. A virtual machine allows Turing complete code to be run on a blockchain (as smart contracts) whereas a transaction script can be limited in its operation. Virtual machines are not available on all blockchains; however, various blockchains use virtual machines to run programs, for example **Ethereum Virtual Machine (EVM)** and **Chain Virtual Machine (CVM)**.

State machine

A blockchain can be viewed as a state transition mechanism whereby a state is modified from its initial form to the next and eventually to a final form as a result of a transaction execution and validation process by nodes.

Nodes

A node in a blockchain network performs various functions depending on the role it takes. A node can propose and validate transactions and perform mining to facilitate consensus and secure the blockchain. This is done by following a consensus protocol. (Most commonly this is PoW.) Nodes can also perform other functions such as simple payment verification (lightweight nodes), validators, and many others functions depending on the type of the blockchain used and the role assigned to the node.

Smart contracts

These programs run on top of the blockchain and encapsulate the business logic to be executed when certain conditions are met. The smart contract feature is not available in all blockchains but is now becoming a very desirable feature due to the flexibility and power it provides to the blockchain applications.

Features of a blockchain

A blockchain performs various functions. These are described below in detail.

Distributed consensus

Distributed consensus is the major underpinning of a blockchain. This enables a blockchain to present a single version of truth that is agreed upon by all parties without the requirement of a central authority.

Transaction verification

Any transactions posted from nodes on the blockchain are verified based on a predetermined set of rules and only valid transactions are selected for inclusion in a block.

Platforms for smart contracts

A blockchain is a platform where programs can run that execute business logic on behalf of the users. As explained earlier, not all blockchains have a mechanism to execute smart contracts; however, this is now a very desirable feature.

Transferring value between peers

Blockchain enables the transfer of value between its users via tokens. Tokens can be thought of as a carrier of value.

Generating cryptocurrency

This is an optional feature depending on the type of blockchain used. A blockchain can generate cryptocurrency as an incentive to its miners who validate the transactions and spend resources in order to secure the blockchain.

Smart property

For the first time it is possible to link a digital or physical asset to the blockchain in an irrevocable manner, such that it cannot be claimed by anyone else; you are in full control of your asset and it cannot be double spent or double owned. Compare it with a digital music file, for example, which can be copied many times without any control; on a blockchain, however, if you own it no one else can claim it unless you decide to transfer it to someone. This feature has far-reaching implications especially in **Digital Rights Management (DRM)** and electronic cash systems where double spend detection is a key requirement. The double spend problem was first solved in bitcoin.

Provider of security

Blockchain is based on proven cryptographic technology that ensures the integrity and availability of data. Generally, confidentiality is not provided due to the requirements of transparency. This has become a main barrier for its adaptability by financial institutions and other industries that need privacy and confidentiality of transactions. As such it is being researched very actively and there is already some good progress made. It could be argued that in many situations confidentiality is not really needed and transparency is preferred instead. For example, in bitcoin confidentiality is not really required; however, it is desirable in some scenarios. Research in this area is very ripe and already major progress has been made towards providing confidentiality and privacy on blockchain. A more recent example is Zcash, which will be discussed in more detail in later chapters. Other security services such as nonrepudiation and authentication are also provided by blockchain as all actions are secured by using private keys and digital signatures.

Immutability

This is another key feature of blockchain: records once added onto the blockchain are immutable. There is the possibility of rolling back the changes but this is considered almost impossible to do as it will require an unaffordable amount of computing resources. For example, in much desirable case of bitcoin if a malicious user wants to alter the previous blocks then it would require computing the PoW again for all those blocks that have already been added to the blockchain. This difficulty makes the records on a blockchain practically immutable.

Uniqueness

This feature of blockchain ensures that every transaction is unique and has not been spent already. This is especially relevant in cryptocurrencies where much desirable detection and avoidance of double spending are a key requirement.

Smart contracts

Blockchain provides a platform to run smart contracts. These are automated autonomous programs that reside on the blockchain and encapsulate business logic and code in order to execute a required function when certain conditions are met. This is indeed a revolutionary feature of blockchain as it allows flexibility, programmability, and much desirable control of actions that users of blockchain need to perform according to their specific business requirements.

Applications of blockchain technology

Blockchain technology has a multitude of applications in various sectors including but not limited to finance, government, media, law, and arts. More light will be shed on these aspects in `Chapter 9`, *Hyperledger* where practical use cases will be discussed in detail for various industries. It is sufficient to say for now that almost all industries have already realized the potential and promise of blockchain and have already embarked, or soon will embark, on the journey to benefit from the blockchain technology.

In the following section, a general scheme of creating blocks is discussed. This is presented here to give readers a general idea of how blocks are generated and what the relationship is between transactions and blocks.

How blockchains accumulate blocks

1. A node starts a transaction by signing it with its private key.
2. The transaction is propagated (flooded) by using much desirable Gossip protocol to peers, which validates the transaction based on pre-set criteria. Usually, more than one node is required to validate the transactions.
3. Once the transaction is validated, it is included in a block, which is then propagated on to the network. At this point, the transaction is considered confirmed.
4. The newly created block now becomes part of the ledger and the next block links itself cryptographically back to this block. This link is a hash pointer. At this stage, the transaction gets its second confirmation and the block gets its first.
5. Transactions are then reconfirmed every time a new block is created. Usually, six confirmations in the bitcoin network are required to consider the transaction final.

Steps 4 and 5 can be considered non-compulsory as the transaction itself is finalized in step 3; however, block confirmation and further transaction reconfirmations, if required, are then carried out in steps 4 and 5.

Tiers of blockchain technology

In this section, various tiers of blockchain technology are discussed. It is envisaged that, due to the rapid development and progress made in blockchain technology, many applications will evolve over time. Some have already been realized while some can be envisioned for the future based on the current rate of advancement in the blockchain technology.

First, the three levels discussed below were originally described by *Melanie Swan* in her book *Blockchain, Blueprint for a New Economy* as tiers of blockchain categorized on the basis of applications in each category. In addition to this, Tier X or Generation X is discussed later. This is what the author thinks will become a reality when the blockchain technology becomes advanced enough.

Blockchain 1.0

This was introduced with the invention of bitcoin and is basically used for cryptocurrencies. Also, as bitcoin was the first implementation of cryptocurrencies it makes sense to categorize Generation 1 of blockchain technology to only include cryptographic currencies. All alternative coins and bitcoin fall into this category. This includes core applications such as payments and applications.

Blockchain 2.0

Generation 2.0 blockchains are used by financial services and contracts are introduced in this generation. This includes various financial assets, for example derivatives, options, swaps, and bonds. Applications that are beyond currency, finance, and markets are included at this tier.

Blockchain 3.0

Generation 3 blockchains are used to implement applications beyond the financial services industry and are used in more general-purpose industries such as government, health, media, the arts, and justice.

Generation X (Blockchain X)

This is a vision of blockchain singularity where one day we will have a public blockchain service available that anyone can use just like the Google search engine. It will provide services in all realms of society. This is a public open distributed ledger with general-purpose rational agents (Machina Economicus) running on blockchain, making decisions and interacting with other intelligent autonomous agents on behalf of humans and regulated by code instead of law or paper contracts. This will be elaborated in detail in Chapter 13, *Current Landscape and What's Next*.

Types of blockchain

Based on the way blockchain has evolved over the last few years, it can be divided into multiple types with distinct but sometimes partly overlapping attributes.

Public blockchains

As the name suggests, these blockchains are open to the public and anyone can participate as a node in the decision-making process. Users may or may not be rewarded for their participation. These ledgers are not owned by anyone and are publicly open for anyone to participate in. All users of the permission-less ledger maintain a copy of the ledger on their local nodes and use a distributed consensus mechanism in order to reach a decision about the eventual state of the ledger. These blockchains are also known as permission-less ledgers.

Private blockchains

Private blockchains as the name implies are private and are open only to a consortium or group of individuals or organizations that has decided to share the ledger among themselves.

Semi-private blockchains

Here part of the blockchain is private and part of it is public. The private part is controlled by a group of individuals whereas the public part is open for participation by anyone.

Sidechains

More precisely known as pegged sidechains, this is a concept whereby coins can be moved from one blockchain to another and moved back. Common uses include the creation of new altcoins (alternative cryptocurrencies) whereby coins are *burnt* as a proof of adequate stake. There are two types of sidechain. The example provided above for *burning* coins is applicable to a one-way pegged sidechain. The second type is called a two-way pegged sidechain, which allows the movement of coins from the main chain to the sidechain and back to the main chain when required.

Permissioned ledger

A permissioned ledger is a blockchain whereby the participants of the network are known and already trusted. Permissioned ledgers do not need to use a distributed consensus mechanism, instead an *agreement protocol* can be used to maintain a shared version of truth about the state of the records on the blockchain. There is also no requirement for a permissioned blockchain to be private as it can be a public blockchain but with regulated access control.

Distributed ledger

As the name suggests, this ledger is distributed among its participants and spread across multiple sites or organizations. This type can either be private or public. The key idea is that, unlike many other blockchains, the records are stored contiguously instead of sorted into blocks. This concept is used in Ripple.

Shared ledger

This is generic term that is used to describe any application or database that is shared by the public or a consortium.

Fully private and proprietary blockchains

These blockchains perhaps have no mainstream application as they deviate from the core idea of decentralization in blockchain technology. Nonetheless in specific private settings within an organization there might be a need to share data and provide some level of guarantee of the authenticity of the data. These blockchains could be useful in that scenario. For example, for collaboration and sharing data between various government departments.

Tokenized blockchains

These blockchains are standard blockchains that generate cryptocurrency as a result of a consensus process via mining or via initial distribution.

Tokenless blockchains

These are probably not real blockchains because they lack the basic unit of transfer of value but are still valuable in situations where there is no need to transfer value between nodes and only sharing some data among various already trusted parties is required.

In the next section, the idea of consensus from a blockchain perspective will be discussed. Consensus is the backbone of a blockchain and provides decentralization of control as a result through an optional process known as mining. The choice of consensus algorithm is also governed by the type of blockchain in use. Not all consensus mechanisms are suitable for all types of blockchains. For example, in public permission-less blockchains it would make sense to use PoW instead of some basic agreement mechanism that perhaps is based on proof of authority. Therefore it is essential to choose a consensus algorithm appropriately for a blockchain project.

Consensus in blockchain

Consensus is basically a distributed computing concept that has been used in blockchain in order to provide a means of agreeing to a single version of truth by all peers on the blockchain network. This concept was discussed in the distributed systems section earlier in this chapter.

Roughly, the following two categories of consensus mechanism exist:

1. Proof-based, leader-based, or the *Nakamoto consensus* whereby a leader is elected and proposes a final value
2. Byzantine fault tolerance-based, which is a more traditional approach based on rounds of votes

Consensus algorithms that are available today or are being researched in the context of blockchain are presented later. This is not an exhaustive list but an attempt has been made to present all important algorithms.

Proof of Work

This type of consensus mechanism relies on proof that enough computational resources have been spent before proposing a value for acceptance by the network. This is used in bitcoin and other cryptocurrencies. Currently, this is the only algorithm that has proven astonishingly successful against Sybil attacks.

Proof of Stake

This algorithm works on the idea that a node or user has enough stake in the system; for example the user has invested enough in the system so that any malicious attempt would outweigh the benefits of performing an attack on the system. This idea was first introduced by Peercoin and is going to be used in the Ethereum blockchain. Another important concept in **Proof of Stake (PoS)** is coin age, which is a derived from the amount of time and the number of coins that have not been spent. In this model, the chances of proposing and signing the next block increase with the coin age.

Delegated Proof of Stake

Delegated Proof of Stake (DPOS) is an innovation over standard PoS whereby each node that has stake in the system can delegate the validation of a transaction to other nodes by voting. This is used in the bitshares blockchain.

Proof of Elapsed Time

Introduced by Intel, it uses **Trusted Execution Environment (TEE)** to provide randomness and safety in the leader election process via a guaranteed wait time. It requires the Intel **SGX (Software Guard Extensions)** processor in order to provide the security guarantee and for it to be secure. This concept is discussed in more detail in Chapter 9, *Hyperledger* in the context of the Intel Sawtooth Lake blockchain project.

Deposit-based consensus

Nodes that wish to participate on the network have to put in a security deposit before they can propose a block.

Proof of importance

This idea is important and different from Proof of Stake. Proof of importance not only relies on how much stake a user has in the system but it also monitors the usage and movement of tokens by the user to establish a level of trust and importance. This is used in Nemcoin.

Federated consensus or federated Byzantine consensus

Used in the stellar consensus protocol, nodes in this protocol keep a group of publicly trusted peers and propagates only those transactions that have been validated by the majority of trusted nodes.

Reputation-based mechanisms

As the name suggests, a leader is elected on the basis of the reputation it has built over time on the network. This can be based on the voting from other members.

Practical Byzantine Fault Tolerance

Practical Byzantine Fault Tolerance (**PBFT**) achieves state machine replication, which provides tolerance against Byzantine nodes. Various other protocols, including but are not limited to PBFT, PAXOS, RAFT, and **Federated Byzantine Agreement** (**FBA**), are also being used or have been proposed for use in many different implementations of distributed systems and blockchains.

CAP theorem and blockchain

Strangely, it seems that the CAP theorem is violated in blockchain, and especially in the most successful implementation: bitcoin, but this is not the case. In blockchains consistency is sacrificed in favor of availability and partition tolerance. In this scenario, **Consistency** (**C**) on the blockchain is not achieved simultaneously with **Partition tolerance** (**P**) and **Availability** (**A**), but it is achieved over time. This is called *eventual consistency*, where consistency is achieved as a result of validation from multiple nodes over time. For this purpose, the concept of mining was introduced in bitcoin; this is a process that facilitates the achievement of consensus by using a consensus algorithm called PoW. At a higher level, mining can be defined as a process that is used to add more blocks to the blockchain.

Benefits and limitations of blockchain

Numerous benefits of blockchain technology are being discussed in the industry and proposed by thought leaders around the world in blockchain space. The top 10 benefits are listed and discussed as follows.

Decentralization

This is a core concept and benefit of blockchain. There is no need for a trusted third party or intermediary to validate transactions; instead a consensus mechanism is used to agree on the validity of transactions.

Transparency and trust

As blockchains are shared and everyone can see what is on the blockchain, this allows the system to be transparent and as a result trust is established. This is more relevant in scenarios such as the disbursement of funds or benefits where personal discretion should be restricted.

Immutability

Once the data has been written to the blockchain, it is extremely difficult to change it back. It is not truly immutable but, due to the fact that changing data is extremely difficult and almost impossible, this is seen as a benefit to maintaining an immutable ledger of transactions.

High availability

As the system is based on thousands of nodes in a peer-to-peer network, and the data is replicated and updated on each and every node, the system becomes highly available. Even if nodes leave the network or become inaccessible, the network as a whole continues to work, thus making it highly available.

Highly secure

All transactions on a blockchain are cryptographically secured and provide integrity.

Simplification of current paradigms

The current model in many industries such as finance or health is rather disorganized, wherein multiple entities maintain their own databases and data sharing can become very difficult due to the disparate nature of the systems. But as a blockchain can serve as a single shared ledger among interested parties, this can result in simplifying this model by reducing the complexity of managing the separate systems maintained by each entity.

Faster dealings

In the financial industry, especially in post-trade settlement functions, blockchain can play a vital role by allowing the quicker settlement of trades as it does not require a lengthy process of verification, reconciliation, and clearance because a single version of agreed upon data is already available on a shared ledger between financial organizations.

Cost saving

As no third party or clearing houses are required in the blockchain model, this can massively eliminate overhead costs in the form of fees that are paid to clearing houses or trusted third parties.

Challenges and limitations of blockchain technology

As with any technology there are challenges that need to be addressed in order to make a system more robust, useful, and accessible. Blockchain technology is no exception; in fact a lot of effort is being made in Academia and Industry to overcome the challenges posed by blockchain technology. A selection of the most sensitive challenges are presented as follows:

- Scalability
- Adaptability
- Regulation
- Relatively immature technology
- Privacy

All these and more will be discussed in detail with possible solutions in Chapter 13, *Current Landscape and What's Next*.

This chapter has been kept generic and less technical on purpose. Once cryptography has been explained in detail in Chapter 3, *Cryptography and Technical Foundations*, specific blockchain solutions will be discussed in appropriate technical depth and detail.

Summary

This chapter introduced blockchain technology at a high level to the readers. First some basic ideas regarding distributed systems were discussed then the history of blockchain was introduced. Concepts such as electronic cash and hashcash were discussed. Furthermore, various definitions of blockchain from different points of views were presented. Some applications of blockchain technology were also discussed briefly. Next in the chapter, different types of blockchain were introduced. Finally, the benefits and limitations of this new technology were also introduced. Some topics were introduced only lightly on purpose as they will be discussed in depth in later chapters. For example, challenges and limitations were only mentioned in the chapter but no details were provided as there is a full chapter dedicated to this later in the book. In the next chapter, readers will be introduced to the concept of decentralization, which is central to the concept of blockchains and their vast number of applications.

2
Decentralization

Decentralization is not a new concept; it has been used in strategy, management, and governance for a long time. The basic idea of decentralization is to distribute control and authority to peripheries instead of one central authority being in full control of the organization. This results in several benefits for organizations. such as increased efficiency, quicker decision making, better motivation, and a reduced burden on top management.

In this chapter, the concept of decentralization will be discussed in the context of blockchain; the goals of both are similar, whereby no single central authority is in control. Methods of decentralization and routes to decentralization with some examples will also be presented. Also, the decentralization of the blockchain ecosystem, decentralized applications, and platforms for decentralization will be discussed in detail. Many exciting applications and ideas emerge out of the decentralized blockchain technology, and will be introduced in this chapter.

Decentralization using blockchain

Decentralization is a core benefit and service provided by the blockchain technology. Blockchain by design is a perfect vehicle for providing a platform that does not need any intermediaries and can function with many different leaders chosen via consensus mechanisms. This model allows anyone to compete to become the decision-making authority. This competition is governed by a consensus mechanism and the most commonly used method is known as **Proof of Work (PoW)**.

Decentralization is applied in varying degrees from semi-decentralized to fully decentralized depending on the requirements and circumstances. Decentralization can be viewed from a blockchain perspective as a mechanism that provides a way to remodel existing applications and paradigms or build new applications in order to give full control to users.

Information and communication technology (ICT) has conventionally been based on a centralized paradigm whereby database or application servers are under the control of a central authority, such as a system administrator. With bitcoin and the advent of the blockchain technology, this model has changed and now the technology that allows anyone to start a decentralized system (and operate it with no single point of failure or single trusted authority) is available. It can either be run autonomously or by requiring some human intervention depending on the type and model of governance used in the decentralized application running on the blockchain.

An upcoming diagram shows different types of system that currently exist, that is, central, distributed, and decentralized. This concept was first published in 1964 in a paper by *Paul Baran* on *distributed communication networks* in the context of communication networks.

Centralized systems are conventional (client–server) IT systems whereby there is a single authority that controls the system and is solely in-charge of all operations on the system. All users of a central system are dependent on a single source of service. Online service providers, such as eBay, Google, Amazon, Apple's App Store, and the majority of other providers, use this common model of delivering services. On the other hand, in a distributed system, the data and computation are spread across multiple nodes in the network. Sometimes, this term is confused with parallel computing. While there is an overlap in the definition, the main difference between both these systems is that in a parallel system, computation is performed by all nodes simultaneously in order to achieve a result, whereas in a distributed system, computation may not happen in parallel and data is only replicated on multiple nodes that users view as a single coherent system. Both of these models are used with variations in order to achieve failure tolerance and speed. In this model, there is still a central authority that has control over all nodes and governs processing. This means that the system is still centralized in nature.

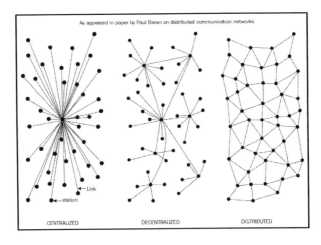

Different types of network/system

The key difference between a decentralized system and distributed system is that in a distributed system, there still exists a central authority that governs the entire system, whereas in a decentralized system, no such authority exists. A decentralized system is a type of network whereby nodes are not dependent on a single master node; instead, control is distributed among many nodes. For example, this is analogous to a model where each department in an organization has its own database server that they are in charge of, thus taking away the power from the central server and distributing it to the sub-departments that manage their own databases.

A real innovation in the decentralized paradigm that has started this new era of decentralization applications is decentralized consensus, which was introduced with bitcoin. This enables a user to agree on something via a consensus algorithm without the need for a central trusted third party, intermediary, or service provider.

Methods of decentralization

There are two methods that can be used to achieve decentralization. These methods are discussed in detail in the following sections.

Disintermediation

This can be explained with the help of an example. Imagine you want to send money to your friend in another country. You go to a bank that will transfer your money to the bank in the country of your choice for a fee. In this case, the bank keeps a central database that is updated, confirming that you have sent the money. With blockchain technology, it is possible to send this money directly to your friend without the need for a bank. All you need is the address of your friend on the blockchain. This way, the intermediary is no longer required and decentralization is achieved by disintermediation. However, it is debatable how practical decentralization is in the financial sector by disintermediation due to heavy regulatory and compliance requirements. Nevertheless, this model can be used not only in finance but also in many other different industries.

Through competition

In this method, a group of service providers compete with each other in order to be selected for the provision of services by the system. This paradigm does not achieve complete decentralization, but to a certain degree ensures that an intermediary or service provider is not monopolizing the service. In the context of blockchain technology, a system can be envisioned in which smart contracts can choose an external data provider from a large number of providers based on their reputation, previous score, reviews, and quality of service. This will not result in full decentralization, but it allows smart contracts to make a free choice based on the criteria mentioned earlier. This way, an environment of competition is cultivated among service providers, whereby they compete with each other to become the data provider of choice.

In the following diagram, varying levels of decentralization are shown. On the left-hand side, there is a conventional approach where a central system is in control; on the right-hand side, complete disintermediation is achieved; and in middle, competing intermediaries or service providers are shown. In the middle, intermediaries or service providers are selected based on reputation or voting, thus achieving partial decentralization.

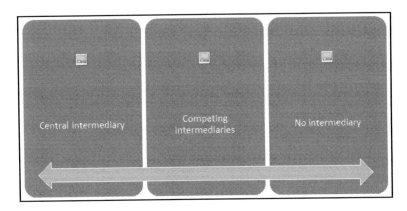

Scale of decentralization

While there are many benefits of decentralization–including but not limited to transparency, efficiency, cost saving, development of trusted ecosystems, and in some cases privacy and anonymity–some challenges, such as security requirements, software bugs, and human errors, also need to be looked at thoroughly. For example, in a decentralized system such as bitcoin or Ethereum, where security is usually provided by private keys, how can it be ensured that a smart property associated with these private keys cannot be rendered useless if, due to a human error, the private keys are lost or if, due to a bug in the smart contract code, the decentralized application is vulnerable to attack by adversaries? Before we embark on a journey to decentralize everything using blockchain and decentralized applications, it is important to understand that not everything is required to (or can be) decentralized.

Routes to decentralization

Even though there are systems that existed before bitcoin or blockchain that can be classed as decentralized to a certain degree, such as BitTorrent or Gnutella file sharing, with the advent of the blockchain technology many initiatives are being taken in order leverage this new technology for decentralization. Usually, the bitcoin blockchain is the first choice for many as it has proven to be the most resilient and secure blockchain with a market cap of almost 12 billion dollars. An alternative approach is to use other blockchains, such as Ethereum, which is currently the tool of choice of many developers for building decentralized applications.

How to decentralize

A framework has been proposed by *Arvind Narayanan* and others that can be used to evaluate the decentralization requirements of a variety of things in the context of blockchain technology. The framework basically proposes four questions that, once answered, provide a clear idea as to how a system can be decentralized. These questions are listed as follows:

1. What is being decentralized?
2. What level of decentralization is required?
3. What blockchain is used?
4. What security mechanism is used?

The first question simply asks what system is being decentralized. This can be any system, for example an Identity system or trading. The next question can be answered by specifying the level of decentralization required by looking at the scale of decentralization discussed earlier. It can be full disintermediation or partial disintermediation. The third question is quite straightforward, where developers can make a choice as to which blockchain is suitable for a particular application. It can be bitcoin blockchain, Ethereum blockchain, or any other blockchain that is deemed fit for a specific application. Finally, a key question needs to be answered about the security mechanism as to how the security of a decentralized system can be guaranteed. It can be Atomicity, for example, whereby either the transaction executes in full or does not execute at all. In other words, it is all or nothing. This ensures the integrity of the system. Other mechanisms can include reputation, which allows varying degrees of trust in a system.

Examples

In this section, an example of the application of the afore mentioned framework is provided.

In the first example, a money transfer system is selected, which is required to be decentralized. In this case, the four questions mentioned earlier can be answered in order to evaluate the decentralization requirements. The answers are shown as follows:

1. **Answer 1**: Money transfer system.
2. **Answer 2**: Disintermediation.
3. **Answer 3**: Bitcoin.
4. **Answer 4**: Atomicity.

By answering these four questions, it can be shown how a payment system can be decentralized. Based on the preceding answers, it can be stated that the money transfer system can be decentralized by removing the intermediary and will be implemented on the Bitcoin blockchain with security guarantee provided via Atomicity.

Similarly, this framework can be used for any other system that needs to be evaluated for decentralization. By answering these four simple questions, it becomes quite clear as to what approach can be taken to decentralize the system.

Blockchain and full ecosystem decentralization

In order to achieve complete decentralization, it is necessary that the environment around the blockchain is also decentralized. Blockchain itself is a distributed ledger that runs on top of conventional systems. These elements include storage, communication, and computation. There are other factors, such as Identity and Wealth, that are traditionally based on centralized paradigms and there's a need to decentralize these aspects too in order to achieve a fully decentralized ecosystem.

Storage

Data can be stored directly in a blockchain, and with this, it does achieve decentralization, but a major disadvantage of this approach is that blockchain is not suitable for storing large amounts of data by design. It can store simple transactions and some arbitrary data but is certainly not suitable for storing images or large blobs of data, as is the case in traditional database systems. A better alternative is to use **distributed hash tables (DHTs)**. DHTs were originally used in peer-to-peer file sharing software, such as BitTorrent, Napster, Kazaa, and Gnutella. DHT research was made popular by CAN, Chord, Pastry, and Tapestry projects. BitTorrent turns out to be the most scalable and fast network, but the issue is that there is no incentive for users to keep the files indefinitely. Users do not usually keep files permanently, and if nodes leave the network that has data required by someone, there is no way to retrieve it except having the required nodes rejoin the network again so that the files become available once more. Two main requirements here are high availability and link stability, which means that data should be available when required and network links should also always be accessible. **Inter Planetary File System (IPFS)** by *Juan Benet* possesses both of these properties and the vision is to provide a decentralized World Wide Web by replacing the HTTP protocol. IPFS uses Kademlia DHT and merkle **DAG (Directed Acyclic Graph)** to provide the storage and searching functionality, respectively.

The incentive mechanism is based on a protocol known as Filecoin that pays incentives to nodes that store data using the BitSwap mechanism. The BitSwap mechanism allows nodes to keep a simple ledger of bytes sent or bytes received under a one-to-one relationship. Also, a Git-based version control mechanism is used in IPFS to provide structure and control over the versioning of data.

There are other alternatives, such as Ethereum swarm, storj, and maidsafe. Ethereum has its own decentralized and distributed ecosystem that uses Swarm for storage and the whisper protocol for communication. Maidsafe is aiming to provide a decentralized World Wide Web. All these projects will be discussed later in the book in more detail.

BigChainDB is another storage layer decentralization project aimed at providing a scalable, fast, and linearly scalable decentralized database as opposed to a traditional filesystem. BigChainDB complements decentralized processing platforms and file systems such as Ethereum and IPFS.

Communication

It is generally considered that the Internet (the communication layer in blockchain) is decentralized. This is true to some extent as the original vision of the Internet was to develop a decentralized system. Services such as e-mail and online storage are all now based on a paradigm where the service provider is in control and users trust them to give them access to the service when required. This model is based on the trust of the central authority (the service provider) and users are not in control of their data; even passwords are stored on trusted third-party systems. There is a need to provide control to individual users in such a way that access to their data is guaranteed and is not dependent on a single third party. Access to the Internet (the communication layer) is based on Internet service providers (ISPs) that act as a central hub for Internet users. If the ISP is shut down for political or any other reasons, then no communication is possible in this model. An alternative is to use mesh networks. Even though they are limited in functionality as compared to the Internet, they still provide a decentralized alternative where nodes can talk directly to each other without a central hub such as an ISP.

 An example of a Meshnet is Firechat (http://www.opengarden.com/firec hat.html), which allows iPhone users to communicate with each other directly in a peer-to-peer fashion without the Internet.

Now imagine a network that allows users to be in control of their communication; no one can shut it down for political or censorship reasons. This could be the next step toward decentralizing communication networks in the blockchain ecosystem. It must be noted that this model may only be required in a jurisdiction where the Internet is censored and controlled by the government.

As mentioned earlier, the original vision of the Internet was to build a decentralized network; however, over the years, with the advent of large-scale service providers such as Google, Amazon, and eBay, the control is shifting toward the big players. For example, e-mail is a decentralized system at its core; anyone can run an e-mail server with minimal effort and can start sending and receiving e-mails, but there is a better alternative available that is already providing a managed service for end users, so there is a natural inclination toward selecting a centralized service as it is more convenient and free. Free services, however, are being offered at the cost of valuable personal data and many users are not aware of this fact. This is one example that shows how the Internet has moved toward centralization. Blockchain has once again given this vision of decentralization to the world and now concerted efforts are being made to harness this technology and gain the benefits that it can provide.

Computation

Decentralization of computing or processing is achieved by a blockchain technology such as Ethereum, where smart contracts with embedded business logic can run on the network. Other blockchain technologies also provide similar processing layer platforms where business logic can run over the network in a decentralized manner.

The following diagram shows the decentralized ecosystem overview where, on the bottom layer, Internet or Meshnets provides a decentralized communication layer, then a storage layer uses technologies such as IPFS and BigChainDB to enable decentralization, and finally, you see the blockchain that serves as a decentralized processing layer. Blockchain can, in a limited way, provide a storage layer too, but that seriously hampers the speed and capacity of the system; therefore, other solutions such as IPFS and BigChainDB are more suitable to store large amounts of data in a decentralized way. At the top, the Identity and Wealth layers are shown. Identity on the Internet is a very big topic and systems such as bitAuth and OpenID have provided authentication and identification services with varying degrees of decentralization and security assumptions.

Blockchain is capable of providing solutions to various problems. A concept relevant to Identity known as *Zooko's Triangle* requires that a naming system in a network protocol be secure, decentralized, and meaningful to humans. It is conjectured that a system can have only two of these properties simultaneously, but with the advent of blockchain, in the form of Namecoin, this problem was resolved. This, however, is not a panacea and comes with its own challenges, such as reliance on users to store and maintain private keys securely. This opens up other general questions about the suitability of decentralization. Perhaps decentralization is not appropriate in every scenario. Well-reputed centralized systems tend to work better in many cases.

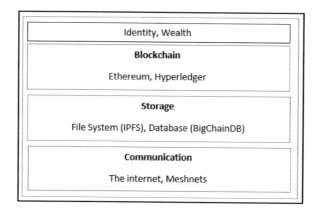

There are many projects underway that are developing solutions for a wider distributed blockchain system.

With the emergence of the decentralization paradigm, different terminologies and buzz words are now appearing in the media and in academic literature. With the advent of the blockchain technology, it is now possible to build software versions of traditional physical organizations. In the context of decentralization, the upcoming concepts are worth discussing.

Smart contract

A smart contract can be thought of as a small decentralized program. Smart contracts do not necessarily need a blockchain to run; however, due to the security benefits that the blockchain technology provides, it is now becoming almost a standard to use blockchain as a decentralized execution platform for smart contracts. A smart contract usually contains some business logic and a limited amount of data. Actors or participants in the blockchain use these smart contracts or they run autonomously on behalf of the network participants.

These small programs reside on the blockchain and execute business logic if some specific criteria are met. More information on smart contracts will be provided in `Chapter 6`, *Smart Contracts*, which is dedicated to a detailed discussion of smart contracts.

Decentralized organizations

Decentralized organization (DOs) are software programs that run on a blockchain and are based on the idea of real human organizations with people and protocols. Once a DO, in the form of a smart contract or a set of smart contracts, is added to the blockchain, it becomes decentralized and parties interact with each other based on the code defined within the DO software.

Decentralized autonomous organizations

Just like DOs, a **Decentralized autonomous organization (DAO)** is also a computer program than runs on top of a blockchain and embedded within it are governance and business logic rules. DAO and DO are basically the same thing, but the main difference is that DAOs are autonomous, which means that they are fully automated and contain artificially intelligent logic, whereas DOs lack this feature and rely on human input in order to execute business logic.

Ethereum blockchain led the way with the introduction of DAOs for the first time. In DAO, the code is considered the governing entity rather than humans or paper contracts. A *Curator*, however, is a human entity that participates as someone who maintains this code and acts as a proposal evaluator for the community. DAOs are capable of hiring external *Contractors* if enough input is received from the token holders (participants). The most famous DAO project is *The DAO* (`https://daohub.org`) as it raised 168 million US dollars in its crowd-funding phase. The DAO project was designed to be a venture capital fund which was aimed at providing a decentralized business model with no single entity as an owner. Unfortunately, this was hacked due to a bug in the DAO code and millions of dollars' worth of **Ether currency (ETH)** were siphoned out of the DAO into a child DAO created by the hackers. It required a hard fork on the Ethereum blockchain to reverse the impact of the hack and initiate the recovery of the funds. This incident opened up a debate on the security, quality, and the need for thorough testing of the code in smart contracts in order to ensure integrity and adequate control. There are projects underway, especially in Academia, that are looking to formalize smart contract coding.

Currently, DAOs do not have any legal status even though they may contain some intelligent code that enforces some protocols and conditions, but these rules have no value in the current real-world legal system. One day, perhaps an *autonomous agent* that is commissioned and permissioned by a law enforcement agency or a regulator containing rules and regulations could be embedded in a DAO, to ensure the integrity of the DAO from a legal and compliance perspective. An **Autonomous Agent (AA)** is a piece of code that runs without human intervention. The fact that DAOs are purely decentralized entities makes it possible to run them in any physical jurisdiction. Therefore, they raise a big question as to how a current legal system would work with such a varied mix of different jurisdictions and geographies.

Decentralized autonomous corporations

DAOs, **Decentralized autonomous corporations** (DACs) are a similar concept but are considered a smaller subset of DAOs. The definitions of DACs and DAOs can sometimes overlap, but a general difference is that DAOs are usually considered to be nonprofit, whereas DACs can make money via shares offered to the participants and by paying dividends. These corporations can run a business automatically without human intervention based on the logic programmed within them.

Decentralized autonomous societies

Decentralized autonomous societies (DASs) are a concept whereby entire societies can function on a blockchain with the help of multiple complex smart contracts and a combination of DAOs and **Decentralized applications** (DAPPs) running autonomously. This model does not mean an outlaw approach, nor is it based on a totally libertarian ideology; instead, many services that a government offers can be delivered via blockchain, such as Government Identity Card systems, passport issuance, and records of deeds, marriages, and births. Another theory is that, if a government is corrupt and central systems do not provide the satisfactory levels of trust that a society needs, then the society can start its own virtual society on a blockchain that is driven by decentralized consensus and is transparent. This might be seen as a libertarian or cypherpunk dream but is entirely possible on a blockchain.

Decentralized applications

All ideas mentioned earlier come under the larger umbrella of decentralized applications. All DAOs, DACs, and DOs are basically decentralized applications that run on top of a blockchain in a peer-to-peer network. This is the latest advancement in technology with regard to decentralization. Decentralized applications or DAPPs are software programs that can run on their own blockchain, use another already existing established blockchain, or use only protocols of an existing blockchain solution. These are called Type I, Type II, and Type III DAPPs.

Requirements of a decentralized application

In order for an application to be considered a decentralized application, it must meet the following criteria. This definition was provided by *David Johnston* and others in their whitepaper called *The General Theory of Decentralized Applications, Dapps*:

1. The DAPP should be fully open source and autonomous and no single entity should be in control of a majority of its tokens. All changes to the application must be consensus-driven based on the feedback given by the community.

2. Data and records of operations of the application must be cryptographically secured and stored on a public, decentralized blockchain in order to avoid any central points of failure.

3. A cryptographic token must be used by the application in order to provide access and rewards to those who contribute value to the applications, for example, miners in bitcoin.

4. The tokens must be generated by the decentralized application according to a standard cryptographic algorithm. This generation of tokens acts as a proof of the value to contributors (for example, miners).

Operations of a DAPP

Establishment of consensus by a DAPP can be achieved using consensus algorithms such as Proof of Work and Proof of Stake. So far, only PoW has been found to be incredibly resistant to 51% attacks, as is evident from bitcoin. Furthermore, a DAPP can distribute tokens (coins) via mining, fundraising, and development.

Examples

Examples of some decentralized applications are provided here.

KYC-Chain

This application provides a facility to manage **Know Your Customer** (**KYC**) data in a secure and convenient way based on smart contracts.

OpenBazaar

This is a decentralized peer-to-peer network that allows commercial activities directly between sellers and buyers instead of relying on a central party, as opposed to conventional providers such as eBay and Amazon. It should be noted that this system is not built on top of a blockchain; instead, distributed hash tables are used in a peer-to-peer network in order to enable direct communication and data sharing between peers. It makes use of bitcoin as a payment network, however.

Lazooz

This is a decentralized equivalent of Uber. It allows peer-to-peer ride sharing and users can be incentivized by *proof of movement* and can earn Zooz coins.

 There are many other DAPPS that have been built on the Ethereum blockchain and are showcased at `http://dapps.ethercasts.com/`.

Platforms for decentralization

There are many platforms available for decentralization now. Many companies around the world have introduced platforms that promise to make distributed application development easy, accessible, and secure for users. Some prominent names are discussed here.

Ethereum

Ethereum tops the list as being the first blockchain that introduced a Turing-complete language and the concept of a virtual machine. This is in contrast to the limited scripting language in bitcoin and many other cryptocurrencies. With the availability of this Turing-complete language called Solidity, endless possibilities have opened for the development of decentralized applications. This was proposed in 2013 by *Vitalik Buterin* and provides a public blockchain to develop smart contracts and decentralized applications. Currency tokens on Ethereum are called Ethers.

Maidsafe

Maidsafe provides a **SAFE (Secure Access for Everyone)** network that is made up of unused computing resources, such as storage, processing power, and the data connections of its users. The files on the network are divided into small chunks of data that are encrypted and distributed throughout the network randomly. This data can only be retrieved by its respective owner. One key innovation is that duplicate files are automatically rejected on the network, which helps reduce the need for additional computing resources to manage the load. It uses Safecoin as a token to incentivize its contributors.

Lisk

Lisk is a blockchain application development and cryptocurrency platform. It allows developers to use JavaScript to build decentralized applications and host them in their own respective sidechains. Lisk uses the **Delegated Proof of Stake (DPOS)** mechanism for consensus whereby 101 nodes can be elected to secure the network and propose blocks. It uses the Node.js and JavaScript backend whereas the frontend allows the use of standard technologies, such as CSS3, HTML5, and JavaScript. Lisk uses LSK coin as a currency on the blockchain. Another derivative of Lisk is Rise, which is a Lisk-based decentralized application and digital currency platform. It has more focus on the security of the system.

A more practical introduction to these platforms and others will be supplied in later chapters.

Summary

This chapter introduced the concept of decentralization, which is the core service offered by the blockchain technology. Although the concept of decentralization is not new, it gained renewed significance in the world of blockchain. As such, various applications based on decentralized architecture have been introduced recently. The chapter started with an introduction to the idea of decentralization. Next, decentralization from the blockchain perspective was discussed. Moreover, ideas related to different layers of decentralization in the blockchain ecosystem were introduced. There are several new concepts and terms that have emerged with the advent of the blockchain technology and decentralization from the blockchain perspective, such as DAOs, DAPPs, and various others. An introduction to all these terms was also provided in this chapter. Finally, decentralized applications with some examples were discussed. In the next chapter, fundamental concepts that are necessary to understand the Blockchain ecosystem will be presented. Mainly, cryptography will be introduced, which provides a crucial foundation for the blockchain technology.

3
Cryptography and Technical Foundations

In this chapter, you will be introduced to the concepts, theory, and practical aspects of cryptography. More focus will be given to aspects that are specifically relevant in the context of the blockchain technology. Moreover, concepts from financial markets will also be discussed in order to provide a basis for the material covered in later chapters.

You will also be introduced to the practical implementations of cryptographic algorithms so that you can experience the cryptographic functions practically. For this, the **OpenSSL** command line is used.

Before starting the theoretical foundations, the installation of OpenSSL is discussed in the following section so that you can do some practical work as you read through the theoretical material.

On Ubuntu Linux distribution, OpenSSL is usually already available; however, it can be installed using the following commands:

```
$ sudo apt-get install openssl
```

In the upcoming sections, first, the theoretical foundation will be discussed and then relevant practical experiments will be introduced.

Introduction

Cryptography is the science of making information secure in the presence of adversaries. It provides a means of secure communication in the presence of adversaries with assumed limitless resources. Ciphers are used to encrypt data so that if intercepted by an adversary, the data is meaningless to them without decryption, which requires the secret key.

Cryptography is generally used to provide a confidentiality service. On its own, it cannot be considered a complete solution but serve as a crucial building block within a larger security system to address a security problem.

Cryptography provides various security services, such as **Confidentiality, Integrity, Authentication**, (Entity Authentication and Data origin authentication) and **non-repudiation**. Additionally, accountability is also required in various security systems.

Before discussing cryptography further, there are some mathematical terms and concepts that need to be explained first in order to fully understand the material provided later in this chapter. The next section introduces these concepts. It should be noted that this section is intended as a basic introduction. An explanation with proofs and relevant background for all these terms will require rather involved mathematics, which is beyond the scope of this book. More details on these topics can be found in any standard number theory, algebra, or cryptography text book.

Mathematics

As the subject of cryptography is based on mathematics, this section will introduce some basic concepts that will help you understand the concepts later in the chapter.

Set

A set is a collection of distinct objects, for example, X= {1, 2, 3, 4, 5}.

Group

A group is a commutative set with one operation that combines two elements of the set. The group operation is closed and associated with an identity element defined. Additionally, each element in the set has an inverse. Closure (closed) means that if, for example, elements A and B are in the set, then the resultant element after performing operation on the elements is also in the set. Associative means that the grouping of elements does not affect the result of the operation.

Field

A field is a set that contains both additive and multiplicative groups. More precisely, all elements in the set form an additive and multiplicative group. It satisfies specific axioms for addition and multiplication. For all group operations, the distributive law is also applied. The law dictates that the same sum or product will be produced even if any terms or factors are reordered.

A finite field

A finite field is a field with a finite set of elements. Also known as Galois fields, these structures are of particular importance in cryptography as they can be used to produce accurate and error-free results of arithmetic operations. For example, prime finite fields are used in elliptic curve cryptography to construct discrete logarithm problem.

Order

This is the number of elements in a field. It is also known as the cardinality of the field.

Prime fields

This is a finite field with a prime number of elements. It has specific rules for addition and multiplication, and each nonzero element in the field has an inverse. Addition and multiplication operations are performed modulo p.

Ring

If more than one operation can be defined over an abelian group, that group becomes a ring. There are also certain properties that need to be satisfied. A ring must have closure and associative and distributive properties.

A cyclic group

A cyclic group is a type of group that can be generated by a single element called the group generator. In other words, if the group operation is repeatedly applied to a particular element in the group, then all elements in the group can be generated.

An abelian group

An abelian group is formed when the operation on the elements of a set is commutative. Commutative law basically means that changing the order of the elements does not affect the result of the operation, for example, *A X B = B X A*.

Modular arithmetic

Also known as clock arithmetic, numbers in modular arithmetic wrap around when they reach a certain fixed number. This fixed number is a positive number called modulus and all operations are performed with regard to this fixed number. In an analogy to a clock, there are number from 1 to 12. When it reaches 12, the number 1 starts again. In other words, this arithmetic deals with the remainders after the division operation. For example, 50 mod 11 is 6 because 50 / 11 leaves a remainder of 6.

This completes a basic introduction to some mathematical concepts; in the next section, you will be introduced to cryptography.

Cryptography

As discussed earlier, cryptography provides various security services, and these security services are discussed here.

Confidentiality

Confidentiality is the assurance that information is only available to authorized entities.

Integrity

Integrity is the assurance that information is modifiable only by authorized entities.

Authentication

Authentication provides assurance about the identity of an entity or the validity of a message. There are two types of authentications, discussed here.

Entity authentication

Entity authentication is the assurance that an entity is currently involved and active in a communication session. Traditionally, users are issued a username and password, which are used to gain access to the platforms they are using. This is called single factor authentication as there is only one factor, namely *something you know*, that is, the password and username. This type of authentication is not very secure due to various reasons, such as password leakage; therefore, additional factors are now commonly used to provide better security. The use of additional techniques for user identification is known as multifactor authentication or two-factor authentication if only two methods are used. If more than two factors are used for authentication, that is called multifactor authentication. Various factors are described here:

1. The first factor is something you have, such as a hardware token or smart card. In this case, a user can use a hardware token in addition to login credentials to gain access to a system. This provides protection by requiring two factors of authentication. A user who has access to the hardware token and knows the log-on credentials will be able to access the system. Both factors should be available in order to gain access to the system, thus making this method a two-factor authentication mechanism.

2. The second factor is something you are, which uses biometric features in order to identify the user. In this method, a user uses fingerprint, retina, iris, or hand geometry to provide an additional factor for authentication. This way, it can be ensured that a user was indeed present during the authentication mechanism as biometric features are unique to an individual. However, careful implementation is required in order to ensure a high level of security as some research has suggested that biometric systems can be circumvented in certain scenarios.

Data origin authentication

Also known as message authentication, this is an assurance that the source of information is verified. Data origin authentication implies data integrity because if a source is corroborated, then data must not have been altered. Various methods, such as **Message Authentication Codes (MACs)** and digital signatures are most commonly used. These terms will be explained in detail later in the chapter.

Non-repudiation

Non-repudiation is the assurance that an entity cannot deny a previous commitment or action by providing unforgeable evidence. It is a security service that provides unforgeable evidence that a particular action has occurred. This property is very necessary in disputable situations whereby an entity has denied actions performed, for example, placing an order on an e-commerce system. This service produces cryptographic evidence in electronic transactions so that in case of disputes, it can be used as a confirmation of an action. Non-repudiation has been an active research area for many years. Disputes in electronic transactions are a common issue and there is a need to address them in order to increase the confidence level of consumers in the service.

The non-repudiation protocol usually runs in a communication network and is used to provide evidence that an action has been taken by an entity (originator or recipient) on the network. In this context, there are two communication models that can be used to transfer messages from originator A to recipient B:

1. Message is sent directly from originator A to recipient B.
2. Message is sent to a delivery agent from originator A, which then delivers the message to recipient B.

The main requirements of a non-repudiation protocol are fairness, effectiveness, and timeliness. In many scenarios, there are multiple participants involved in a transaction as opposed to only two parties. For example, in electronic trading systems, there can be many entities, such as clearing agents, brokers, and traders that can be involved in a single transaction. In this case, two-party non-repudiation protocols are not appropriate. To address this problem **Multi-party nonrepudiation protocols (MPNR)** has been developed.

Accountability

Accountability is the assurance that actions affecting security can be traced to the responsible party. This is usually provided by logging and audit mechanisms in systems where a detailed audit is required due to the nature of the business, for example, in electronic trading systems. Detailed logs are vital to trace an entity's actions, for example, when a trade is placed in an audit record with the date and time stamp and the entity's identity is generated and saved in the log file. This log file can optionally be encrypted and can be part of the database or a standalone ASCII text log file on a system.

Cryptographic primitives

Cryptographic primitives are the basic building blocks of a security protocol or system. In the following section, you are introduced to cryptographic algorithms that are essential for the building of secure protocols and systems. A **security protocol** is a set of steps taken in order to achieve required security goals by utilizing appropriate security mechanisms.

Various types of security protocols are in use, such as **authentication protocols**, **non-repudiation protocols**, and **key management protocols**.

A generic cryptography model is shown in the following diagram:

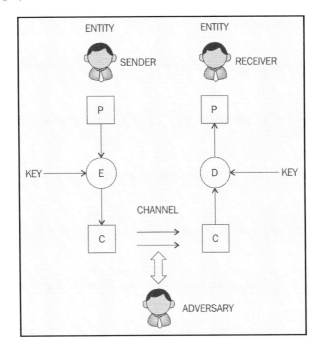

A model showing the generic encryption and decryption model

In the preceding diagram, **P**, **E**, **C**, and **D** represents Plain text, Encryption, Cipher text, and Decryption, respectively. Also, based on the model shown earlier, it is worth explaining various concepts such as entity, sender, receiver, adversary, key, and a channel.

- **Entity**: It is either a person or a system that sends, receives, or performs operations on data
- **Sender**: Sender is an entity that transmits the data
- **Receiver**: Receiver is an entity that takes delivery of the data

- **Adversary**: This is an entity that tries to circumvent the security service
- **Key**: A key is some data that is used to encrypt or decrypt data
- **Channel**: Channel provides a medium of communication between entities

Cryptography is mainly divided into two categories, namely symmetric and asymmetric cryptography.

Symmetric cryptography

Symmetric cryptography refers to a type of cryptography whereby the key that is used to encrypt the data is the same for decrypting the data, and thus it is also known as a shared key cryptography. The key must be established or agreed on before the data exchange between the communicating parties. This is the reason it is also called **secret key cryptography**.

There are two types of symmetric ciphers, stream ciphers and block ciphers. **Data Encryption Standard (DES)** and **Advanced Encryption Standard (AES)** are common examples of block ciphers, whereas RC4 and A5 are commonly used stream ciphers.

Stream ciphers

These ciphers are encryption algorithms that apply encryption algorithms on a bit-by-bit basis to plain text using a key stream. There are two types of stream ciphers: synchronous and asynchronous. Synchronous stream ciphers are ones where key stream is dependent only on the key, whereas asynchronous stream ciphers have a key stream that is also dependent on the encrypted data.

In stream ciphers, encryption and decryption are basically the same function because they are simple modulo 2 additions or XOR operation. The key requirement in stream ciphers is the security and randomness of key streams. Various techniques have been developed to generate random numbers, and it's vital that all key generators be cryptographically secure:

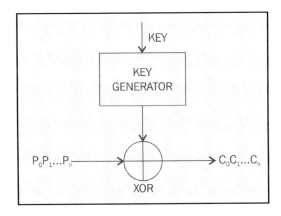

Operation of a stream cipher

Block ciphers

These are encryption algorithms that break up a text to be encrypted (plain text) into blocks of fixed length and apply encryption block by block. Block ciphers are usually built using a design strategy known as Fiestel cipher. Recent block ciphers, such as AES (Rijndael) have been built using a combination of substitution and permutation called **substitution-permutation network (SPN)**.

Fiestel ciphers are based on the Fiestel network, which is a structure developed by *Horst Fiestel*. This structure is based on the idea of combining multiple rounds of repeated operations to achieve desirable cryptographic properties knows as confusion and diffusion. Fiestel networks operate by dividing data into two blocks (left and right) and process these blocks via keyed round functions.

Confusion makes the relationship between the encrypted text and plaintext complex. This is achieved by substitution in practice. For example, 'A' in plain text is replaced by 'X' in encrypted text. In modern cryptographic algorithms, substitution is performed using lookup tables called S-boxes. The diffusion property spreads the plain text statistically over the encrypted data, which ensures that even if a single bit is changed in the input text, it results in changing at least half (on average) of the bits in the cipher text. Confusion is required to make finding the encryption key very difficult even if many encrypted and decrypted data pairs are created using the same key. In practice, this is achieved by transposition or permutation.

A key advantage of using Fiestel cipher is that encryption and decryption operations are almost identical and only require a reversal of the encryption process in order to achieve decryption. DES is a prime example of Fiestel-based ciphers:

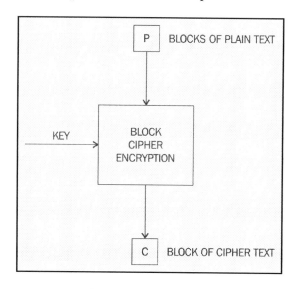

Simplified operation of a block cipher

Various modes of operation for block ciphers are **Electronic Code Book (ECB)**, **Cipher block chaining (CBC)**, **Output Feedback Mode (OFB)**, or **Counter mode (CTR)**. These modes are used to specify the way in which an encryption function would be applied to the plain text. These modes will be explained later in this section, but the first four categories of block cipher encryption modes are introduced here.

Block encryption mode

In this mode, plaintext is divided into blocks of fixed length depending on the type of cipher used and then the encryption function is applied on each block.

Keystream generation modes

In this mode, the encryption function generates a keystream that is then XORed with the plaintext stream in order to achieve encryption.

Message authentication modes

In this mode, a message authentication code is computed as a result of an encryption function. MAC is basically a cryptographic checksum that provides an integrity service. The most common method to generate MAC using block ciphers is CBC-MAC, where some part of the last block of the chain is used as a MAC.

Cryptographic hashes

Hash functions are basically used to compress a message to a fixed length digest. In this mode, block ciphers are used as a compression function to produce a hash of plain text.

The most common block encryption modes are discussed briefly.

Electronic code book

This is a basic mode of operation in which the encrypted data is produced as a result of applying the encryption algorithm one by one separately to each block of plain text. This is the simplest mode but should not be used in practice as it is insecure and can reveal information:

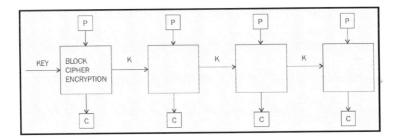

Electronic code book mode for block ciphers

Cipher block chaining

In this mode, each block of plain text is XORed with the previous encrypted block. The CBC mode uses initialization vector IV to encrypt the first block. It is recommended that IV be randomly chosen:

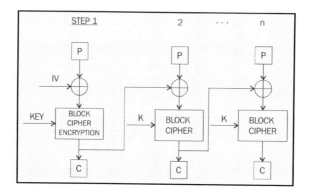

Cipher block chaining mode

Counter mode

The CTR mode effectively uses a block cipher as a stream cipher. In this case, a unique nonce is supplied that is concatenated with the counter value in order to produce a **key stream**:

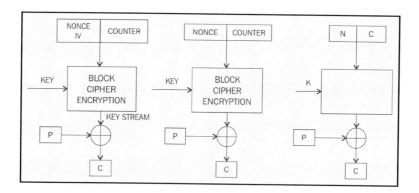

Counter mode

There are other modes, such as **Cipher Feedback mode (CFB)**, **Galois Counter mode (GCM)**, and Output Feedback mode, which are also used in various scenarios.

In the following section, you will be introduced to the design and mechanism of a currently dominant block cipher know as AES. First, some history will be presented with regard to Data Encryption Standard (DES) that led to the development of a new AES standard.

Data Encryption Standard (DES)

DES was introduced by the US **National Institute of Standards and Technology** (**NIST**) as a standard algorithm for encryption and was in main use during 1980s and 1990s, but it has been not proven to be very resistant against brute force attacks, due to advances in technology and cryptography research. Especially in July 1998, **Electronic Frontier Foundation** (**EFF**) broke DES using a special purpose machine. DES uses a key of only 56 bits, which has raised some concerns. This problem was addressed with the introduction of **Triple DES** (**3DES**), which proposed the usage of a 168-bit key using three 56-bit keys and the same number of executions of the DES algorithm, thus making brute force attacks almost impossible. But other limitations, such as slow performance and 64-bit block size, are not desirable.

Advanced Encryption Standard (AES)

In 2001, after an open competition, an encryption algorithm named Rijndael that was invented by cryptographers *Joan Daemen* and *Vincent Rijmen* was standardized as AES with minor modifications by NIST in 2001. So far, no attack has been found against AES that is better than the brute force method. Original Rijndael allows different key and block sizes of 128-bit, 192-bit, and 256-bits, but in the AES standard, only a 128-bit block size is allowed. However, key sizes of 128-bit, 192-bit, and 256-bit are allowed.

AES steps

During the AES Algorithm processing, a 4 by 4 array of bytes knows as *state* is modified using multiple rounds. Full encryption requires 10 to 14 rounds depending on the size of the key. The following table shows the key sizes and the required number of rounds:

Key size	Number of rounds required
128-bit	10 rounds
192-bit	12 rounds
256-bit	14 rounds

Once the state is initialized with the input to the cipher, four operations are performed in four stages in order to encrypt the input. These stages are `AddRoundKey`, `SubBytes`, `ShiftRows,` and `MixColumns`:

1. In the `AddRoundKey` step, the state array is XORed with a subkey, which is derived from the master key.
2. This is the substitution step where a lookup table (S-box) is used to replace all bytes of the state array.
3. This step is used to shift each row except the first one in the state array to the left in a cyclic and incremental manner.
4. Finally, all bytes are mixed in this step in a linear fashion column-wise.

The preceding steps describe one round of AES. In the final round (either 10, 12, or 14 depending on the key size), stage 4 is replaced with `Addroundkey` to ensure that the first three steps cannot be simply inverted back:

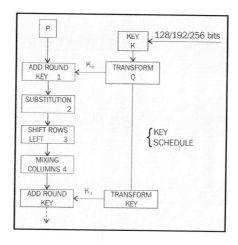

AES block diagram, showing 1st round, in last round mixing step is not performed

Various cryptocurrency wallets use AES encryption to encrypt locally stored data. Especially in bitcoin wallet, AES 256 in the CBC mode is used.

An OpenSSL example of how to encrypt and decrypt using AES

```
:~/Crypt$ openssl enc -aes-256-cbc -in message.txt -out message.bin
enter aes-256-cbc encryption password:
Verifying - enter aes-256-cbc encryption password:
:~/Crypt$ ls -ltr
total 12
```

```
-rw-rw-r-- 1 drequinox drequinox 14 Sep 21 05:54 message.txt
-rw-rw-r-- 1 drequinox drequinox 32 Sep 21 05:57 message.bin
:~/Crypt$ cat message.bin

Salted__w     s_ÿ  h~     :~/Crypt$
:~/Crypt$
```

Note that `message.bin` is a binary file; sometimes, it is desirable to encode this binary file into a text format for compatibility/interoperability reasons. The following command can be used to do that:

```
:~/Crypt$ openssl enc -base64 -in message.bin -out message.b64
:~/Crypt$ ls -ltr
-rw-rw-r-- 1 drequinox drequinox 14 Sep 21 05:54 message.txt
-rw-rw-r-- 1 drequinox drequinox 32 Sep 21 05:57 message.bin
-rw-rw-r-- 1 drequinox drequinox 45 Sep 21 06:00 message.b64
:~/Crypt$ cat message.b64
U2FsdGVkX193uByIcwZf0Z7J1at+4L+Fj8/uzeDAtJE=
:~/Crypt$
```

In order to decrypt an AES-encrypted file, the following commands can be used. An example of `message.bin` from a previous example is taken:

```
:~/Crypt$ openssl enc -d -aes-256-cbc -in message.bin -out message.dec
enter aes-256-cbc decryption password:
:~/Crypt$ ls -ltr
-rw-rw-r-- 1 drequinox drequinox 14 Sep 21 05:54 message.txt
-rw-rw-r-- 1 drequinox drequinox 32 Sep 21 05:57 message.bin
-rw-rw-r-- 1 drequinox drequinox 45 Sep 21 06:00 message.b64
-rw-rw-r-- 1 drequinox drequinox 14 Sep 21 06:06 message.dec
:~/Crypt$ cat message.dec
datatoencrypt
:~/Crypt$
```

Astute readers would have noticed that no initialization vector has been provided even though it's required in all block encryption modes of operation except ECB. The reason is that OpenSSL automatically derives the initialization vector from the given password. Users can specify the initialization vector using the switch:

```
-K/-iv   , (Initialization Vector) should be provided in Hex.
```

In order to decode from base64, the following commands are used. Take the `message.b64` file from the previous example:

```
:~/Crypt$ openssl enc -d -base64 -in message.b64 -out message.ptx
:~/Crypt$ ls -ltr
-rw-rw-r-- 1 drequinox drequinox 14 Sep 21 05:54 message.txt
-rw-rw-r-- 1 drequinox drequinox 32 Sep 21 05:57 message.bin
```

```
-rw-rw-r-- 1 drequinox drequinox 45 Sep 21 06:00 message.b64
-rw-rw-r-- 1 drequinox drequinox 14 Sep 21 06:06 message.dec
-rw-rw-r-- 1 drequinox drequinox 32 Sep 21 06:16 message.ptx

:~/Crypt$ cat message.ptx
Salted__w    s_ÿ  h~      :~/Crypt$
```

There are many types of ciphers that are supported in OpenSSL; you can explore these options based on the examples provided earlier. A list of supported cipher types is shown in the following screenshot:

Screenshot displaying rich library options available in OpenSSL.

Asymmetric cryptography

Asymmetric cryptography refers to a type of cryptography whereby the key that is used to encrypt the data is different from the key that is used to decrypt the data. Also known as public key cryptography, it uses public and private keys in order to encrypt and decrypt data, respectively. Various asymmetric cryptography schemes are in use, such as RSA, DSA, and El-Gammal.

An overview of public key cryptography is shown in the following diagram:

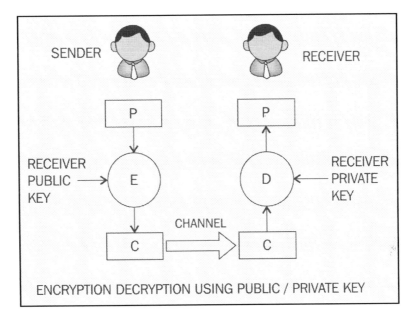

Encryption decryption using public/private key

The diagram explains how a sender encrypts the data using a recipient's public key and is then transmitted over the network to the receiver. Once it reaches the receiver, it can be decrypted using the receiver's private key. This way, the private key remains on the receiver's side and there is no need to share keys in order to perform encryption and decryption, which is the case with symmetric encryption.

Another diagram shows how public key cryptography can be used to verify the integrity of the received message by the receiver. In this model, the sender signs the data using their private key and transmits the message across to the receiver. Once the message is received on the receiver's side, it can be verified for its integrity by the sender's public key. Note that there is no encryption being performed in this model. This model is only used for message authentication and validation purposes:

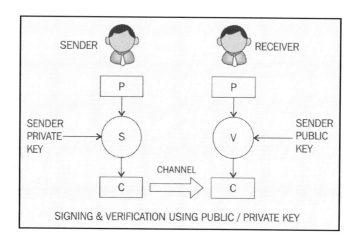

Model of a public key cryptography signature scheme

Security mechanisms offered by public key cryptosystem include key establishment, digital signatures, identification, encryption, and decryption.

Key establishment mechanisms are concerned with the design of protocols that allow setting up of keys over an insecure channel. Non-repudiation service, a very desirable property in many scenarios, can be provided using digital signatures. Sometimes, it is important to not only authenticate a user, but to also identify the entity involved in a transaction; this can also be achieved by a combination of digital signatures and challenge-response protocols. Finally, the encryption mechanism to provide confidentiality can also be realized using public key cryptosystems, such as RSA, ECC, or El-Gammal.

Public key algorithms are slower in computation as compared to symmetric key algorithms. Therefore, they are not commonly used in the encryption of large files or the actual data that needs encryption. They are usually used to exchange keys for symmetric algorithms and once the keys are established securely, symmetric key algorithms can be used to encrypt the data.

Public key cryptography algorithms are based on various underlying mathematical problems. There are three main families of asymmetric algorithms that are described here.

Integer factorization

These schemes are based on the fact that large integers are very hard to factor. RSA is the prime example of this type of algorithm.

Discrete logarithm

This is based on a problem in modular arithmetic that it is easy to calculate the result of modulo function but it is computationally infeasible to find the exponent of the generator. In other words, it is extremely difficult to find the input from the result. This is a one-way function.

For example, consider the following equation:

$$3^2 \bmod 10 = 9$$

Now given 9 finding 2, the exponent of the generator 3 is very hard. This hard problem is commonly used in **Diffie-Hellman** key exchange and digital signature algorithms.

Elliptic curves

This is based on the discrete logarithm problem discussed earlier, but in the context of elliptic curves. Elliptic curve is an algebraic cubic curve over a field, which can be defined by an equation shown here. The curve is non-singular, which means that it has no cusps or self-intersections. It has two variables a, b, along with a point of infinity.

$$y^2 = x^3 + ax + b$$

Here, a, b are integers that can have various values and are elements of the field on which the elliptic curve is defined. Elliptic curves can be defined over reals, rational numbers, complex numbers, or finite fields. For cryptographic purposes, elliptic curve over prime finite fields is used instead of real numbers. Additionally, the prime should be greater than 3. Different curves can be generated by varying the value of a, b.

Mostly prominently used cryptosystems based on elliptic curves are **Elliptic Curve Digital Signatures Algorithm (ECDSA)** and **Elliptic Curve Diffie-Hellman (ECDH)** key exchange.

Public and private keys

In order to understand public key cryptography, the first concept that needs to be looked at is the idea of public and private keys.

A private key, as the names suggests, is basically a randomly generated number that is kept secret and held privately by the users. Private key needs to be protected and no unauthorized access should be granted to that key; otherwise, the whole scheme of public key cryptography will be jeopardized as this is the key that is used to decrypt messages. Private keys can be of various lengths depending upon the type and class of algorithms used. For example, in RSA, typically, a key of 1024-bit or 2048-bits is used. 1024-bit key size is no longer considered secure and at least 2048 bit is recommended to be used in practice.

A public key is the public part of the private-public key pair. A public key is available publicly and published by the private key owner. Anyone who would then like to send the publisher of the public key an encrypted message can do so by encrypting the message using the published public key and sending it to the holder of the private key. No one else would be able to decrypt the message because the corresponding private key is held securely by the intended recipient. Once the public key encrypted message is received, the recipient can decrypt the message using the private key. There are a few concerns regarding public keys, such as authenticity and identification of the publisher of the public keys.

RSA

A description of RSA is discussed here. RSA was invented in 1977 by *Ron Rivest, Adi Shamir,* and *Leonard Adelman,* hence the name RSA. This is based on the integer factorization problem, where the multiplication of two large prime numbers is easy but difficult to factor it back to the two original numbers.

The crux of the work in the RSA algorithm is during the key generation process. An RSA key pair is generated by performing the steps described here.

Modulus generation:

- Select p and q very large primes

- Multiply p and q , $n=p.q$ to generate modulus n

Generate co-prime:

- Assume a number called e.

- It should satisfy certain conditions, that is, it should be greater than 1 and less than *(p-1) (q-1)*. In other words, e must be such a number that no number other than 1 can be divided into *e* and *(p-1) (q-1)*. This is called co-prime, that is, *e* is the co-prime of *(p-1)(q-1)*.

Generate public key:

- Modulus generated in step 1 and e generated in step 2 is pair that, together, is a public key. This part is the public part that can be shared with anyone; however, *p* and *q* need to be kept secret.

Generate private key:

- Private key called d here and is calculated from *p*, *q* and *e*. Private key is basically the inverse of e modulo *(p-1)(q-1)*. In the equation form, it is this:

$$ed = 1\ mod(p\text{-}1)(q\text{-}1)$$

Usually, an extended Euclidean algorithm is used to calculate *d*; this algorithm takes *p*, *q* and *e* and calculates *d*. The key idea in this scheme is that anyone who knows *p* and *q* can calculate private key *d* easily, by applying the extended Euclidean algorithm, but someone who doesn't know the value of *p* and *q* cannot generate *d*. This also implies that *p* and *q* should be large enough for the modulus *n* to become very difficult (computationally infeasible) to factor.

Encryption and decryption using RSA

RSA uses the following equation to produce cipher text:

$$C = P^e\ mod\ n$$

This means that plain text *P* is raised to *e* number of times and then reduced to modulo *n*.

Decryption in RSA is given by the following equation:

$$P = C^d\ mod\ n$$

This means that the receiver who has a public key pair *(n, e)* can decipher the data by raising *C* to the value of the private key *d* and reducing to modulo *n*.

Elliptic curve cryptography (ECC)

ECC is based on the discrete logarithm problem that is based on elliptic curves over finite fields (Galois fields). The main benefit of ECC over other types of public key algorithms is that it needs a smaller key size while providing the same level of security as, for example, RSA. Two notable schemes that originate from ECC are **Elliptic Curve Diffie-Hellman (ECDH)** for key exchange and **Elliptic Curve Digital Signature Algorithm (ECDSA)** for digital signatures. It can also be used for encryption but is not usually used for this purpose in practice; instead, key exchange and digital signatures are more commonly used. As ECC needs less space to operate, it is becoming very popular on embedded platforms or in systems where storage resources are limited. As a comparison, the same level of security can be achieved in ECC by only using 256-bit operands as compared to 3072-bits in RSA.

Mathematics behind ECC

In order to understand ECC, a basic introduction to the underlying mathematics is necessary. Elliptic curve is basically a type of polynomial equation known as weierstrass equation that generates a curve over a finite field. The most commonly used field is where all arithmetic operations are performed modulo *a* prime *p*. Elliptic curve groups consist of points on the curve over a finite field.

An elliptic curve can be defined as an equation here:

$$y^2 = x^3 + Ax + B \bmod p$$

Here, *A* and *B* belong to a finite field *Zp* or *FP* (prime finite field) along with a special value called point of infinity. Point of infinity ∞ is used to provide identity operations for points on the curve.

Furthermore, a condition also needs to be met that ensures that the equation mentioned earlier has no repeated roots. This means that the curve is non-singular.

The condition is described here in the equation, which is a standard requirement that needs to be met. More precisely, this ensures that the curve is nonsingular:

$$4a^3 + 27b^2 \neq 0 \bmod p$$

A real number representation of elliptic curve can be visualized as shown in the following graph. This is a graph of equation over real numbers:

$$y^2 = x^3 + ax + b$$

The actual curves used in elliptic curve cryptography are over finite prime fields, but here, they are shown over real number as it becomes easier to visualize the operations when graphed over *R*:

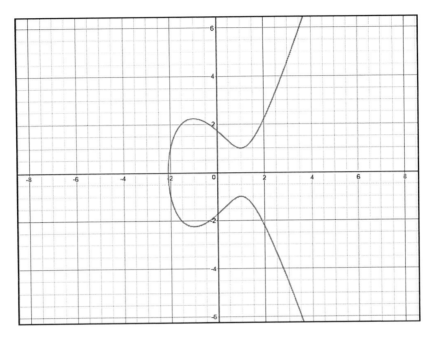

Elliptic curve over reals, a = -3 and b = 3

In order to construct the discrete logarithm problem based on elliptic curves, a large enough cyclic group is required. First, the group elements are identified as a set of points that satisfy the earlier equation. After this, group operations need to be defined on these points.

Group operations on elliptic curves are point addition and point doubling. Point addition is a process where two different points are added and point doubling means that the same point is added to itself. Both of these operations can be visualized as shown in the following diagrams.

Point addition

Point addition is shown in the following diagram. This is a geometric representation of point addition on elliptic curves. In this method, a line is drawn through the curve that intersects the curve at two points shown below *P* and *Q*, which yields a third point between the curve and the line. This point is mirrored as *P+Q*, which represent the result of addition as *R*. This is shown as *P+Q* in the following diagram:

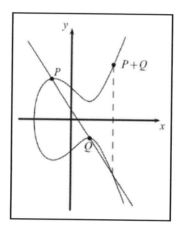

Point addition visualized over R

Group operation denoted by sign + for addition yields the following equation:

$$P + Q = R$$

In this case, two points are added in order to compute the coordinates of the third point on the curve:

$$P + Q = R$$

More precisely, this means that coordinates are added as shown in the following equation:

$$(x1, y1) + (x2, y2) = (x3, y3)$$

The equation of point addition is as follows:

$$x_3 = s^2 - x_1 - x^2 \bmod p$$

$$y_3 = s(x_1 - x_3) - y_1 \bmod p$$

Here, this is the result:

$$S = \frac{(y_2 - y_1)}{(x_2 - x_1)} \bmod p$$

S in the preceding equation depicts the line going through P and Q.

An example of point addition shown here is produced using Certicom's online calculator. This example shows the addition and solutions for the equation over finite field F_{23}. This is in contrast to the example shown earlier, which is over real numbers and only shows the curve but no solutions to the equation:

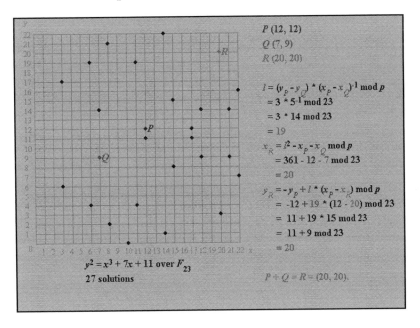

Example of point addition using Certicom's online calculator tool

In the example, the graph on the left-hand side shows the points that satisfy the equation shown here:

$$y^2 = x^3 + 7x + 11$$

There are 27 solutions to the equation shown earlier over a finite field F_{23}. P and Q are chosen to be added to produce the point R. Calculations are shown on the right-hand side, which calculates the third point R. Note that here, l is used to depict the line going through P and Q.

As an example to show how the equation is satisfied by the points shown in the graph, a point (x, y) is picked up where $x = 3$ and $y = 6$.

Using these values in the equation shows that the equation is satisfied indeed. This is shown as follows:

$$y^2 mod\ 23 = x^3 + 7x + 11\ mod\ 23$$

$$6^2 mod\ 23 = 3^3 + 7(3) + 11\ mod\ 23$$

$$36\ mod\ 23 = 59\ mod\ 23$$

$$13 = 13$$

The next section will introduce the concept of point doubling, which is another operation that can be performed on elliptic curves.

Point doubling

The other group operation on elliptic curves is called point doubling and is described in the following diagram. This is a process where P is added into itself. In this method, a tangent line is drawn through the curve, as shown in the following graph. The second point is obtained, which is at the intersection of the tangent line drawn and the curve. This point is then mirrored to yield the result, which is shown as $2P = P + P$:

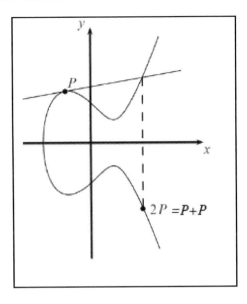

Graph representing point doubling over real numbers

In case of point doubling, the equation becomes as follows:

$$x_3 = s^2 - x_1 - x^2 \bmod p$$

$$y_3 = s(x_1 - x_3) - y_1 \bmod p$$

$$S = \frac{(y_2 - y_1)}{(x_2 - x_1)} \bmod p$$

Here, S is the slope of tangent (tangent line) going through P. It is the line on top shown in the preceding figure. In the preceding example, the curve is plotted over reals as a simple example and no solution to the equation is shown.

An example is shown here, which shows the solutions and point doubling of elliptic curve over finite field F_{23}. The graph on the left-hand side shows the points that satisfy the equation:

$$y^2 = x^3 + 7x + 11$$

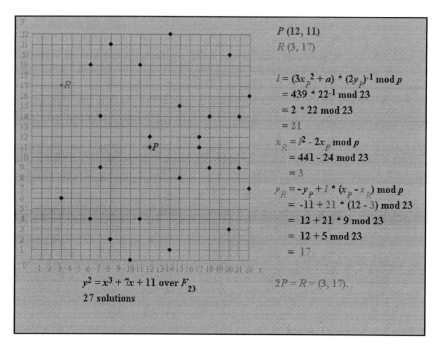

$P\,(12, 11)$

$R\,(3, 17)$

$l = (3x_p{}^2 + a) * (2y_p)^{-1} \bmod p$
$= 439 * 22^{-1} \bmod 23$
$= 2 * 22 \bmod 23$
$= 21$

$x_R = l^2 - 2x_p \bmod p$
$= 441 - 24 \bmod 23$
$= 3$

$y_R = -y_p + l * (x_p - x_R) \bmod p$
$= -11 + 21 * (12 - 3) \bmod 23$
$= 12 + 21 * 9 \bmod 23$
$= 12 + 5 \bmod 23$
$= 17$

$y^2 = x^3 + 7x + 11$ over F_{23}

27 solutions

$2P = R = (3, 17)$.

Example of point doubling using certicom's online calculator tool

As shown earlier, on the right-hand side, a calculation is shown that finds the R after P is added into itself (point doubling). There is no Q as here, the same point P is used for doubling. Note that in the calculation, l is used to depict the tangent line going through P.

In the next section, an introduction to the discrete logarithm problem will be presented.

Discrete logarithm problem

The discrete logarithm problem in ECC is based on the idea that under certain conditions, all points on an elliptic curve form a cyclic group.

On an elliptic curve, the public key is a random multiple of the generator point, whereas the private key is a randomly chosen integer used to generate the multiple. In other words, a private key is a randomly chosen integer, whereas the public key is a point on the curve. The discrete logarithm problem is used to find the private key (an integer) where that integer falls within all points on the elliptic curve. An upcoming equation shows this precisely.

Consider an elliptic curve E, with two elements P and T. The discrete logarithmic problem is to find the integer d, where $1 <= d <= \#E$, such that:

$$P + P + \ldots + P = d\,P = T$$

Here, T is the public key (point on the curve) and d is the private key. In other words, public key is a random multiple of generator, whereas the private key is the integer that is used to generate the multiple. $\#E$ represents the order of the elliptic curve, which basically means the number of points that are present in the cyclic group of the elliptic curve. A cyclic group is formed by a combination of points on the elliptic curve and point at infinity.

A key pair is linked with specific domain parameters of an elliptic curve. Domain parameters include a field size, field representation, two elements from the field a and b, two field elements Xg and Yg, order n of point G that is calculated as $G=(Xg, Yg)$ and the co-factor $h = \#E(Fq)/n$. A practical example using OpenSSL will be described later in this section.

There are various parameters that are recommended and standardized to use as curves with ECC. You are shown an example of SECP256K1 specifications here. This is the specification that has been used in bitcoin:

The elliptic curve domain parameters over $\mathbb{F}_p$ associated with a Koblitz curve `secp256k1` are specified by the sextuple $T = (p, a, b, G, n, h)$ where the finite field $\mathbb{F}_p$ is defined by:

$$p \;=\; \text{FFFFFFFF FFFFFFFF FFFFFFFF FFFFFFFF FFFFFFFF FFFFFFFF FFFFFFFE FFFFFC2F}$$

$$=\; 2^{256} - 2^{32} - 2^9 - 2^8 - 2^7 - 2^6 - 2^4 - 1$$

The curve $E: y^2 = x^3 + ax + b$ over $\mathbb{F}_p$ is defined by:

$$a \;=\; \text{00000000 00000000 00000000 00000000 00000000 00000000 00000000 00000000}$$

$$b \;=\; \text{00000000 00000000 00000000 00000000 00000000 00000000 00000000 00000007}$$

The base point G in compressed form is:

$$G \;=\; \text{02 79BE667E F9DCBBAC 55A06295 CE870B07 029BFCDB 2DCE28D9 59F2815B 16F81798}$$

and in uncompressed form is:

$$G \;=\; \text{04 79BE667E F9DCBBAC 55A06295 CE870B07 029BFCDB 2DCE28D9 59F2815B 16F81798 483ADA77 26A3C465 5DA4FBFC 0E1108A8 FD17B448 A6855419 9C47D08F FB10D4B8}$$

Finally the order n of G and the cofactor are:

$$n \;=\; \text{FFFFFFFF FFFFFFFF FFFFFFFF FFFFFFFE BAAEDCE6 AF48A03B BFD25E8C D0364141}$$

$$h \;=\; 01$$

Specification of SECP256K1 taken from http://www.secg.org/sec2-v2.pdf

An explanation of all these values in the sextuple is given here.

P is the prime p that specifies the size of the finite field.

a and *b* are the coefficients of the elliptic curve equation.

G is the base point that generates the required subgroup, also known as generator. Base point can be represented in either compressed or uncompressed form. There is no need to store all points on the curve in practical implementations. The compressed generator works because points on the curve can be identified by using only the x coordinate and the least significant bit of the y coordinate.

n is the order of the subgroup.

h is the cofactor of the subgroup.

In the following section, an example using OpenSSL is shown to help you understand the practical aspects of RSA.

In the following section, it is shown how RSA public and private key pairs can be generated using OpenSSL.

How to generate public and private key pairs

First, it is shown how the RSA private key can be generated using OpenSSL.

Private key

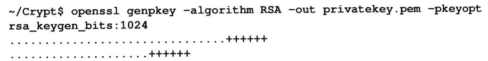

```
~/Crypt$ openssl genpkey -algorithm RSA -out privatekey.pem -pkeyopt
rsa_keygen_bits:1024
.............................++++++
...................++++++
```

After executing the command, a file named `privatekey.pem` is produced, which contains the generated private key. This is shown as follows:

```
~/Crypt$ cat privatekey.pem
-----BEGIN PRIVATE KEY-----
MIICdgIBADANBgkqhkiG9w0BAQEFAASCAmAwggJcAgEAAoGBAKJOFBzPy2vOd6em
Bk/UGrzDy7TvgDYnYxBfiEJId/r+EyMt/F14k2fDTOVwxXaXTxiQgD+BKuiey/69
9itnrqW/xy/pocDMvobj8QCngEntOdNoVSaN+t0f9nRM3iVM94mz3/C/v4vXvoac
PyPkr/0jhIV0woCurXGTghgqIbHRAgMBAAECgYEAlB3s/N4lJh0l1TkOSYunWtzT
6isnNkR7g1WrY9H+rG9xx4kP5b1DyE3SvxBLJA6xgBle8JVQMzm3sKJrJPFZzzT5
NNNnugCxairxcF1mPzJAP3aqpcSjxKpTv4qgqYevwgW1A0R3xKQZzBKU+bTO2hXV
D1oHxu75mDY3xCwqSAECQQDUYV04wNSEjEy9tYJ0zaryDAcvd/VG2/U/6qiQGajB
eSpSqoEESigbusKku+wVtRYgWWEomL/X58t+K01eMMZZAkEAw6PUR9YLebsm/Sji
iOShV4AKuFdi7t7DYWE5Ulb1uqP/i28zN/ytt4BXKIs/KcFykQGeAC6LDHZyycyc
ntDIOQJAVqrE1/wYvV5jkqcXbYLgV5YA+KYDOb9Y/ZRM5UETVKCVXNanf5CjfW1h
MMhfNxyGwvy2YVK0Nu8oY3xYPi+5QQJAUGcmORe4w6Cs12JUJ5p+zG0s+rG/URhw
B7djTXm7p6b6wR1EWYAZDM9MArenj8uXAA1AGCcIsmiDqHfU7lgz0QJAe9mOdNGW
7qRppgmOE5nuEbxkDSQI7OqHYbOLuwfCjHzJBrSgqyi6pj9/9CbXJrZPgNDwdLEb
GgpDKtZs9gLv3A==
-----END PRIVATE KEY-----
```

Generate public key

As the private key is mathematically linked to the public key, it is possible to generate or derive the public key out of the private key. Taking the example of the preceding private key, the public key can be generated as shown here:

```
:~/Crypt$ openssl rsa -pubout -in privatekey.pem -out publickey.pem
writing RSA key
```

Public key can be viewed using a file reader or any text viewer, as shown here:

```
:~/Crypt$ cat publickey.pem
-----BEGIN PUBLIC KEY-----
MIGfMA0GCSqGSIb3DQEBAQUAA4GNADCBiQKBgQCiThQcz8trznenpgZP1Bq8w8u0
74A2J2MQX4hCSHf6/hMjLfxdeJNnw0zlcMV2l08YkIA/gSronsv+vfYrZ66lv8cv
6aHAzL6G4/EAp4BJ7TnTaFUmjfrdH/Z0TN4lTPeJs9/wv7+L176GnD8j5K/9I4SF
dMKArq1xk4IYKiGx0QIDAQAB
-----END PUBLIC KEY-----
```

In order to see more details about the various components, such as modulus, prime numbers that are used in the process, exponents and coefficients of the generated private key, the following command can be used (the complete output is not shown as it is too large):

```
:~/Crypt$ openssl rsa -text -in privatekey.pem
Private-Key: (1024 bit)
modulus:
        00:a2:4e:14:1c:cf:cb:6b:ce:77:a7:a6:06:4f:d4:
        1a:bc:c3:cb:b4:ef:80:36:27:63:10:5f:88:42:48:
        77:fa:fe:13:23:2d:fc:5d:78:93:67:c3:4c:e5:70:
        c5:76:97:4f:18:90:80:3f:81:2a:e8:9e:cb:fe:bd:
        f6:2b:67:ae:a5:bf:c7:2f:e9:a1:c0:cc:be:86:e3:
        f1:00:a7:80:49:ed:39:d3:68:55:26:8d:fa:dd:1f:
        f6:74:4c:de:25:4c:f7:89:b3:df:f0:bf:bf:8b:d7:
        be:86:9c:3f:23:e4:af:fd:23:84:85:74:c2:80:ae:
        ad:71:93:82:18:2a:21:b1:d1
publicExponent: 65537 (0x10001)
privateExponent:
        00:94:1d:ec:fc:de:25:26:1d:25:d5:39:0e:49:8b:
        a7:5a:dc:d3:ea:2b:27:36:44:7b:83:55:ab:63:d1:
        fe:ac:6f:71:c7:89:0f:e5:bd:43:c8:4d:d2:bf:10:
        4b:24:0e:b1:80:19:5e:f0:95:50:33:39:b7:b0:a2:
        6b:24:f1:59:cf:34:f9:34:d3:67:ba:00:b1:6a:2a:
        f1:70:5d:66:3f:32:40:3f:76:aa:a5:c4:a3:c4:aa:
        53:bf:8a:a0:a9:87:af:c2:05:b5:03:44:77:c4:a4:
        19:cc:12:94:f9:b4:ce:da:15:d5:0f:5a:07:c6:ee:
        f9:98:36:37:c4:2c:2a:48:01
```

```
prime1:
        00:d4:61:5d:38:c0:d4:84:8c:4c:bd:b5:82:74:cd:
        aa:f2:0c:07:2f:77:f5:46:db:f5:3f:ea:a8:90:19:
        a8:c1:79:2a:52:aa:81:04:4a:28:1b:ba:c2:a4:bb:
        ec:15:b5:16:20:59:61:28:98:bf:d7:e7:cb:7e:2b:
        4d:5e:30:c6:59
prime2:
        00:c3:a3:d4:47:d6:0b:79:bb:26:fd:28:e2:88:e4:
        a1:57:80:0a:b8:57:62:ee:de:c3:61:61:39:52:56:
        f5:ba:a3:ff:8b:6f:33:37:fc:ad:b7:80:57:28:8b:
        3f:29:c1:72:91:01:9e:00:2e:8b:0c:76:72:c9:cc:
        9c:9e:d0:c8:39
```

Similarly, the public key can be explored using the following commands. Public and Private keys are base64-encoded:

```
~/Crypt$ openssl pkey -in publickey.pem -pubin -text
-----BEGIN PUBLIC KEY-----
MIGfMA0GCSqGSIb3DQEBAQUAA4GNADCBiQKBgQCiThQcz8trznenpgZP1Bq8w8u0
74A2J2MQX4hCSHf6/hMjLfxdeJNnw0zlcMV2l08YkIA/gSronsv+vfYrZ66lv8cv
6aHAzL6G4/EAp4BJ7TnTaFUmjfrdH/Z0TN4lTPeJs9/wv7+L176GnD8j5K/9I4SF
dMKArq1xk4IYKiGx0QIDAQAB
-----END PUBLIC KEY-----
Public-Key: (1024 bit)
Modulus:
        00:a2:4e:14:1c:cf:cb:6b:ce:77:a7:a6:06:4f:d4:
        1a:bc:c3:cb:b4:ef:80:36:27:63:10:5f:88:42:48:
        77:fa:fe:13:23:2d:fc:5d:78:93:67:c3:4c:e5:70:
        c5:76:97:4f:18:90:80:3f:81:2a:e8:9e:cb:fe:bd:
        f6:2b:67:ae:a5:bf:c7:2f:e9:a1:c0:cc:be:86:e3:
        f1:00:a7:80:49:ed:39:d3:68:55:26:8d:fa:dd:1f:
        f6:74:4c:de:25:4c:f7:89:b3:df:f0:bf:bf:8b:d7:
        be:86:9c:3f:23:e4:af:fd:23:84:85:74:c2:80:ae:
        ad:71:93:82:18:2a:21:b1:d1
Exponent: 65537 (0x10001)
```

Now the public key can be shared openly and anyone who wants to send us a message can use the public key to encrypt the message and send it to us. We can then use the corresponding private key to decrypt the file.

How to encrypt and decrypt using RSA with OpenSSL

First in the section, an example will presented, which demonstrates how encryption can be performed using RSA.

Encryption

Taking the private key generated in the earlier example, the command to encrypt a text file `message.txt` can be constructed, as shown here:

```
:~/Crypt$ openssl rsautl -encrypt -inkey publickey.pem -pubin -in
message.txt -out message.rsa
```

This will produce a file named `message.rsa`, which is in a binary format. If we open `message.rsa` in the nano editor, it will show some garbage:

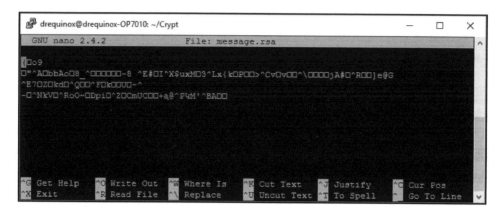

message.rsa showing garbage data

Decrypt

In order to decrypt the RSA-encrypted file, the following command can be used:

```
:~/Crypt$ openssl rsautl -decrypt -inkey privatekey.pem -in message.rsa -
out message.dec
```

Now if the file is read using cat, decrypted plain text can be seen, as shown here:

```
:~/Crypt$ cat message.dec
datatoencrypt
```

ECC using OpenSSL

OpenSSL provides a very rich library of functions to perform elliptic curve cryptography. The following section shows how to practically use ECC functions in OpenSSL.

ECC private and public key pair

In this example, first, an example is presented that demonstrates the creation of a private key using ECC functions available in the OpenSSL library.

Private key

ECC is based on domain parameters defined by various standards. We can see the list of all available standards' defined and recommended curves available in OpenSSL using the following command:

```
Crypt$ openssl ecparam -list_curves
    secp112r1 : SECG/WTLS curve over a 112 bit prime field
    secp112r2 : SECG curve over a 112 bit prime field
    secp128r1 : SECG curve over a 128 bit prime field
    secp128r2 : SECG curve over a 128 bit prime field
    secp160k1 : SECG curve over a 160 bit prime field
    secp160r1 : SECG curve over a 160 bit prime field
    secp160r2 : SECG/WTLS curve over a 160 bit prime field
    secp192k1 : SECG curve over a 192 bit prime field
    secp224k1 : SECG curve over a 224 bit prime field
    secp224r1 : NIST/SECG curve over a 224 bit prime field
    secp256k1 : SECG curve over a 256 bit prime field
    secp384r1 : NIST/SECG curve over a 384 bit prime field
    secp521r1 : NIST/SECG curve over a 521 bit prime field
    prime192v1: NIST/X9.62/SECG curve over a 192 bit prime field
    .
    .
    .
    .
    brainpoolP384r1: RFC 5639 curve over a 384 bit prime field
    brainpoolP384t1: RFC 5639 curve over a 384 bit prime field
    brainpoolP512r1: RFC 5639 curve over a 512 bit prime field
    brainpoolP512t1: RFC 5639 curve over a 512 bit prime field
```

As this produces a long output, the complete output is not shown and truncated in between. In the following example, SECP256k1 is used to demonstrate ECC usage.

Private key generation

```
~/Crypt$ openssl ecparam -name secp256k1 -genkey -noout -out ec-
privatekey.pem
~/Crypt$ cat ec-privatekey.pem
-----BEGIN EC PRIVATE KEY-----
MHQCAQEEIJHUIm9NZAgfpUrSxUk/iINq1ghM/ewn/RLNreuR52h/oAcGBSuBBAAK
oUQDQgAE0G33mCZ4PKbg5EtwQjk6ucv9Qc9DTr8JdcGXYGxHdzr0Jt1NInaYE0GG
ChFMT5pK+wfvSLkY15ul0oczwWKjng==
-----END EC PRIVATE KEY-----
```

The file named `ec-privatekey.pem` now contains the EC private key that is generated based on the SECP256K1 curve.

In order to generate a public key out of a private key, issue the following command:

```
~/Crypt$ openssl ec -in ec-privatekey.pem -pubout -out ec-pubkey.pem
read EC key
writing EC key
```

Reading the file produces the following output, displaying the generated public key:

```
~/Crypt$ cat ec-pubkey.pem
-----BEGIN PUBLIC KEY-----
MFYwEAYHKoZIzj0CAQYFK4EEAAoDQgAE0G33mCZ4PKbg5EtwQjk6ucv9Qc9DTr8J
dcGXYGxHdzr0Jt1NInaYE0GGChFMT5pK+wfvSLkY15ul0oczwWKjng==
-----END PUBLIC KEY-----
```

Now the `ec-pubkey.pem` file contains the public key derived out of `ec-privatekey.pem`.

The private key can be further explored using the following command:

```
~/Crypt$ openssl ec -in ec-privatekey.pem -text -noout
read EC key
Private-Key: (256 bit)
priv:
    00:91:d4:22:6f:4d:64:08:1f:a5:4a:d2:c5:49:3f:
    88:83:6a:d6:08:4c:fd:ec:27:fd:12:cd:ad:eb:91:
    e7:68:7f
pub:
    04:d0:6d:f7:98:26:78:3c:a6:e0:e4:4b:70:42:39:
    3a:b9:cb:fd:41:cf:43:4e:bf:09:75:c1:97:60:6c:
    47:77:3a:f4:26:dd:4d:22:76:98:13:41:86:0a:11:
    4c:4f:9a:4a:fb:07:ef:48:b9:18:97:9b:a5:d2:87:
```

```
    33:c1:62:a3:9e
ASN1 OID: secp256k1
```

Similarly, the public key can be explored further with the following command:

```
drequinox@drequinox-OP7010:~/Crypt$ openssl ec -in ec-pubkey.pem -pubin -
text -noout
read EC key
Private-Key: (256 bit)
pub:
    04:d0:6d:f7:98:26:78:3c:a6:e0:e4:4b:70:42:39:
    3a:b9:cb:fd:41:cf:43:4e:bf:09:75:c1:97:60:6c:
    47:77:3a:f4:26:dd:4d:22:76:98:13:41:86:0a:11:
    4c:4f:9a:4a:fb:07:ef:48:b9:18:97:9b:a5:d2:87:
    33:c1:62:a3:9e
ASN1 OID: secp256k1
drequinox@drequinox-OP7010:~/Crypt$
```

It is also possible to generate a file with the required parameters-in this case, SECP256K1-and then explore it further to understand the underlying parameters:

```
~/Crypt$ openssl ecparam -name secp256k1 -out secp256k1.pem
drequinox@drequinox-OP7010:~/Crypt$ cat secp256k1.pem
-----BEGIN EC PARAMETERS-----
BgUrgQQACg==
-----END EC PARAMETERS-----
```

The file now contains all SECP256K1 parameters and can be analyzed using the following command:

```
drequinox@drequinox-OP7010:~/Crypt$ openssl ecparam -in secp256k1.pem -text
-param_enc explicit -noout
Field Type: prime-field
Prime:
    00:ff:ff:ff:ff:ff:ff:ff:ff:ff:ff:ff:ff:ff:ff:
    ff:ff:ff:ff:ff:ff:ff:ff:ff:ff:ff:ff:ff:fe:ff:
    ff:fc:2f
A:    0
B:    7 (0x7)
Generator (uncompressed):
    04:79:be:66:7e:f9:dc:bb:ac:55:a0:62:95:ce:87:
    0b:07:02:9b:fc:db:2d:ce:28:d9:59:f2:81:5b:16:
    f8:17:98:48:3a:da:77:26:a3:c4:65:5d:a4:fb:fc:
    0e:11:08:a8:fd:17:b4:48:a6:85:54:19:9c:47:d0:
    8f:fb:10:d4:b8
Order:
    00:ff:ff:ff:ff:ff:ff:ff:ff:ff:ff:ff:ff:ff:ff:
    ff:fe:ba:ae:dc:e6:af:48:a0:3b:bf:d2:5e:8c:d0:
```

```
        36:41:41
  Cofactor:  1 (0x1)
```

The preceding example shows the prime number used and values of A and B the with generator, order, and cofactor of the SECP256K1 curve domain parameters.

There is another category of cryptographic primitives that is known as hash functions. Hash functions are not used to encrypt; data instead, they produce a fixed length digest of text.

Cryptographic primitives

This taxonomy of cryptographic primitives can be visualized as shown here:

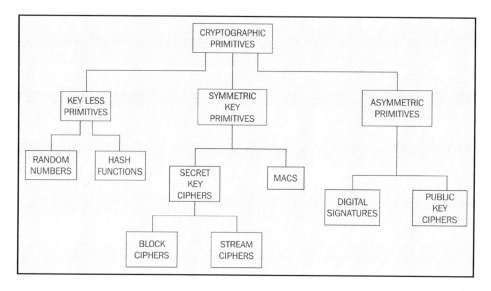

Cryptographic primitives

Hash functions

Hash functions are used to create fixed length digests of arbitrarily long input strings. Hash functions are keyless and provide the data integrity service. They are usually built using iterated and dedicated hash function construction techniques. Various families of hash functions are available, such as MD, SHA1, SHA-2, SHA-3, RIPEMD, and Whirlpool. Hash functions are commonly used in digital signatures and message authentication codes, such as HMACs. They have three security properties, namely pre-image resistance, second pre-image resistance, and collision resistance. These properties are explained later in the section.

Hash functions are typically used to provide data integrity services. These can be used as one-way functions and to construct other cryptographic primitives, such as MACs and digital signatures. Some applications used hash functions as a means of generating **pseudo random numbers (PRNGs)**. Hash functions do not require a key. There are two practical and three security properties of hash functions that must be met depending on the level of requirements of integrity.

Compression of arbitrary messages into fixed length digest

This property is concerned with the fact that a hash function must be able to take a long input text of any length and output a fixed length compressed message. Hash functions produce a compressed output in various bit sizes, usually between 128-bits and 512-bits.

Easy to compute

Hash functions are efficient and fast one-way functions. The requirement is that they be very quick to compute regardless of the message size. The efficiency may decrease if the message is too big but the function should still be fast enough for practical use.

In the following section, security properties of hash functions are discussed.

Pre-image resistance

Consider an equation:

$$h(x) = y$$

Here, h is the hash function, x is the input, and y is the hash. The first security property requires that y cannot be reverse computed to x. x is considered a *pre-image* of y, hence the name pre-image resistance. This is also called one-way property.

Second pre-image resistance

This property requires that given x and $h(x)$, it is almost impossible to find any other message m, where $m \mathrel{!=} x$ and *hash of m = hash of x*. $h(m) = h(x)$. This property is also known as weak collision resistance.

Collision resistance

This property requires that two different input messages should not hash to the same output. In other words, $h(x) != h(z)$. This property is also known as strong collision resistance.

Hash functions, due to their very nature, will always have some collisions, and that is where two different messages hash to the same output, but they should be computationally infeasible to find. A concept known as **avalanche effect** is desirable in all hash functions. Avalanche effect specifies that a small change, even a single character change in the input text, will result in a totally different hash output.

Hash functions are usually designed by following iterated hash functions approach. In this method, the input message is compressed in multiple rounds on a block-by-block basis to produce the compressed output. A popular type of iterated hash function is Merkle-Damgard construction. This construction is based on the idea of dividing the input data into equal sizes of blocks and then feeding them through the compression functions in an iterative manner. The collision resistance of the property of compression functions ensures that the hash output is also collision-resistant. Compression functions can be built using block ciphers. In addition to Merkle-Damgard, there are various other constructions of compression functions proposed by researchers, for example, *Miyaguchi-Preneel* and *Davies-Meyer*.

There are multiple hash function categories. You will be introduced to these categories in the upcoming section.

Message Digest (MD)

Message Digest functions were very popular in early 1990s. MD4 and MD5 are members of this category. Both MD functions are found to be insecure and not recommended for use any more. MD5 is a 128-bit hash function that was commonly used for file integrity checks.

Secure Hash Algorithms (SHAs)

SHA-0: This is a 160-bit function introduced by NIST in 1993.

SHA-1: SHA-1 was introduced later by NIST as a replacement of SHA-0. This is also a 160-bit hash function. SHA-1 is used commonly in SSL and TLS implementations. It should be noted that SHA-1 is now considered insecure and is being deprecated by certificate authorities. Its usage is now discouraged in any new implementations.

SHA-2: This category includes four functions defined by the number of bits of the hash: SHA-224, SHA-256, SHA-384 and SHA-512.

SHA-3: This is the latest family of SHA functions. SHA3-224, SHA3-256, SHA3-384 and SHA3-512 are members of this family. SHA3 is a NIST-standardized version of Keccak. Keccak uses a new approach called *sponge construction* instead of the commonly used Merkle-Damgard transformation.

RIPEMD: RIPEMD is the acronym for *RACE Integrity Primitives Evaluation Message Digest*. It is based on the design ideas used to build MD4. There are multiple versions of RIPEMD, including 128-bit, 160-bit, 256-bit, and 320-bit.

Whirlpool: This is based on a modified version of Rijndael cipher known as W. It uses the Miyaguchi-Preneel compression function, which is a type of one-way function used for the compression of two fixed length inputs into a single fixed length output. It is a single block length compression function:

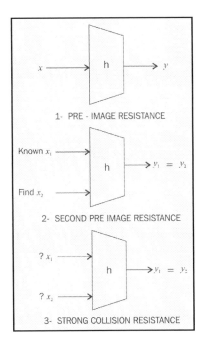

Three security properties of hash functions

Hash functions have many practical applications ranging from simple file integrity checks and password storage to be used in cryptographic protocols and algorithms. They are used in hash tables, distributed hash tables, bloom filters, virus finger printing, peer-to-peer P2P file sharing, and many other applications.

In blockchain, hash functions play a very vital role. Especially, the proof of work function uses SHA-256 twice in order to verify the computational effort spent by miners. RIPEMD 160 is used to produce bitcoin addresses. This will be discussed in more detail in later chapters.

Design of Secure Hash Algorithms (SHA)

In the following section, you will be introduced to the design of SHA-256 and SHA-3. Both of these are used in bitcoin and Ethereum, respectively. Ethereum doesn't use NIST Standard SHA-3 but Keccak, which is the original algorithm presented to NIST. NIST, after some modifications such as increase in the number of rounds and simpler message padding, standardized Keccak as SHA-3.

SHA-256

SHA-256 has the input message size < 2^64-bits. Block size is 512-bits and has a word size of 32-bits. Output is 256-bit digest.

The compression function processes a 512-bit message block and a 256-bit intermediate hash value. There are two main components of this function: compression function and a message schedule.

The algorithm works as follows:

- Pre-processing:

1. Padding of the message, which is used to make the length of a block to 512-bits if it is smaller than the required block size of 512-bits.
2. Parsing the message into message blocks that ensure that the message and its padding is divided into equal blocks of 512-bits.
3. Setting up the initial hash value, which is the eight 32-bit words obtained by taking the first 32-bits of the fractional parts of the square roots of the first eight prime numbers. These initial values are randomly chosen in order to initialize the process and gives a level of confidence that no backdoor exists in the algorithm.

- Hash computation:

1. Each message block is processed in a sequence and requires 64 rounds to compute the full hash output. Each round uses slightly different constants to ensure that no two rounds are the same.
2. First, the message schedule is prepared.
3. Then, eight working variables are initialized.
4. Then, the intermediate hash value is calculated.
5. Finally, the message is processed and the output hash is produced:

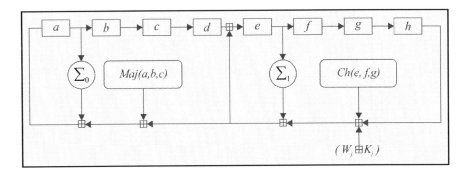

one round of SHA 256 compression function

In the preceding diagram, *a*, *b*, *c*, *d*, *e*, *f*, *g*, and *h* are the registers. **Maj** and **Ch** are applied bitwise. Σ_0 and Σ_1 performs bitwise rotation. Round constants are $\mathbf{W}_j$ and $\mathbf{K}_j$, which are added *mod 2^32*.

Design of SHA3 (Keccak)

The structure of SHA-3 is very different from the usual SHA-1 and SHA-2. The key idea behind SHA-3 is based on un-keyed permutations as opposed to other usual hash functions' constructions that used keyed permutations. Keccak also does not make use of the Merkle-Damgard transformation that is commonly used to handle arbitrary length input messages in hash functions. A newer approach called sponge and squeeze construction is used in Keccak, which is basically a random permutation model. Different variants of SHA3 have been standardized, such as SHA3-224, SHA3-256, SHA3-384, SHA3-512, SHAKE128, and SHAKE256. SHAKE128 and SHAKE256 are extendable output functions that are also standardized by `NIST`. `XOF` functions that allow the output to be extended to any desired length.

The following diagram shows the sponge and squeeze model that is the basis of SHA3 or Keccak. As an analogy to sponge, first, the data is absorbed into the sponge after applying padding, where it is then changed into a subset of permutation state using XOR and then the output is squeezed out of the sponge function that represents the transformed state. Rate is the input block size of a sponge function, whereas capacity determines the generic security level:

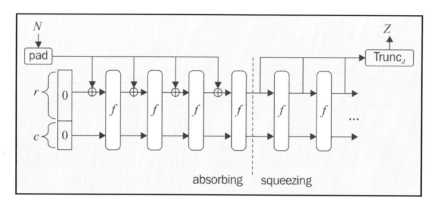

SHA-3 absorbing and squeezing function in SHA3

OpenSSL example of hash functions

The following command will produce a hash of 256-bits of Hello messages using the SHA256 algorithm:

```
:~/Crypt$ echo -n 'Hello' | openssl dgst -sha256
(stdin)= 185f8db32271fe25f561a6fc938b2e264306ec304eda518007d1764826381969
```

Note that even a small change in the text, such as changing the case of *H*, results in a big change in the output hash. This is known as *avalanche effect*, as discussed earlier:

```
:~/Crypt$ echo -n 'hello' | openssl dgst -sha256
(stdin)= 2cf24dba5fb0a30e26e83b2ac5b9e29e1b161e5c1fa7425e73043362938b9824
```

Note that both outputs are completely different:

```
Hello:
18:5f:8d:b3:22:71:fe:25:f5:61:a6:fc:93:8b:2e:26:43:06:ec:30:4e:da:51:80:07:
d1:76:48:26:38:19:69
hello:
2c:f2:4d:ba:5f:b0:a3:0e:26:e8:3b:2a:c5:b9:e2:9e:1b:16:1e:5c:1f:a7:42:5e:73:
04:33:62:93:8b:98:24
```

Message Authentication codes (MACs)

MACs are sometimes called keyed hash functions and can be used to provide message integrity and authentication. In others words, they are used to provide data origin authentication. These are symmetric cryptographic primitives using a shared key between the sender and the receiver. MACs can be constructed using block ciphers or hash functions.

MACs using block ciphers

In this approach, block ciphers are used in the **Cipher block chaining mode (CBC mode)** in order to generate a MAC. Any block cipher-for example, AES in the CBC mode-can be used. The MAC of the message is in fact the output of the last round of the CBC operation. The length of the MAC output is the same as the block length of the block cipher used to generate MAC. MACs are verified simply by computing the MAC of the message and comparing it with the received MAC. If they are the same, then the message integrity is confirmed; otherwise, the message is considered altered. It should also be noted that MACs work like digital signatures, but they cannot provide the nonrepudiation service due to their symmetric nature.

HMACs (hash-based MACs)

Similar to the hash function, they produce a fixed length output and take an arbitrarily long message as the input. In this scheme, the sender signs a message using MAC and the receiver verifies it using the shared key. The key is hashed with the message using either of the two methods known as secret prefix or the secret suffix method. In the first method, the key is concatenated with the message, that is, the key comes first and the message comes after, whereas in the latter method, the key comes after the message:

Secret prefix: $M = MACk(x) = h(k||x)$

Secret suffix: $M=MACk(x) = h(x||k)$

There are pros and cons of both methods. Some attacks on both schemes have been discovered. There are HMAC constructions schemes that use various techniques, such as **ipad** and **opad** (inner padding and outer padding) proposed by researchers that are considered secure with some assumptions:

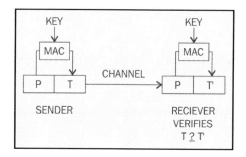

Operation of a MAC function

Merkle trees

The concept of Merkle tree was introduced by *Ralph Merkle*. A visualization of Merkle tree is shown here, which makes it easy to understand. Merkle trees allow secure and efficient verification of large data sets.

It is a binary tree in which first, the inputs are placed at the leaves (node with no children), and then values of pairs of child nodes are hashed together in order to produce a value for the parent node (internal node) until a single hash value known as Merkle root is achieved:

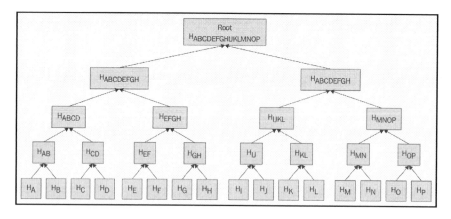

A Merkle tree

Patricia trees

In order to understand Patricia trees, first, you will be introduced to the concept of a **trie**. A trie or a digital tree is an ordered tree data structure used to store a dataset.

Practical Algorithm to Retrieve Information Coded in Alphanumeric (Patricia), also known as Radix tree, is a compact representation of a trie in which a node that is the only child of a parent is merged with its parent.

Merkle-Patricia tree, based on the definitions of Patricia and Merkle, is a tree that has a root node that contains the hash value of the entire data structure.

Distributed hash tables (DHTs)

A hash table is a data structure that is used to map keys to values. Internally, a hash function is used to calculate an index into an array of buckets, from which the required value can be found. Buckets have records stored in them using a hash key and are organized in a particular order.

With the definition provided earlier in mind, one can think of the distributed hash table as a data structure where data is spread across various nodes and nodes are equivalent to buckets in a peer-to-peer to network.

The following diagram visually shows how a DHT works. The example shows that data is passed through a hash function, which results in generating a compact key. This key is then linked with the data (values) on the peer-to-peer network. When users on the network request the data (via the filename), the filename can be hashed again to produce the same key and any node on the network can then be requested to find the corresponding data. DHTs provides decentralization, fault tolerance, and scalability:

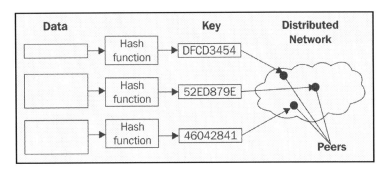

Distributed hash tables

Digital signatures

Digital signatures provide a means of associating a message with an entity from which the message has been originated. Digital signatures are used to provide data origin authentication and nonrepudiation. They are calculated in two steps. High-level steps of an RSA digital signature scheme is given as follows:

1. Calculate the hash value of the data packet. This will provide the data integrity guarantee as hash can be computed at the receiver's end again and matched with the original hash to check whether the data has been modified in transit. Technically, message signing can work without hashing the data first, but is not considered secure.
2. The second step signs the hash value with the signer's private key. As only the singer has the private key, the authenticity of the signature and the signed data is ensured.

Digital signatures have some important properties, such as authenticity, unforgeability, and nonreusability. Authenticity means that the digital signatures are verifiable by a receiving party. The unforgeability property ensures that only the sender of the message is able to use the signing functionality using the private key. In other words, no one else should be able to produce the signed message that has been produced by the legitimate sender. Non reusability means that the digital signature cannot be separated from a message and used for another message again.

The operation of a generic digital signature function is shown in the following diagram:

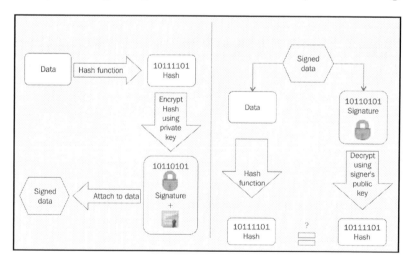

Digital signing (left) and verification process (right) (Example of RSA digital signatures)

If a sender wants to send an authenticated message to a receiver, there are two methods that can be used. These two approaches to use digital signatures with encryption are introduced here.

Sign then encrypt

In this approach, the sender digitally signs the data using the private key, appends the signature to the data, and then encrypts the data and the digital signature using the receiver's public key. This is considered a more secure scheme as compared to the encrypt then sign scheme described next.

Encrypt then sign

In this approach, the sender encrypts the data using the receiver's public key and then digitally signs the encrypted data.

In practice, a digital certificate that contains the digital signature is issued by a **certificate authority (CA)** that associates a public key with an identity.

Various schemes, such as RSA, Digital Signature Algorithm, and Elliptic Curve Digital Signature Algorithm-based digital signature schemes are used in practice. RSA is the most commonly used; however, with the traction of elliptic curve cryptography, ECDSA-based schemes are also becoming quite popular.

The ECDSA scheme is described in detail here.

Elliptic Curve Digital signature algorithm (ECDSA)

In order to sign and verify using the ECDSA scheme, the first key pair needs to be generated:

1. First, define an elliptic curve E:

   1. With modulus P.

   2. Coefficients a and b.

   3. Generator point A that forms a cyclic group of prime order q.

2. An integer d is chosen randomly so that $0 < d < q$.
3. Calculate public key B so that $B = d\ A$.

Public key is the sextuple of the form shown here:

$$Kpb = (p,a,b,q,A,B)$$

Private key is randomly chosen d in Step 2:

$$Kpr = d$$

Now the signature can be generated using the private and public key.

1. First, an ephemeral key Ke is chosen, where $0 < Ke < q$. It should be ensured that Ke is truly random, and no two signatures have the same key; otherwise, the private key can be calculated.
2. Another value R is calculated using $R = Ke\ A$, that is, by multiplying A (the generator point) and the random ephemeral key.
3. Initialize a variable r with the x coordinate value of point R. $r = xR$.
4. The signature can be calculated as follows:

$$S = (h(m) + dr)K_{e-1}\bmod q$$

Here, m is the message for which the signature is being computed and $h(m)$ is the hash of the message m.

Signature verification is carried out by following this process.

1. Auxiliary value w is calculated as $w = s^{-1} mod\ q$.
2. Auxiliary value $u1 = w.\ h(m)\ mod\ q$.
3. Auxiliary value $u2 = w.\ r\ mod\ q$.
4. Calculate Point P, $P = u1A + u2B$.
5. Verification is carried out as follows.
6. r, s is accepted as a valid signature if x-coordinate of the point P calculated in Step 4 has the same value as the signature parameter $r\ mod\ q$.

that is:

$$Xp = r\ mod\ q\ means\ valid\ signature$$

Xp != r mod q means invalid signature

Various practical examples are shown here, which shows how the RSA digital signature can be generated, used, and verified using OpenSSL.

How to generate a digital signature

The first step is to generate a hash of the message file:

```
:~/Crypt$ openssl dgst -sha256 message.txt
SHA256(message.txt)=
eb96d1f89812bf4967d9fb4ead128c3b787272b7be21dd2529278db1128d559c
```

Both hash generation and signing can be done in a single step, as shown here. Note that `privatekey.pem` is generated in the steps provided previously:

```
:~/Crypt$ openssl dgst -sha256 -sign privatekey.pem -out signature.bin
message.txt
```

Now let's display the directory showing relevant files:

```
:~/Crypt$ ls -ltr
total 36
-rw-rw-r-- 1 drequinox drequinox  14 Sep 21 05:54 message.txt
-rw-rw-r-- 1 drequinox drequinox  32 Sep 21 05:57 message.bin
-rw-rw-r-- 1 drequinox drequinox  45 Sep 21 06:00 message.b64
-rw-rw-r-- 1 drequinox drequinox  32 Sep 21 06:16 message.ptx
-rw-rw-r-- 1 drequinox drequinox 916 Sep 21 06:28 privatekey.pem
-rw-rw-r-- 1 drequinox drequinox 272 Sep 21 06:30 publickey.pem
-rw-rw-r-- 1 drequinox drequinox 128 Sep 21 06:43 message.rsa
-rw-rw-r-- 1 drequinox drequinox  14 Sep 21 06:49 message.dec
-rw-rw-r-- 1 drequinox drequinox 128 Sep 21 07:05 signature.bin
:~/Crypt$ cat signature.bin
V _[h]ht+T~Ols{Cq"#AQU,ufp*□*7T'ueAy
$x<$a`:LqWhuG=$:~/Crypt$
```

In order to verify the signature, the following operation can be performed:

```
:~/Crypt$ openssl dgst -sha256 -verify publickey.pem -signature
signature.bin message.txt
Verified OK
:~/Crypt$
```

Similarly, if some other signature file that is not valid is used, the verification will fail, as shown here:

```
:~/Crypt$ openssl dgst -sha256 -verify publickey.pem -signature
someothersignature.bin message.txt
Verification Failure
```

Now you are introduced to an example that shows how OpenSSL can be used to perform ECDSA-related operations.

ECDSA using OpenSSL

First, the private key is generated using the following commands:

```
~/Crypt$ openssl ecparam -genkey -name secp256k1 -noout -out
eccprivatekey.pem
~/Crypt$ cat eccprivatekey.pem
-----BEGIN EC PRIVATE KEY-----
MHQCAQEEIMVmyrnEDOs7SYxS/AbXoIwqZqJ+gND9Z2/nQyzcpaPBoAcGBSuBBAAK
oUQDQgAEEKKS4E4+TATIeBX8o2J6PxKkjcoWrXPwNRo/k4Y/CZA4pXvlyTgH5LYm
QbU0qUtPM7dAEzOsaoXmetqB+6cM+Q==
-----END EC PRIVATE KEY-----
```

Now the public key is generated out of the private key:

```
~/Crypt$ openssl ec -in eccprivatekey.pem -pubout -out eccpublickey.pem
read EC key
writing EC key
~/Crypt$ cat eccpublickey.pem
-----BEGIN PUBLIC KEY-----
MFYwEAYHKoZIzj0CAQYFK4EEAAoDQgAEEKKS4E4+TATIeBX8o2J6PxKkjcoWrXPw
NRo/k4Y/CZA4pXvlyTgH5LYmQbU0qUtPM7dAEzOsaoXmetqB+6cM+Q==
-----END PUBLIC KEY-----
~/Crypt$
```

Now suppose a file named `testsign.txt` needs to be signed and verified. This can be achieved as follows:

1. Create a test file:

   ```
   ~/Crypt$ echo testing > testsign.txt
   ~/Crypt$ cat testsign.txt
   testing
   ```

2. Run the following command to generate a signature using a private key for the `testsign.txt` file:

   ```
   ~/Crypt$ openssl dgst -ecdsa-with-SHA1 -sign eccprivatekey.pem
   testsign.txt > ecsign.bin
   ```

3. Finally, the command for verification can be run as shown here:

   ```
   ~/Crypt$ openssl dgst -ecdsa-with-SHA1 -verify eccpublickey.pem
   -signature ecsign.bin testsign.txt
   Verified OK
   ```

A certificate can also be generated using the private key generated earlier:

```
~/Crypt$ openssl req -new -key eccprivatekey.pem -x509 -nodes -days 365 -
out ecccertificate.pem
You are about to be asked to enter information that will be incorporated
into your certificate request.
What you are about to enter is what is called a Distinguished Name or a DN.
There are quite a few fields but you can leave some blank
For some fields there will be a default value,
If you enter '.', the field will be left blank.
-----
Country Name (2 letter code) [AU]:GB
State or Province Name (full name) [Some-State]:Cambridge
Locality Name (eg, city) []:Cambridge
Organization Name (eg, company) [Internet Widgits Pty Ltd]:Dr.Equinox!
Organizational Unit Name (eg, section) []:NA
Common Name (e.g. server FQDN or YOUR name) []:drequinox
Email Address []:drequinox@drequinox.com
```

The certificate can be explored using the command below:

```
~/Crypt$ openssl x509 -in ecccertificate.pem -text -noout
```

X509 certificate that uses ECDSA algorithm with SHA-256

There are other topics in cryptography that are presented here due to their relevance to blockchain or potential use in future blockchain ecosystems.

Homomorphic encryption

Usually, public key cryptosystems, such as RSA, are multiplicative homomorphic or additive homomorphic, such as Paillier cryptosystem, and are called **partially homomorphic** systems. Additive PHEs are suitable for e-voting and banking applications. Until recently, there has been no system that supported both operations, but in 2009, a **fully homomorphic** system was discovered by *Craig Gentry*. As these schemes allow the processing of encrypted data without the need for decryption, they have many different possible applications, especially in scenarios where privacy is required to be maintained but data is also required to be processed by potentially untrusted parties, for example, cloud computing and online search engines. Recent development in homomorphic encryption has been very promising and researchers are actively working to make it efficient and more practical. This is of particular interest in the blockchain technology, as described later in the book, because it can solve the problem of confidentiality and privacy in blockchain.

Signcryption

Signcryption is a public key cryptography primitive that provides all the functions of the digital signature and encryption. It was invented by *Yuliang Zheng* and is now an ISO standard ISO/IEC 29150:2011. Traditionally, signature then encrypt or encrypt then sign schemes are used to provide unforgeability, authentication, and nonrepudiation, but with Signcryption, all services of digital signatures and encryption are provided with cost less than that of sign then encrypt schemes.

This is **Cost (signature & encryption) << Cost (signature) + Cost (Encryption)** in a single logical step.

Zero knowledge proofs

Zero knowledge proofs were introduced by *GoldWasser, Micali*, and *Rackoff*. These proofs are used to prove the validity of an assertion without revealing any information whatsoever about the assertion. There are three properties of ZKPs that are required, namely completeness, soundness, and zero-knowledge property.

Completeness ensures that if a certain assertion is true, then the verifier will be convinced of this claim by the prover. The soundness property makes sure that if an assertion is false, then no dishonest prover can convince the verifier otherwise. Zero-knowledge property, as the name implies, is the key property of zero knowledge proofs whereby it is ensured that absolutely nothing is revealed about the assertion except whether it is true or false.

Zero knowledge proofs have sparked a special interest among researchers in the blockchain space due to its privacy properties that are very much desirable in financial and many other fields, such as law and medicine. A recent example of the successful implementation of the zero knowledge proof mechanism is the Zcash crypto currency. In Zcash, a specific type of zero knowledge proof, known as **zero-knowledge Succinct Non-interactive Argument of Knowledge (ZK-Snark)**, is implemented. This will be discussed in detail in `Chapter 5,` *Alternative Coins.*

Blind signatures

Blind signatures were introduced by *David Chaum* in 1982 and are based on public key digital signature schemes, such as RSA. The key idea behind blind signatures is to get the message signed by the signer without actually revealing the message. This is achieved by disguising or blinding the message before signing it, hence the name blind signatures. This blind signature can then be verified against the original message just like a normal digital signature. Blind signatures were introduced as a mechanism to allow the development of digital cash schemes.

Encoding schemes

Other than cryptographic primitives, binary to text encoding schemes are also used in various scenarios. The most common usage is to convert binary data into text so that it can be either processed, saved, or transmitted via a protocol that does not support the processing of binary data. For example, sometimes, images are stored in the database as base64 encoding, which allows a text field to be able to store a picture. A commonly used encoding scheme is base64. Another encoding named base58 was popularized by its usage in bitcoin.

Cryptography is a vast field and this section has introduced basic concepts that are essential to understand cryptography in general and specifically from the blockchain and cryptocurrency point of view. In the next section, you are introduced to basic financial markets concepts.

The upcoming section describes general terminologies about trading, exchanges, and trade life cycle. More relevant information will be provided in later chapters where specific use cases are discussed.

Financial markets and trading

Financial markets exist to facilitate the transfers of savings from savers to investors. In an economic system, there are two sectors, namely household and business. Financial markets, at their core, act as an intermediary between the savers and the investors. Basically, there are three types of markets, namely money markets, credit markets, and capital markets. Money markets are short-term markets where money is lent to companies or banks to do interbank lending. Foreign exchange or FX is another category of money markets where currencies are traded. Credit markets consist mostly of retail banks where they borrow money from central banks and loan it to companies or households in the form of mortgages or loans.

Capital markets facilitate the buying and selling of financial instruments, mainly stocks and bonds. Capital markets can be divided into two types, primary and secondary markets. Stocks are issued directly by the companies to investors in primary markets, whereas in secondary markets, investors resell their securities to investors via stock exchanges. Various electronic trading systems are used by exchanges to facilitate the trading of financial instruments.

Trading

A market is a place where traders come to trade. It can ent asset classes.

Trading can be defined as an activity in which traders buy or sell various financial instruments to generate profit and hedge risk. Investors, borrowers, hedgers, asset exchangers, and gamblers are a few types of traders. Traders have a short position when they owe something, for example, if they have sold a contract and have a long position when they buy a contract. There are various ways to transact trades, such as through brokers or directly on the exchange or over the counter. Brokers are agents who arrange trades for their customers. Brokers act on clients' behalf to deal at a given price or at the best possible price.

Exchanges

Exchanges are usually considered to be a very safe, regulated, and reliable place for trading. Recently, electronic trading has gained high popularity as compared to traditional floor-based trading. Now traders send orders to a central electronic order book from where the orders, prices, and related attributes are published to all associated systems using communication networks thus, in essence, creating a virtual marketplace. Exchange trades can be performed only by members of the exchange. In order to trade without these limitations, the counter parties can participate in **OTC (Over the Counter)** trading directly.

Orders and order properties

Orders are instructions to trade and are the main building blocks of a trading system. They have the following general attributes:

1. The instrument name.
2. Quantity.
3. Direction (buy or sell).

4. The type of the order that represents various conditions, for example, limit orders and stop orders, an example of which is 1500 Royal Bank of Scotland ordinary shares for GBP £15.50.

Orders are traded on the basis of bid prices and offer prices. Traders show their intention to buy or sell by attaching bid and offer prices to their orders. The price at which a trader will buy is known as the bid price. The price at which a trader is willing to sell is known as the offer price.

Order management and routing systems

Order routing systems routes and deliver orders to various destinations depending on the business logic. Customers use them to send orders to their brokers, who then send these orders to dealers, clearing houses, and exchanges.

There are different types of orders; the two most common ones are markets orders and limit orders. A market order is an instruction to trade at the best price currently available in the market, and these orders get filled immediately at spot prices. On the other hand, a limit order is an instruction to trade at the best price available but only if it is not lower than the limit price set by the trader. This can also be higher depending on the direction of the order, either sell or buy. All these orders are managed in an order book, which is a list of orders maintained by an exchange, and records the intention of buying or selling by the traders.

A position is a commitment to sell or buy an amount of financial instruments, such as securities, currencies, or commodities for a given price. The contracts, securities, commodities, and currencies that traders buy or sell are commonly known as trading instruments and come under the large umbrella of asset classes. The most common classes are real assets, financial assets, derivative contracts, and insurance contracts.

Components of a trade

A trade ticket is the combination of all details related to a trade. However, there is some variation depending on the type of the instrument and asset class, but generally, all instruments have the attributes discussed in the next section.

The underlying instrument
The underlying instrument is the basis of the trade. It can be a currency, a bond, interest rate, commodity, or equities.

General attributes

This includes general identification information and basic features associated with every trade. Common attributes include a unique ID, instrument name, type, status, trade date, and time.

Economic

These are features related to the value of the trade, for example, buy or sell value, ticker, exchange, price, and quantity.

Sales

Sales refers to the sales-characteristic-related details, such as the name of the sales person, and is just an information field, usually without any impact on the trade life cycle.

Counterparty

Counterparty is an important component of a trade as it shows the other side of the trade and is required to settle the trade successfully. Usual attributes include counterparty name, address, payment type, any reference IDs, settlement date, and delivery type.

Trade life cycle

A general trade life cycle includes various stages from order placement to execution and then settlement. This life cycle is described step by step as follows:

- **Pre-execution**: An order is placed at this stage.
- **Execution and booking**: When the order is matched and executed, it converts into a trade. At this stage, the contract between counter parties is matured.
- **Confirmation**: This is where both counter parties agree to particulars of the trade.
- **Post booking**: This stage is concerned with various scrutiny and verification processes to ascertain the correctness of the trade.
- **Settlement**: This is the most vital part during trade and at this stage, the trade is final.

- **Overnight (end of day processing)**: End of day processes include report generation, profit and loss calculations, and various risk calculations.

- In all the mentioned processes, many people and business functions are involved. Most commonly, these functions are divided into functions such as front office, middle office, and back office.

In the following section, you are introduced to some concepts that are essential in order to understand the strict and necessary rules and regulations that govern the financial industry. Some concepts are described here and in later chapters when specific use cases are discussed, and these ideas will help you understand the scenarios described.

Order anticipators

Order anticipators try to make profit before other traders can carry out trading. This is based on the anticipation where a trader knows how trading activities of other trades will affect prices. Frontrunners, sentiment-oriented technical traders, and squeezers are some examples of order anticipators.

Market manipulation

Market manipulation is strictly illegal in the UK and other countries. Fraudulent traders can spread false information in the market, which can result in price movements thus making illegal profits. Usually, manipulative market conduct is trade-based and it includes generalized and time-specific manipulations. Actions that can create an artificial shortage of stock, impression of false activity, and price manipulation to gain criminal benefit are included in this category.

Both of the terms discussed earlier are relevant to financial crime. and there is a possibility of developing blockchain-based systems that can thwart market abuse. This will be discussed in detail in later chapters, where specific use cases will be discussed.

Summary

This chapter aimed at introducing concepts of cryptography and financial markets in order to provide background information for you to be able to understand the material provided in later chapters. First, you were introduced to the basics of cryptography, and then various schemes such as symmetric and asymmetric ciphers were introduced. Practical examples using OpenSSL command line were shown so that you could experiment with various commands and experience various cryptographic functions firsthand. Also, some mathematical background was provided at the beginning of the chapter and where necessary, especially with the elliptic curve cryptography. All cryptography concepts presented in this chapter are related to the blockchain technology and are implemented or have been proposed to be implemented in various blockchains, cryptocurrencies, and relevant ecosystems. Moreover, you were given a quick introduction to the financial industry as it sets the scene for various examples that will be discussed in relation to the distributed ledger technology later in the book. As cryptography and finance are vast subjects, the material covered in his chapter is aimed to be introductory in nature (with some exceptions) and specific topics will be expanded upon in more detail, where relevant and required, in the next chapters.

4
Bitcoin

Bitcoin is the first application of the blockchain technology. In this chapter, readers will be introduced to bitcoin technology in detail.

Bitcoin has started a revolution with the introduction of the very first fully decentralized digital currency, and one that has proven to be extremely secure and stable. This has also sparked a great interest in academic and industrial research and introduced many new research areas. Since its introduction in 2008, bitcoin has gained much popularity and is currently the most successful digital currency in the world with billions of dollars invested in it. It is built on decades of research in the field of cryptography, digital cash, and distributed computing. In the following section, a brief history is presented in order to provide the background required to understand the foundations behind the invention of bitcoin.

Digital currencies have always been an active area of research for many decades. Early proposals to create digital cash go as far back as the early 1980s. In 1982, *David Chaum* proposed a scheme that used blind signatures to build untraceable digital currency. In this scheme, a bank would issue digital money by signing a blind and random serial number presented to it by the user. The user could then use the digital token signed by the bank as currency. The limitation in this scheme was that the bank had to keep track of all used serial numbers. This was a central system by design and required to be trusted by the users. Later on in 1990, *David Chaum* proposed a refined version named e-cash that not only used blinded signature, but also some private identification data to craft a message that was then sent to the bank. This scheme allowed the detection of double spending but did not prevent it. If the same token was used at two different locations, then the identity of the double spender would be revealed. e-cash could only represent a fixed amount of money. *Adam Back's* hashcash, introduced in 1997, was originally proposed to thwart e-mail spam. The idea behind hashcash was to solve a computational puzzle that was easy to verify but comparatively difficult to compute.

The idea was that for a single user and a single e-mail, extra computational effort was not noticeable, but someone sending a large number of spam e-mails would be discouraged as the time and resources required to run the spam campaign would increase substantially.

B-money was proposed by *Wei Dai* in 1998, which introduced the idea of using Proof of Work to create money. A major weakness in the system was that an adversary with higher computational power could generate unsolicited money without allowing the network to adjust to an appropriate difficulty level. The system lacked details on the consensus mechanism between nodes and some security issues such as Sybil attacks were also not addressed. At the same time, *Nick Szabo* introduced the concept of BitGold, which was also based on the Proof of Work mechanism but had the same problems as b-money with the exception that the network difficulty level was adjustable. *Tomas Sander* and *Ammon TaShama* introduced an e-cash scheme in 1999 that, for the first time, used Merkle trees to represent coins and zero knowledge proofs to prove the possession of coins. In the scheme, a central bank was required that kept a record of all used serial numbers. This scheme allowed users to be fully anonymous albeit at a computational cost. **RPOW (Reusable Proof of Work)** was introduced by *Hal Finney* in 2004 and used the hashcash scheme by *Adam Back* as a proof of computational resources spent to create the money. This was also a central system that kept a central database to keep track of all used POW tokens. This was an online system that used remote attestation made possible by a **trusted computing platform (TPM hardware)**.

All the previously mentioned schemes are intelligently designed but were weak from one aspect or another. Especially, all these schemes rely on a central server that is required to be trusted by the users.

Bitcoin

In 2008, a paper on bitcoin, *Bitcoin: A Peer-to-Peer Electronic Cash System* was written by *Satoshi Nakamoto*. The first key idea introduced in the paper was that purely peer-to-peer electronic cash that does need an intermediary bank to transfer payments between peers.

Bitcoin is built on decades of cryptographic research such as the research in Merkle trees, hash functions, public key cryptography, and digital signatures. Moreover, ideas such as BitGold, b-money, hashcash, and cryptographic time stamping provided the foundations for bitcoin invention. All these technologies are cleverly combined in bitcoin to create the world's first decentralized currency. The key issue that has been addressed in bitcoin is an elegant solution to the Byzantine Generals problem along with a practical solution of the double-spend problem.

The value of bitcoin has increased significantly since 2011, as shown in the following graph:

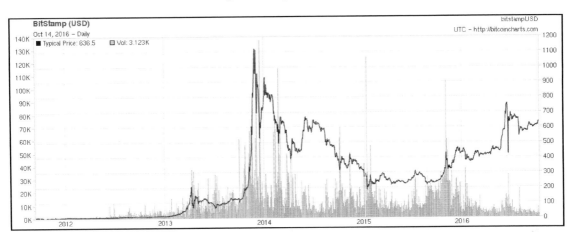

Bitcoin price and volume since 2012 (on logarithmic scale)

The regulation of bitcoin is a controversial subject and as much as it is a libertarian's dream, law enforcement agencies and governments are proposing various regulations to control it, such as BitLicense issued by New York's state department of financial services. This is a license issued to businesses that perform activities related to virtual currencies.

The growth of Bitcoin is also due to so-called *Network Effect*. Also called demand-side economies of scale, it is a concept that basically means more users who use the network, the more valuable it becomes. Over time, an exponential increase has been seen in the Bitcoin network growth. Even though the price of bitcoin is quite volatile, it has increased significantly over the last few years. Currently (at the time of writing this), bitcoin price is 815 GBP.

Bitcoin definition

Bitcoin can be defined in various ways; it's a protocol, a digital currency, and a platform. It is a combination of peer-to-peer network, protocols, and software that facilitate the creation and usage of the digital currency named bitcoin. Note that Bitcoin with a capital *B* is used to refer to the Bitcoin protocol, whereas bitcoin with a lowercase *b* is used to refer to bitcoin, the currency. Nodes in this peer-to-peer network talk to each other using the Bitcoin protocol.

Decentralization of currency was made possible for the first time with the invention of bitcoin. Moreover, the double spending problem was solved in an elegant and ingenious way in bitcoin. Double spending problem arises when, for example, a user sends coins to two different users at the same time and they are verified independently as valid transactions.

Keys and addresses

Elliptic curve cryptography is used to generate public and private key pairs in the Bitcoin network. The bitcoin address is created by taking the corresponding public key of a private key and hashing it twice, first with the SHA256 algorithm and then with RIPEMD160. The resultant 160-bit hash is then prefixed with a version number and finally encoded with a Base58Check encoding scheme. The bitcoin addresses are 26-35 characters long and begin with digit 1 or 3. A typical bitcoin address looks like a string shown here:

1ANAguGG8bikEv2fYsTBnRUmx7QUcK58wt

This is also commonly encoded in a QR code for easy sharing. The QR code of the preceding address is shown in the following image:

QR code of a bitcoin address 1ANAguGG8bikEv2fYsTBnRUmx7QUcK58wt

Currently, there are two types of addresses, the commonly used P2PKH and another P2SH type, starting with 1 and 3, respectively. In the early days, bitcoin used direct Pay-to-Pubkey, which is now superseded by P2PKH. However, direct Pay-to-Pubkey is still used in bitcoin for coinbase addresses. Addresses should not be used more than once; otherwise, privacy and security issues can arise. Avoiding address reuse circumvents anonymity issues to an extent, bitcoin has some other security issues as well, such as transaction malleability, which requires different approaches to resolve.

From bitaddress.org private key and bitcoin address in a paper wallet

Public keys in bitcoin

In public key cryptography, public keys are generated from private keys. Bitcoin uses ECC based on the SECP256K1 standard. A private key is randomly selected and is 256-bit in length. Public keys can be presented in an uncompressed or compressed format. Public keys are basically x and y coordinates on an elliptic curve and in an uncompressed format and are presented with a prefix of 04 in a hexadecimal format. X and Y coordinates are both 32-bit in length. In total, the compressed public key is 33 bytes long as compared to 65 bytes in the uncompressed format. The compressed version of public keys basically includes only the X part, since the Y part can be derived from it. The reason why the compressed version of public keys works is that the bitcoin client initially used uncompressed keys, but starting from bitcoin core client 0.6, compressed keys are used as the standard.

Keys are identified by various prefixes, described as follows:

- Uncompressed public keys used 0x04 as the prefix
- Compressed public key starts with 0x03 if the y 32-bit part of the public key is odd
- Compressed public key starts with 0x02 if the y 32-bit part of the public key is even

The more detailed mathematical description and the reason why it works is described here. If the ECC graph is visualized, it reveals that the y coordinate can be either below the x axis or above the x axis and as the curve is symmetric, only the location in the prime field is required to be stored.

Private keys in bitcoin

Private keys are basically 256-bit numbers chosen in the range specified by the SECP256K1 ECDSA recommendation. Any randomly chosen 256-bit number from 0x1 to 0xFFFF FFFF FFFF FFFF FFFF FFFF FFFF FFFE BAAE DCE6 AF48 A03B BFD2 5E8C D036 4140 is a valid private key.

Private keys are usually encoded using **Wallet Import Format** (**WIF**) in order to make them easier to copy and use. WIF can be converted into private key and vice versa. The steps are described here.

Also, **Mini Private Key Format** is sometimes used to encode the key in under 30 characters in order to allow storage where physical space is limited, for example, etching on physical coins or damage-resistant QR codes. The bitcoin core client also allows the encryption of the wallet that contains the private keys.

Bitcoin currency units

Bitcoin currency units are described as follows. The smallest bitcoin denomination is the Satoshi.

DENOMINATION	ABBREVIATION	FAMILIAR NAME	VALUE IN BTC
Satoshi	SAT	Satoshi	0.00000001 BTC
Microbit	µBTC (uBTC)	Microbitcoin or Bit	0.000001 BTC
Millibit	mBTC	Millibitcoin	0.001 BTC
Centibit	cBTC	Centibitcoin	0.01 BTC
Decibit	dBTC	Decibitcoin	0.1 BTC
Bitcoin	BTC	Bitcoin	1 BTC
DecaBit	daBTC	Decabitcoin	10 BTC
Hectobit	hBTC	Hectobitcoin	100 BTC
Kilobit	kBTC	Kilobitcoin	1000 BTC
Megabit	MBTC	Megabitcoin	1000000 BTC

Base58Check encoding

This encoding is used to limit the confusion between various characters, such as 0OIl as they can look the same in different fonts. The encoding basically takes the binary byte arrays and converts them into human-readable strings. This string is composed by utlilizing a set of 58 alphanumeric symbols. More explanation and logic can be found in the `base58.h` source file in the bitcoin source code.

```
 6   /**
 7    * Why base-58 instead of standard base-64 encoding?
 8    * - Don't want 0OI1 characters that look the same in some fonts and
 9    *     could be used to create visually identical looking data.
10    * - A string with non-alphanumeric characters is not as easily accepted as input.
11    * - E-mail usually won't line-break if there's no punctuation to break at.
12    * - Double-clicking selects the whole string as one word if it's all alphanumeric.
13    */
14   #ifndef BITCOIN_BASE58_H
```

Explanation from the bitcoin source code

Bitcoin addresses are encoded using the Base58check encoding.

Vanity addresses

As bitcoin addresses are based on base 58 encoding, it is possible to generate addresses that contain human-readable messages. An example is shown as follows:

1BasHiry2VoCQCdX6X
64oxvKRuf7fW6qGr

Public address encoded in QR

Vanity addresses are generated using a purely brute-force method. An example is shown in the following screenshot:

Vanity address generated from https://bitcoinvanitygen.com/

Transactions

Transactions are at the core of the bitcoin ecosystem. Transactions can be as simple as just sending some bitcoins to a bitcoin address, or it can be quite complex depending on the requirements. Each transaction is composed of at least one input and output. Inputs can be thought of as coins being spent that have been created in a previous transaction and outputs as coins being created. If a transaction is minting new coins, then there is no input and therefore no signature is needed. If a transaction is to sends coins to some other user (a bitcoin address), then it needs to be signed by the sender with their private key and a reference is also required to the previous transaction in order to show the origin of the coins. Coins are, in fact, unspent transaction outputs represented in Satoshis.

Transactions are not encrypted and are publicly visible in the blockchain. Blocks are made up of transactions and these can be viewed using any online blockchain explorer.

The transaction life cycle

1. A user/sender sends a transaction using wallet software or some other interface.

2. The wallet software signs the transaction using the sender's private key.
3. The transaction is broadcasted to the Bitcoin network using a flooding algorithm.
4. Mining nodes include this transaction in the next block to be mined.
5. Mining starts once a miner who solves the Proof of Work problem broadcasts the newly mined block to the network. Proof of Work is explained in detail later in this chapter.
6. The nodes verify the block and propagate the block further, and confirmation starts to generate.
7. Finally, the confirmations start to appear in the receiver's wallet and after approximately six confirmations, the transaction is considered finalized and confirmed. However, six is just a recommended number; the transaction can be considered final even after the first confirmation. The key idea behind waiting for six confirmations is that the probability of double spending is virtually eliminated after six confirmations.

The transaction structure

A transaction at a high level contains metadata, inputs, and outputs. Transactions are combined to create a block. The transaction structure is shown in the following table:

Field	Size	Description
Version Number	4 bytes	Used to specify rules to be used by the miners and nodes for transaction processing.
Input counter	1 bytes – 9 bytes	The number of inputs included in the transaction.
list of inputs	variable	Each input is composed of several fields, including Previous transaction hash, Previous Txout-index, Txin-script length, Txin-script, and optional sequence number. The first transaction in a block is also called a coinbase transaction. It specifies one or more transaction inputs.
Out-counter	1 bytes – 9 bytes	A positive integer representing the number of outputs.
list of outputs	variable	Outputs included in the transaction.
lock_time	4 bytes	This defines the earliest time when a transaction becomes valid. It is either a Unix timestamp or a block number.

- **MetaData**: This part of the transaction contains some values such as the size of the transaction, the number of inputs and outputs, the hash of the transaction, and a `lock_time` field. Every transaction has a prefix specifying the version number.

- **Inputs**: Generally, each input spends a previous output. Each output is considered an **Unspent Transaction Output (UTXO)** until an input consumes it.

- **Outputs**: Outputs have only two fields, and they contain instructions for the sending of bitcoins. The first field contains the amount of Satoshis, whereas the second field is a locking script that contains the conditions that need to be met in order for the output to be spent. More information on transaction spending using locking and unlocking scripts and producing outputs is discussed later in this section.

- **Verification**: Verification is performed using bitcoin's scripting language.

A sample transaction is shown as follows:

```
{
  "txid": "08af7960ca9255c67686296fb65452ed3f96f18831c9a3d8ea552e4ccee5c4af",
  "hash": "08af7960ca9255c67686296fb65452ed3f96f18831c9a3d8ea552e4ccee5c4af",
  "size": 226,
  "vsize": 226,
  "version": 1,
  "locktime": 969523,
  "vin": [
    {
  "txid": "3e553260a0a94860f7043eb6576e15e6cfeb2990aea961210ae1fde328bb08b0",
  "vout": 1,
  "scriptSig": {
  "asm":
"3045022100cfb31edabc62c82b41d12f651d2e3e013ee1a7ee2bb4526f3dda640e6d8d224502207d8d1d8e41350b9cdf36f389f942ab68c12
f113fe99014f5d6df6610407877d2[ALL] 037bc82d0078993f6943e7ff6e82e82da600f34edc8bca136331a9901c8bb60b0d",
  "hex":
"483045022100cfb31edabc62c82b41d12f651d2e3e013ee1a7ee2bb4526f3dda640e6d8d224502207d8d1d8e41350b9cdf36f389f942ab68c
12f113fe99014f5d6df6610407877d20121037bc82d0078993f6943e7ff6e82e82da600f34edc8bca136331a9901c8bb60b0d"
      },
      "sequence": 4294967294
    }
  ],
  "vout": [
    {
      "value": 2.30000000,
      "n": 0,
      "scriptPubKey": {
        "asm": "OP_DUP OP_HASH160 07e78644a61343068fa8d4940a79976e758ac6ef OP_EQUALVERIFY OP_CHECKSIG",
        "hex": "76a91407e78644a61343068fa8d4940a79976e758ac6ef88ac",
        "reqSigs": 1,
        "type": "pubkeyhash",
        "addresses": [
          "mgEkNzxV3qbYtDKEKTvo1VpgJ63Au619q2"
}}}
```

A sample decoded transaction, showing various fields described earlier

The script language

Bitcoin uses a simple stack-based language called *script* to describe how bitcoins can be spent and transferred. It is not Turing complete and has no loops to avoid any undesirable effects of long running/hung scripts on the bitcoin network. This scripting language is based on a Forth-like syntax and uses a reverse polish notation in which every operand is followed by its operators. It is evaluated from the left to the right using a **Last in First Out** (**LIFO**) stack.

Scripts use various Opcodes or instructions to define their operation. Opcodes are also known as words, commands, or functions. Earlier versions of the bitcoin node had a few Opcodes that are no longer used due to bugs discovered in their design.

The various categories of the scripting Opcodes are constants, flow control, stack, bitwise logic, splice, and arithmetic, cryptography, and lock time.

A transaction script is evaluated by combining `ScriptSig` and `ScriptPubKey`. `ScriptSig` is the unlocking script, whereas `ScriptPubKey` is the locking script. This is how a transaction is evaluated to be spent; first, it is unlocked and then it is spent. `ScriptSig` is provided by the user who wishes to unlock the transaction. `ScriptPubkey` is part of the transaction output and specifies the conditions that need to be fulfilled in order to spend the output. In other words, outputs are locked by the `ScriptPubKey` (Locking script) that contains the conditions, when met will unlock the output, and coins can then be redeemed.

Commonly used Opcodes

All Opcodes are declared in the script.h file in the bitcoin reference client source code. This can be accessed from the link at `https://github.com/bitcoin/bitcoin/blob/master/src/script/script.h` under the following comment:

/ Script opcodes */**

A description of the most commonly used Opcodes is listed here. This table is taken from the bitcoin developer's guide:

Opcode	Description
OP_CHECKSIG	This takes a public key and signature and validates the signature of the hash of the transaction. If it matches, then TRUE is pushed onto the stack; otherwise, FALSE is pushed.
OP_EQUAL	This returns 1 if the inputs are exactly equal; otherwise, 0 is returned.
OP_DUP	This duplicates the top item in the stack.
OP_HASH160	The input is hashed twice, first with SHA-256 and then with RIPEMD-160.
OP_VERIFY	This marks the transaction as invalid if the top stack value is not true.
OP_EQUALVERIFY	This is the same as OP_EQUAL, but it runs OP_VERIFY afterwards.
OP_CHECKMULTISIG	This takes the first signature and compares it against each public key until a match is found and repeats this process until all signatures are checked. If all signatures turn out to be valid, then a value of 1 is returned as a result; otherwise, 0 is returned.

Types of transaction

There are various scripts available in bitcoin to handle the value transfer from the source to the destination. These scripts range from very simple to quite complex depending upon the requirements of the transaction. Standard transaction types are discussed here. Standard transactions are evaluated using IsStandard() and IsStandardTx() tests and only standard transactions that pass the test are generally allowed to be mined or broadcasted on the bitcoin network. However, nonstandard transactions are valid and allowed on the network.

- **Pay to Public Key Hash (P2PKH)**: P2PKH is the most commonly used transaction type and is used to send transactions to the bitcoin addresses. The format of the transaction is shown as folows:

  ScriptPubKey: OP_DUP OP_HASH160 <pubKeyHash> OP_EQUALVERIFY OP_CHECKSIG

  ScriptSig: <sig> <pubKey>

The `ScriptPubKey` and `ScriptSig` parameters are concatenated together and executed. An example will follow shortly in this section, where this is explained in more detail.

- **Pay to Script Hash (P2SH)**: P2SH is used in order to send transactions to a script hash (that is, the addresses starting with 3) and was standardized in BIP16. In addition to passing the script, the redeem script is also evaluated and must be valid. The template is shown as follows:

    `ScriptPubKey`: OP_HASH160 <redeemScriptHash> OP_EQUAL

    `ScriptSig`: [<sig>...<sign>] <redeemScript>

- **MultiSig (Pay to MultiSig)**: M of n multisignature transaction script is a complex type of script where it is possible to construct a script that required multiple signatures to be valid in order to redeem a transaction. Various complex transactions such as escrow and deposits can be built using this script. The template is shown here:

    `ScriptPubKey`: <m> <pubKey> [<pubKey>...] <n> OP_CHECKMULTISIG

    `ScriptSig`: 0 [<sig >... <sign>]

Raw multisig is obsolete, and multisig is usually part of the P2SH redeem script, mentioned in the previous bullet point.

- **Pay to Pubkey**: This script is a very simple script that is commonly used in coinbase transactions. It is now obsolete and was used in an old version of bitcoin. The public key is stored within the script in this case, and the unlocking script is required to sign the transaction with the private key.

The template is shown as follows:

<PubKey> OP_CHECKSIG

- **Null data/OP_RETURN**: This script is used to store arbitrary data on the blockchain for a fee. The limit of the message is 40 bytes. The output of this script is unredeemable because OP_RETURN will fail the validation in any case. `ScriptSig` is not required in this case.

The template is very simple and is shown as follows:

OP_RETURN <data>

A P2PKH script execution is shown as follows:

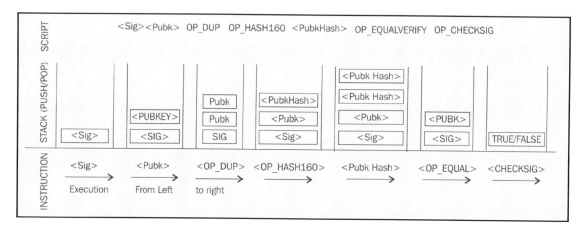

P2PKH script execution

All transactions are eventually encoded into the hex before transmitting over the bitcoin network. A sample transaction is shown in hex that is retrieved using bitcoin-cli on the bitcoin testnet by using the following command:

```
drequinox@drequinox-OP7010:~$ bitcoin-cli --testnet getrawtransaction
"08af7960ca9255c67686296fb65452ed3f96f18831c9a3d8ea552e4ccee5c4af"
0100000001b008bb28e3fde10a2161a9ae9029ebcfe6156e57b63e04f76048a9a06032553e0
10000006b483045022100cfb31edabc62c82b41d12f651d2e3e013ee1a7ee2bb4526f3dda64
0e6d8d224502207d8d1d8e41350b9cdf36f389f942ab68c12f113fe99014f5d6df661040787
7d20121037bc82d0078993f6943e7ff6e82e82da600f34edc8bca136331a9901c8bb60b0dfe
ffffff028085b50d000000001976a91407e78644a61343068fa8d4940a79976e758ac6ef88a
c95bddc1c000000001976a914dad770cccb1026ebf87acacfe35f2d6f2d336faa88ac33cb0e
00
```

Coinbase transactions

A coinbase transaction or generation transaction is always created by a miner and is the first transaction in a block. It is used to create new coins. It includes a special field, also called *coinbase*, which acts as an input to the coinbase transaction. This transaction also allows up to 100 bytes of arbitrary data that can be used to store arbitrary data. In the genesis block, this included the most famous comment taken from The Times newspaper:

"The Times 03/Jan/2009 Chancellor on brink of second bailout for banks"

This message is proof that the genesis block was not mined earlier than January 3, 2009.

What is UTXO?

Unspent Transaction Output (UTXO) is an unspent transaction output that can be spent as an input to a new transaction. Other concepts related to transactions in bitcoin are described below.

Transaction fee

Transaction fees are charged by the miners. The fee charged is dependent upon the size of the transaction. Transaction fees are calculated by subtracting the sum of the inputs and the sum of the outputs. The fees are used as an incentive for miners to encourage them to include a user transaction in the block the miners are creating. All transactions end up in the memory pool, from where miners pick up transactions based on their priority to include them in the proposed block. The calculation of priority is introduced later in this chapter; however, from a transaction fee point of view, a transaction with a higher fee will be picked up sooner by the miners. There are different rules based on which fee is calculated for various types of actions, such as sending transactions, inclusion in blocks, and relaying by nodes. Fees are not fixed by the Bitcoin protocol and are not mandatory; even a transaction with no fee will be processed in due course but may take a very long time.

Contracts

As defined in the bitcoin core developer guide, contracts are basically transactions that use the bitcoin system to enforce a financial agreement. This is a simple definition but has far-reaching consequences as it allows users to design complex contracts that can be used in many real-world scenarios. Contracts allow the development of a completely decentralized, independent, and reduced risk platform. Various contracts, such as escrow, arbitration, and micropayment channels, can be built using the bitcoin scripting language. The current implementation of a script is very limited, but various types of contracts are still possible to develop. For example, the release of funds only if multiple parties sign the transaction or perhaps the release of funds only after a certain time has elapsed. Both of these scenarios can be realized using `multiSig` and transaction lock time options.

Transaction malleability

Transaction malleability in bitcoin was introduced due to a bug in the bitcoin implementation. Due to this bug, it becomes possible for an adversary to change the Transaction ID of a transaction, thus resulting in a scenario where it would appear that a certain transaction has not been executed. This can allow scenarios where double deposits or withdrawals can occur. In other words, this bug allows the changing of the unique ID of a bitcoin transaction before it is confirmed.

If the ID is changed before confirmation, it would seem that the transaction did not happen at all, which can then allow double deposits or withdrawal attacks.

Transaction pools

Also known as *memory pools*, these pools are basically created in local memory by nodes in order to maintain a temporary list of transactions that are not yet confirmed in a block. Transactions are included in a block after passing verification and based on their priority.

Transaction verification

This verification process is performed by bitcoin nodes. The following is described in the bitcoin developer guide:

1. Check the syntax and ensure that the syntax of the transaction is correct.
2. Verify that inputs and outputs are not empty.
3. Check whether the size in bytes is less than the maximum block size, which is 1 MB currently.
4. The output value must be in the allowed money range (0 to 21 million BTC).
5. All inputs must have a specified previous output, except for coinbase transactions, which should not be relayed.
6. Verify that nLockTime must not exceed 31-bits. For a transaction to be valid, it should not be less than 100 bytes. Also, the number of signature operands in a standard signature should be less than or not more than 2.
7. Reject *nonstandard* transactions; for example, ScriptSig is allowed to only push numbers on the stack. ScriptPubkey not passing the isStandard() checks.
8. A transaction is rejected if there is already a matching transaction in the pool or in a block in the main branch.
9. The transaction will be rejected if the referenced output for each input exists in any other transaction in the pool.
10. For each input, there must exist a referenced output transaction. This is searched in the main branch and the transaction pool to find whether the output transaction is missing for any input, and this will be considered an orphan transaction. It will be added to the orphan transactions pool if a matching transaction is not in the pool already.
11. For each input, if the referenced output transaction is the coinbase, it must have at least 100 confirmations; otherwise, the transaction will be rejected.
12. For each input, if the referenced output does not exist or has been spent already, the transaction will be rejected.

13. Using the referenced output transactions to get input values, verify that each input value, as well as the sum, is in the allowed range of 0-21 million BTC.
14. Reject the transaction if the sum of input values is less than the sum of output values.
15. Reject the transaction if the transaction fee would be too low to get into an empty block.

Blockchain

Blockchain is a public ledger of a timestamped, ordered, and immutable list of all transactions on the bitcoin network. Each block is identified by a hash in the chain and is linked to its previous block by referencing the previous block's hash.

In the following structure of a block, a block header is described, followed by a detailed diagram that provides an insight into the blockchain structure.

The structure of a block

Bytes	Name	Description
80	Block header	This includes fields from the block header described in the next section.
variable	Transaction counter	The field contains the total number of transactions in the block, including the coinbase transaction.
variable	Transactions	All transactions in the block.

The structure of a block header

Bytes	Name	Description
4	Version	The block version number that dictates the block validation rules to follow.
32	previous block header hash	This is a double SHA256 hash of the previous block's header.
32	merkle root hash	This is a double SHA256 hash of the merkle tree of all transactions included in the block.

4	Timestamp	This field contains the approximate creation time of the block in the Unix epoch time format. More precisely, this is the time when the miner has started hashing the header (the time from the miner's point of view).
4	Difficulty target	This is the difficulty target of the block.
4	Nonce	This is an arbitrary number that miners change repeatedly in order to produce a hash that fulfills the difficulty target threshold.

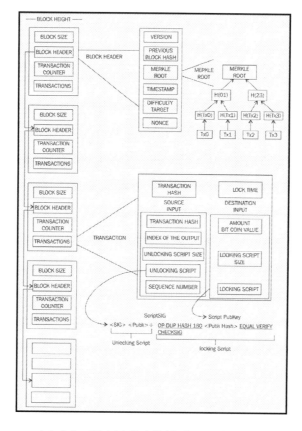

A visualization of blockchain, block, block header, transaction and script

As shown in the preceding diagram, blockchain is a chain of blocks where each block is linked to its previous block by referencing the previous block header's hash. This linking makes sure that no transaction can be modified unless the block that records it and all blocks that follow it are also modified. The first block is not linked to any previous block and is known as the genesis block.

The genesis block

This is the first block in the bitcoin blockchain. The genesis block was hardcoded in the bitcoin core software. It is in the `chainparams.cpp` file.

```
https://github.com/bitcoin/bitcoin/blob/master/src/chainparams.cpp
```

```
48   *       CTxOut(nValue=50.00000000, scriptPubKey=0x5F1DF16B2B704C8A578D08)
49   *   vMerkleTree: 4a5e1e
50   */
51   static CBlock CreateGenesisBlock(uint32_t nTime, uint32_t nNonce, uint32_t nBits, int32_t nVersion, const CAmount& genesisReward)
52   {
53       const char* pszTimestamp = "The Times 03/Jan/2009 Chancellor on brink of second bailout for banks";
54       const CScript genesisOutputScript = CScript() << ParseHex("04678afdb0fe5548271967f1a67130b7105cd6a828e03909a67962e0ea1f61deb649
55       return CreateGenesisBlock(pszTimestamp, genesisOutputScript, nTime, nNonce, nBits, nVersion, genesisReward);
56   }
57
58   /**
```

Bitcoin provides protection against double spending by enforcing strict rules on transaction verification and via mining. Blocks are added in the blockchain only after strict rule checking and successful Proof of Work solution. Block height is the number of blocks before a particular block in the blockchain. The current height (at the time of writing this) of the blockchain is 434755 blocks. Proof of Work is used to secure the blockchain. Each block contains one or more transactions, out of which the first transaction is a coinbase transaction. There is a special condition for coinbase transactions that prevent them to be spent until at least 100 blocks in order to avoid a situation where the block may be declared stale later on.

Stale blocks are created when a block is solved and every other miner who is still working to find a solution to the hash puzzle is working on that block. Mining and hash puzzles will be discussed later in the chapter in detail. As the block is no longer required to be worked on, this is considered a stale block.

Orphan blocks are also called detached blocks and were accepted at one point in time by the network as valid blocks but were rejected when a proven longer chain was created that did not include this initially accepted block. They are not part of the main chain and can occur at times when two miners manage to produce the blocks at the same time.

The latest block version is version 4, which was proposed with BIP65 and has been used since bitcoin core client 0.11.2 since the implementation of BIP9 bits in `nVersion` field are being used to indicate softfork changes.

Because of the distributed nature of bitcoin, network forks can occurs naturally. In cases where two nodes simultaneously announce a valid b lock can result in a situation where there are two blockchains with different transactions. This is an undesirable situation but can be addressed by the bitcoin network only by accepting the longest chain. In this case, the smaller chain will be considered orphaned. If an adversary manages to gain 51% control of the network hashrate (computational power), then they can impose their own version of transaction history.

Forks in blockchain can occur with the introduction of changes in the Bitcoin protocol. In case of *soft fork*, only previous valid blocks are no longer acceptable, thus making soft fork backward compatible. In case of soft fork, only miners are required to upgrade to the new client software in order to make use of the new protocol rules. Planned upgrades do not necessarily create forks because all users should have updated already. A hard fork, on the other hand, invalidates previously valid blocks and requires all users to upgrade. New transaction types are sometimes added as a soft fork, and any changes such as block structure change or major protocol changes results in hard fork.

The current size of the bitcoin blockchain as on February 4, 2017, stands at approximately 101 GB. The following figure shows the size increase of blockchain as a function of time:

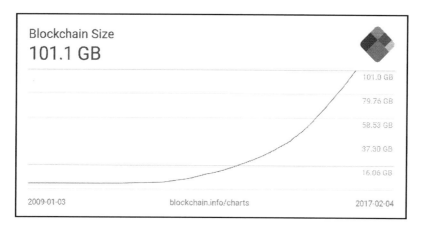

Current size of blockchain as of 06/02/2017

New blocks are added to the blockchain approximately every 10 minutes and network difficulty is adjusted dynamically every 2016 blocks in order to maintain a steady addition of new blocks to the network.

Network difficulty is calculated using the following equation:

*Target = Previous target * Time/2016 * 10 minutes*

Difficulty and target are interchangeable and represent the same thing. Previous target represents the old target value, and time is the time spent to generate previous 2016 blocks. Network difficulty basically means how hard it is for miners to find a new block, that is, how difficult the hashing puzzle is now.

In the section, mining is discussed, which will explain how a hashing puzzle is solved.

Mining

Mining is a resource-intensive process by which new blocks are added to the blockchain. Blocks contain transactions that are validated via the mining process by mining nodes and are added to the blockchain. This process is resource-intensive in order to ensure that the required resources have been spent by miners in order for a block to be accepted. New coins are minted by the miners by spending the required computing resources. This also secures the system against frauds and double spending attacks while adding more virtual currency to the bitcoin ecosystem.

Roughly one new block is created (mined) every 10 minute. Miners are rewarded with new coins if and when they create new blocks and are paid transaction fees in return of including transactions in their blocks. New blocks are created at an approximate fixed rate. Also, the rate of creation of new bitcoins decreases by 50%, every 210,000 blocks, roughly every 4 years. When bitcoin was initially introduced, the block reward was 50 bitcoins; then in 2012, this was reduced to 25 bitcoins. In July 2016, this was further reduced to 12.5 coins (12 coins) and the next reduction is estimated to be on July 4, 2020. This will reduce the coin reward further down to approximately six coins.

Approximately 144 blocks, that is, 1,728 bitcoins are generated per day. The number of actual coins can vary per day; however, the number of blocks remains at 144 per day. Bitcoin supply is also limited and in 2140, almost 21 million bitcoins will be finally created and no new bitcoins can be created after that. Bitcoin miners, however, will still be able to profit from the ecosystem by charging transaction fees.

Task of miners

Once a node connects with the bitcoin network, there are several tasks that a bitcoin miner performs.

Synching up with the network

Once a new node joins the bitcoin network, it downloads the blockchain by requesting historical blocks from other nodes. This is mentioned here in the context of the bitcoin miner; however, this not necessarily a task only for a miner.

- **Transaction validation**: Transactions broadcasted on the network are validated by full nodes by verifying and validating signatures and outputs.

- **Block validation**: Miners and full nodes can start validating blocks received by them by evaluating them against certain rules. This includes the verification of each transaction in the block along with verification of the nonce value.

- **Create a new block**: Miners propose a new block by combining transactions broadcasted on the network after validating them.

- **Perform Proof of Work**: This task is the core of the mining process and this is where miners find a valid block by solving a computational puzzle. The block header contains a 32-bit nonce field and miners are required to repeatedly vary the nonce until the resultant hash is less than a predetermined target.

- **Fetch reward**: Once a node solves the hash puzzle, it immediately broadcasts the results, and other nodes verify it and accept the block. There is a slight chance that the newly minted block will not be accepted by other miners due to a clash with another block found at roughly the same time, but once accepted, the miner is rewarded with 12.5 bitcoins (as of 2016) and any associated transaction fees.

Proof of Work

This is a proof that enough computational resources have been spent in order to build a valid block. **Proof of Work (PoW)** is based on the idea that a random node is selected every time to create a new block. In this model, nodes compete with each other in order to be selected in proportion to their computing capacity. The following equation sums up the Proof of Work requirement in bitcoin:

$$H (N \parallel P\_hash \parallel Tx \parallel Tx \parallel \ldots Tx) < Target$$

Where N is a nonce, *P_hash* is a hash of the previous block, *Tx* represents transactions in the block, and *Target* is the target network difficulty value. This means that the hash of the previously mentioned concatenated fields should be less than the target hash value. The only way to find this nonce is the brute force method. Once a certain pattern of a certain number of zeroes is met by a miner, the block is immediately broadcasted and accepted by other miners.

The mining algorithm

The mining algorithm consists of the following steps.

- The previous hash block is retrieved from the bitcoin network.
- Assemble a set of potential transactions broadcasted on the network into a block.
- Compute the double hash of the block header with a nonce and the previous hash using the SHA256 algorithm.
- If the resultant hash is lower than the current difficulty level (target), then stop the process.
- If the resultant hash is greater than the current difficulty level (target), then repeat the process by incrementing the nonce. As the hash rate of the bitcoin network increased, the total amount of 32-bit nonces was exhausted too quickly. In order to address this issue, the *extra nonce* solution was implemented, whereby the coinbase transaction is used as a source of extra nonce to provide a larger range of nonces to be searched by the miners.

- Mining difficulty increased over time and bitcoins that could be mined by single CPU laptop computers now require dedicated mining centers to solve the hash puzzle. The current difficulty level can be queried using the bitcoin command line interface using the following command:

```
$ bitcoin-cli getdifficulty
258522748404.5154
```

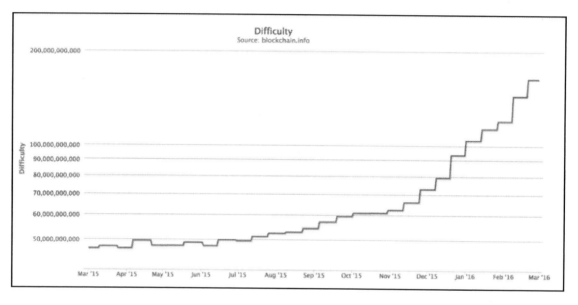

Mining difficulty over time

The value returned by the `getdifficulty` command.

The hashing rate

The hashing rate basically represents the rate of calculating hashes per second. In early days of bitcoin, it used to be quite small as CPUs were used, but with dedicated mining pools and ASICs now, this has gone up exponentially in the last few years. This has resulted in increased difficulty. The following hash rate graph shows the hash rate increase over time and is currently measured in Exa hashes. This means that in 1 second, bitcoin network miners are computing more than 1 000 000 000 000 000 000 hashes per second.

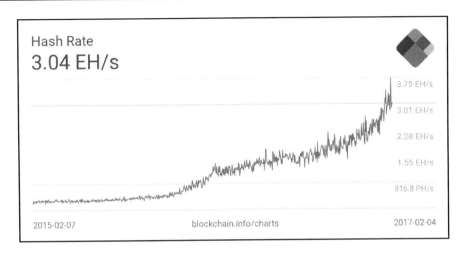

Hash Rate
3.04 EH/s

3.75 EH/s

3.01 EH/s

2.28 EH/s

1.55 EH/s

816.8 PH/s

2015-02-07   blockchain.info/charts   2017-02-04

Hashing rate as of 06/02/2017, shown over a period of two years

Mining systems

Over time, bitcoin miners have used various methods to mine bitcoins. As the core principle behind mining is based on the double SHA256 algorithm, overtime miners have developed sophisticated systems to calculate the hash faster and faster. The following is a review of the different types of mining methods used in bitcoin and how they evolved with time.

CPU

CPU mining was the first type of mining available in the original bitcoin client. Users could even use laptop or desktop computers to mine bitcoins. CPU mining is no longer profitable and now more advanced mining methods such as ASIC-based mining are used.

GPU

Due to the increased difficulty of the bitcoin network and general tendency of finding faster methods to mine, miners started to use GPUs or graphics cards available in PCs to perform mining. GPUs support faster and parallelized calculations that are usually programmed using the OpenCL language. This turned out to be a faster option as compared to CPUs. Users also used techniques such as overclocking to gain maximum benefit of the GPU power. Also, the possibility of using multiple graphics cards increased the popularity of graphics cards' usage for bitcoin mining. GPU mining, however, has some limitations, such as overheating and the requirement for specialized motherboards and extra hardware to house multiple graphics cards.

FPGA

Even GPU mining did not last long, and soon miners found another way to perform mining using FPGAs. **Field Programmable Gate Array (FPGA)** is basically an integrated circuit that can be programmed to perform specific operations. FPGAs are usually programmed in **hardware description languages (HDLs)**, such as Verilog and VHDL. Double SHA256 quickly became an attractive programming task for FPGA programmers and several open source projects started too. FPGA offered much better performance as compared to GPUs; however, issues such as accessibility, programming difficulty, and the requirement for specialized knowledge to program and configure FPGAs resulted in a short life of the FPGA era for bitcoin mining. Also, the arrival of ASICs resulted in quickly phased out FPGA-based systems for mining. Mining hardware such as X6500 miner, Ztex, and Icarus were developed during the time when FPGA mining was profitable. Various FPGA manufacturers, such as Xilinx and Altera, produce FPGA hardware and development boards that can be used to program mining algorithms.

ASICs

Application Specific Integrated Circuit (ASIC) was designed to perform the SHA-256 operation. These special chips were sold by various manufacturers and offered a very high hashing rate. This worked for some time, but due to the quickly increasing mining difficulty level, single-unit ASICs are no longer profitable.

Currently, mining is out of the reach of individuals and now professional mining centers using thousands of ASIC units in parallel are offering mining contracts to users to perform mining on their behalf. There is no technical limitation, that's why a single user cannot run thousands of ASICs in parallel, but it will require dedicated data centers and hardware and cost for a single individual can become prohibitive.

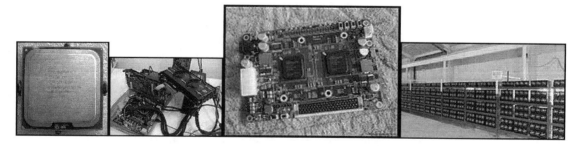

Four types of mining (CPU, GPU, FPGA, and ASIC)

Mining pools

A mining pool forms when group miners work together to mine a block. The *Pool manager* receives the coinbase transaction if the block is successfully mined, which is then responsible for distributing the reward to the group of miners who invested resources to mine the block. This is profitable as compared to solo mining, where only one sole miner is trying to solve the partial hash inversion function (hash puzzle) because in mining pools, the reward is paid to each member of the pool regardless of whether they (more specifically, their individual node) solved the puzzle or not.

There are various models that a mining pool manager can use to pay to the miners, such as the pay-per-share model and the proportional model. In the pay per share model, the mining pool manager pays a flat fee to all miners who participated in the mining exercise, whereas in the proportional model, the share is calculated based on the amount of computing resources spent to solve the hash puzzle.

Many commercial pools now exist and provide mining service contracts via the cloud and easy-to-use web interfaces. The most commonly used ones are **AntPool**, **F2Pool**, and **BW.COM**. A comparison of hashing power for all major mining pools is shown in the following image:

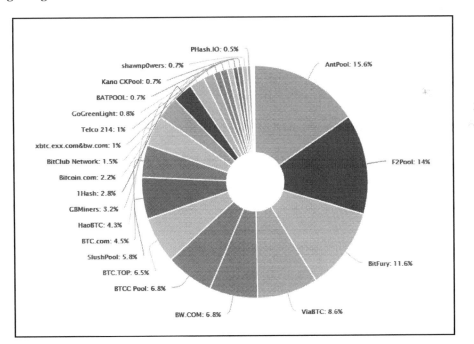

Mining pools and their hashing power (hash rate) as of 06/02/2017, taken from https://blockchain.info/pools

Mining centralization is a major concern that can occur if a pool manages to control more than 51% of the network by generating more than 51% hash rate of the bitcoin network. As discussed earlier in the introduction section, 51% attack can result in double spending attacks, and it can impact consensus and in fact impose another version of transaction history on the bitcoin network.

This has happened once in the bitcoin history, when GHash.IO, a large mining pool, managed to acquire more than 51% of the network capacity. Theoretical solutions , such as two-phase Proof of Work, have been proposed in academia to disincentivize large mining pools. This scheme introduces a second cryptographic puzzle that results in mining pools to reveal their private keys or providing a considerable portion of the hashrate of their mining pool, thus reducing the overall hashrate of the pool.

Various types of hardware are commercially available for mining purposes. Currently, the most profitable one is ASIC mining, and specialized hardware is available from a number of vendors. Solo mining is not much profitable now unless a vast amount of money and energy is spent to build your own mining rig or even center. With the current difficulty factor (Oct 2016), if a user manages to produce a hash rate of 12 TH/s, they can hope to make 0.01366887 BTC (around $8) per day, which is very low as compared to the investment required to source the equipment that can produce 12 TH. Including running costs such as electricity, this turns out to be not very profitable.

The bitcoin network

The bitcoin network is a P2P network where nodes exchange transactions and blocks. There are different types of nodes on the network. There are two main types of nodes, full nodes and SPV nodes. Full nodes, as the name implies, are implementations of bitcoin core clients performing the wallet, miner, full blockchain storage, and network routing functions. However, it is not necessary to perform all these functions. SPV nodes or lightweight clients perform only wallet and network routing functionality. The latest version of Bitcoin protocol is 70014 and was introduced with bitcoin core client 0.13.0.

Some nodes prefer to be full blockchain nodes only and contain complete blockchain and perform network routing functions but do not perform mining or store private keys (the wallet function). Another type is solo miner nodes that can perform mining, store full blockchain, and act as a bitcoin network routing node.

There are a few nonstandard but heavily used nodes that are called pool protocol servers. These nodes make use of alternative protocols, such as the stratum protocol. Some nodes perform only mining functions and are called mining nodes. Nodes that only compute hashes use the stratum protocol to submit their solutions to the mining pool. It is possible to run an SPV client runs a wallet and network routing function without a blockchain.

Most protocols on the Internet are line-based, which means that each line is delimited by a carriage return and newline \r \n character. Stratum is also a line-based protocol that makes use of plain TCP sockets and human-readable JSON-RPC to operate and communicate between nodes.

Bitcoin network is identified by its different magic values. A list is shown as follows:

Network	Magic value	Hex
main	0xD9B4BEF9	F9 BE B4 D9
testnet3	0x0709110B	0B 11 09 07

Bitcoin network magic values

Magic values are used to indicate the message origin network.

A full node performs four functions: wallet, miner, blockchain, and the network routing node.

When a bitcoin core node starts up, first, it initiates the discovery of all peers. This is achieved by querying DNS seeds that are hardcoded into the bitcoin core client and are maintained by bitcoin community members. This lookup returns a number of DNS A records. The bitcoin protocol works on TCP port 8333 by default for the main network and TCP 18333 for testnet.

```
vSeeds.push_back(CDNSSeedData("bitcoin.sipa.be", "seed.bitcoin.sipa.be", true)); // Pieter Wuille
vSeeds.push_back(CDNSSeedData("bluematt.me", "dnsseed.bluematt.me")); // Matt Corallo
vSeeds.push_back(CDNSSeedData("dashjr.org", "dnsseed.bitcoin.dashjr.org")); // Luke Dashjr
vSeeds.push_back(CDNSSeedData("bitcoinstats.com", "seed.bitcoinstats.com")); // Christian Decker
vSeeds.push_back(CDNSSeedData("xf2.org", "bitseed.xf2.org")); // Jeff Garzik
vSeeds.push_back(CDNSSeedData("bitcoin.jonasschnelli.ch", "seed.bitcoin.jonasschnelli.ch", true)); // Jonas Schnelli
```

DNSSeeds in chainparams.cpp

First, the client sends a protocol message *Version* that contains various fields, such as version, services, timestamp, network address, nonce, and some other fields. The remote node responds with its own version message followed by verack message exchange between both nodes, indicating that the connection has been established.

After this, **Getaddr** and **addr** messages are exchanged to find the peers that the client do not know. Meanwhile, either of the nodes can send a ping message to see whether the connection is still live.

Now the block download can begin. If the node already has all blocks fully synchronized, then it listens for new blocks using the *Inv* protocol message; otherwise, it first checks whether it has a response to *inv* messages and have inventories already. If yes, then it requests the blocks using the **Getdata** protocol message; if not, then it requests inventories using the *GetBlocks* message. This method was used until version 0.9.3.

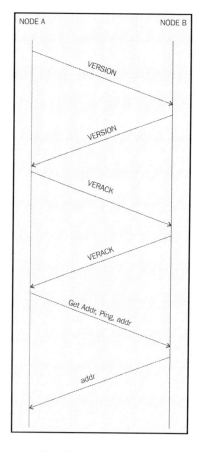

Protocol visualization node discovery

Initial block download can use blocks first or the headers-first method to synchronize blocks depending on the version of the bitcoin core client. The blocks-first method is very slow and was discontinued since version 0.10.0.

Since version 0.10.0, the initial block download method named headers-first was introduced. This resulted in major performance improvement and the blockchain synchronization that used to take days to complete started taking only a few hours. The core idea is that the new node-first asks peers for block headers and validates them. Once this is completed, blocks are requested in parallel from all available peers as the blueprint of the complete chain is already downloaded in the form of the block header chain.

In this method, when the client starts up, it checks whether the block chain is fully synchronized already if the header chain is already synchronized; if not, which is the case the first time the client starts up, it requests headers from other peers using the **getHeaders** message. If the block chain is fully synchronized, it listens for new blocks via *Inv* messages, and if it already has a fully synchronized header chain, then it requests blocks using *Getdata* protocol messages. The node also checks whether the header chain has more headers than blocks and then it requests blocks by issuing the *Getdata* protocol message.

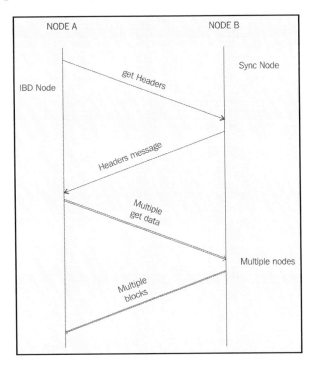

Bitcoin Core Client >= 0.10.0 header and block synchronization, IBD = Initial block download and sync node means the node from where the blocks are being requested from

Getblockchaininfo and getpeerinfo RPCs were updated with a new functionality to cater for this change. An RPC, *getchaintips*, is used to list all known branches of the blockchain. This also includes headers only blocks. Getblockchaininfo is used to provide the information about the current state of the blockchain. Getpeerinfo is used to list both the number of blocks and the headers that are in common between peers.

Wireshark can also be used to visualize message exchange between peers and can serve as an invaluable tool to learn about the Bitcoin protocol. A sample is shown here. This is a basic example showing the version, verack, getaddr, ping, addr, and inv messages.

In the details, valuable information such as the packet type, command name, and results of the protocol messages can be seen.

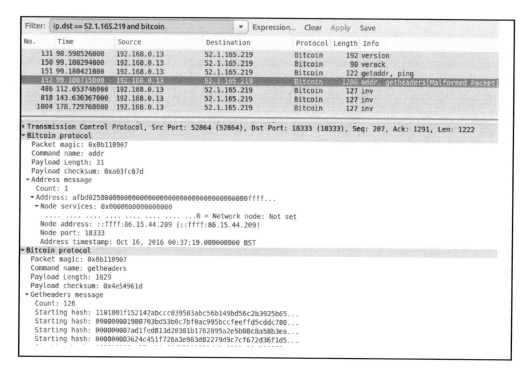

A sample block message in wireshark

A protocol graph showing the flow of data between the two peers is shown here. This can help you understand when a node starts up and what type of messages are used.

In the following example, the bitcoin dissector is used to analyze the traffic and identify the Bitcoin protocol commands.

Exchange of messages such as the **version**, **getaddr**, and **getdata** can be seen in the following example along with the appropriate comment describing the message name. This exercise can be very useful in order to learn bitcoin and it is recommended that the experiments be carried out on the bitcoin testnet, where various messages and transactions can be sent over the network and then be analyzed by Wireshark.

Time	192.168.0.13 → 136.243.139.96	Comment
97.734135000	(57868) version (18333)	Bitcoin: version
98.025045000	(57868) verack (18333)	Bitcoin: verack
98.025177000	(57868) getaddr, pin... (18333)	Bitcoin: getaddr, ping, addr
98.025468000	(57868) getheaders... (18333)	Bitcoin: getheaders, [unknown command], [unknown command], [unknown command], headers
98.160419000	(57868) [TCP Retran... (18333)	Bitcoin: [TCP Retransmission] , getheaders, [unknown command], [unknown command], [unknown command]
98.598399000	(57868) getdata (18333)	Bitcoin: getdata
144.343544000	(57868) inv (18333)	Bitcoin: inv
176.152240000	(57868) getdata (18333)	Bitcoin: getdata
179.493755000	(57868) getdata (18333)	Bitcoin: getdata
218.101646000	(57868) ping (18333)	Bitcoin: ping
218.192004000	(57868) [unknown co... (18333)	Bitcoin: [unknown command]
218.444431000	(57868) [TCP Retran... (18333)	Bitcoin: [TCP Retransmission] , [unknown command]
336.234936000	(57868) getdata (18333)	Bitcoin: getdata
337.843423000	(57868) [unknown co... (18333)	Bitcoin: [unknown command]
338.143885000	(57868) ping (18333)	Bitcoin: ping
448.764093000	(57868) getdata (18333)	Bitcoin: getdata
457.894823000	(57868) [unknown co... (18333)	Bitcoin: [unknown command]
458.195265000	(57868) ping (18333)	Bitcoin: ping
578.011774000	(57868) [unknown co... (18333)	Bitcoin: [unknown command]
578.212044000	(57868) ping (18333)	Bitcoin: ping
585.587671000	(57868) inv (18333)	Bitcoin: inv
647.169633000	(57868) inv (18333)	Bitcoin: inv
671.962545000	(57868) getdata (18333)	Bitcoin: getdata
698.037067000	(57868) [unknown co... (18333)	Bitcoin: [unknown command]
698.237350000	(57868) ping (18333)	Bitcoin: ping
701.563581000	(57868) inv (18333)	Bitcoin: inv
701.986269000	(57868) inv (18333)	Bitcoin: inv
705.022173000	(57868) inv (18333)	Bitcoin: inv
812.115878000	(57868) inv (18333)	Bitcoin: inv
818.198570000	(57868) [unknown co... (18333)	Bitcoin: [unknown command]
818.298733000	(57868) ping (18333)	Bitcoin: ping

There are 27 types of protocol messages in total, but they're likely to increase over time as the protocol grows. The most commonly used protocol messages and their explanation are listed as follows:

- **Version**: This is the first message that a node sends out to the network, advertising its version and block count. The remote node then replies with the same information and the connection is then established.
- **Verack :** This is the response of the version message accepting the connection request.
- **Inv:** This is used by nodes to advertise their knowledge of blocks and transactions.

- **Getdata** : This is a response to inv, requesting a single block or transaction identified by its hash.
- **Getblocks:** This returns an *inv* packet containing the list of all blocks starting after the last known hash or 500 blocks.
- **Getheaders** : This is used to request block headers in a specified range.
- **Tx** : This is used to send a transaction as a response to the getdata protocol message.
- **Block:** This sends a block in response to the *getdata* protocol message.
- **Headers:** This packet returns up to 2,000 block headers as a reply to the getheaders request.
- **Getaddr:** This is sent as a request to get information about known peers.
- **Addr:** This provides information about nodes on the network. It contains the number of addresses and address list in the form of IP address and port number.
- **Full client and SPV client**: Full clients are thick clients or full nodes that download the entire blockchain; this is the most secure method of validating the blockchain as a client. Bitcoin network nodes can operate in two fundamental modes: full client or lightweight SPV client. SPV clients are used to verify payments without requiring the download of a full blockchain. SPV nodes only keep a copy of block headers of the current valid longest blockchain. Verification is performed by looking at the merkle branch that links the transactions to the original block the transaction was accepted in. This is not very practical and requires a more practical approach, which was implemented with BIP37, where bloom filters were used to filter out relevant transactions only.

- **Bloom filters**: Bloom filter is basically a data structure (a bit vector with indexes) that is used to test the membership of an element in a probabilistic manner. It basically provides probabilistic lookup with false positives but no false negatives. Elements are added to the bloom filter after hashing them several times and then set the corresponding bits in the bit vector to 1 via the corresponding index. In order to check the presence of the element in the bloom filter, the same hash functions are applied and compared with the bits in the bit vector to see whether the same bits are set to 1. Not every hash function (such as SHA1) is suitable for bloom filters as they need to be fast, independent, and uniformly distributed. The most commonly used hash functions for bloom filters are fnv, mumur, and Jenkins.

These filters are mainly used by simple payment verification SPV clients to request transactions and the merkle blocks they are interested in. A merkle block is a lightweight version of the block, which includes a block header, some hashes, a list of 1-bit flags, and a transaction count. This information can then be used to build a merkle tree. This is achieved by creating a filter that matches only those transaction and blocks that have been requested by the SPV client. Once version messages have been exchanged and connection has been established between peers, the nodes can set filters according to their requirements. These probabilistic filters offer a varying degree of privacy or precision depending upon how accurately or loosely they have been set. A strict bloom filter will only filter transactions that have been requested by the node but at the expense of the possibility of revealing the user addresses to adversaries who can correlate transactions with their IP addresses, thus compromising privacy. On the other hand, a loosely set filter can result in retrieving more unrelated transactions but will offer more privacy. Also, for SPV clients, bloom filters allow them to use low bandwidth as opposed to downloading all transactions for verification.

- **BIP 37** proposed the bitcoin implementation of bloom filters and introduced three new messages to the Bitcoin protocol.
- **Filterload:** This is used to set the bloom filter on the connection.
- **Filteradd:** This adds a new data element to the current filter.
- **FilterClear**: This deletes the currently loaded filter.

More details can be found in the BIP37 specification.

Wallets

The wallet software is used to store private or public keys and bitcoin address. It performs various functions, such as receiving and sending bitcoins. Nowadays, software usually offers both functionalities: bitcoin client and wallet. On the disk, the bitcoin core client wallets are stored as the Berkeley DB file:

```
:~/.bitcoin$ file wallet.dat
```

`wallet.dat`: Berkeley DB (Btree, version 9, native byte-order)

Private keys can be generated in different ways and are used by different types of wallets. Wallets do not store any coins, and there is no concept of wallets storing balance or coins for a user. In fact, in the bitcoin network, *coins* do not exist; instead, only transaction information is stored on the blockchain (more precisely, UTXO, unspent outputs), which are then used to calculate the amount of bitcoins.

Wallet types

In bitcoin, there are different types of wallets that can be used to store private keys. As a software program, they also provide some functions to the users to manage and carry out transactions on the bitcoin network.

Non-deterministic wallets

These wallets contain randomly generated private keys and are also called *Just a Bunch of Key wallets*. The bitcoin core client generates some keys when first started and generates keys as and when required. Managing a large number of keys is very difficult and an error-prone process can lead to theft and loss of coins. Moreover, there is a need to create regular backups of the keys and protect them appropriately in order to prevent theft or loss.

Deterministic wallets

In this type of wallet, keys are derived out of a seed value via hash functions. This seed number is generated randomly and is commonly represented by human-readable *mnemonic code* words. Mnemonic code words are defined in BIP39. This phrase can be used to recover all keys and makes private key management comparatively easier.

Hierarchical deterministic wallets

Defined in BIP32 and BIP44, HD wallets store keys in a tree structure derived from a seed. The seed generates the parent key (master key), which is used to generate child keys and, subsequently, grandchild keys. Key generation in HD wallets does not generate keys directly; instead, it produces some information (private key generation information) that can be used to generate a sequence of private keys. The complete hierarchy of private keys in an HD wallet is easily recoverable if the master private key is known. It is because of this property that HD wallets are very easy to maintain and are highly portable.

Brain wallets

The master private key can also be derived from the hash of passwords that are memorized. The key idea is that this passphrase is used to derive the private key and if used in HD wallets, this can result in a full HD wallet that is derived from a single memorized password. This is known as brain wallet. This method is prone to password guessing and brute force attacks but techniques such as *key stretching* can be used to slow down the progress made by the attacker.

Paper wallets

As the name implies, this is a paper-based wallet with the required key material printed on it. It requires physical security to be stored. Paper wallets can be generated online from various service providers, such as `https://bitcoinpaperwallet.com/` or `https://www.bitaddress.org/`.

Hardware wallets

Another method is to use a tamper-resistant device to store keys. This tamper-resistant device can be custom-built or with the advent of NFC-enabled phones, this can also be a **secure element** (**SE**) in NFC phones. Trezor and Ledger wallets (various types) are the most commonly used bitcoin hardware wallets.

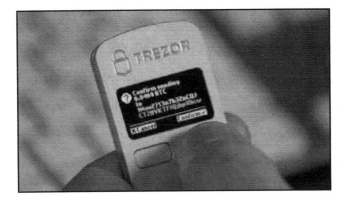

Trezor Wallet

Online wallets

Online wallets, as the name implies, are stored entirely online and are provided as a service usually via cloud. They provide a web interface to the users to manage their wallets and perform various functions such as making and receiving payments. They are easy to use but imply that the user trust the online wallet service provider.

Mobile wallets

Mobile wallets, as the name suggests, are installed on mobile devices. They can provide various methods to make payments, most notably the ability to use smart phone cameras to scan QR codes quickly and make payments. Mobile wallets are available for the Android platform and iOS, for example, breadwallet, copay, and Jaxx.

Jaxx Mobile wallet

Bitcoin payments

Bitcoins can be accepted as payments using various techniques. Bitcoin is not recognized as a legal currency in many jurisdictions, but it is increasingly being accepted as a payment method by many online merchants and e-commerce websites. There are a numbers of ways in which buyers can pay the business that accepts bitcoins. For example, in an online shop, bitcoin merchant solutions can be used, whereas in traditional physical shops, point of sale terminals and other specialized hardware can be used. Customers can simply scan the QR barcode with the seller's payment URI in it and pay using their mobile devices. Bitcoin URIs allow users to make payments by simply clicking on links or scanning QR codes. **URI (Uniform Resource Idenfier)** is basically a string that represents the transaction information. It is defined in BIP21. The QR code can be displayed near the point of the sale terminal. Nearly all bitcoin wallets support this feature.

Business can use the following screenshot to advertise that they can accept bitcoins as payment.

bitcoin accepted here logo

Various payment solutions, such as xbtterminal and 34 bytes bitcoin POS terminal are available commercially.

34 bytes POS solution.

Bitcoin payment processor, offered by many online service providers, allows integration with e-commerce websites. A simple Internet search can reveal many options.

Various BIPs have been proposed and finalized in order to introduce and standardize bitcoin payments. Most notably, BIP 70 (secure payment protocol) describes the protocol for secure communication between a merchant and customers. This protocol uses X.509 certificates for authentication and runs over HTTP and HTTPS. There are three messages in this protocol: PaymentRequest, Payment, and PaymentACK. The key features of this proposal is defence against man-in-the-middle attacks and secure proof of payment. Man in-the-middle attacks can result in a scenario where the attacker is sitting between the merchant and the buyer and it would seem to the buyer that they are talking to the merchant, but in fact, the *man in the middle* is interacting with the buyer instead of the merchant. This can result in manipulation of the merchant's bitcoin address to defraud the buyer.

Several others BIPs, such as BIP71 and BIP72, have also been proposed to standardize payment message encapsulation and URI scheme to support BIP70.

Bitcoin lightning network, a solution for scalable off-chain instant payments, was introduced in early 2016, which allows off-blockchain payments. The network makes use of payments channels that run off the blockchain. This allows greater speed and scalability of bitcoin. This paper is available at `https://lightning.network/` and interested readers are encouraged to read the paper in order to understand the theory and rationale behind this invention.

Bitcoin investment and buying and selling bitcoins

There are many online exchanges where users can buy and sell bitcoins. This is a big business on the Internet now and it offers bitcoin trading, CFDs, spread betting, margin trading, and various other choices. Traders can buy bitcoins or trade by opening long or short positions to make profit when bitcoin's price goes up or down. Several other features, such as exchanging bitcoins for other virtual currencies, are also possible, and many online bitcoin exchanges provide this function. Advanced market data, trading strategies, charts, and relevant data to support traders is also available. An example is shown from **CEX.IO** here. Other exchanges offer similar types of services.

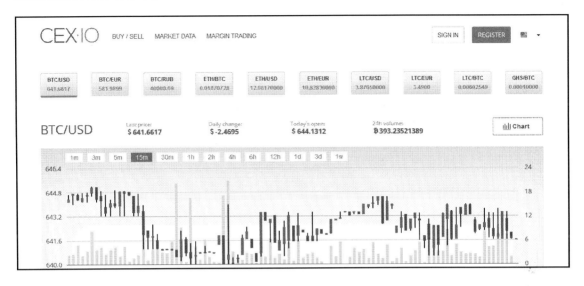

Example of bitcoin exchange cex.io

The following screenshot shows the order book at the exchange where all buy and sell orders are listed:

Example of bitcoin order book at exchange cex.io

Bitcoin installation

The bitcoin core client can be installed from `https://bitcoin.org/en/download`. This is available for different architectures and platforms ranging from x86 windows to ARM Linux, as shown in the following image:

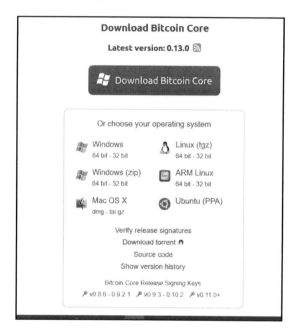

Setting up a bitcoin node

A sample run of the bitcoin core installation on Ubuntu is shown here; for other platforms, you can get details from `www.bitcoin.org`.

```
drequinox@drequinox-OP7010: ~                                    —    □    ×
drequinox@drequinox-OP7010:~$ sudo apt-add-repository ppa:bitcoin/bitcoin
[sudo] password for drequinox:
 Stable Channel of bitcoin-qt and bitcoind for Ubuntu, and their dependencies
 More info: https://launchpad.net/~bitcoin/+archive/ubuntu/bitcoin
Press [ENTER] to continue or ctrl-c to cancel adding it

gpg: keyring `/tmp/tmpzs14ltrx/secring.gpg' created
gpg: keyring `/tmp/tmpzs14ltrx/pubring.gpg' created
gpg: requesting key 8842CE5E from hkp server keyserver.ubuntu.com
gpg: /tmp/tmpzs14ltrx/trustdb.gpg: trustdb created
gpg: key 8842CE5E: public key "Launchpad PPA for Bitcoin" imported
gpg: no ultimately trusted keys found
gpg: Total number processed: 1
gpg:               imported: 1  (RSA: 1)
OK
drequinox@drequinox-OP7010:~$ ▌
```

Step 2:

```
drequinox@drequinox-OP7010:~$ sudo apt-get update
```

Depending on the client required, users can use either of the following commands, or they can issue both commands at once:

```
sudo apt-get install bitcoind
sudo apt-get install bitcoin-qt
drequinox@drequinox-OP7010:~$ sudo apt-get install bitcoin-qt bitcoind
Reading package lists... Done
Building dependency tree
Reading state information... Done
.......
```

Setting up the source code

The bitcoin source code can be downloaded and compiled if users wish to participate in the bitcoin code or for learning purpose. Git can be used to download the bitcoin source code:

```
$ sudo apt-get install git
$ mkdir bcsource
$ cd bcsource
drequinox@drequinox-OP7010:~/bcsource $ git clone
https://github.com/bitcoin/bitcoin.git
Cloning into 'bitcoin'...
remote: Counting objects: 78960, done.
```

```
remote: Compressing objects: 100% (3/3), done.
remote: Total 78960 (delta 0), reused 0 (delta 0), pack-reused 78957
Receiving objects: 100% (78960/78960), 72.53 MiB | 1.85 MiB/s, done.
Resolving deltas: 100% (57908/57908), done.
Checking connectivity... done.
drequinox@drequinox-OP7010:~/bcsource$
```

Change the directory to bitcoin:

```
drequinox@drequinox-OP7010:~/bcsource$ cd bitcoin
```

After the preceding steps are completed, the code can be compiled:

```
drequinox@drequinox-OP7010:~/bcsource/bitcoin$ ./autogen.sh
drequinox@drequinox-OP7010:~/bcsource/bitcoin$ ./configure.sh
drequinox@drequinox-OP7010:~/bcsource/bitcoin$ make
drequinox@drequinox-OP7010:~/bcsource/bitcoin$ sudo make install
```

Setting up bitcoin.conf

bitcoin.conf file is a configuration file that is used by the bitcoin core client to save configuration settings. All command line options for the bitcoind client with the exception of -conf switch can be set up in the configuration file, and when bitcoin-qt or bitcoind will start up, it will take the configuration information from that file.

In Linux systems, this is usually found in $HOME/.bitcoin/, or it can also specified in the command line using the -conf=<file> switch to bitcoind core client software.

Starting up a node in testnet

The bitcoin node can be started in the testnet mode if you want to test the bitcoin network and run an experiment. This is a faster network as compared to the live network and has relaxed rules for mining and transactions.

Various faucet services are available for the bitcoin test network. One example is Bitcoin TestNet sandbox, where users can request bitcoins to be paid to their testnet bitcoin address. This can be accessed via https://testnet.manu.backend.hamburg/. This is very useful for experimentation with transactions on test net.

The command line to start up test net is as follows:

```
bitcoind --testnet -daemon
bitcoin-cli --testnet <command>
bitcoin-qt --testnet
```

Starting up a node in regtest

The regtest mode (regression testing mode) can be used to create a local blockchain for testing purposes.

The following commands can be used to start up a node in the reg test mode:

```
bitcoind -regtest -daemon
Bitcoin server starting
```

Blocks can be generated using the following command:

```
bitcoin-cli -regtest generate 200
```

Relevant log messages can be viewed in the `.bitcoin/regtest` directory on a Linux system under `debug.log`.

After block generation, the balance can be viewed as follows:

```
drequinox@drequinox-OP7010:~/.bitcoin/regtest$ bitcoin-cli -regtest
getbalance
8750.00000000
```

The node can be stopped using this:

```
drequinox@drequinox-OP7010:~/.bitcoin$ bitcoin-cli -regtest stop
Bitcoin server stopping
```

Starting up a node in live mainnet

Bitcoind is the core client software that can be run as a daemon, and it provides the JSON RPC interface.

Bitcoin-cli is the command line feature-rich tool to interact with the daemon; the daemon then interacts with the blockchain and performs various functions. Bitcoin-cli calls only JSON-RPC functions and does not perform any actions on its own on the blockchain.

Bitcoin-qt is the bitcoin core client GUI. When the wallet software starts up first, it verifies the blocks on the disk and then starts up and shows the following GUI:

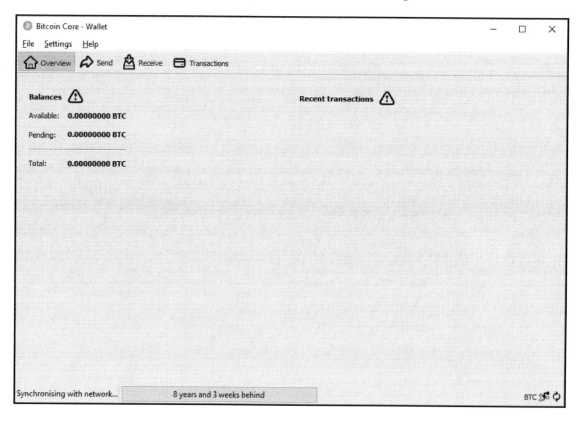

Bitcoin Core QT client, just after installation, showing that blockchain is not in sync

The verification process is not specific to the Bitcoin-qt client; it is performed by the *bitcoind* client as well.

Experimenting with bitcoin-cli

Bitcoin-cli is the command-line interface available with the bitcoin core client and can be used to perform various functions using the RPC interface provided by the bitcoin core client.

A sample run of bitcoin-cli getinfo; the same format can be used to invoke other commands

A list of all commands can be shown via the following command:

Testnet bitcoin-cli, this is just the first few lines of the output, actual output has many commands

- **HTTP REST**: Starting from bitcoin core client 0.10.0, the HTTP REST interface is also available. By default, this runs on the same TCP port 8332 as JSON-RPC.

Bitcoin programming and the command-line interface

Bitcoin programming is a very rich field now. The bitcoin core client exposes various JSON RPC commands that can be used to construct raw transactions and perform other functions via custom scripts or programs. Also, the command line tool Bitcoin-cli is available, which makes use of the JSON-RPC interface and provides a rich toolset to work with Bitcoin.

These APIs are also available via many online service provider in the form of bitcoin APIs, and they provide a simple HTTP REST interface. Bitcoin APIs, such as `blockchain.info` and bitpay, block.io, and many others, offer a myriad of options to develop bitcoin-based solutions.

Various libraries are available for bitcoin programming. A list is shown as follows, and those if you interested can further explore the libraries.

Libbitcoin: Available at `https://libbitcoin.dyne.org/` and provides powerful command line utilities and clients.
Pycoin: Available at `https://github.com/richardkiss/pycoin`, is a library for Python.

Bitcoinj: This library is available at `https://bitcoinj.github.io/` and is implemented in Java.

There are many online bitcoin APIs available; the most commonly used APIs are listed as follows:

```
https://bitcore.io/
```

```
https://bitcoinjs.org/
```

```
https://blockchain.info/api
```

All APIs offer more or less the same type of functionality, and it gets difficult to choose which API is the best.

Bitcoin improvement proposals (BIPs)

These documents are used to propose or inform the bitcoin community about the improvements suggested, the design issues, or information about some aspects of the bitcoin ecosystem. There are three types of bitcoin improvement proposals, abbreviated as BIPs:

- **Standard BIP**: Used to describe the major changes that have a major impact on the bitcoin system, for example, block size changes, network protocol changes, or transaction verification changes.
- **Process BIP**: A major difference between standard and process BIPs is that standard BIPs cover protocol changes, whereas process BIPs usually deal with proposing a change in a process that is outside the core Bitcoin protocol. These are implemented only after a consensus among bitcoin users.
- **Informational BIP**: These are usually used to just advise or record some information about the bitcoin ecosystem, such as design issues.

Summary

This chapter introduced bitcoin and related concepts. It started with some history and basic definitions related to bitcoin. Concepts such as keys and addresses along with public keys and private keys were introduced. How transactions work in the bitcoin network (and related concepts such as scripts, Opcodes, and types of transactions) were also discussed. Moreover, blockchain, which underpins the bitcoin network, was also introduced. Along with that, related concepts such as mining, proof of work, mining systems, and wallets were presented. Finally, some practical information regarding setting up bitcoin clients, the usage of bitcoin-cli, and an introduction to different bitcoin networks was also provided. In the next chapter, alternative currencies, and related concepts will be introduced.

5
Alternative Coins

Since the initial success of bitcoin, many alternative currency projects have been launched. Bitcoin was released in 2009 and the first alternative coin project (named Namecoin) was introduced in 2011. In 2013 and 2014, the altcoin market grew exponentially and many different types of alternative coin project were started. A few of those became a success, whereas many were unpopular and did not succeed. A few were *pump and dump* scams that surfaced for some time but soon disappeared. Alternative approaches to bitcoin can be divided broadly into two categories, based on the primary purpose of their development. If the primary purpose is to build a decentralized blockchain platform, they are called alternative chains; if the sole purpose of the alternative project is to introduce a new virtual currency, it's called an altcoin. Alternative blockchains will be discussed in detail in later chapters in this book.

This chapter is mainly dedicated to alternative coins (altcoins) whose main purpose is to introduce a new virtual currency (coin) although some material will also be presented on the topic of alternate protocols built on top of bitcoin in order to provide various services. These include concepts such as Namecoin, where the primary purpose is to provide decentralized naming and identity services instead of currency.

Currently, as of late 2016, there are hundreds of altcoins on the market and they hold a certain monetary value. Many of these alternative projects are direct forks of bitcoin source code although some of those have been written from scratch. Some altcoins set out to address bitcoin limitations such as privacy. Some others offer different types of mining, changes in block times, and distribution schemes.

By definition an altcoin is generated in the case of a hard fork. If bitcoin has a hard fork then the other, older chain is effectively considered another coin. However there is no established rule as to which chain becomes the altcoin. This has happened recently with Ethereum, where a hard fork caused a new currency **ETC (Ethereum classic)** to come into existence in addition to the **Ethereum (ETH)** currency. Ethereum classic is the old chain and Ether is the new chain after the fork. Such a contentious hard fork is not desirable for a number of reasons. First it is against the true spirit of decentralization as the Ethereum foundation, a central entity, decided to go ahead with the hardfork even though not everyone agreed to the proposition; second it also splits the user community due to disagreement over the hard fork. Although a hard fork in theory generates an altcoin, it is limited in what it can offer due to the fact that, even if the change results in a hard fork, usually there are no drastic changes around the fundamental parameters of the coin. They usually remain the same. For this reason, it is desirable to either write a new coin from scratch or fork the bitcoin (or another coin's source code) to create a new currency with the desired parameters and features.

Altcoins must be able to attract new users, trades, and miners otherwise the currency will have no value. Currency gains its value, especially in the virtual currency space, due to the network effect and its acceptability by the community. If a coin fails to attract enough users then soon it will be forgotten. Users can be attracted by providing an initial amount of coins and can be achieved by using various methods. Methods of providing an initial number of altcoins are discussed as follows:

- **Create a new blockchain**: Altcoins can create a new blockchain and allocate coins to initial miners but this approach is now unpopular due to many scam schemes or *pump and dump* schemes where initial miners made a profit with the launch of a new currency and then disappeared.
- **Proof of burn**: Another approach to allocating initial funds to a new altcoin is *Proof of burn*, also called a one-way peg or price ceiling. In this method users permanently destroy a certain quantity of bitcoins in proportion to the quantity of altcoins to be claimed. For example if 10 bitcoins were destroyed then altcoins can have a value no greater than the amount of bitcoins destroyed. This basically means that bitcoins are being *converted* into altcoins by burning them.
- **Proof of Ownership**: Instead of permanently destroying bitcoins, an alternative method is to prove that users own a certain number of bitcoins. This proof of ownership can be used to claim altcoins by tethering altcoin blocks to bitcoin blocks. For example, this can be achieved by merged mining in which effectively bitcoin miners can mine altcoin blocks while mining for bitcoin without any extra work.

- **Pegged sidechains**: Sidechains, as the name suggests, are blockchains separate from the bitcoin network but bitcoins can be transferred to them. Altcoins can also be transferred back to the bitcoin network. This concept is called a two-way peg.

Investing and trading these alternative coins is also a big business, albeit not as big as bitcoin but enough to attract new investors and traders and provide liquidity to the market. Combined altcoin market capitalization is shown as follows in the graph generated from `http://coinmarketcap.com`:

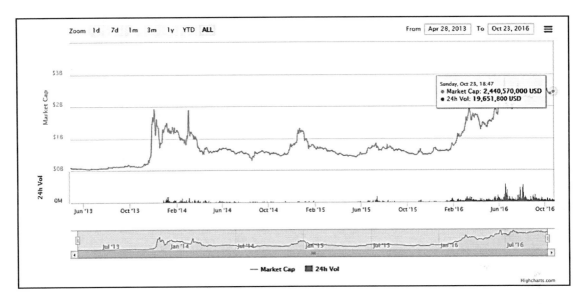

This shows that at the time of writing the Combined Altcoin Market Capitalization is more than 2 billion US Dollars

Current market cap (as of Oct 2016) of the top 10 coins is shown as follows:

Name	Market Cap	Price
Bitcoin	£8,983,068,268	£563.40
Ethereum	£806,208,216	£9.44
Ripple	£248,473,625	£0.01
Litecoin	£159,226,903	£3.31
Ethereum Classic	£69,366,041	£0.81
Monero	£67,664,027	£5.12
Dash	£54,675,636	£8.00
Augur	£45,221,626	£4.11
MaidSafeCoin	£30,929,833	£0.07
NEM	£28,761,896	£0.00

The data is taken from https://coinmarketcap.com/

There are various factors and new concepts introduced with alternative coins. Many concepts were invented even before bitcoin but with bitcoin not only were new concepts, such as a solution to the Byzantine Generals' problem, introduced for the first time but also previous concepts such as hashcash and Proof of Work were used in an ingenious way and came into the limelight. Since then, with the introduction of alternative coin projects, various new techniques and concepts have been developed and introduced. In order to appreciate the current landscape of alternative cryptocurrencies, it is essential to understand some theoretical concepts first. In the following section, some new concepts that have been introduced with altcoin projects are introduced to the reader.

Theoretical foundations

In this section, various theoretical concepts are introduced to the reader that have been developed with the introduction of different altcoins in the past few years.

Alternatives to Proof of Work

The **Proof of Work (PoW)** scheme in the context of cryptocurrency was first used in bitcoin and served as a mechanism to provide assurance that a miner had completed the required number of work in order to find a block. This in return provided decentralization, security, and stability for the blockchain. Also, this is the main vehicle in bitcoin for providing decentralized distributed consensus. PoW schemes are required to have a much desired property called *progress freeness*, which basically means that the reward for consuming computational resources should be random and proportional to the contribution made by the miners. In this case, some chance of winning the block reward is given to even those miners who have comparatively less computational power. The term *progress freeness* was introduced by *Arvind Narayanan .et.al* in the book *Bitcoin and Cryptocurrency Technologies*. Other requirements for mining computational puzzles include adjustable difficulty and quick verification. Adjustable difficulty ensures that the difficulty target for mining on the blockchain is regulated in response to increased hashing power and the number of users. Quick verification is a property which means that mining computational puzzles should be easy and quick to verify. Another aspect of the PoW scheme, especially the one used in Bitcoin (Double SHA-256), is that since the introduction of ASICs the power is shifting towards miners or mining pools who can afford to operate large-scale ASIC farms and this challenges the core philosophy of the decentralization of bitcoin.

There are a few alternatives that have been proposed such as ASIC-resistant puzzles and are designed in such a way that building ASICs for solving this puzzle is infeasible and does not result in a major performance gain over commodity hardware. A common technique used for this purpose is to apply a class of computational hard problems called *memory hard* computational puzzles. The core idea behind this method is that as puzzle solving requires a large amount of memory, it is not feasible to be implemented on ASIC-based systems. This technique was initially used in litecoin and Tenebrix where the Scrypt hash function was used as an ASIC-resistant PoW scheme. Even though this scheme was initially advertised as ASIC resistant, recently Scrypt ASICs have now become available disproving the original claim by litecoin.

Another approach to ASIC resistance is where multiple hash functions are required to be calculated in order to provide PoW. This is also called a chained hashing scheme. The rationale behind this idea is that designing multiple hash functions on an ASIC is not very feasible. The most common example is the X11 memory hard function implemented in Dash. X11 comprises 11 SHA3 contestants where one algorithm outputs the calculated hash to the next algorithm until all 11 algorithms are used in a sequence. These algorithms include blake, bmw, groestl, jh, keccak, skein, luffa, cubehash, shavite, simd, and echo.

This approach did provide some resistance to ASIC development initially but now ASIC miners are available commercially and support mining of X11 and similar schemes. A recent example is ASIC Baikal Miner, which supports X11, X13, X14, and X15 mining. Other examples include miners such as iBeLink DM384M X11 miner and Pinidea X11 ASIC miner.

Perhaps another approach could be to design *self-mutating puzzles* that intelligently or randomly change the PoW scheme or its requirements as a function of time. This will make it almost impossible to be implemented in ASICs as it will require multiple ASICs to be designed for each function and also randomly changing schemes would be almost impossible to handle in ASICs. At the moment, it is unclear how this can be achieved practically.

PoW has various drawbacks and the biggest of all is energy consumption. It is estimated that the total electricity consumed by bitcoin miners will be equivalent to that of Denmark by 2020. This is huge and all that power is in a way wasted; in fact no useful purpose is served except for of mining. Environmentalists have raised real concerns about this situation.

It has been proposed that PoW puzzles can be designed in such a way that they serve two purposes. First their primary purpose is in consensus mechanisms and second to perform some useful scientific computation. This way not only can the schemes be used in mining but they can also help to potentially solve other scientific problems too. This proof of useful work has been recently put into practice by Primecoin where the requirement is to find special prime number chains known as Cunningham chains and bi-twin chains. As the study of prime number distribution has special significance in scientific disciplines such as physics, by mining Primecoin miners not only achieve the block reward but also help in finding the special prime numbers.

Proof of Storage

Also known as proof of irretrievability, this is another type of proof of useful work that requires storage of large number of data. Introduced by Microsoft Research, this scheme provides a useful benefit of distributed storage of archival data. Miners are required to store a pseudo, randomly-selected subset of large data in order to perform mining.

Proof of Stake

This proof is also called virtual mining. This is another type of mining puzzle that has been proposed as an alternative to traditional PoW schemes. It was first proposed in PeerCoin in August, 2012. In this scheme, the idea is that users are required to demonstrate possession of a certain amount of currency (coins) thus proving that they have a stake in the coin. The simplest form of stake is where mining is made comparatively easier for those users who demonstrably own larger amounts of digital currency. The benefits of this scheme are twofold; first acquiring large amounts of digital currency is relatively difficult as compared to buying high-end ASIC devices and second it results in saving computational resources. Various forms of stake have been proposed and are briefly discussed below.

Proof of coinage

The age of a coin is the time since the coins were last used or held. This is a different approach from the usual form of Proof of Stake where mining is made easier for users who have the highest stake in the altcoin. In the coin-age-based approach the age of the coin (coinage) is reset every time a block is mined. The miner is rewarded for holding and not spending coins for a time period. This mechanism has been implemented in Peercoin combined with PoW in a creative way. The difficulty of mining puzzles (PoW) is inversely proportional to the coin-age, meaning that if miners consume some coin-age using *coin-stake* transactions then the PoW requirements are relieved.

Proof of deposit

The core idea behind this scheme is that newly minted blocks by miners are made un-spendable for a certain period of time. More precisely the coins get locked for a set number of blocks during the mining operation. The scheme works by allowing miners to perform mining at the cost of freezing a certain number of coins for some time. This is a type of Proof of Stake.

Proof of burn

As an alternate expenditure to computing power, proof of burn in fact destroys a certain amount of bitcoins in order to get equivalent altcoins. This is commonly used when starting up new coin projects as a means to provide a fair initial distribution. This can be considered an alternative mining scheme where the value of the new coins comes from the fact that previously a certain number of coins have been destroyed.

Proof of activity

This scheme is a hybrid of PoW and Proof of Stake. In this scheme, blocks are initially produced by using PoW but then each block randomly assigns three stakeholders that are required to digitally sign it. The validity of subsequent blocks is dependent on the successful signing of previously randomly chosen blocks.

There is, however a possible issue known as the *nothing at stake* problem where it would be trivial to create a fork of the blockchain. This is possible because in PoW appropriate computational resources are required to mine whereas in Proof of Stake there is no such requirement; as a result, an attacker can try to mine on multiple chains using the same coin.

Non-outsourceable puzzles

The key motivation behind this puzzle is to develop resistance again the development of mining pools. Mining pools as previously discussed offer rewards to all participants in proportion to the computing power they consume. However, in this model the mining pool operator is a central authority to whom all the rewards go and who can enforce certain rules. Also, in this model all miners only trust each other because they are working towards a common goal together in the hope of the pool manager getting the reward. Non-outsourceable puzzles are a scheme that allows miners to claim rewards for themselves; consequently pool formation becomes unlikely due to inherent mistrust between anonymous miners.

Difficulty adjustment and retargeting algorithms

Another concept that has been introduced with the advent of bitcoin and altcoins is difficulty in retargeting algorithms. In bitcoin a difficulty target is calculated simply by the following equation; however other coins have either developed their own algorithms or implemented modified versions of the bitcoin difficulty algorithm:

$$T = Time\ previous * time\ actual\ /\ 2016 * 10\ min$$

The idea behind difficulty regulation in bitcoin is that a generation of 2016 blocks should take roughly around 2 weeks (inter-block time should be around 10 minutes). If it takes longer than 2 weeks to mine 2016 blocks then the difficulty is decreased and if it takes less than two weeks to mine 2016 blocks then the difficulty is increased. When ASICs were introduced due to a high block generation rate the difficulty increased exponentially and that is one drawback of PoW algorithms that are not ASIC resistant. This leads to mining power centralization. This also poses another problem; if a new coin starts now with the same Proof of Work based on SHA256 as bitcoin uses, then it would be easy for a malicious user to just simply use an ASIC miner and control the entire network. This attack would be more practical if there is less interest in the new altcoin and someone decides to take over the network by consuming adequately high computing resources. This may not be a feasible attack if other miners with similar computing power also join the the altcoin network because then miners will be competing with each other. Also, multipools pose a greater threat where a group of miners can automatically switch to the currency that is becoming profitable. This phenomenon is known as **pool hopping** and can adversely affect a blockchain, and consequently the growth of the altcoin. Pool hopping impacts the network adversely because pool hoppers join the network only when the difficulty is low and they can gain quick rewards; the moment difficulty goes up (or is readjusted) they *hop off* and then come back again when the difficulty is adjusted back. For example if a multipool consumes its resources in quickly mining a new coin, the difficulty will increase very quickly; when the multipool leaves the currency network; it becomes almost unusable because of the fact that now the difficulty has increased to such a level that it is no longer profitable for solo miners and can no longer be maintained. The only fix for this problem is to initiate a hard fork which is usually undesirable for the community.

There are a few algorithms that have come into existence to address this issue and are discussed later. All these algorithms are based on the idea of readjusting various parameters in response to hash rate changes; these parameters include the number of previous blocks, difficulty of previous blocks, ratio of adjustment, and the number by which the difficulty can be readjusted back or up. In the following section, readers will be introduced to the few difficulty algorithms being used in and proposed for various altcoins.

Kimoto Gravity Well

This algorithm is used in various altcoins to regulate difficulty. This was first introduced in Megacoin and used to adaptively adjust difficulty of the network every block. The logic of the algorithm is shown as follows:

KGW = 1 + (0.7084 * pow((double(PastBlocksMass)/double(144)), -1.228))

Basically, the algorithm runs in a loop that goes through a set of predetermined blocks (`PastBlockMass`) and calculates a new readjustment value. The core idea behind this algorithm is to develop an adaptive difficulty regulation mechanism that can readjust the difficulty in response to rapid spikes in hash rates. **Kimoto Gravity Well (KGW)** ensures that the time between blocks remains approximately the same. In bitcoin the difficulty is adjusted every 2016 blocks but in KGW the difficulty is adjusted at every block.

This algorithm is vulnerable to time warp attacks, which allow an attacker to temporarily enjoy less difficulty in creating new blocks. This attack allows a time window where the difficulty becomes low and the attacker can easily generate many coins at a fast rate.

Dark Gravity Wave

Dark Gravity Wave (DGW) is a new algorithm designed to address certain flaws such as the time warp attack in the KGW algorithm. This was first introduced in Dash, previously known as Darkcoin. It makes use of multiple exponential moving averages and simple move averages to achieve a smoother readjustment mechanism. The formula is shown as follows:

$$2222222/ \; (((Difficulty+2600)/9)^{\wedge}2)$$

This formula is implemented in Dash coin and various other altcoins as a mechanism to readjust difficulty.

DGW version 3.0 is the latest implementation of this algorithm and allows improved difficulty retargeting compared to KGW.

DigiShield

This is another difficulty retargeting algorithm that has recently been used in Zcash with slight variations and after adequate experimentation. This algorithm works by going through a fixed number of previous blocks to calculate the time they took to be generated and then readjusts the difficulty to the difficulty of the previous block by dividing the actual time span by averaging the target time. In this scheme, the retargeting is calculated much much rapidly and also the recovery from a sudden increase or decrease in hashrate is quick. This algorithm protects against multipools, which can result in rapid hashrate increases. The network difficulty is readjusted every block or every minute depending on the implementation. The key innovation is faster readjust times as compared to KGW.

MIDAS

Multi Interval Difficulty Adjustment System (**MIDAS**) is an algorithm that is comparatively more complex than the algorithms discussed previously. This method responds much more rapidly to abrupt changes in hash rates. This algorithm also provides protection against time warp attacks.

Many currencies have emerged as an attempt to address various limitations in bitcoin. A brief discussion of bitcoin limitations is provided as follows.

Bitcoin limitations

Various limitations in bitcoin have also sparked some interest in altcoins, which were developed specifically to address limitations in bitcoin. The most prominent and widely discussed limitation is the lack of anonymity in bitcoin. This limitation is discussed in detail as follows.

Privacy and anonymity

As the blockchain is a public ledger of all transactions and is openly available it becomes trivial to analyse it. Combined with traffic analyses, transactions can be linked back to their source IP addresses, thus possibly revealing a transaction's originator. This is a big concern from a privacy point of view. Even though in bitcoin it is a recommended and common practice to generate a new address for every transaction, thus allowing some level of unlinkability, this is not enough and various techniques have been developed and successfully used to trace the flow of transactions throughout the network and link them back to their originator. Various methods to analyse blockchains such as transaction graphs, address graphs, and entity graphs have been used by researchers to link users to the transactions, thus raising privacy concerns. The afore mentioned analysis techniques can be further enriched by using publicly available information about transactions and linking them to the actual users. There are open source block parsers available that can be used to extract transaction information, balances, and scripts from the blockchain database. A parser available at `https://github.com/mikispag/rusty-blockparser` is written in Rust and provides advanced blockchain analysis capabilities. An earlier version of this work is called BitIodine but is no longer being actively developed.

Various proposals have been made to address the privacy issue in bitcoin. These proposals fall into three categories: mixing protocols, third-party mixing networks, and inherent anonymity. A brief discussion of each category is presented as follows.

Mixing protocols

These schemes are used to provide anonymity to bitcoin transactions. In this model, a mixing service provider (an intermediary or a shared wallet) is used. Users send coins to this shared wallet as a deposit and the shared wallet then can send some other coins (of the same value deposited by some other users) to the destination. Users can also receive coins that were sent by others via this intermediary. This way the link between outputs and inputs is no longer there and transaction graph analysis will not be able to reveal the true relationship between senders and receivers.

CoinJoin is one example of mixing protocols, where two transactions are joined together to form a single transaction while keeping the inputs and outputs unchanged. The core idea behind CoinJoin is to build a shared transaction that is signed by all participants. This technique improves privacy for all participants involved in the transactions:

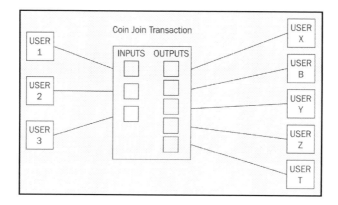

CoinJoin transaction with three users joining their transaction into a single larger CoinJoin transaction

Third-party mixing protocols

Various third-party mixing services are available but if the service is centralized then it poses the threat of tracing the mapping between senders and receivers, because the mixing service knows about all inputs and outputs. In addition to this, fully centralized miners even pose the risk of the administrators of the service stealing the coins.

Various services, with varying degrees of complexity, such as CoinShuffle, Coinmux, and dark send in Dash (coin) are available that are based on the idea of CoinJoin (mixing) transactions. CoinShuffle is a decentralized alternative to traditional mixing services as it does not require a trusted third party.

CoinJoin-based schemes, however, have some weaknesses, most prominently the possibility of launching a Denial of Service attack by users who committed to signing the transactions initially but now are not providing their signature, thus delaying or stopping joint transaction a altogether.

Inherent anonymity

This category includes coins that support privacy inherently and is built into the design of the currency. The most popular is Zcash, which is discussed in detail later in the chapter. Other examples include Monero, which makes use of ring signatures to provide anonymous services.

The next section introduces various enhancements that have been made, or are proposed, in order to extend the bitcoin protocol.

Extended protocols on top of bitcoin

Several protocols have been proposed and implemented on top of bitcoin in order to enhance and extend the bitcoin protocol and use for various other purposes instead of just as a virtual currency.

Colored coins

Colored coins is a set of methods that have been developed to represent digital assets on the bitcoin blockchain. Coloring a bitcoin refers colloquially to updating it with some metadata representing a digital asset (smart property). The coin still works and operates as a bitcoin but additionally carries some metadata that represents some assets. This mechanism allows issuing and tracking specific bitcoins. Metadata can be recorded using the bitcoins `OP_RETURN` opcode or optionally in multi-signature addresses. This metadata can also be encrypted if required to address any privacy concerns. Colored coins can be used to represent a multitude of assets including but not limited to commodities, certificates, shares, bonds, and voting. It should also be noted that, in order to work with colored coins, a wallet that interprets colored coins is necessary and normal bitcoin wallets will not work. Colored coin wallets can be set up online using a service available at `https://www.coinprism.com/`. Using this service, any type of digital asset can be created and issued via a colored coin.

The idea of colored coins is very appealing as it does not require any modification to the existing bitcoin protocol and can make use of the already existing secure bitcoin network. In addition to the traditional representation of digital assets, there is also the possibility of creating *smart assets* that behave according to the parameters and conditions defined for them. These parameters includes time validation, restrictions on transferability, and fees. This opens the possibility of creating smart contracts.

A major use case can be the issuance of financial instruments on the blockchain. This will ensure low transaction fees, valid and mathematically secure proof of ownership, fast transferability without requiring an intermediary, and instant dividend pay outs to the investors.

A rich API is available for coloured coins at `http://coloredcoins.org/`.

Counterparty

This is another service that can be used to create custom tokens that act as a cryptocurrency and can be used for various purposes such as issuing digital assets on top of bitcoin blockchain. This is quite a powerful platform and runs on bitcoin blockchains at their core but has developed its own client and other components to support issuing digital assets. The architecture consists of a counterparty server, counterblock, counter wallet, and armory_utxsvr. Counterparty works based on the same idea as coloured coins by embedding data into regular bitcoin transactions but provides a much richer library and set of powerful tools to support the handling of digital assets. This embedding is also called embedded consensus because the counterparty transactions are embedded within bitcoin transactions. The method of embedding the data is by using OP_RETURN opcode in bitcoin.

The currency produced and used by counterparty is known as XCP and is used by smart contracts as the fee for running the contract. At the time of writing its price is 2.78 USD. XCPs were created by using the proof of burn method discussed previously.

Counterparty allows the development of smart contracts on Ethereum using solidity language and allows interaction with bitcoin blockchain. In order to achieve this, BTC Relay is used as a means to provide interoperability between Ethereum and bitcoin. This is a clever concept where Ethereum contracts can talk to bitcoin blockchain and transactions through BTC Relay. The relayers (nodes that are running BTC Relay) fetch the bitcoin block headers and relay them to a smart contract on the Ethereum network that verifies the PoW. This process verifies that a transaction has occurred on the bitcoin network. This is available at `http://btcrelay.org/`.

Technically, this is basically an Ethereum contract that is capable of storing and verifying bitcoin block headers just like bitcoin simple payment verification lightweight clients do by using bloom filters. SPV clients were discussed in detail in the previous chapter. The idea can be visualized with the following diagram:

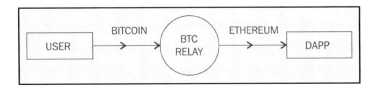

BTC relay concept

 Counterparty is available at `http://counterparty.io/`.

Development of altcoins

Altcoin projects can be started very easily from a coding point of view by simply forking the bitcoin or another coin's source code but this probably is not enough. When a new coin project is started, there are several things that need to be considered in order to ensure a successful launch and the coin's longevity. Usually, the code base is written in C++ as was the case with bitcoin but almost any language can be used to develop coin projects, for example Golang or Rust.

Writing code or forking the code for an existing coin is the trivial part, the challenging issue is how to start a new currency so that new investors and users can be attracted to it. Generally, the following steps are taken in order to start a new coin project.

From a technical point of view, in the case of forking the code of another coin, for example bitcoin, there are various parameters that can be changed to effectively create a new coin. These parameters are required to be *tweaked* or introduced in order to create a new coin. These parameters can include but are not limited to the following.

Consensus algorithms

There is a choice of consensus algorithm: **Proof of Work (PoW)** as used in bitcoin or **Proof of Stake (PoS)**, as in Peercoin.

Hashing algorithms

This is either SHA256, Scrypt, X11, X13, X15, or any other hashing algorithm that is adequate for use as a consensus algorithm.

Difficulty adjustment algorithms

Various options are available in this category to provide difficulty retargeting mechanisms. The most prominent examples are KGW, DGW, Nite's Gravity Wave, and DigiShield. Also all these algorithms can be tweaked based on requirements to produce different results; therefore many variants are possible.

Inter-block time

This is the time elapsed between the generation of each block. For bitcoin the blocks are generated every 10 minutes, for litecoin it's 2.5 minutes. Any value can be used but an appropriate value is usually between a few minutes; if the generation time is too fast it might destabilize the blockchain, if it's too slow it may not attract many users.

Block rewards

A block reward is for the miner who solves the mining puzzle and is allowed to have a Coinbase transaction that contains the reward. This used to be 50 coins in bitcoin initially and now many altcoins set this parameter to a very high number; for example in Dogecoin it is 10,000, currently.

Reward halving rate

This is another important factor; in bitcoin it is halved every 4 years and now is set to 12.5 bitcoins. It's a variable number that can be set to any time period or none at all depending on the requirements.

Block size and transaction size

This is another important factor that determines how high or low the transaction rate can be on the network. Block sizes in bitcoin are limited to 1 MB but in altcoins it can vary depending on the requirements.

Interest rate

This property applies only to PoS systems where the owner of the coins can earn interest at a rate defined by the network in return for the amount of coins that are held on the network as a PoS to protect the network.

Coin age

This parameter defines how long the coin has to remain unspent in order for it to become eligible to be considered stakeworthy.

Total supply of coins

This number sets the total limit of the coins that can ever be generated. For example in bitcoin the limit is 21 million, whereas in Dogecoin it's unlimited. This limit is fixed by the block reward and halving schedule discussed above.

There are two options to create your own virtual currency: forking existing established cryptocurrency source code or writing a new one from scratch. The latter option is less popular but the first option is easier and has allowed the creation of many virtual currencies over the last few years. Fundamentally, the idea is that first a cryptocurrency source code is forked and then appropriate changes are made at different strategic locations in the source code to effectively create a new currency.

In the next section, readers are introduced to some altcoin projects. It is not possible to cover all alternative currencies in this chapter, but a few selected coins are discussed below. Selection is based on longevity, market cap, and innovation. Each coin is discussed from different angles such as theoretical foundations, trading, and mining.

Namecoin

Namecoin is the first fork of the bitcoin source code. The key idea behind Namecoin is not to produce an altcoin but instead to provide improved decentralization, censorship resistance, privacy, security, and faster decentralized naming. Decentralized naming services are intended to provide a response to inherent limitations such as slowness and centralized control in the traditional **Domain Name System** (DNS) protocols used on the Internet. Namecoin is also the first solution to Zooko's triangle, which was briefly discussed in previous chapters.

Namecoin is used to essentially provide a service to register a key/value pair. One major use case of Namecoin is that it can provide a decentralized **Transport Layer Security (TLS)** certificate validation mechanism, driven by blockchain-based distributed and decentralized consensus.

It is based on the same technology introduced with bitcoin, but with its own blockchain and wallet software. The source code for the Namecoin core is available at `https://github.com/namecoin/namecoin-core`.

In summary, Namecoin provides the following three services:

- Secure storage and transfer of names (keys)
- Attachment of some value to the names by attaching up to 520 bytes of data
- Production of a digital currency (Namecoin)

Namecoin also for the first time introduced merged mining, which allows a miner to mine on more than one chain simultaneously. The idea is simple but very effective: miners create a Namecoin block and produce a hash of that block. Then the hash is added to a bitcoin block and miners solve that block at equal to or greater than the Namecoin block difficulty in order to prove that enough work has been contributed towards solving the Namecoin block.

More precisely the Coinbase transaction is used to include the hash of the transactions from Namecoin (or any other altcoin). The mining task is to solve bitcoin blocks whose Coinbase scripSig contains a hash pointer to Namecoin (or any other altcoin) block. This is shown in the diagram below. If a miner manages to solve a hash at the bitcoin blockchain difficulty level, the bitcoin block is built and becomes part of the bitcoin network. In this case, the Namecoin hash is ignored by the bitcoin blockchain. On the other hand, if a miner solves a block at Namecoin blockchain difficulty level a new block is created in the Namecoin blockchain. The core benefit of this scheme is that all the computational power spent by the miners contributes towards securing both Namecoin and bitcoin:

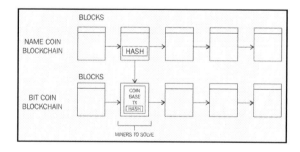

Merged mining diagram

Trading Namecoins

The current market cap of Namecoin is £2,736,537 as per `https://coinmarketcap.com/` and it can be bought and sold at various exchanges such as `https://cryptonit.net/`. Various other exchanges can be found via a simple online search.

Obtaining Namecoins

Even though Namecoins can be mined independently, they are usually mined as part of bitcoin mining by utilizing the merged mining technique as explained above. This way Namecoin can be mined as a by-product of bitcoin mining. Solo mining is no longer profitable as is evident from the following difficulty graph; instead it is recommended to merge-mine, use a mining pool, or even use a cryptocurrency exchange to buy Namecoin.

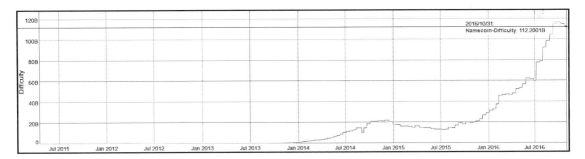

Namecoin difficulty as shown at: https://bitinfocharts.com/comparison/difficulty-nmc.html

Various mining pools such `https://slushpool.com` also offer the option of merged mining. This allows a miner to mine primarily bitcoin but also as a result earn Namecoin too.

Another method that can be used to quickly get some Namecoins is to swap your existing coins with Namecoins, for example, if you already have some bitcoins or an other cryptocurrency that can be used to exchange with Namecoin. An online service, `https://shapeshift.io/`, is available that provides this service. This service allows conversion from one cryptocurrency to another, using a simple user-friendly interface.

For example, paying BTC to receive NMC is shown as follows:

Once **Start Transaction** is clicked, the transaction starts and instructs the user to send the bitcoins to a specific bitcoin address. When the user sends the required amount, the conversion process starts as shown:

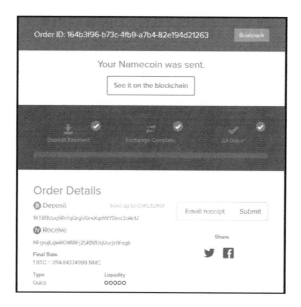

When the process completes, the transactions can be viewed in the Namecoin wallet:

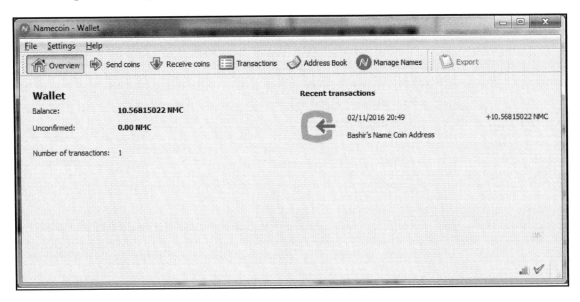

It may take some time to confirm the transactions; until that time it is not possible to use the Namecoins to manage names. Once Namecoins are available in the wallet, the **Manage Names** option can be used to generate Namecoin records.

Generating Namecoin records

Namecoin records are in the form of key and value pairs. A name is a lower-case string of the form `d/examplename` whereas a value is a case-sensitive, UTF-8 encoded JSON object with a maximum of 520 bytes. The name should be RFC1035 (`https://tools.ietf.org/html/rfc1035`)-compliant. A general namecoin name can be an arbitrary binary string up to 255 bytes long with, 1024-bits of associated identifying information. A record on a Namecoin chain is only valid for around 200 days or 36,000 blocks after which it needs to be renewed. Namecoin also introduced .bit top level domains that can be registered using Namecoin and can be browsed using specialized Namecoin-enabled resolvers. Namecoin wallet software as shown in the following screenshot can be used to register `.bit` domain names.

The name is entered and, after the **Submit** button is pressed, it will ask for configuration information such as DNS, IP, or Identity:

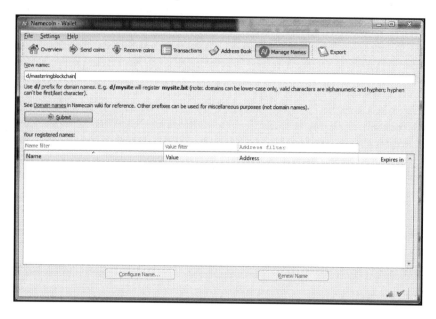

As shown in the following screenshot, **masteringblockchain** will register as masteringblockchain.bit on the Namecoin blockchain:

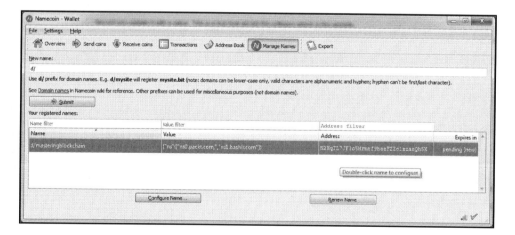

Litecoin

Litecoin is a fork of the bitcoin source code released in 2011. It uses Scrypt as PoW, originally introduced in the Tenebrix coin. Litecoin allows for faster transactions as compared to bitcoin due to its faster block generation time of 2.5 minutes. Also difficulty readjustment is achieved every 3.5 days roughly due to faster block generation time. The total coin supply is 84 million.

Scrypt is a sequentially memory hard function that is the first alternative to the SHA-256-based PoW algorithm. It was originally proposed as a password-based key derivation function PBKDF. The key idea is that if the function requires large number of memory to run then custom hardware such as ASICs will require more VLSI area, which would be unfeasible to build. The Scrypt algorithm requires a large array of pseudo random bits to be held in memory and a key is derived from this in a pseudo random fashion. The algorithm is based on a phenomenon called **Time-Memory Tradeoff** (**TMTO**). If memory requirements are relaxed then it results in increased computational cost. Put another way, TMTO shortens the running time of a programme if more memory is given to it. This tradeoff makes it unfeasible for an attacker to gain more memory because it's expensive and difficult to implement on custom hardware, or if the attacker chooses to not increase memory, then it results in the algorithm running slowly due to high processing requirements.

Scrypt uses the following parameters to generate a derived key (Kd):

- Passphrase: This is a string of characters to hash
- Salt: This is a random string that is provided to Scrypt functions (generally all hash functions) in order to provide a defence against brute-force dictionary attacks using rainbow tables
- N: This is a memory/CPU cost parameter that must be a power of $2 > 1$
- P: The parallelization parameter
- R: The block size parameter
- dkLen: The intended length of the derived key in bytes

Formally, this function can be written as follows:

$$Kd = scrypt\ (P, S, N, P, R, dkLen)$$

Before applying the core Scrypt function, the algorithm takes P and S as input and applies **PBKDF2** and SHA-256-based HMAC. Then the output is fed to an algorithm called **ROMix,** which internally uses the Blockmix algorithm utilizing the Salsa20/8 core stream cipher to fill up the memory which requires large memory to operate, thus enforcing the sequentially memory hard property.

The output from this step of the algorithm is finally fed to the PBKDF2 function again in order to produce a derived key. This process is shown in the following diagram:

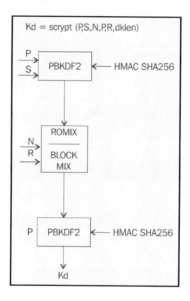

Scrypt algorithm

Scrypt is used in litecoin mining with specific parameters where N= 1024, R = 1, P=1, and S= random 80 bytes producing a 256-bit output.

It appears that, due to the selection of these parameters, the development of ASICs for Scrypt for litecoin mining turned out to be not very difficult. In an ASIC for litecoin mining, a sequential logic can be developed that takes the data and nonce as input and applies the **PBKDF2** algorithm with **HMAC-SHA256**; then the resultant bit stream is fed into the SALSA20/8 function which produces a hash that again is fed down to the PBKDF2 and HMAC-256 functions to produce a 256-bit hash output. As is the case with bitcoin PoW, in Scrypt also if the output hash is less that the target hash (already passed as input at the start, stored in memory, and checked with every iteration) then the function terminates; otherwise, the nonce is incremented and the process is repeated again until a hash is found that is lower than the difficulty target:

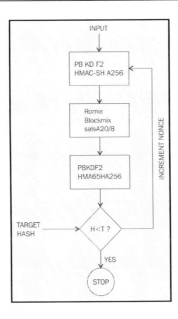

Scrypt ASIC design simplified flowchart

- **Trading Litecoin**: As with other coins, trading litecoin is easily carried out on various online exchanges. The current market cap of litecoin is £161,239,005. The current price of litecoin is £3.25/LTC.

- **Mining**: Litecoin mining can be carried out solo or in pools. At the moment, ASICs for Scrypt are available that are commonly used to mine litecoin.

Litecoin mining on a CPU is no longer profitable as is the case with many other digital currencies. There are online cloud mining providers and ASIC miners available that can be used to mine litecoin. Litecoin mining started from the CPU, progressed through GPU mining rigs, and eventually now has reached a point where specialized ASIC miners such as Asic Scrypt Miner Wolf available from EhsMiner are now required to be used in the hope of being able to make some coins. Generally, it is true that even with ASICs it is better to mine in pools instead of solo as solo mining is not as profitable as mining in pools due to the proportional rewards scheme used by mining pools. These miners are capable of producing a hashing rate of 2 Gh/s for Scrypt algorithms.

- **Software source code and wallet**: The source code for litecoin is available at `https://github.com/litecoin-project/litecoin`. The litecoin wallet can be downloaded from `https://litecoin.org/` and can be used just like the bitcoin core client software.

Primecoin

Primecoin is the first digital currency on the market that introduced a useful PoW, as opposed to bitcoin's SHA256-based PoW. Primecoin uses searching prime numbers as a PoW. Not all types of prime number meet the requirements to be selected as PoW. Three types of prime numbers (known as Cunningham chain of first kind, Cunningham chain of second kind, and bi-twin chains) meet the requirements of a PoW algorithm to be used in cryptocurrencies. The difficulty is dynamically adjusted via a continuous difficulty evaluation scheme in Primecoin blockchain. The efficient verification of PoW based on prime numbers is also of high importance, because if verification is slow then PoW is not suitable. Therefore prime chains are selected as a PoW because finding prime chains gets difficult as the chain increases in length whereas verification remains quick enough to warrant being used as an efficient PoW algorithm. It is also important that once a PoW has been verified on a block it must not be reusable on another block. This is accomplished in Primecoin by a combination of *Proof of Work certificates* and hashing it with the header of the parent block in the child block. The PoW certificate is produced by linking the prime chain to the block header hash. It also requires that the block header's origin is divisible by the block header hash. If it is, it is divided and after division the quotient is used as a PoW certificate. Another property of the adjustable difficulty of PoW algorithms is met by introducing difficulty adjustment every block instead of every 2,016, as is the case with bitcoin. This is a *smoother* approach as compared to bitcoin and allows readjustment in the case of sudden increases in hash power. Also the total number of coins generated is community-driven and there is no concrete limit on the number of coins Primecoin can generate.

Trading Primecoin

Primecoins can be traded on major virtual currency trading exchanges. The current market cap of Primecoin is £828,002 at the time of writing. It is not very large but, due to the fact that Primecoin is based on a novel idea and there is a dedicated community behind it, this continues to hold some market share.

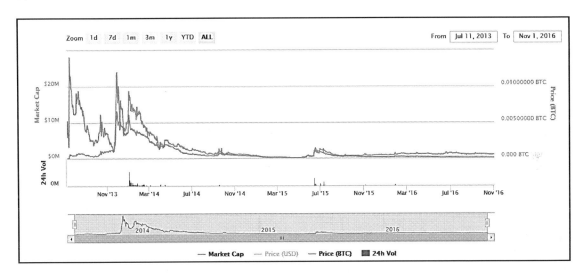

Mining guide

The first step is to download a wallet. Primecoin supports native mining within the wallet, just like original bitcoin clients, but also can be mined on the cloud via various online mining service providers.

A quick Windows guide is presented as follows:

1. The first step is to download the Primecoin wallet from:
   ```
   http://primecoin.io/index.php.
   ```

2. Once the wallet is installed and synched with the network, mining can be started by following the next step. A debug window can be opened in the Primecoin wallet by clicking on the **Help** menu and selecting the **Debug** window menu item. Additional help can be invoked through typing `help` in the console window:

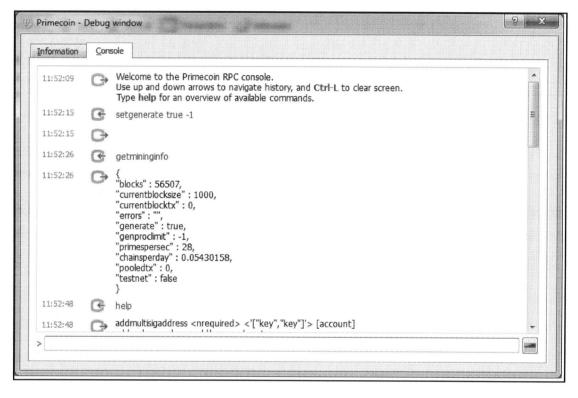

Debug window used to enable the Primecoin mining function

3. Once the preceding commands are successfully executed mining will start in solo mode. This may not be very profitable but the miner can use mining pools available online:

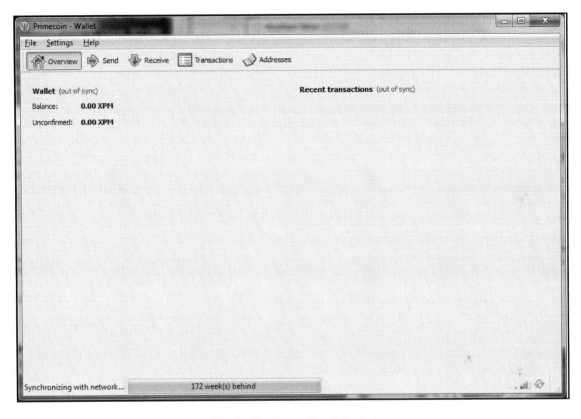

Primecoin wallet software, synching with the network

The Primecoin source code is available at `https://github.com/primecoin/primecoin`. Although it's a novel concept and the PoW that Primecoin has introduced does have scientific significance, it seems that no active development is being carried out to further develop Primecoin. Readers can further explore Primecoin by reading the Primecoin white paper by *Sunny King* (pseudonym) at: `http://primecoin.io/bin/primecoin-paper.pdf`.

Zcash

Zcash was launched on 28th of October, 2016. This is the first currency that uses a specific type of zero knowledge proofs known as **zero-knowledge Succinct Non-interactive Arguments of Knowledge (zk-SNARKs)** to provide complete privacy to the user. These proofs are very short and easy to verify; however, setting up the initial public parameters is a complex process. The latter include two keys: the proving key and verifying key. The process requires sampling some random numbers in order to construct the public parameters. The issue is that these random numbers, also called *toxic waste*, must be destroyed after the parameter generation in order to prevent counterfeiting of Zcash. For this purpose, the Zcash team came up with a multi-party computation protocol to generate the required public parameters in a collaborative manner from independent locations to ensure that *toxic waste* is not created. Due to the fact that these public parameters are required to be created by the Zcash team, it means that the participants in the ceremony are trusted. This is the reason why the ceremony was very open and conducted by making use of a multi-party computation mechanism. This mechanism has a property whereby all of the participants in the ceremony will have to be compromised in order to compromise the final parameters. When the ceremony is completed all participants physically destroy the equipment used for private key generation. This action eliminates any trace of the participants' part of the private key on the equipment.

zk-SNARKs must satisfy the properties of completeness, soundness, succinctness, and non-interactivity. *Completeness* means that there is a definite strategy for a prover to satisfy a verifier that an assertion is true. On the other hand, *soundness* means that no prover can convince the verifier that a false statement is true. *Succinctness* means that messages passed between the prover and verifier are very small in size. Finally, the property non-interactive means that the verification of correctness of an assertion can be carried out without any interaction or very little interaction. Also, being a zero knowledge proof, the property of *zero-knowledge* (discussed in `Chapter 3`, *Cryptography and Technical Foundations*) needs to be met too.

Zcash developers have introduced the concept of a **Decentralized Anonymous Payments scheme (DAP scheme)** that is used in the Zcash network to enable direct and private payments. The transactions reveal no information about the origin, destination, and amount of the payments. There are two types of addresses available in Zcash, z-addr and t-addr. Z addresses are based on zero knowledge proofs and provide privacy protection whereas T addresses are similar to those of bitcoin.

Zcash uses an efficient PoW scheme named **Asymmetric PoW (Equihash)**, which is based on the Generalized Birthday Problem. It allows very efficient verification. It is a memory-hard and ASIC-resistant function. A novel idea (initial slow mining) has been introduced with Zcash, which means that the block reward increases gradually over a period of time until it reaches the 20,000[th] block. This allows for initial scaling of the network and experimentation by early miners, and adjustment by Zcash developers if required. The slow start did have an impact on price due to scarcity as the price of ZEC on its first day of launch reached roughly 25,000 USD. A slightly modified version of the Digishield difficulty adjustment algorithm has been implemented in Zcash. The formula is shown as follows:

(next difficulty) = (last difficulty) x SQRT [(150 seconds) / (last solve time)]

A snapshot of various attributes of Zcash (after an initial slow start) is shown as follows:

Attribute	Value
Name	Zcash
Launch date	28/10/16
Main purpose	Currency
Currency Code	ZEC
Maximum coins	21 million
Block time	10 minutes
Consensus facilitation algorithm	Proof of Work (equihash)
Difficulty adjustment algorithm	DigiShield V3 (modified)
Mining hardware	CPU, GPU
Difficulty adjustment period	1 block

Trading Zcash

Zcash can be bought on major digital currency exchanges. At the time of writing, the price of Zcash is very high. As shown in the following graph, the price soared as high as approximately 10 bitcoins per Zcash. Some exchanges carried out orders as high as 2,500 BTC per ZEC:

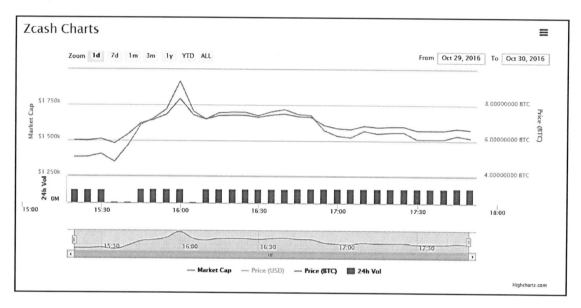

Mining guide

There are multiple methods to mine Zcash. Currently, CPU and GPU mining are possible. Various commercial cloud mining pools also offer contracts for mining Zcash. In order to perform solo mining using a CPU, the following steps can be followed:

1. The first step is to install prerequisites using the following command:

```
sudo apt-get install \
build-essential pkg-config libc6-dev m4 g++-multilib \
autoconf libtool ncurses-dev unzip git python \
zlib1g-dev wget bsdmainutils automake
```

If the prerequisites are already installed, a message will display indicating that components are already the newest version. If not already installed or older than the latest package, then the installation will continue, the required packages will be downloaded, and the installation will be completed.

2. Next, run the commands to clone Zcash from `git` as shown in the following screenshot:

```
$ git clone https://github.com/zcash/zcash.git
```

This command will clone the Zcash git repository locally. The output is shown in the following screenshot:

```
drequinox@drequinox-OP7010:~$ git clone https://github.com/zcash/zcash.git
Cloning into 'zcash'...
remote: Counting objects: 56593, done.
remote: Total 56593 (delta 0), reused 0 (delta 0), pack-reused 56593
Receiving objects: 100% (56593/56593), 42.78 MiB | 2.11 MiB/s, done.
Resolving deltas: 100% (43020/43020), done.
Checking connectivity... done.
drequinox@drequinox-OP7010:~$ cd zcash/
drequinox@drequinox-OP7010:~/zcash$ git checkout v1.0.0
Note: checking out 'v1.0.0'.

You are in 'detached HEAD' state. You can look around, make experimental
changes and commit them, and you can discard any commits you make in this
state without impacting any branches by performing another checkout.

If you want to create a new branch to retain commits you create, you may
do so (now or later) by using -b with the checkout command again. Example:

  git checkout -b <new-branch-name>

HEAD is now at 1feaefa... Update network magics for 1.0.0 
```

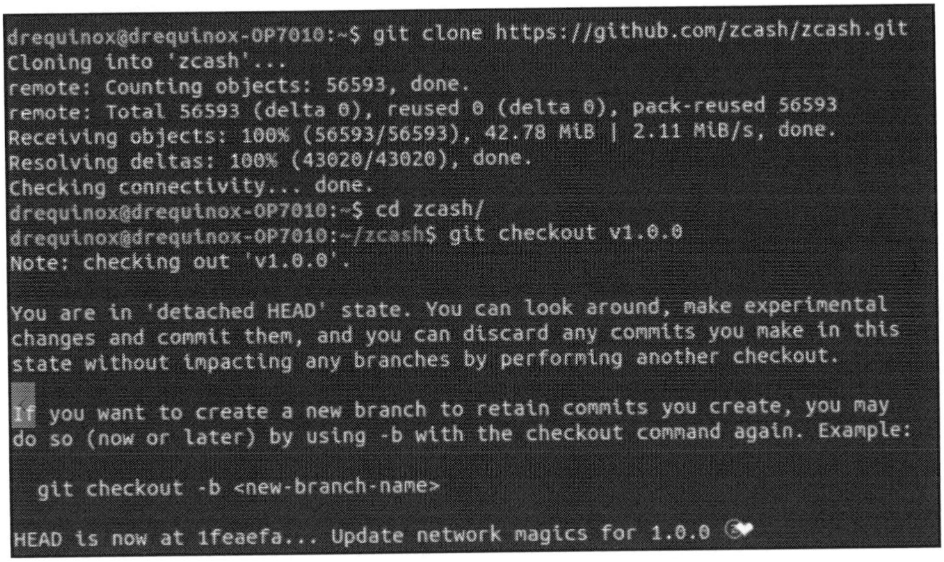

3. The next step is to download proving and verifying keys, by using the following command from the screenshot:

```
drequinox@drequinox-OP7010:~/zcash$ ./zcutil/fetch-params.sh
Zcash - fetch-params.sh

This script will fetch the Zcash zkSNARK parameters and verify their
integrity with sha256sum.

The parameters are currently just under 911MB in size, so plan accordingly
for your bandwidth constraints. If the files are already present and
have the correct sha256sum, no networking is used.

Creating params directory. For details about this directory, see:
/home/drequinox/.zcash-params/README

Retrieving: https://z.cash/downloads/sprout-proving.key
--2016-10-28 21:46:21--  https://z.cash/downloads/sprout-proving.key
Resolving z.cash (z.cash)... 104.236.171.172
Connecting to z.cash (z.cash)|104.236.171.172|:443... connected.
HTTP request sent, awaiting response... 301 Moved Permanently
Location: https://s3.amazonaws.com/zcashfinalmpc/sprout-proving.key [following]
--2016-10-28 21:46:22--  https://s3.amazonaws.com/zcashfinalmpc/sprout-proving.key
Resolving s3.amazonaws.com (s3.amazonaws.com)... 54.231.40.114
Connecting to s3.amazonaws.com (s3.amazonaws.com)|54.231.40.114|:443... connected.
HTTP request sent, awaiting response... 200 OK
Length: 910173851 (868M) [application/octet-stream]
Saving to: '/home/drequinox/.zcash-params/sprout-proving.key.dl'

     OK ........ ........ ........ ........   3% 2.71M 5m8s
 32768K ........ ........ ........ ........   7% 3.58M 4m20s
 65536K ........ ........ ........ ........  11% 2.53M 4m28s
 98304K ........ ........ ........ ........  14% 1.75M 4m59s
131072K ........ ........ ........ ▯
```

4. Once this command runs it will download around 911 MBs of keys into the `~/.zcash-params/` directory. The directory contains files for proving and verifying keys:

```
drequinox@drequinox-OP7010:~/.zcash-params$ pwd
/home/drequinox/.zcash-params
drequinox@drequinox-OP7010:~/.zcash-params$ ls -ltr
-rw-rw-r-- 1 drequinox drequinox      1449 Oct 24 16:46 sprout-
verifying.key
-rw-rw-r-- 1 drequinox drequinox 910173851 Oct 24 16:46 sprout-
proving.key
```

5. Once the preceding commands are completed successfully, the source code can be built using the following command:

```
./zcutil/build.sh -j$(nproc)
```

This will produce very long output; if everything goes well it will produce a `zcashd` binary file. Note that this command takes `nproc` as the parameter, which is basically a command that finds the number of cores or processors in the system and displays that number. If you don't have that command then replace `nproc` with the number of processors in your system.

Once the build is completed, the next step is to configure Zcash. This is achieved by creating a configuration file with the name `zcash.conf` in the `~/.zcash/` directory.

A sample configuration file is shown as follows:

```
addnode=mainnet.z.cash
rpcuser=drequinox
rpcpassword=xxxxxxoJNo4o5c+F6E+J4P2C1D5izlzIKPZJhTzdW5A=
gen=1
genproclimit=8
equihashsolver=tromp
```

The preceding configuration enables various features. The first line adds the mainnet node and enables mainnet connectivity. `rpcuser` and `rpcpassword` are the username and password for the RPC interface. `gen = 1` is used to enable mining. `genproclimit` is the number of processors that can be used for mining. The last line enables a faster mining solver; this is not required if you want to use standard CPU mining.

Now Zcash can be started using the following command:

```
./zcashd --daemon
```

Once started this will allow interaction with the RPC interface via the Zcash-cli command-line interface. This is almost the same as the bitcoin command-line interface. Once the Zcash daemon is up-and-running, various commands can be run to query different attributes of Zcash. Transactions can be viewed locally by using the CLI or via a blockchain explorer. A blockchain explorer for Zcash is available at: `https://explorer.zcha.in/`.

Address generation

New Z addresses can be generated using the command below:

```
$:~/zcash/src$ ./zcash-cli z_getnewaddress
zcPDBKuuwHJ4gqT5Q59zAMXDHhFoihyTC1aLE5Kz4GwgUXfCBWG6SDr45SFLUsZhpcdvHt7nFmC
3iQcn37rKBcVRa93DYrA
```

Running the Zcash-cli command with the `getinfo` parameter produces the output shown in the following screenshot. It displays valuable information such as blocks, difficulty, and balance:

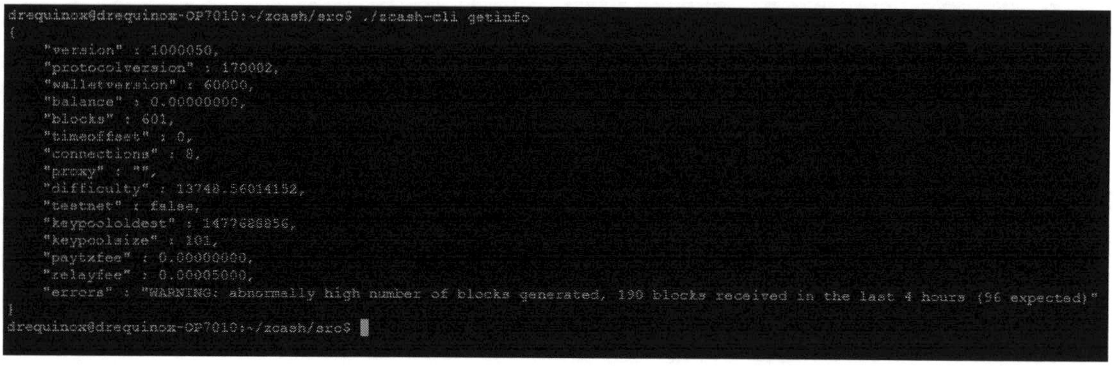

Screenshot displaying the output of getinfo

New T addresses can be generated using the following command:

```
drequinox@drequinox-OP7010:~/zcash/src$ ./zcash-cli getnewaddress
t1XRCGMAw36yPVCcxDUrxv2csAAuGdS8Nny
```

GPU mining

Other than CPU mining, a GPU mining option is also available. There is no official GPU miner yet; however open source developers have produced various proofs of concepts and working miners. The Zcash Company held an open competition to encourage developers to build and submit CPU and GPU miners. No winning entry has been announced as of the time of writing. Readers can get more information by visiting the website, `https://zcashminers.org/`.

There is another mining: using cloud mining contracts available from various online cloud mining providers. The cloud mining service providers perform mining on the customers' behalf. In addition to cloud mining contracts, miners can use their own equipment to mine via mining pools using stratum or other protocols. One key example is Zcash pool by nice hash. Using this pool, miners can sell their hash power. An example of building and using a CPU miner on a Zcash mining pool is shown as follows.

Downloading and compiling nheqminer

The following steps can be used to download and compile `nheqminer` on an Ubuntu Linux distribution:

```
sudo apt-get install cmake build-essential libboost-all-dev
git clone https://github.com/nicehash/nheqminer.git
cd nheqminer/nheqminer
mkdir build
cd build
cmake ..
make
```

Once all the steps are completed successfully, nhequminer can be run using the following command:

```
./nhequminer -l eu -u <btc address> -t <number of threads>
```

Nhequminer releases are available for Windows at:
`https://github.com/nicehash/nheqminer/releases`.

Nheqminer takes several parameters such as location (`-l`), username (`-u`), and the number of threads to be used for mining (`-t`).

A sample run of Windows miner for Zcash is shown as follows:

Using the BTC address to receive pay-outs for selling hash power

Using Zcash T address to receive pay-outs for selling hash power

This completes the introduction to Zcash; readers can explore more about Zcash online as it is very volatile at the moment and things can change very quickly. One thing is for sure; Zcash's zero knowledge proofs are a major innovation and they pave the way for future applications that require inherent privacy, such as banking, medicine, or the law.

Summary

In this chapter, readers have been introduced to the overall cryptocurrency landscape. A few altcoins have been discussed in detail, especially Zcash and Namecoin. Cryptocurrencies are a very active area for research, especially around scalability, privacy, and security aspects. Some research has also been conducted in order to invent new difficulty retargeting algorithms in order to thwart the threat of centralization in cryptocurrencies. Further research can be carried out in the areas of privacy and specially scalability. Readers now should be able to appreciate the concept of altcoins and various motivations behind them. Some practical aspects, such as mining and starting a new currency project, have also been discussed, which hopefully will give readers a strong foundation and enable them to further explore these areas. Altcoins are a fascinating field of research and open a lot of possibilities for a decentralized future.

6
Smart Contracts

This chapter provides an introduction to smart contracts. This is not a new concept, but, with the advent of blockchain, interest in this concept has revived, and this is now an active area of research in the blockchain space. Due to the cost saving benefits that smart contracts can bring to the financial services industry by reducing the cost of transactions and simplifying complex contracts, rigorous research is being carried out by various financial and academic institutions in order to formalize and make the implementation of smart contracts easy and practical, as soon as possible.

History

Smart contracts were first theorized by *Nick Szabo* in the late 1990s, but it was almost 20 years before the true potential and benefits of them were truly appreciated. Smart contracts are described by *Szabo* as follows:

> *"A smart contract is a computerized transaction protocol that executes the terms of a contract. The general objectives are to satisfy common contractual conditions (such as payment terms, liens, confidentiality, and even enforcement), minimize exceptions both malicious and accidental, and minimize the need for trusted intermediaries. Related economic goals include lowering fraud loss, arbitrations and enforcement costs, and other transaction costs."*

This idea of smart contracts was implemented in a limited fashion in bitcoin in 2009, where bitcoin transactions can be used to transfer the value between users, over a peer-to-peer network where users do not necessarily trust each other and there is no need for a trusted intermediary.

Definition

There is no consensus on a standard definition of smart contracts. It is essential to define what a smart contract is, and the following is the author's attempt to provide a generalized definition of a smart contract.

 A smart contract is a secure and unstoppable computer program representing an agreement that is automatically executable and enforceable.

Dissecting this definition further reveals that a smart contract is in fact a computer program that is written in a language that a computer or target machine can understand. Also, it encompasses agreements between parties in the form of business logic. Another key idea is that smart contracts are automatically executed when certain conditions are met. They are enforceable, which means that all contractual terms are executed as defined and expected, even in the presence of adversaries. Enforcement is a broader term that encompasses traditional enforcement in the form of law, along with implementation of certain measures and controls that make it possible to execute contract terms without requiring any mediation. It should be noted that true smart contracts should not rely on traditional methods of enforcement. Instead, they should work on the principle that *code is law*, meaning that there is no need for an arbitrator or a third party to control or influence the execution of the smart contract. Smart contracts are self-enforcing as opposed to legally enforceable. This might be regarded as a libertarian's dream, but it is entirely possible, and is in line with the true spirit of smart contracts.

Moreover, they are secure and unstoppable, which means that these computer programmes are required to be designed in such a fashion that they are fault tolerant and executable in reasonable amount of time. These programmes should be able to execute and maintain a healthy internal state, even if external factors are unfavorable. For example, imagine a normal computer programme which is encoded with some logic and executes according to the instruction coded within it, but if the environment it is running in or external factors it relies on deviate from the normal or expected state, the programme may react arbitrarily or simply abort. It is important that smart contracts are immune to this type of issue.

Secure and unstoppable may well be considered requirements or desirable features but it will provide greater benefits in the long run if security and unstoppable properties are included in the smart contract definition from the beginning. This will allow researchers to focus on these aspects from the start and will help to build strong foundations on which further research can then be based. There is also a suggestion by some researchers that smart contracts need not be automatically executable; instead they can be what's called *automatable*, due to manual human input required in certain scenarios. Whilst it's true that in some cases human input and control is desirable, it is not absolutely necessary; and, for a contract to be truly *smart*, in the authors opinion, it has to be fully automated. Certain inputs that need to be provided by people can and should also be automated via the use of Oracles. Oracles will be discussed later in this chapter in greater detail.

Smart contracts usually operate by managing their internal state using a state machine model. This allows development of an effective framework for programming smart contracts, where the state of a contract is advanced further based on some predefined criteria and conditions.

There is also on-going debate on the question of whether code is acceptable as a contract in a court of law. This is totally different in presentation from traditional legal prose, albeit they do represent and enforce all contractual clauses but a court of law does not understand code. This raises several questions around how a smart contract can be legally binding: can it be developed in such a way that it is readily acceptable and understandable in a court of law? How can dispute resolution be implemented within the code, and is it possible? Moreover, regulatory and compliance requirements is another topic that needs to be addressed before smart contracts can be used as effectively as traditional legal documents.

The preceding questions open up various possibilities, such as making smart contract code readable not only by machines but also by people. If humans and machines can both understand the code written in a smart contract it might be more acceptable in legal situations, as opposed to just a piece of code that no-one understands except for programmers. This desirable property is an area ripe for research and much research effort has been expended in this area to answer questions around semantics, meaning and interpretation of a contract.

Smart contracts are inherently required to be deterministic in nature. This property will allow a smart contract to be run by any node on a network and achieve the same result. If the result differs even slightly between nodes, consensus then cannot be achieved and a whole paradigm of distributed consensus on blockchain can fail. Moreover, it is also desirable that the contract language itself is deterministic thus ensuring the integrity and stability of the smart contracts. By which I mean, deterministic in the sense that there are no non-deterministic functions used in the language which can produce varied results on different nodes. For example, various floating point operations calculated by various functions in a variety of programming languages can produce different results in different runtime environments. Another example is of some math functions in JavaScript which can produce different results for the same input on different browsers, and which can in turn lead to various bugs. This is highly undesirable in smart contracts because, if results are inconsistent between nodes, then consensus will never be achieved. A deterministic feature ensures that smart contracts always produce the same output for a specific input. In other words, programs once compiled produce a solid and accurate business logic that is completely in line with the requirements programmed in the high level code.

In summary, a smart contract has the following four properties:

- Automatically executable
- Enforceable
- Semantically sound
- Secure and unstoppable.

The first two properties are required as a minimum, whereas the latter two may not be required or implementable in certain scenarios and can be relaxed. For example, a derivatives contract does not perhaps need to be semantically sound and unstoppable but should at least be automatically executable and enforceable at a basic level. On the other hand, a title deed needs to be semantically sound and complete therefore, in order for it to be implemented as a smart contract, the language must be understood by both computers and people. This issue of interpretation was addressed by *Ian Grigg* with his invention of **Ricardian contracts**, which we will look at in more detail in the next section.

Ricardian contracts

Ricardian contracts were originally proposed in the *Financial Cryptography in 7 Layers* paper by *Ian Grigg* in late 1990s. These contracts were used initially in a bond trading and payment system called **Ricardo**. The key idea is to write a document which is understandable and acceptable by both a court of law and computer software. Ricardian contracts address the challenge of issuance of value over the Internet. It identifies the issuer and captures all the terms and clauses of the contract in a document in order to make it acceptable as a legally binding contract.

Based on the original definition by *Ian Grigg* at `http://iang.org/papers/ricardian_contract.html`, a Ricardian contract is a document that has several of the following properties:

- A contract offered by an issuer to holders
- A valuable right held by holders, and managed by the issuer
- Easily readable by people (like a contract on paper)
- Readable by programs (parseable, like a database)
- Digitally signed
- Carries the keys and server information
- Allied with a unique and secure identifier

In practice, the contracts are implemented by producing a single document that contains the terms of the contract in legal prose and the required machine-readable tags. This document is digitally signed by the issuer using their private key. This document is then hashed using a message digest function to produce a hash by which the document can be identified. This hash is then further used and signed by parties during the performance of the contract in order to link each transaction, with the identifier hash thus serving as evidence of intent. This is depicted in the diagram below, usually called a *bowtie* model.

The diagram below shows the **World of Law** on the left hand side from where the document originates. It is then hashed and the resultant message digest is used as an indentifier throughout the **World of Accountancy**. The **World of Accountancy** can basically represent any or multiple accounting, trading and information systems that are being used in a business to perform various business operations. The idea behind this flow is that the message digest generated by hashing the document is first used in a so called *genesis transaction*, or first transaction, and then used in every transaction as an indentifier throughout the operational execution of the contract.

This way, a secure link is created between the original written contract and every transaction in the *World of Accounting.*

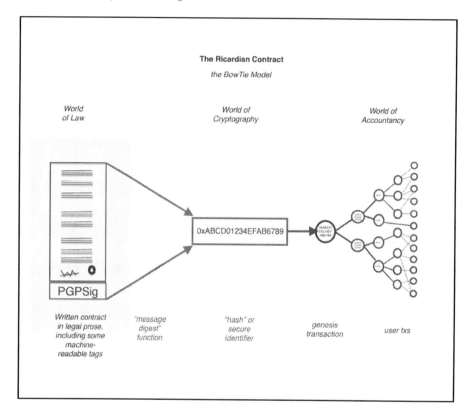

Ricardian contracts, bowtie diagram

A Ricardian contract is different from a smart contract in the sense that a smart contract does not include any contractual document and is focused purely on the execution of the contract. A Ricardian contract, on the other hand, is more concerned with the semantic richness and production of a document that contains contractual legal prose. The semantics of a contract can be divided into two types: operational semantics and denotational semantics. The first type defines the actual execution, correctness and safety of the contract, and the latter is concerned with the real-world meaning of the full contract. Some researchers have differentiated between smart contract code and smart legal contracts where a smart contract is only concerned with the execution of the contract and the second type encompasses both the denotational and operational semantics of a legal agreement. It makes sense to perhaps categorize smart contracts based on the difference between semantics, but it is better to consider smart contracts as a standalone entity that is capable of encoding legal prose and code (business logic) in it.

At bitcoin, a very simple implementation of a smart contract can be observed which is fully oriented towards the execution of the contract, whereas a Ricardian contract is more geared towards producing a document that is understandable by humans, with some parts that a computer program can understand. This can be viewed as legal semantics vs operational performance (semantics vs performance) as shown in the following diagram. This was originally proposed by *Ian Grigg* in his paper *On the intersection of Ricardian and smart contracts*.

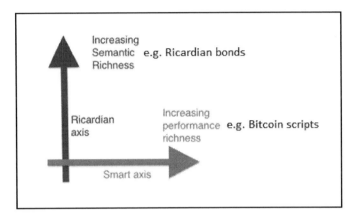

Diagram explaining performance v. semantics are orthogonal issues as described by Ian Grigg; slightly modified to show examples of different types of contracts on both axis

A smart contract is made up to have both of these elements (performance and semantics) embedded together, which completes an ideal model of a smart contract.

A Ricardian contract can be represented as a tuple of three objects, namely *Prose, parameters* and *code*. Prose represents the legal contract in regular language; code represents the program that is a computer-understandable representation of legal prose; and parameters join the appropriate parts of the legal contract to the equivalent code.

Ricardian contracts have been implemented in many systems, such as CommonAccord, OpenBazaar, OpenAssets, and Askemos.

Smart contract templates

Smart contracts can be implemented for any industry where required but most current use cases are related to the financial industry. Recent work in smart contract space specific to the financial industry has proposed the idea of smart contract templates. The idea is to build standard templates that provide a framework to support legal agreements for financial instruments. This was proposed by *Clack et al* in their paper named *Smart Contract Templates: Foundations, design landscape and research directions*. The paper also proposed that domain-specific languages should be built in order to support design and implementation of smart contract templates. A language named *CLACK*, a common language for augmented contract knowledge has been proposed and research has begun to develop the language. This language is intended to be very rich and provide a large variety of functions ranging from supporting legal prose to the ability to be executed on multiple platforms and cryptographic functions.

Contracts in the finance industry is not a new concept and various domain-specific language DSLs are already in use in the financial industry to provide specific language for a specific domain. For example, there are DSLs available that support development of insurance products, represent energy derivatives, or are being used to build trading strategies. The list goes on and a comprehensive list of financial domain-specific languages can be found at `http://www.dslfin.org/resources.html`.

It's important to understand the concept of domain-specific languages. These languages are developed with limited expressiveness for a particular application or area of interest. **Domain-specific languages (DSLs)** are different from **general-purpose programming languages (GPLs)**: DSLs have a small set of features that are sufficient and optimized for the domain they are intended to be used in and, unlike GPLs, are usually not used to build general purpose large application programmes. Based on the design philosophy of DSLs it can be envisaged that such languages can be developed specifically to write smart contracts. Some work has already been done and Solidity is one such language that has been introduced with Ethereum blockchain to write smart contracts. Serpent is another language that has been introduced with Ethereum even though it's not used as much as Solidity.

This idea of domain-specific languages for smart contract programming can be further extended to a graphical domain-specific language, a smart contract modelling platform where a domain expert (not a programmer) can use a graphical user interface and a canvas to define and draw the semantics and performance of a financial contract. Once the flow has been drawn and completed, it can be emulated first to test and then to deploy from the same system to the target platform, which can be a blockchain. This is also not a new concept and a similar approach is used in the Tibco streambase product, which is a Java based system used for building event-driven high frequency trading systems.

It is proposed that research should also be conducted in the area of developing high level DSLs that can be used to programme a smart contract in a user friendly graphical user interface thus allowing a non-programmer to design a smart contract.

Oracles

Oracles are an important component of the smart contract ecosystem. The limitation with smart contracts is that they cannot access external data which might be required to control the execution of the business logic; for example, the stock price of a security that is required by the contract to release the dividend payments. Oracles can be used to provide external data to smart contracts. An Oracle is an interface that delivers data from an external source to smart contracts. Depending on the industry and requirements, Oracles can deliver different types of data ranging from weather reports, real-world news, and corporate actions to data coming from **Internet of Things (IoT)** devices. Oracles are trusted entities that use a secure channel to transfer data to a smart contract.

Oracles are also capable of digitally signing the data proving that the source of the data is authentic. Smart contracts can then subscribe to the Oracles, and the smart contracts can either pull the data, or Oracles can push the data to the smart contracts. It is also necessary that Oracles should not be able to manipulate the data they provide and must be able to provide authentic data. Even though Oracles are trusted, it may still be possible in some cases that the data is incorrect due to manipulation. Therefore, it is necessary that Oracles are unable to change the data. This validation can be provided by using various notary schemes, discussed later in the chapter. In this approach an issue can already be seen which perhaps is not desirable in some cases, and that is the issue of trust. How do you trust a third party about the quality and authenticity of data they provide? This is especially true in the financial world, where market data must be accurate and reliable. It might be acceptable for a smart contract designer to accept data for an oracle that is provided by a large reputable trusted third party, but the issue of centralization still remains. These types of Oracles can be called standard or simple Oracles.

Another type of Oracle, which essentially emerged due to the decentralization requirements, can be called *decentralized* Oracles. These types of Oracles can be built based on some distributed mechanism. It can also be envisaged that the Oracles can themselves source data from another blockchain which is driven by distributed consensus, thus ensuring the authenticity of data. For example, one institution running their own private blockchain can publish their data feed via an Oracle that can then be consumed by other blockchains.

Another concept of hardware Oracles is also introduced by researchers where real-world data from physical devices is required. For example, this can be used in telemetry and IoT. However, this approach however requires a mechanism in which hardware devices cannot be tampered with. This can be achieved by using tamper-proof devices.

There are platforms available now to enable a smart contract to get external data using an Oracle. There are different methods used by an Oracle to write data into the blockchain depending on the type of blockchain used. For example in bitcoin blockchain, an oracle can write data to a specific transaction via an OP_RETURN Opcode, and a smart contract can monitor that transaction and read the data. Various online services such as http://www.oraclize.it/ and https://www.realitykeys.com/ are available that provide oracle services. Also, another service at https://smartcontract.com/ is available which provides external data and the ability to make payments using smart contracts. The aim of all these services is to enable the smart contract to get the data it needs to execute and make decisions. In order to prove the authenticity of the data retrieved by the Oracles from external sources, mechanisms like TLSnotary can be used which produce proof of communication between the data source and the oracle. This ensures that the data fed back to the smart contract is definitely retrieved from the source. More details about TLSnotary can be found here https://tlsnotary.org/.

The following diagram shows a generic model of an oracle and smart contract ecosystem:

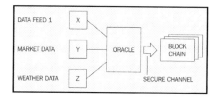

A simplified model of an oracle interacting with smart contract on blockchain

Smart Oracles

An idea of Smart Oracle has also been proposed and implemented in *Codius*. Smart Oracles are basically entities just like Oracles, but with the added capability of contract code execution. Smart Oracles proposed by Codius run using Google Native Client. which is a sandboxed environment for running untrusted x86 native code. Codius is available at https://www.codius.org/.

Deploying smart contracts on a blockchain

Smart contracts may or may not be deployed on a blockchain but it makes sense to deploy them on a blockchain due to the distributed consensus mechanism provided by blockchain. Ethereum is an example of a blockchain that natively supports the development and deployment of smart contracts. Smart contracts on Ethereum blockchain are usually part of a larger application such as **Decentralized Autonomous organization (DAOs)**.

As a comparison, in bitcoin blockchain the `lock_time` field in the bitcoin transaction can be seen as an enabler of a basic version of a smart contract. The `lock_time` field enables a transaction to be locked until a specified time or after a number of blocks, thus enforcing a basic contract that a certain transaction can only be unlocked if certain conditions (elapsed time or number of blocks) is met. However, this is very limited in nature and should be only viewed as an example of a basic smart contract. In addition to the above mentioned example, bitcoin scripting language, though limited, can be used to construct basic smart contracts. One possibility is to fund a bitcoin address that can be spent by anyone who demonstrates a hash collision attack. This idea was presented on the Bitcointalk forum and more information can be found at `https://bitcointalk.org/index.php?topic=293382.0`. This can also be considered a basic form of smart contract.

The DAO

The DAO is one of the highest crowdfunded projects, and started in April 2016. This was basically a set of smart contracts written in order to provide a platform for investment. Due to a bug in the code this was hacked in June 2016 and an equivalent of 50 million dollars was siphoned out of the DAO into another account. This resulted in a hard fork on Ethereum in order to recover from the attack. It should be noted that the notion of *code is law*, or unstoppable smart contracts, should be viewed with some scepticism as the implementation of these concepts is not mature enough to warrant full and unquestionable trust. This is evident from the recent events where the Ethereum foundation was able to stop and change the execution of *The DAO* by introducing a hard fork. Though this hard fork was introduced for genuine reasons, it goes against the true spirit of decentralization and the notion of *code is law*. On the other hand, resistance against this hard fork and some miners who decided to keep mining on the original chain resulted in the creation of Ethereum Classic. This is the original, non-forked Ethereum blockchain where *code is still law*.

This attack highlights the dangers of smart contracts and the absolute need to develop a formal language for smart contracts. The attack also highlighted the importance of thorough testing. There have been various vulnerabilities discovered in Ethereum recently around the smart contract development language. Therefore it is of utmost importance that a standard framework is developed to address all these issues. Some work has already begun as discussed previously, but this area is ripe for more research in order to address limitations in smart contract languages.

Summary

This chapter started by introducing a history of smart contracts, and was followed by a detailed discussion on the definition of a smart contract. As there is no agreement on the standard definition of a smart contract, we attempted to introduce a definition that encompasses the crux of smart contracts. An introduction to Ricardian contracts was also provided, and the difference between Ricardian contracts and smart contracts was explained, highlighting the fact that Ricardian contracts are concerned with the definition of the contract whereas smart contracts are geared towards the actual execution of the contract. The concept of smart contract templates was discussed, on the subject of which high quality active research is currently being conducted in academia and industry. Some ideas about the possibility of creating high level domain-specific languages were also discussed to create smart contracts or smart contract templates. In later sections of the chapter, the concepts of Oracles was introduced followed by a brief discussion on the DAO, and security issues in DAO and smart contracts.

7
Ethereum 101

This chapter is intended to be an introduction to the Ethereum blockchain. You will be introduced to the fundamentals and advanced theoretical concepts behind Ethereum. A discussion on various components, protocols, and algorithms relevant to the Ethereum blockchain will be given in detail so that you can understand the theory behind this blockchain paradigm. Also, a practical and in-depth introduction to wallet software, mining, and setting up Ethereum nodes will be covered in this chapter. Some material on various challenges, such as security and scalability faced by Ethereum, will also be introduced. Additionally, trading and market dynamics will be discussed.

Introduction

Ethereum was conceptualized by *Vitalik Buterin* in November 2013. The key idea proposed was the development of a Turing-complete language that allows the development of arbitrary programs (smart contracts) for blockchain and decentralized applications. This is in contrast to bitcoin, where the scripting language is very limited and allows basic and necessary operations only.

Ethereum clients and releases

Various Ethereum clients have been developed using different languages and currently most popular are go-Ethereum and parity. go-Ethereum was developed using Golang, whereas parity was built using Rust. There are other clients available too, but usually, the go-Ethereum client known as *geth* is sufficient for all purposes. Mist is a user-friendly **Graphical User Interface (GUI)** wallet that runs geth in the background to sync with the network. More details on this will be provided later in the chapter, in the installation and mining section.

The first release of Ethereum was known as *Frontier*, and the current release of Ethereum is called *homestead release*. The next version is named metropolis and it focuses on protocol simplification and performance improvement. The final release is named *serenity*, which is envisaged to have a Proof of Stake algorithm (Casper) implemented with it. Other areas of research targeted with serenity include scalability, privacy, and **Ethereum virtual machine (EVM)** upgrade. As this is a continuous development effort and the Ethereum ecosystem will undergo constant improvement and development, serenity should not really be considered a *final* version but a major milestone in a long journey of continuous improvement. Further releases are envisaged but have not been named yet. The vision of *web 3.0* has already been proposed and is being discussed in the community. Web 3.0 is a concept that basically proposes a semantic and intelligent web as an evolution of the existing web 2.0 technology. This is the vision of an ecosystem where people, applications, data, and web are all connected together and are able to interact with each other in an intelligent fashion. With the advent of the blockchain technology, an idea of decentralized web has also emerged, which in fact was the original vision of the Internet. The core idea is that all major services, such as DNS, search engines, and identity on the Internet will be decentralized in web 3.0. This is where Ethereum is being envisaged as a platform that can help realize this vision.

The Ethereum stack

The Ethereum stack consists of various components. At the core, there is the Ethereum blockchain running on the P2P Ethereum network. Secondly, there's an Ethereum client (usually geth) that runs on the nodes and connects to the peer-to-peer Ethereum network from where blockchain is downloaded and stored locally. It provides various functions, such as mining and account management. The local copy of the blockchain is synchronized regularly with the network. Another component is the `web3.js` library that allows interaction with geth via the **Remote Procedure Call (RPC)** interface.

This can be visualized in the following diagram:

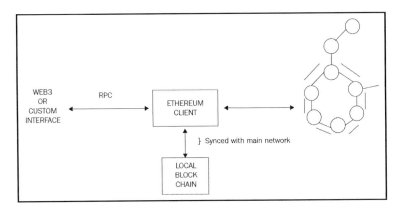

The Ethereum stack showing various components

Ethereum blockchain

Ethereum, just like any other blockchain, can be visualized as a transaction-based state machine. This is mentioned in the Ethereum yellow paper written by *Dr. Gavin Wood*. The idea is that a genesis state is transformed into a final state by executing transactions incrementally. The final transformation is then accepted as the absolute undisputed version of the state. In the following diagram, the Ethereum state transition function is shown, where a transaction execution has resulted in a state transition.

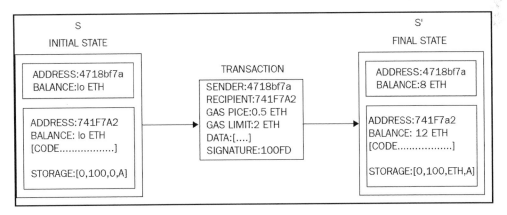

Ethereum State transition function

In the preceding example, a transfer of 2 Ether from **Address 4718bf7a** to **Address 741f7a2** is initiated. The initial state represents the state before the transaction execution and the final state is what the morphed state looks like. This will be discussed in more detail later in the chapter, but the aim of this example is to introduce the core idea of state transition in Ethereum.

Currency (ETH and ETC)

As an incentive to the miners, Ethereum also rewards its native currency called Ether, abbreviated as ETH. After the DAO hack (described later), a hard fork was proposed in order to mitigate the issue; therefore, there are now two Ethereum blockchains: one is called Ethereum classic and its currency is represented by ETC, whereas the hard-forked version is ETH, which continues to grow and on which active development is being carried out. ETC, however, has its own following with a dedicated community that is further developing ETC, which is the nonforked original version of Ethereum. This chapter is focused mainly on ETH, which is the currently the most active and official Ethereum blockchain.

Forks

With the latest release of homestead, due to major protocol upgrades, it resulted in a hard fork. The protocol was upgraded at block number 1,150,000, resulting in the migration from the first version of Ethereum known as Frontier to the second version of Ethereum called homestead.

A recent unintentional fork that occurred on November 24, 2016, at 14:12:07 UTC was due to a bug in the geth client's journaling mechanism. Network fork occurred at block number 2,686,351. This bug resulted in geth failing to revert empty account deletions in the case of the empty out-of-gas exception. This was not an issue in parity (another popular Ethereum client). This means that from block number 2686351, the Ethereum blockchain is split into two, one running with parity clients and the other with geth. This issue was resolved with the release of geth version 1.5.3.

Gas

Another key concept in Ethereum is that of gas. All transactions on the Ethereum blockchain are required to cover the cost of computation they are performing. The cost is covered by something called *gas* or *crypto fuel*, which is a new concept introduced by Ethereum. This gas as *execution fee* is paid upfront by the transaction originators. The *fuel* is consumed with each operation. Each operation has a predefined amount of gas associated with it. Each transaction specifies the amount of gas it is willing to consume for its execution. If it runs *out of gas* before the execution is completed, any operation performed by the transaction up to that point is rolled back. If the transaction is successfully executed, then any remaining gas is refunded to the transaction originator.

This concept should not be confused with mining fee, which is a different concept that is used to pay *gas* as a fee to the miners. More information on the concept and calculations related to gas and operations will be provided later in the chapter.

The consensus mechanism

The consensus mechanism in Ethereum is based on the GHOST protocol originally proposed by *Zohar* and *Sompolinsky* in December 2013. Those of you interested in it can explore the detailed original paper at http://eprint.iacr.org/2013/881.pdf.

Ethereum uses a simpler version of this protocol, where the chain that has most computational effort spent on it in order to build it is identified as the definite version. Another way of looking at it is to find the longest chain, as the longest chain must have been built by consuming adequate mining effort. **Greedy Heaviest Observed Subtree (GHOST)** was first introduced as a mechanism to alleviate the issues arising out of fast block generation times that led to stale or orphan blocks. In GHOST, stale blocks are added in calculations to figure out the longest and heaviest chain of blocks. Stale blocks are called Uncles or Ommers in Ethereum.

The following diagram shows a quick comparison between the longest and heaviest chain:

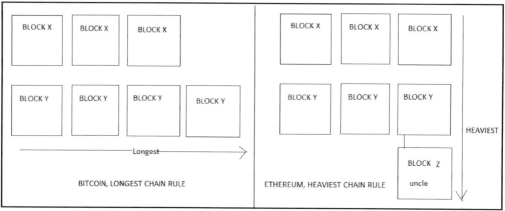

Longest versus heaviest chain

The world state

The world state in Ethereum represents the global state of the Ethereum blockchain. It is basically a mapping between Ethereum addresses and account states. The addresses are 20 bytes long. This mapping is a data structure that is serialized using **Recursive Length Prefix (RLP)**. RLP is a specially developed encoding scheme that is used in Ethereum to serialize binary data for storage or transmission over the network and also to save the state in a Patricia tree. The RLP function takes an item as an input, which can be a string or a list of items, and produces raw bytes that are suitable for storage and transmission over the network. RLP does not encode data; instead, its main purpose is to encode structures.

The account state

The account state consists of four fields: nonce, balance, storageroot and codehash and is described in detail here.

Nonce

This is a value that is incremented every time a transaction is sent from the address. In case of contract accounts, it represents the number of contracts created by the account. Contract accounts are one of the two types of accounts that exist in Ethereum; they will be explained later on in the chapter in more detail.

Balance

This value represents the number of Weis which is the smallest unit of the currency (Ether) in Ethereum held by the address.

Storageroot

This field represents the root node of a Merkle Patricia tree that encodes the storage contents of the account.

Codehash

This is an immutable field that contains the hash of the smart contract code that is associated with the account. In the case of normal accounts, this field contains the Keccak 256-bit hash of an empty string. This code is invoked via a message call.

The world state and its relationship with accounts trie, accounts, and block header can be visualized in the following diagram. It shows the account data structure in the middle of the diagram, which contains a storage root hash derived from the root node of the account storage trie shown on the left. The account data structure is then used in the world state trie, which is a mapping between addresses and account states. Finally, the root node of the world state trie is hashed using the Keccak 256-bit algorithm and made part of the block header data structure, which is shown on the right-hand side of the diagram as state root hash.

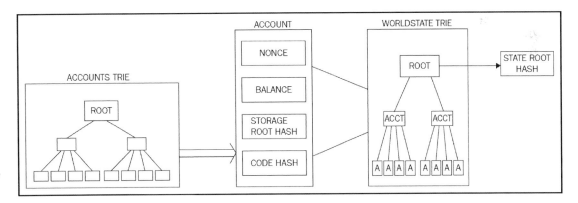

Accounts trie (storage contents of account), account tuple, world state trie, and state root hash and their relationship

Accounts trie is basically a Merkle Patricia tree used to encode the storage contents of an account. The contents are stored as a mapping between keccak 256-bit hashes of 256-bit integer keys to the RLP-encoded 256-bit integer values.

Transactions

A transaction in Ethereum is a digitally signed data packet using a private key that contains the instructions that, when completed, either result in a message call or contract creation. Transactions can be divided into two types based on the output they produce:

- **Message call transactions**: This transaction simply produces a message call that is used to pass messages from one account to another.
- **Contract creation transactions**: As the name suggests, these transactions result in the creation of a new contract. This means that when this transaction is executed successfully, it creates an account with the associated code.

Both of these transactions are composed of a number of common fields, which are described here.

Nonce

Nonce is a number that is incremented by one every time a transaction is sent by the sender. It must be equal to the number of transactions sent and is used as a unique identifier for the transaction. A nonce value can only be used once.

gasPrice

The `gasPrice` field represents the amount of Wei required in order to execute the transaction.

gasLimit

The `gasLimit` field contains the value that represents the maximum amount of gas that can be consumed in order to execute the transaction. The concept of gas and gas limit will be covered later in the chapter in more detail. For now, it is sufficient to say that this is the amount of fee in Ether that a user (for example, the sender of the transaction) is willing to pay for computation.

To

As the name suggests, the `to` field is a value that represents the address of the recipient of the transaction.

Value

`Value` represents the total number of Wei to be transferred to the recipient; in the case of a contract account, this represents the balance that the contract will hold.

Signature

Signature is composed of three fields, namely *v*, *r*, and *s*. These values represent the digital signature (*R*, *S*) and some information that can be used to recover the public key (*V*). Also of the transaction from which the sender of the transaction can also be determined. The signature is based on ECDSA scheme and makes use of the SECP256k1 curve. The theory of elliptic curve cryptography was discussed in `Chapter 3`, *Cryptography and technical foundations*. In this section, ECDSA will be presented in the context of its usage in Ethereum.

V is a single byte value that depicts the size and sign of the elliptic curve point and can be either 27 or 28. *V* is used in the ECDSA recovery contract as a recovery ID. This value is used to recover (derive) the public key from the private key. In secp256k1, the recovery ID is expected to be either 0 or 1. In Ethereum, this is offset by 27. More details on the ECDSARECOVER function will be provided later in this chapter.

R is derived from a calculated point on the curve. First, a random number is picked up, which is multiplied with the generator of the curve to calculate a point on the curve. The *x* coordinate part of this point is *R*. *R* is encoded as a 32 byte sequence. *R* must be greater than 0 and less than the secp256k1n limit (115792089237316195423570985008687907852837564279074904382605163141518161494337).

S is calculated by multiplying *R* with the private key and adding it into the hash of the message to be signed and by finally dividing it with the random number chosen to calculate *R*. *S* is also a 32 byte sequence. *R* and *S* together represent the signature.

In order to sign a transaction, the `ECDSASIGN` function is used, which takes the message to be signed and the private key as an input and produces *V*, a single byte value; *R*, a 32 byte value, and *S*, another 32 byte value. The equation is as follows:

ECDSASIGN (Message, Private Key) = (V, R, S)

Init

The Init field is used only in transactions that are intended to create contracts. This represents a byte array of unlimited length that specifies the EVM code to be used in the account initialization process. The code contained in this field is executed only once, when the account is created for the first time, and gets destroyed immediately after that.

Init also returns another code section called *body*, which persists and runs in response to message calls that the contract account may receive. These message calls may be sent via a transaction or an internal code execution.

Data

If the transaction is a message call, then the data field is used instead of init, which represents the input data of the message call. It is also unlimited in size and is organized as a byte array.

This can be visualized in the following diagram, where a transaction is a tuple of the fields mentioned earlier, which is then included in a transaction trie (a modified Merkle-Patricia tree) composed of the transactions to be included. Finally, the root node of transaction trie is hashed using a Keccak 256-bit algorithm and is included in the block header along with a list of transactions in the block.

Transactions can be found in either transaction pools or blocks. When a mining node starts its operation of verifying blocks, it starts with the highest paying transactions in the transaction pool and executes them one by one. When the gas limit is reached or no more transactions are left to be processed in the transaction pool, the mining starts. In this process, the block is repeatedly hashed until a valid nonce is found that, once hashed with the block, results in a value less than the difficulty target. Once the block is successfully mined, it will be broadcasted immediately to the network, claiming success, and will be verified and accepted by the network. This process is similar to Bitcoin's mining process discussed in the previous chapter. The only difference is that Ethereum's Proof of Work algorithm is ASIC-resistant, known as *Ethash*, where finding a nonce requires large memory.

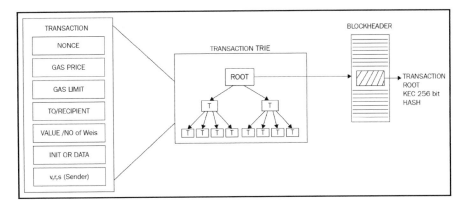

Relationship between transaction, transaction trie and block header

Contract creation transaction

There are a few essential parameters that are required when creating an account. These parameters are listed as follows:

- Sender
- Original transactor
- Available gas
- Gas price
- Endowment, which is the amount of ether allocated initially
- A byte array of arbitrary length
- Initialization EVM code
- Current depth of the message call/contract-creation stack (current depth means the number of items that are already there in the stack)

Addresses generated as a result of contract creation transaction are 160-bit in length. Precisely, as defined in the yellow paper, they are the rightmost 160-bits of the Keccak hash of the RLP encoding of the structure containing only the sender and the nonce. Initially, the nonce in the account is set to zero. The balance of the account is set to the value passed to the contract. Storage is also set to empty. Code hash is Keccak 256-bit hash of the empty string.

The account is initialized when the EVM code (Initialization EVM code) is executed. In the case of any exception during code execution, such as not having enough gas, the state does not change. If the execution is successful, then the account is created after the payment of appropriate gas costs. The current version of Ethereum (homestead) specifies that the result of contract transaction is either a new contract with its balance, or no new contract is created with no transfer of value. This is in contrast to previous versions, where the contract could be created regardless of the contract code deployment being successful or not due to an out-of-gas exception.

Message call transaction

A message call requires several parameters for execution, which are listed as follows:

- Sender
- The transaction originator
- Recipient
- The account whose code is to be executed
- Available gas
- Value
- Gas price
- Arbitrary length byte array
- Input data of the call
- Current depth of the message call/contract creation stack

Message calls result in state transition. Message calls also produce output data, which is not used if transactions are executed. In cases where message calls are triggered by VM code, the output produced by the transaction execution is used.

In the following diagram, the segregation between two types of transaction is shown:

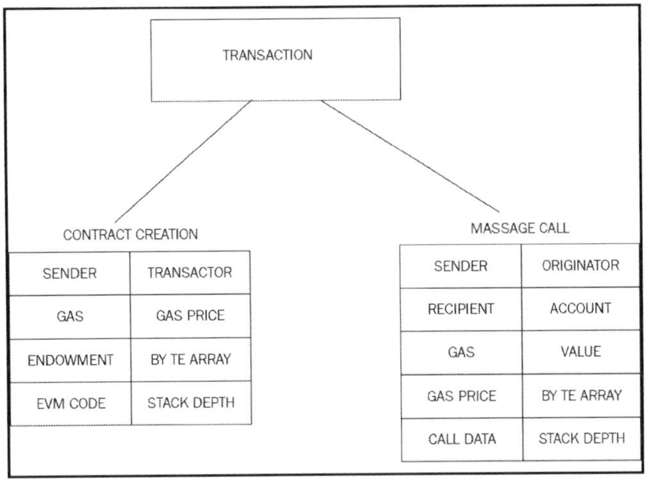

Types of transactions, required parameters for execution

Elements of the Ethereum blockchain

In the following section, you will be introduced to various components of the Ethereum network and the blockchain. First, the basic concept of the EVM is given in the next section.

Ethereum virtual machine (EVM)

EVM is a simple stack-based execution machine that runs bytecode instructions in order to transform the system state from one state to another. The word size of the virtual machine is set to 256-bit. The stack size is limited to 1024 elements and is based on the **LIFO (Last in First Out)** queue. EVM is a Turing-complete machine but is limited by the amount of gas that is required to run any instruction. This means that infinite loops that can result in denial of service attacks are not possible due to gas requirements. EVM also supports exception handling in case exceptions occur, such as not having enough gas or invalid instructions, in which case the machine would immediately halt and return the error to the executing agent.

EVM is a fully isolated and sandboxed runtime environment. The code that runs on the EVM does not have access to any external resources, such as a network or filesystem.

As discussed earlier, EVM is a stack-based architecture. EVM is big-endian by design and it uses 256-bit wide words. This word size allows for Keccak 256-bit hash and elliptic curve cryptography computations.

There are two types of storage available to contracts and EVM. The first one is called memory, which is a byte array. When a contract finishes the code execution, the memory is cleared. It is akin to the concept of RAM. The other type, called storage, is permanently stored on the blockchain. It is a key value store.

Memory is unlimited but constrained by gas fee requirements. The storage associated with the virtual machine is a word addressable *word array* that is nonvolatile and is maintained as part of the system state. Keys and value are 32 bytes in size and storage. The program code is stored in a **virtual read-only memory (virtual ROM)** that is accessible using the CODECOPY instruction. The CODECOPY instruction is used to copy the program code into the main memory. Initially, all storage and memory is set to zero in the EVM.

The following diagram shows the design of the EVM where the virtual ROM stores the program code that is copied into main memory using **CODECOPY**. The main memory is then read by the EVM by referring to the program counter and executes instructions step by step. The program counter and EVM stack are updated accordingly with each instruction execution.

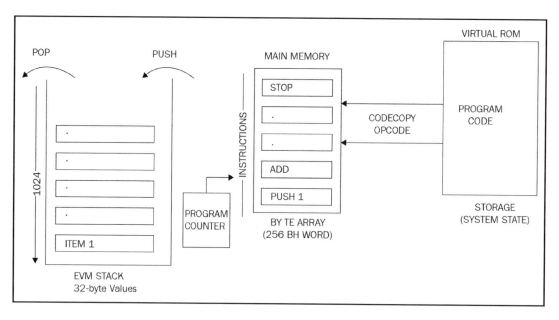

EVM operation

EVM optimization is an active area of research and recent research has suggested that EVM can be optimized and tuned to a very fine degree in order to achieve high performance. Research into the possibility of using **Web assembly (WASM)** is underway already. WASM is developed by Google, Mozilla, and Microsoft and is now being designed as an open standard by the W3C community group. The aim of WASM is to be able to run machine code in the browser that will result in execution at native speed. Similarly, the aim of EVM 2.0 is to be able to run the EVM instruction set (Opcodes) natively in CPUs, thus making it faster and efficient.

Execution environment

There are some key elements that are required by the execution environment in order to execute the code. The key parameters are provided by the execution agent, for example, a transaction. These are listed as follows:

1. The address of the account that owns the executing code.
2. The address of the sender of the transaction and the originating address of this execution.
3. The gas price in the transaction that initiated the execution.
4. Input data or transaction data depending on the type of executing agent. This is a byte array; in the case of a message call, if the execution agent is a transaction, then the transaction data is included as input data.
5. The address of the account that initiated the code execution or transaction sender. This is the address of the sender in case the code execution is initiated by a transaction; otherwise, it's the address of the account.
6. The value or transaction value. This is the amount in Wei. If the execution agent is a transaction, then it is the transaction value.
7. The code to be executed presented as a byte array that the iterator function picks up in each execution cycle.
8. The block header of the current block
9. The number of message calls or contract creation transactions currently in execution. In other words, this is the number of CALLs or CREATEs currently in execution.

The execution environment can be visualized as a tuple of nine elements, as follows:

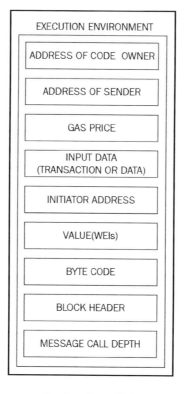

Execution environment Tuple

In addition to the previously mentioned nine fields, system state and the remaining gas are also provided to the execution environment. The execution results in producing the resulting state, gas remaining after the execution, self-destruct or suicide set (described later), log series (described later), and any gas refunds.

Machine state

Machine state is also maintained internally by the EVM. Machine state is updated after each execution cycle of EVM. An iterator function (detailed in the next section) runs in the virtual machine, which outputs the results of a single cycle of the state machine. Machine state is a tuple that consist of the following elements:

- Available gas
- The program counter, which is a positive integer up to 256
- Memory contents

- Active number of words in memory
- Contents of the stack

The EVM is designed to handle exceptions and will halt (stop execution) in case any of the following exceptions occur:

- Not having enough gas required for execution
- Invalid instructions
- Insufficient stack items
- Invalid destination of jump op codes
- Invalid stack size (greater than 1024)

The iterator function

The iterator function mentioned earlier performs various important functions that are used to set the next state of the machine and eventually the world state. These functions include the following:

- It fetches the next instruction from a byte array where the machine code is stored in the execution environment.
- It adds/removes (PUSH/POP) items from the stack accordingly.
- Gas is reduced according to the gas cost of the instructions/Opcodes.
- It increments the **program counter (PC)**.

Machine state can be viewed as a tuple shown in the following diagram:

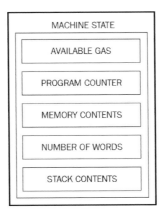

Machine state tuple

The virtual machine is also able to halt in normal conditions if STOP or SUICIDE or RETURN Opcodes are encountered during the execution cycle.

Code written in a high-level language such as serpent, LLL, or Solidity is converted into the byte code that EVM understands in order for it to be executed by the EVM. Solidity is the high-level language that has been developed for Ethereum with JavaScript such as syntax to write code for smart contracts. Once the code is written, it is compiled into byte code that's understandable by the EVM using the Solidity compiler called solc.

LLL (Lisp-like Low-level language) is another language that is used to write smart contract code. Serpent is a Python-like high-level language that can be used to write smart contracts for Ethereum.

For example, a simple program in solidity is shown as follows:

```
pragma solidity ^0.4.0;
contract Test1
  {
     uint x=2;
     function addition1(uint x) returns (uint y) {
     y=x+2;
  }
}
```

This program is converted into bytecode, as shown here. Details on how to compile solidity code with examples will be given in the next chapter.

Runtime byte code

```
606060405260e060020a6000350463989e17318114601c575b6000565b34600057602960043
5603b565b604080519182525190819003602001390f35b600281015b91905056
Opcodes PUSH1 0x60 PUSH1 0x40 MSTORE PUSH1 0x2 PUSH1 0x0 SSTORE CALLVALUE
PUSH1 0x0 JUMPI JUMPDEST PUSH1 0x45 DUP1 PUSH1 0x1A PUSH1 0x0 CODECOPY
PUSH1 0x0 RETURN PUSH1 0x60 PUSH1 0x40 MSTORE PUSH1 0xE0 PUSH1 0x2 EXP
PUSH1 0x0 CALLDATALOAD DIV PUSH4 0x989E1731 DUP2 EQ PUSH1 0x1C JUMPI
JUMPDEST PUSH1 0x0 JUMP JUMPDEST CALLVALUE PUSH1 0x0 JUMPI PUSH1 0x29 PUSH1
0x4 CALLDATALOAD PUSH1 0x3B JUMP JUMPDEST PUSH1 0x40 DUP1 MLOAD SWAP2 DUP3
MSTORE MLOAD SWAP1 DUP2 SWAP1 SUB PUSH1 0x20 ADD SWAP1 RETURN JUMPDEST
PUSH1 0x2 DUP2 ADD JUMPDEST SWAP2 SWAP1 POP JUMP
```

Opcodes and their meaning

There are different opcodes that have been introduced in the EVM. Opcodes are divided into multiple categories based on the operation they perform. The list of opcodes with their meaning and usage is presented here.

Arithmetic operations

All arithmetic in EVM is modulo 2^{256}. This group of opcodes is used to perform basic arithmetic operations. The value of these operations starts from 0x00 up to 0x0b.

Mnemonic	Value	POP	PUSH	Gas	Description
STOP	0x00	0	0	0	Halts execution
ADD	0x01	2	1	3	Adds two values
MUL	0x02	2	1	5	Multiplies two values
SUB	0x03	2	1	3	Subtraction operation
DIV	0x04	2	1	5	Integer division operation
SDIV	0x05	2	1	5	Signed integer division operation
MOD	0x06	2	1	5	Modulo remainder operation
SMOD	0x07	2	1	5	Signed modulo remainder operation
ADDMOD	0x08	3	1	8	Modulo addition operation
MULMOD	0x09	3	1	8	Module multiplication operation
EXP	0x0a	2	1	10	Exponential operation (repeated multiplication of the base)
SIGNEXTEND	0x0b	2	1	5	Extends the length of 2s complement signed integer

Note that STOP is not an arithmetic operation but is categorized in this list of arithmetic operations due to the range of values (0s) it falls in.

Logical operations

Logical operations include operations that are used to perform comparisons and Boolean logic operations. The value of these operations is in the range of 0x10 to 0x1a.

Mnemonic	Value	POP	PUSH	Gas	Description
LT	0x10	2	1	3	Less than
GT	0x11	2	1	3	Greater than
SLT	0x12	2	1	3	Signed less than comparison
SGT	0x13	2	1	3	Signed greater than comparison
EQ	0x14	2	1	3	Equal comparison
ISZERO	0x15	1	1	3	Not operator
AND	0x16	2	1	3	Bitwise AND operation
OR	0x17	2	1	3	Bitwise OR operation
XOR	0x18	2	1	3	Bitwise exclusive OR (XOR) operation
NOT	0x19	1	1	3	Bitwise NOT operation
BYTE	0x1a	2	1	3	Retrieve single byte from word

Cryptographic operations

There is only one operation in this category named SHA3. It is worth noting that this is not the standard SHA3 standardized by NIST but the original Keccak implementation.

Mnemonic	Value	POP	PUSH	Gas	Description
SHA3	0x20	2	1	30	Used to calculate Keccak 256-bit hash.

Environmental information

There are a total of 13 instructions in this category. These opcodes are used to provide information related to addresses, runtime environments, and data copy operations.

Mnemonic	Value	POP	PUSH	Gas	Description
ADDRESS	0x30	0	1	2	Used to get the address of the currently executing account
BALANCE	0x31	1	1	20	Used to get the balance of the given account
ORIGIN	0x32	0	1	2	Used to get the address of the sender of the original transaction
CALLER	0x33	0	1	2	Used to get the address of the account that initiated the execution
CALLVALUE	0x34	0	1	2	Retrieves the value deposited by the instruction or transaction
CALLDATALOAD	0x35	1	1	3	Retrieves the input data that was passed a parameter with the message call
CALLDATASIZE	0x36	0	1	2	Used to retrieve the size of the input data passed with the message call
CALLDATACOPY	0x37	3	0	3	Used to copy input data passed with the message call from the current environment to the memory.
CODESIZE	0x38	0	1	2	Retrieves the size of running the code in the current environment
CODECOPY	0x39	3	0	3	Copies the running code from current environment to the memory
GASPRICE	0x3a	0	1	2	Retrieves the gas price specified by the initiating transaction.
EXTCODESIZE	0x3b	1	1	20	Gets the size of the specified account code
EXTCODECOPY	0x3c	4	0	20	Used to copy the account code to the memory.

Block Information

This set of instructions is related to retrieving various attributes associated with a block:

Mnemonic	Value	POP	PUSH	Gas	Description
BLOCKHASH	0x40	1	1	20	Gets the hash of one of the 256 most recently completed blocks
COINBASE	0x41	0	1	2	Retrieves the address of the beneficiary set in the block
TIMESTAMP	0x42	0	1	2	Retrieves the time stamp set in the blocks
NUMBER	0x43	0	1	2	Gets the block's number
DIFFICULTY	0x44	0	1	2	Retrieves the block difficulty
GASLIMIT	0x45	0	1	2	Gets the gas limit value of the block

Stack, memory, storage and flow operations

Mnemonic	Value	POP	PUSH	Gas	Description
POP	0x50	1	0	2	Removes items from the stack
MLOAD	0x51	1	1	3	Used to load a word from the memory.
MSTORE	0x52	2	0	3	Used to store a word to the memory.
MSTORE8	0x53	2	0	3	Used to save a byte to the memory
SLOAD	0x54	1	1	50	Used to load a word from the storage
SSTORE	0x55	2	0	0	Saves a word to the storage
JUMP	0x56	1	0	8	Alters the program counter
JUMPI	0x57	2	0	10	Alters the program counter based on a condition
PC	0x58	0	1	2	Used to retrieve the value in the program counter before the increment.
MSIZE	0x59	0	1	2	Retrieves the size of the active memory in bytes.
GAS	0x5a	0	1	2	Retrieves the available gas amount
JUMPDEST	0x5b	0	0	1	Used to mark a valid destination for jumps with no effect on the machine state during the execution.

Push operations

These operations include PUSH operations that are used to place items on the stack. The range of these instructions is from 0x60 to 0x7f. There are 32 PUSH operations available in total in the EVM. PUSH operation, which reads from the byte array of the program code.

Mnemonic	Value	POP	PUSH	Gas	Description
PUSH1 . . . PUSH 32	0x60 ... 0x7f	0	1	3	Used to place N right-aligned big-endian byte item(s) on the the stack. N is a value that ranges from 1 byte to 32 bytes (full word) based on the mnemonic used.

Duplication operations

As the name suggests, duplication operations are used to duplicate stack items. The range of values is from 0x80 to 0x8f. There are 16 DUP instructions available in the EVM. Items placed on the stack or removed from the stack also change incrementally with the mnemonic used; for example, DUP1 removes one item from the stack and places two items on the stack, whereas DUP16 removes 16 items from the stack and places 17 items.

Mnemonic	Value	POP	PUSH	Gas	Description
DUP1 . . . DUP16	0x80 ... 0x8f	X	Y	3	Used to duplicate the nth stack item, where N is the number corresponding to the DUP instruction used. X and Y are the items removed and placed on the stack, respectively.

Exchange operations

SWAP operations provide the ability to exchange stack items. There are 16 SWAP instructions available and with each instruction, the stack items are removed and placed incrementally up to 17 items depending on the type of Opcode used.

Mnemonic	Value	POP	PUSH	Gas	Description
SWAP1 . . . SWAP16	0x90 ... 0x9f	X	Y	3	Used to swap the nth stack item, where N is the number corresponding to the SWAP instruction used. X and Y are the items removed and placed on the stack, respectively.

Logging operations

Logging operations provide opcodes to append log entries on the sub-state tuple's log series field. There are four log operations available in total and they range from value 0x0a to 0xa4.

Mnemonic	Value	POP	PUSH	Gas	Description
LOG0 . . . LOG4	0x0a . . . 0xa4	X	Y (0)	375, 750, 1125, 1500, 1875	Used to append log record with N topics, where N is the number corresponding to the LOG Opcode used. For example, LOG0 means a log record with no topics, and LOG4 means a log record with four topics. X and Y represent the items removed and placed on the stack, respectively. X and Y change incrementally, starting from 2, 0 up to 6, 0 according to the LOG operation used.

System operations

System operations are used to perform various system-related operations, such as account creation, message calling, and execution control. There are six Opcodes available in total in this category.

Mnemonic	Value	POP	PUSH	Gas	Description
CREATE	0xf0	3	1	32000	Used to create a new account with the associated code.
CALL	0xf1	7	1	40	Used to initiate a message call into an account.
CALLCODE	0xf2	7	1	40	Used to initiate a message call into this account with an alternative account's code.
RETURN	0xf3	2	0	0	Stops the execution and returns output data.
DELEGATECALL	0xf4	6	1	40	The same as CALLCODE but does not change the current values of the sender and the value.
SUICIDE	0xff	1	0	0	Stops (halts) the execution and the account is registered for deletion later

In this section, all EVM opcodes have been discussed. There are 129 opcodes available in the EVM of the homestead release of Ethereum in total.

Precompiled contracts

There are four precompiled contracts in Ethereum. Here is the list of these contracts and details.

The elliptic curve public key recovery function

ECDSARECOVER (Elliptic curve DSA recover function) is available at address 1. It is denoted as ECREC and requires 3000 gas for execution. If the signature is invalid, then no output is returned by this function. Public key recovery is a standard mechanism by which the public key can be derived from the private key in elliptic curve cryptography.

The ECDSA recovery function is shown as follows:

$$ECDSARECOVER(H, V, R, S) = Public\ Key$$

It takes four inputs: H, which is a 32 byte hash of the message to be signed and V, R, and S, which represent the ECDSA signature with the recovery ID and produce a 64 byte public key. V, R, and S have been discussed in detail previously in this chapter.

The SHA-256 bit hash function

The SHA-256 bit hash function is a precompiled contract that is available at address 2 and produces a SHA256 hash of the input. It is almost like a pass-through function. Gas requirement for SHA-256 (SHA256) depends on the input data size. The output is a 32 byte value.

The RIPEMD-160 bit hash function

The RIPEMD-160 bit hash function is used to provide RIPEMD 160-bit hash and is available at address 3. The output of this function is a 20-byte value. Gas requirement, similar to SHA-256, is dependent on the amount of input data.

The identity function

The identity function is available at address 4 and is denoted by the ID. It simply defines output as input; in other words, whatever input is given to the ID function, it will output the same value. Gas requirement is calculated by a simple formula: $15 + 3 [I_d/32]$ where I_d is the input data. This means that at a high level, the gas requirement is dependent on the size of the input data albeit with some calculation performed, as shown in the preceding equation.

All the previously mentioned precompiled contracts can become native extensions and can be included in the EVM opcodes in the future.

Accounts

Accounts are one of the main building blocks of the Ethereum blockchain. The state is created or updated as a result of the interaction between accounts. Operations performed between and on the accounts represent state transitions. State transition is achieved using what's called the Ethereum state transition function, which works as follows:

1. Confirm the transaction validity by checking the syntax, signature validity, and nonce.

2. Transaction fee is calculated and the sending address is resolved using the signature. Furthermore, sender's account balance is checked and subtracted accordingly and nonce is incremented. An error is returned if the account balance is not enough.

3. Provide enough ether (gas price) to cover the cost of the transaction. This is charged per byte incrementally according to the size of the transaction.

4. In this step, the actual transfer of value occurs. The flow is from the sender's account to receiver's account. The account is created automatically if the destination account specified in the transaction does not exist yet. Moreover, if the destination account is a contract, then the contract code is executed. This also depends on the amount of gas available. If enough gas is available, then the contract code will be executed fully; otherwise, it will run up to the point where it runs out of gas.

5. In cases of transaction failure due to insufficient account balance or gas, all state changes are rolled back with the exception of fee payment, which is paid to the miners.

6. Finally, the remainder (if any) of the fee is sent back to the sender as change and fee is paid to the miners accordingly. At this point, the function returns the resulting state.

Types of accounts

There are two types of accounts in Ethereum:

- Externally owned accounts
- Contract accounts

The first is **externally owned accounts (EOAs)** and the other is contract accounts. EOAs are similar to accounts that are controlled by a private key in bitcoin. Contract accounts are the accounts that have code associated with them along with the private key. An EOA has ether balance, is able to send transactions, and has no associated code, whereas a **Contract Account (CA)** has ether balance, associated code, and the ability to get triggered and execute code in response to a transaction or a message. It is worth noting that due to the Turing-completeness property of the Ethereum blockchain, the code within contract accounts can be of any level of complexity. The code is executed by EVM by each mining node on the Ethereum network. In addition, contract accounts are able to maintain their own permanent state and can call other contracts. It is envisaged that in the serenity release, the distinction between externally owned accounts and contract accounts may be eliminated.

Block

As discussed earlier, blocks are the main building blocks of a blockchain. Ethereum blocks consist of various components, which are described as follows:

- The block header
- The transactions list
- The list of headers of Ommers or Uncles

The transaction list is simply a list of all transactions included in the block. In addition, the list of headers of Uncles is also included in the block. The most important and complex part is the block header, which is discussed here.

Block header

Block headers are the most critical and detailed components of an Ethereum block. The header contains valuable information, which is described in detail here.

Parent hash

This is the Keccak 256-bit hash of the parent (previous) block's header.

Ommers hash

This is the Keccak 256-bit hash of the list of Ommers (Uncles) blocks included in the block.

Beneficiary

Beneficiary field contains the 160-bit address of the recipient that will receive the mining reward once the block is successfully mined.

State root

The state root field contains the Keccak 256-bit hash of the root node of the state trie. It is calculated after all transactions have been processed and finalized.

Transactions root

The transaction root is the Keccak 256-bit hash of the root node of the transaction trie. Transaction trie represents the list of transactions included in the block.

Receipts root

The receipts root is the keccak 256 bit hash of the root node of the transaction receipt trie. This trie is composed of receipts of all transactions included in the block. Transaction receipts are generated after each transaction is processed and contain useful post-transaction information. More details on transaction receipts are provided in the next section.

Logs bloom

The logs bloom is a bloom filter that is composed of the logger address and log topics from the log entry of each transaction receipt of the included transaction list in the block. Logging is explained in detail in the next section.

Difficulty

The difficulty level of the current block.

Number

The total number of all previous blocks; the genesis block is block zero.

Gas limit

The field contains the value that represents the limit set on the gas consumption per block.

Gas used

The field contains the total gas consumed by the transactions included in the block.

Timestamp

Timestamp is the epoch Unix time of the time of block initialization.

Extra data

Extra data field can be used to store arbitrary data related to the block.

Mixhash

Mixhash field contains a 256-bit hash that once combined with the nonce is used to prove that adequate computational effort has been spent in order to create this block.

Nonce

Nonce is a 64-bit hash (a number) that is used to prove, in combination with the mixhash field, that adequate computational effort has been spent in order to create this block.

The following figure shows the detailed structure of the block and block header:

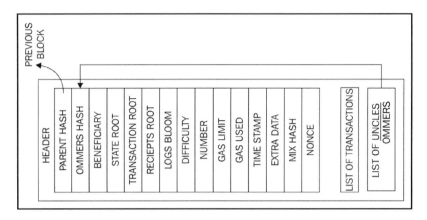

Detailed diagram of block structure with block header

The genesis block

The genesis block varies slightly with regard to the data it contains and the way it has been created from a normal block. It contains 15 items that are described here.

From Etherscan.io, the actual version is shown as follows:

Element	Description
Timestamp	(Jul-30-2015 03:26:13 PM +UTC)
Transactions	8893 transactions and 0 contract internal transactions in this block
Hash	0xd4e56740f876aef8c010b86a40d5f56745a118d0906a34e69aec8c0db1cb8fa3
Parent hash	0x0000000000000000000000000000000000000000000000000000000000000000
Sha3Uncles	0x1dcc4de8dec75d7aab85b567b6ccd41ad312451b948a7413f0a142fd40d49347
Mined by	0x0000000000000000000000000000000000000000 IN 15 secs
Difficulty	17,179,869,184
Total Difficulty	17,179,869,184
Size	540 bytes
Gas Limit	5,000

Gas Used	0
Nonce	0x0000000000000042
Block Reward	5 Ether
Uncles Reward	0
Extra Data	»èÛN4{NŒ"|ƒpäμí3³ÛiËÛz8áå ,ú (Hex:0x11bbe8db4e347b4e8c937c1c8370e4b5ed33adb3db69cbdb7a38e1e50b1b82fa)

Transaction receipts

Transaction receipts are used as a mechanism to store the state after a transaction has been executed. In other words, these structures are used to record the outcome of the transaction execution. It is produced after the execution of each transaction. All receipts are stored in an index-keyed trie. Hash (Keccak 256-bit) of the root of this trie is placed in the block header as the receipts root. It is composed of four elements that are described here.

The post-transaction state

This item is a trie structure that holds the state after the transaction has executed. It is encoded as a byte array.

Gas used

This item represents the total amount of gas used in the block that contains the transaction receipt. The value is taken immediately after the transaction execution is completed. The total gas used is expected to be a non-negative integer.

Set of logs

This field shows the set of log entries created as a result of transaction execution. Log entries contain the logger's address, a series of log topics, and the log data.

The bloom filter

A bloom filter is created from the information contained in the set of logs discussed earlier. A log entry is reduced to a hash of 256 bytes, which is then embedded in the header of the block as the logs bloom. Log entry is composed of the logger's address and log topics and log data. Log topics are encoded as a series of 32 byte data structures. Log data is made up of a few bytes of data.

This process can be visualized in the following diagram:

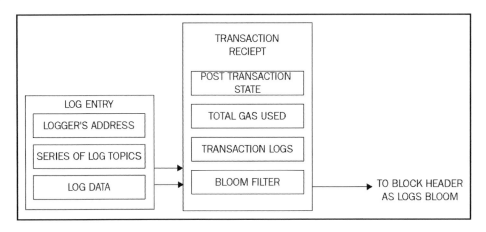

Transaction receipts and logs bloom

Transaction validation and execution

Transactions are executed after verifying the transactions for validity. Initial tests are listed as follows:

- A transaction must be well-formed and RLP-encoded without any additional trailing bytes
- The digital signature used to sign the transaction is valid
- Transaction nonce must be equal to the sender's account's current nonce
- Gas limit must not be less than the gas used by the transaction
- The sender's account contains enough balance to cover the execution cost

The transaction sub state

A transaction sub-state is created during the execution of the transaction that is processed immediately after the execution completes. This transaction sub-state is a tuple that is composed of three items.

Suicide set

This element contains the list of accounts that are disposed of after the transaction is executed.

Log series

This is an indexed series of checkpoints that allow the monitoring and notification of contract calls to the entities external to the Ethereum environment, such as application frontends. It works like a trigger mechanism that is executed every time a specific function is invoked or a specific event occurs. Logs are created in response to events occurring in the smart contract. It can also be used as a cheaper form of storage. Events will be covered with practical examples in `Chapter 8`, *Ethereum development*.

Refund balance

This is the total price of gas in the transaction that initiated the execution. Refunds are not immediately executed; instead, they are used to partially offset the total execution cost.

The following diagram describes the transaction sub-state tuple:

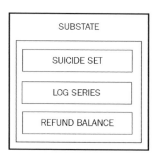

Sub-state tuple

The block validation mechanism

An Ethereum block is considered valid if it passes the following checks:

- Consistent with Uncles and transactions. This means that all Ommers (Uncles) satisfy the property that they are indeed Uncles and also if the Proof of Work for Uncles is valid.
- If the previous block (parent) exists and is valid.
- If the timestamp of the block is valid. This basically means that the current block's timestamp must be higher than the parent block's timestamp. Also, it should be less than 15 minutes into the future. All block times are calculated in epoch time (Unix time).

If any of these checks fails, the block will be rejected.

Block finalization

Block finalization is a process that is run by miners in order to validate the contents of the block and apply rewards. It results in four steps being executed. These steps are described here in detail.

Ommers validation

Validate Ommers (stale blocks also called Uncles). In the case of mining, determine Ommers. The validation process of the headers of stale blocks checks whether the header is valid and the relationship of the Uncle with the current block satisfies the maximum depth of six blocks. A block can contain a maximum of two Uncles.

Transaction validation

Validate transactions. In the case of mining, determine transactions. The process involves checking whether the total gas used in the block is equal to the final gas consumption after the final transaction.

Reward application

Apply rewards, which means updating the beneficiary's account with a reward balance. In Ethereum, a reward is also given to miners for stale blocks, which is 1/32 of the block reward. Uncles that are included in the blocks also receive 7/8 of the total block reward. The current block reward is 5 Ether. A block can have a maximum of two Uncles.

State and nonce validation

Verify the state and nonce. In the case of mining, compute a valid state and nonce.

Block difficulty

Block difficulty is increased if the time between two blocks decreases, whereas it increases if the block time between two blocks decreases. This is required to maintain a roughly consistent block generation time. The difficulty adjustment algorithm in Ethereum's homestead release is shown as follows:

```
block_diff = parent_diff + parent_diff // 2048 *
max(1 - (block_timestamp - parent_timestamp) // 10, -99) +
int(2**((block.number // 100000) - 2))
```

The preceding algorithm means that, if the time difference between the generation of the parent block and the current block is less than 10 seconds, the difficulty goes up. If the time difference is between 10 to 19 seconds, the difficulty level remains the same. Finally, if the time difference is 20 seconds or more, the difficultly level decreases. This decrease is proportional to the time difference.

In addition to timestamp-difference-based difficulty adjustment, there is also another part (shown in the last line of the preceding algorithm) that increases the difficulty exponentially after every 100,000 blocks. This is the so called *difficulty time bomb* or *Ice age* introduced in the Ethereum network, which will make it very hard to mine on the Ethereum blockchain at some point in the future. This will encourage users to switch to Proof of Stake as mining on the POW chain will eventually become prohibitively difficult. According to the latest update and estimates based on the algorithm, the block generation time will become significantly high during the second half of the year 2017 and in 2021, it will become so high that it will be virtually impossible to mine on the POW chain. This way, miners will have no choice but to switch to the Proof of Stake scheme proposed by Ethereum called Casper.

Ether

Ether is minted by miners as a currency reward for the computational effort they spend in order to secure the network by verifying and with validation transactions and blocks. Ether is used within the Ethereum blockchain to pay for the execution of contracts on the EVM. Ether is used to purchase gas as crypto fuel, which is required in order to perform computation on the Ethereum blockchain.

The denomination table is shown as follows:

Unit	Wei Value	Weis
Wei	1 Wei	1
Babbage	1e3 Wei	1,000
Lovelace	1e6 Wei	1,000,000
Shannon	1e9 Wei	1,000,000,000
Szabo	1e12 Wei	1,000,000,000,000
Finney	1e15 Wei	1,000,000,000,000,000
Ether	1e18 Wei	1,000,000,000,000,000,000

Fees are charged for each computation performed by the EVM on the blockchain. A detailed fee schedule is shown in the upcoming section.

Gas

Gas is required to be paid for every operation performed on the ethereum blockchain. This is a mechanism that ensures that infinite loops cannot cause the whole blockchain to stall due to the Turing-complete nature of the EVM. A transaction fee is charged as some amount of Ether and is taken from the account balance of the transaction originator. A fee is paid for transactions to be included by miners for mining. If this fee is too low, the transaction may never be picked up; the more the fee, the higher are the chances that the transactions will be picked up by the miners for inclusion in the block. Conversely, if the transaction that has an appropriate fee paid is included in the block by miners but has too many complex operations to perform, it can result in an out-of-gas exception if the gas cost is not enough. In this case, the transaction will fail but will still be made part of the block and the transaction originator will not get any refund.

Transaction cost can be estimated using the following formula:

$$Total\ cost = gasUsed * gasPrice$$

Here, *gasUsed* is the total gas that is supposed to be used by the transaction during the execution and *gasPrice* is specified by the transaction originator as an incentive to the miners to include the transaction in the next block. This is specified in Ether. Each EVM opcode has a fee assigned to it. It is an estimate because the gas used can be more or less than the value specified by the transaction originator originally. For example, if computation takes too long or the behavior of the smart contract changes in response to some other factors, then the transaction execution may perform more or less operations than originally intended and can result in consuming more or fewer gas. If the execution runs out of gas, everything is immediately rolled back; otherwise, if the execution is successful and there is some remaining gas, then it is returned to the transaction originator.

Each operation costs some gas; a high level fee schedule of a few operations is shown as an example here:

Operation Name	Gas Cost
step	1
stop	0
suicide	0
sha3	30
sload	20
txdata	5
transaction	500
contract creation	53000

Based on the preceding fee schedule and the formula discussed earlier, an example calculation of the SHA3 operation can be calculated as follows:

- SHA3 costs 30 gas
- Current gas price is 25 GWei, which is 0.000000025 Ether
- Multiplying both: *0.000000025 * 30 = 0.00000075* Ether

In total, 0.00000075 Ether is the total gas that will be charged.

Fee schedule

Gas is charged in three scenarios as a prerequisite to the execution of an operation:

- The computation of an operation
- For contract creation or message call
- Increase in the usage of memory

A list of instructions and various operations with the gas values has been provided previously in the chapter.

Messages

Messages, as defined in the yellow paper, are the data and value that are passed between two accounts. A message is a data packet passed between two accounts. This data packet contains data and value (amount of ether). It can either be sent via a smart contract (autonomous object) or from an external actor (externally owned account) in the form of a transaction that has been digitally signed by the sender.

Contracts can send messages to other contracts. Messages only exist in the execution environment and are never stored. Messages are similar to transactions; however, the main difference is that they are produced by the contracts, whereas transactions are produced by entities external (externally owned accounts) to the Ethereum environment.

A message consists of the components mentioned here:

1. Sender of the message
2. Recipient of the message
3. Amount of Wei to transfer and message to the contract address
4. Optional data field (Input data for the contract)
5. Maximum amount of gas that can be consumed

Messages are generated when CALL or DELEGATECALL Opcodes are executed by the contracts.

Calls

A call does not broadcast anything to the blockchain; instead, it is a local call to a contract function and runs locally on the node. It is almost like a local function call. It does not consume any gas as it is a read-only operation. It is akin to a dry run. Calls are executed locally on a node and generally do not result in any state change. As defined in the yellow paper, this is the act of passing a message from one account to another. If the destination account has an associated EVM code, then the virtual machine will start upon the receipt of the message to perform the required operations. If the message sender is an autonomous object, then the call passes any data returned from the virtual machine operation.

State is altered by transactions. These are created by external factors and are signed and then broadcasted to the Ethereum network.

Mining

Mining is the process by which new currency is added to the blockchain. This is an incentive for the miners to validate and verify blocks made up of transactions. The mining process helps secure the network by verifying computations.

At a theoretical level, a miner performs the following functions:

1. Listens for the transactions broadcasted on the Ethereum network and determines the transactions to be processed.
2. Determines stale blocks called Uncles or Ommers and includes them in the block.
3. Updates the account balance with the reward earned from successfully mining the block.
4. Finally, a valid state is computed and block is finalized, which defines the result of all state transitions.

The current method of mining is based on Proof of Work, which is similar to that of bitcoin. When a block is deemed valid, it has to satisfy not only the general consistency requirements, but it must also contain the Proof of Work for a given difficulty.

The Proof of Work algorithm is due to be replaced with the Proof of Stake algorithm with the release of serenity. Considerable research work has been carried out in order to build the Proof of Stake algorithm suitable for the Ethereum Network.

An Algorithm named Casper has been developed, which will replace the existing Proof of Work algorithm in Ethereum. This is a security deposit based on the economic protocol where nodes are required to place a security deposit before they can produce blocks. Nodes have been named bonded validators in Casper, whereas the act of placing the security deposit is named bonding.

Ethash

Ethash is the name of the Proof of Work algorithm used in Ethereum. Originally, this was proposed as the Dagger-Hashimoto algorithm, but much has changed since the first implementation and the PoW algorithm has now evolved into what's known as Ethash now. Similar to bitcoin, the core idea behind mining is to find a nonce that once hashed the result in a predetermined difficulty level. Initially, the difficulty was low when Ethereum was new and even CPU and single GPU mining was profitable to a certain extent, but that is no longer the case. Now either pooled mining is profitable, or large GPU mining farms are used for mining purposes.

Ethash is a memory-hard algorithm, which makes it difficult to be implemented on specialized hardware. As in bitcoin, ASICs have been developed, which have resulted in mining centralization over the years, but memory-hard Proof of Work algorithms are one way of thwarting this threat and Ethereum implements Ethash to discourage ASIC development for mining. This algorithm requires choosing subsets of a fixed resource called **DAG (Directed Acyclic Graph)** depending on the nonce and block headers. DAG is around 2 GB in size and changes every 30000 blocks. Mining can only start when DAG is completely generated the first time a mining node starts. The time between every 30000 blocks is around 5.2 days and is called epoch. This DAG is used as a seed by the Proof of Work algorithm called Ethash. According to current specifications, the epoch time is defined as 30,000 blocks.

The current reward scheme is 5 Ether for successfully finding a valid nonce. In addition to receiving 5 Ethers, the successful miner also receives the cost of the gas consumed within the block and an additional reward for including stale blocks (Uncles) in the block. A maximum of two Uncles are allowed per block and are rewarded 7/8 of the normal block reward. In order to achieve a 12 second block time, block difficulty is adjusted at every block. The rewards are directly proportional to the miner's hash rate, which basically means how fast a miner can hash.

Mining can be performed by simply joining the Ethereum network and running an appropriate client. The key requirement is that the node should be fully synced with the main network before mining can start.

In the upcoming section, various methods of mining are mentioned.

CPU mining

Even though not profitable on the main net, CPU mining is still valuable on the test network or even a private network to experiment with mining and contract deployment. Private and test networks will be discussed with practical examples in the next chapter. A geth example is shown on how to start CPU mining here. Geth can be started with mine switch in order to start mining:

```
geth --mine --minerthreads <n>
```

CPU mining can also be started using the web 3 geth console. Geth console can be started by issuing the following command:

```
geth attach
```

After this, the miner can be started by issuing the following command, which will return true if successful, or false otherwise. Take a look at the following command:

```
Miner.start(4)
True
```

The preceding command will start the miner with four threads. Take a look at the following command:

```
Miner.stop
True
```

The preceding command will stop the miner. The command will return true if successful.

GPU mining

At a basic level, GPU mining can be performed easily by running two commands:

```
geth --rpc
```

Once geth is up and running and the blockchain is fully downloaded, Ethminer can be run in order to start mining. Ethminer is a standalone miner that can also be used in the farm mode to contribute to mining pools. It can be downloaded from `https://github.com/Geno il/cpp-ethereum/tree/master/releases`:

```
ethminer -G
```

Running with G switch assumes that the appropriate graphics card is installed and configured correctly. If no appropriate graphics cards are found, ethminer will return an error, as shown in the following screenshot:

```
drequinox@drequinox-OP7010:~$ ethminer -G
[OPENCL]:No OpenCL platforms found
No GPU device with sufficient memory was found. Can't GPU mine. Remove the -G argument
drequinox@drequinox-OP7010:~$
```

Error in case no appropriate GPUs can be found

GPU mining requires an AMD or Nvidia graphics card and an applicable OpenCL SDK. For NVidia chipset, it can downloaded from `https://developer.nvidia.com/cuda-download s`. For AMD chipsets, it is available at `http://developer.amd.com/tools-and-sdks/openc l-zone/amd-accelerated-parallel-processing-app-sdk`.

Once the graphics cards are installed and configured correctly, the process can be started by issuing the `ethminer -G` command.

Ethminer can also be used to run benchmarking, as shown in the following screenshot. There are two modes that can be invoked for benchmarking. It can either be CPU or GPU. The commands are shown here.

CPU benchmarking

```
$ ethminer -M -C
```

GPU benchmarking

```
$ ethminer -M -G
```

The following screenshot example is shown for CPU mining benchmarking:

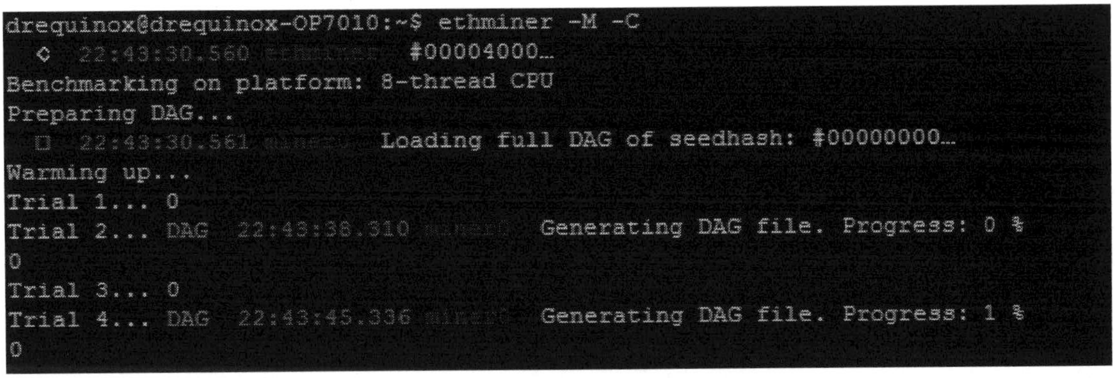

```
drequinox@drequinox-OP7010:~$ ethminer -M -C
  ◇  22:43:30.560            #00004000...
Benchmarking on platform: 8-thread CPU
Preparing DAG...
  □  22:43:30.561            Loading full DAG of seedhash: #00000000...
Warming up...
Trial 1... 0
Trial 2... DAG  22:43:38.310            Generating DAG file. Progress: 0 %
0
Trial 3... 0
Trial 4... DAG  22:43:45.336            Generating DAG file. Progress: 1 %
0
```

CPU benchmarking

The GPU device to be used can also be specified in the command line:

```
$ ethminer -M -G --opencl-device 1
```

As GPU mining is implemented using OpenCL AMD, chipset-based GPUs tend to work faster as compared to NVidia GPUs. Due to the high memory requirements (DAG creation), FPGAs and ASICs will not provide any major advantage over GPUs. This is done on purpose in order to discourage the development of specialized hardware for mining.

Mining rigs

As difficulty increased over time for mining Ether, mining rigs with multiple GPUs were starting to be built by the miners. A mining rig usually contains around five GPU cards, and all of them work in parallel for mining, thus improving the chances of finding valid nonces for mining.

Mining rigs can be built with some effort and are also available commercially from various vendors. A typical mining rig configuration includes the components discussed in the upcoming sections.

Motherboard

A specialized motherboard with multiple PCI-E x1 or x16 slots, for example, BIOSTAR Hi-Fi or ASRock H81, is required.

SSD hard drive

An SSD hard drive is required. The SSD drive is recommended because of its much faster performance over the analog equivalent. This will be mainly used to store the blockchain.

GPU

The GPU is the most important component of the rig as it is the main workhorse that will be used for mining. For example, it can be a Sapphire AMD Radeon R9 380 with 4 GB RAM.

Linux Ubuntu's latest version is usually chosen as the operating system for the rig. There is also another variant of Linux available, called EthOS (available at `http://ethosdistro.com/`), that is especially built for Ethereum mining and supports mining operations natively.

Finally, mining software such as Ethminer and geth are installed. Additionally, some remote monitoring and administration software is also installed so that rigs can be monitored and managed remotely, if required. It is also important to put appropriate air conditioning or cooling mechanisms in place as running multiple GPUs can generate a lot of heat. This also necessitates the need for using an appropriate monitoring software that can alert users if there are any problems with the hardware, for example, if the GPUs are overheating.

A mining rig for Ethereum for sale at eBay

Mining pools

There are many online mining pools that offer Ethereum mining. Ethminer can be used to connect to a mining pool using the following command. Each pool publishes its own instructions, but generally, the process of connecting to a pool is similar. An example from `ethereumpool.co` is shown here:

```
ethminer -C -F
http://ethereumpool.co/?miner=0.1@0x024a20cc5feba7f3dc3776075b3e60c20eb1459
c@DrEquinox
```

Screenshot of ethminer

Clients and wallets

As Ethereum is under heavy development and evolution, there are many components, clients, and tools that have been developed and introduced over the last few years. The following is a list of all main components, client software, and tools that are available with Ethereum. This list is provided in order to reduce the ambiguity around many tools and clients available for Ethereum. The list provided here also explains the usage and significance of various components.

Geth

This is the Go implementation of the Ethereum client.

Eth

This is the C++ implementation of the Ethereum client.

Pyethapp

This is the Python implementation of the Ethereum client.

Parity

This implementation is built using Rust and developed by EthCore. EthCore is a company that works on the development of the parity client. Parity can be downloaded from `https ://ethcore.io/parity.html`.

Light clients

SPV clients download only a small subset of the blockchain. This allows low resource devices, such as mobile phones, embedded devices, or tablets, to be able to verify the transactions. A complete ethereum blockchain and node are not required in this case and SPV clients can still validate the execution of transactions. SPV clients are also called light clients. This idea is similar to bitcoin SPV clients. There is a wallet available from Jaxx (`http s://jaxx.io/`), which can be installed on iOS and Android, which provides the **SPV** (**Simple Payment Verification**) functionality.

Installation

The following installation procedure describes the installation of various Ethereum clients on Ubuntu systems. Instructions for other operating systems are available on Ethereum Wikis. As Ubuntu systems will be used in examples later on, only installation on Ubuntu has been described here.

Geth client can be installed by using the following command on an Ubuntu system:

```
> sudo apt-get install -y software-properties-common
> sudo add-apt-repository -y ppa:ethereum/ethereum
> sudo apt-get update
> sudo apt-get install -y ethereum
```

After installation is completed. Geth can be launched simply by issuing the `geth` command at the command prompt, as it comes preconfigured with all the required parameters to connect to the live Ethereum network (mainnet):

```
> geth
```

Eth installation

Eth is the C++ implementation of the Ethereum client and can be installed using the following command on Ubuntu:

```
> sudo apt-get install cpp-ethereum
```

Mist browser

Mist browser is a user-friendly interface for end users with a feature-rich graphical user interface that is used to browse DAPPS and for account management and contract management. Mist installation is covered in the next chapter.

When Mist is launched for the first time, it will initialize geth in the background and will sync with the network. It can take from a few hours to a few days depending on the speed and type of the network to fully synchronize with the network. If TestNet is used, then syncing completes relatively faster as the size of TestNet (Ropsten) is not as big as MainNet. More information on how to connect to TestNet will be provided in the next chapter.

Mist browser starting up and syncing with the main network

Mist browser is not a wallet; in fact, it is a browser of DAPPS and provides a user-friendly user interface for the creation and management of contracts, accounts, and browsing decentralized applications. Ethereum wallet is a DAPP that is released with Mist.

Wallet is a generic program that can store private keys and associated accounts and, based on the addresses stored within it, it can compute the existing balance of Ether associated with the addresses by querying the blockchain.

Other wallets include but are not limited to MyEtherWallet, which is an open source ether wallet developed in JavaScript. MyEtherWallet runs in the client browser. This is available at `https://www.myetherwallet.com`.

Icebox is developed by Consensys. This is a cold storage browser that provides secure storage of Ether. It depends on whether the computer on which Icebox is run is connected to the Internet or not.

Various wallets are available for ethereum for desktop, mobile, and web platforms. A popular Ethereum iOS Wallet named Jaxx is shown in the following image:

Jaxx Ethereum wallet for iOS showing transactions and current balance

Once the blockchain is synchronized, Mist will launch and show the following interface. In this example, four accounts are displayed with no balance:

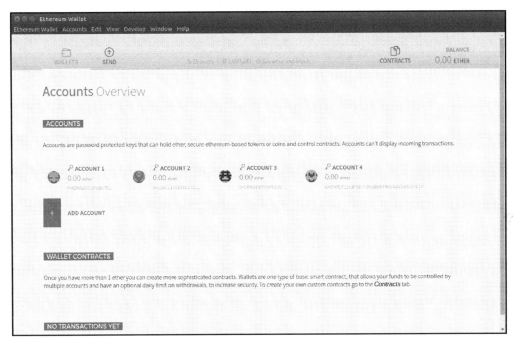

Mist browser

A new accounts can be created in a number of ways. In the Mist browser, it can be created by clicking on the **Accounts** menu and selecting the **New account** or by clicking on the **Add account** option in the Mist Accounts Overview screen.

Add new account

The account will need a password to be set, as shown in the preceding figure; once the account is set up, it will be displayed in the accounts overview section of the Mist browser.

Accounts can also be added via the command line using the geth or parity command-line interface. This process is shown in the next section.

Geth

```
$ geth account new
Your new account is locked with a password. Please give a password. Do not
forget this password.
Passphrase:
Repeat passphrase:
Address: {21c2b52e18353a2cc8223322b33559c1d900c85d}
drequinox@drequinox-OP7010:~$
```

The list of accounts can be shown using geth using the following command:

```
$ geth account list

Account #0: {11bcc1d0b56c57aefc3b52d37e7d6c2c90b8ec35}
/home/drequinox/.ethereum/keystore/UTC--2016-05-07T13-04-15.175558799Z-
-11bcc1d0b56c57aefc3b52d37e7d6c2c90b8ec35

Account #1: {e49668b7ffbf031bbbdab7a222bdb38e7e3e1b63}
/home/drequinox/.ethereum/keystore/UTC--2016-05-10T19-16-11.952722205Z--
e49668b7ffbf031bbbdab7a222bdb38e7e3e1b63

Account #2: {21c2b52e18353a2cc8223322b33559c1d900c85d}
/home/drequinox/.ethereum/keystore/UTC--2016-11-29T22-48-09.825971090Z-
-21c2b52e18353a2cc8223322b33559c1d900c85d
```

The geth console

The geth JavaScript console can be used to perform various functions. For example, an account can be created by attaching geth.

Geth can be attached with the running daemon, as shown in the following figure:

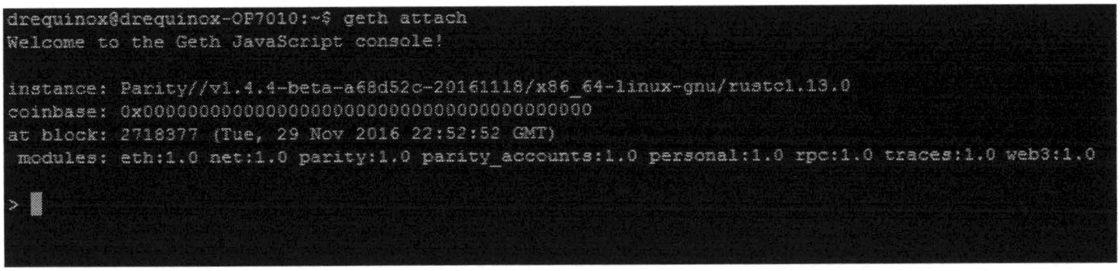

```
drequinox@drequinox-OP7010:~$ geth attach
Welcome to the Geth JavaScript console!

instance: Parity//v1.4.4-beta-a68d52c-20161118/x86_64-linux-gnu/rustc1.13.0
coinbase: 0x0000000000000000000000000000000000000000
at block: 2718377 (Tue, 29 Nov 2016 22:52:52 GMT)
 modules: eth:1.0 net:1.0 parity:1.0 parity_accounts:1.0 personal:1.0 rpc:1.0 traces:1.0 web3:1.0

>
```

Once geth is successfully attached with the running instance of the ethereum client (in this case, parity), it will display command prompt '>', which provides an interactive command line interface to interact with the ethereum client using JavaScript notations.

For example, a new account can be added using the following command in the geth console:

```
> personal.newAccount()
Passphrase:
Repeat passphrase:
"0xc64a728a67ba67048b9c160ec39bacc5626761ce"
>
```

The list of accounts can also be displayed similarly:

```
> eth.accounts
["0x024a20cc5feba7f3dc3776075b3e60c20eb1459c",
 "0x11bcc1d0b56c57aefc3b52d37e7d6c2c90b8ec35",
 "0xdf482f11e3fbb7716e2868786b3afede1c1fb37f",
 "0xe49668b7ffbf031bbbdab7a222bdb38e7e3e1b63",
 "0xf9834defb35d24c5a61a5fe745149e9470282495"]
```

Funding the account with bitcoin

This option is available with the Mist browser by clicking on the account and then selecting the option to fund the account. The backend engine used for this operation is shapeshift.io and can be used to fund the account from bitcoin or other currencies, including the fiat currency option as well.

Once the exchange is completed, the transferred Ether will be available in the account.

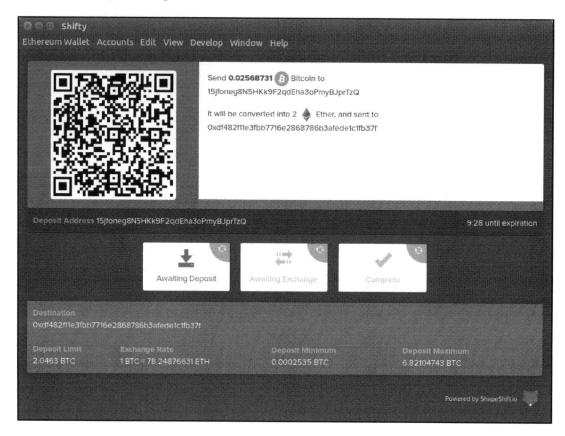

Parity installation

Parity is another implementation of the Ethereum client. It has been written using the Rust programming language. The main aim behind the development of parity is high performance, small footprint, and reliability. Parity can be installed using the following commands on an Ubuntu or Mac system:

```
bash <(curl https://get.parity.io -Lk)
```

This will initiate the download and installation of the parity client. After the installation of parity is completed, the installer will also offer the installation of the netstats client. The netstat client is a daemon that runs in the background and collects important statistics and displays them on stats.ethdev.com.

A sample installation of parity is shown in the following screenshot:

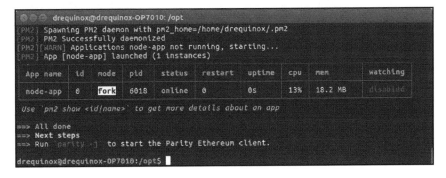

Once the installation is completed successfully, the following message is displayed. Ethereum parity node can then be started using `parity -j`. If compatibility with geth is required in order to use Ethereum wallet (Mist browser) with parity, then the `parity -geth` command should be used to run parity. This will run parity in compatibility mode with the geth client and will consequently allow Mist to run on top of parity.

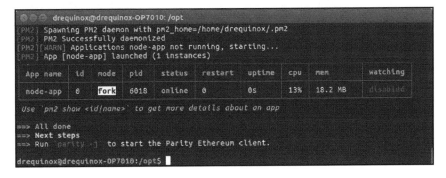

Parity installation

The client can optionally be listed on `https://ethstats.net/`. An example is shown as follows:

All connected clients are listed on the ethstats.net, as shown in the following screenshot. These clients are listed with relevant attributes, such as the node name, node type, latency, mining status, number of peers, number of pending transactions, last block, difficultly, block transactions, and number of Uncles.

Client listed on https://ethstats.net/

Parity also offers a user-friendly web interface from where various tasks, such as account management, address book management, DAPP management, contract management, and status and signer operations, can be managed.

This is accessible by issuing the following command:

```
$ parity ui
```

This will bring up the interface shown as follows:

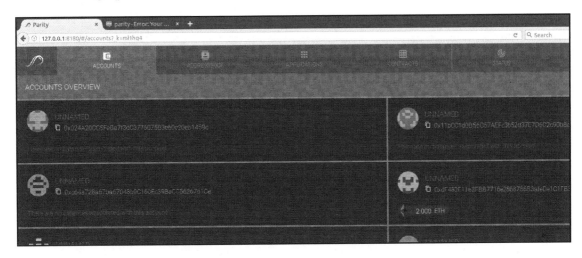

Parity user interface.

If parity is running in the geth compatibility mode, the parity UI is disabled. In order to enable the UI along with geth compatibility, the following command can be used:

```
$ parity --geth --force-ui
```

The preceding command will start parity in the geth compatibility mode and also enable the web user interface.

Creating accounts using the parity command line

The following command can be used to create a new account using parity:

```
$ parity account new
Please note that password is NOT RECOVERABLE.
Type password:
Repeat password:
2016-11-30 02:18:55 UTC c8c92a910cfbce2e655c88d37a89b6657d1498fb
```

Trading and investment

Ether is available at various exchanges for buying and selling. The current market cap of Ethereum is £680,277,967 at the time of writing this, and an Ether is worth £7.89. Recently, the price has been very volatile and has dropped down significantly due to recent Ethereum attacks and subsequent forks on the Ethereum network.

The following chart shows the historical market capitalization details:

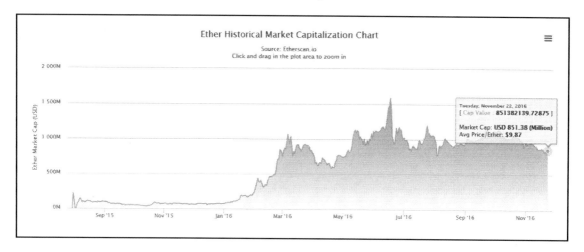

Ether historical market capitalization (source Etherscan.io)

Ether can either be purchased on various exchanges, or it can be mined. There are online services available, such as `shapeshift.io`, that allow conversion from one currency to another.

Various online exchanges, such as kraken, coinbase, and many more, offer ether to be purchased for fiat currency using credit cards or another virtual currency, such as bitcoin.

The yellow paper

The Ethereum yellow paper has been written by *Dr. Gavin Wood* and serves as a formal definition of the Ethereum protocol. Anyone can implement an Ethereum client by following the protocol specifications defined in the paper. This paper can be somewhat difficult to read, especially for the readers who do not have a background in algebra or mathematics and are not familiar with mathematical notations.

The list of all symbols with their meanings used in the paper is provided here with the anticipation that it will make reading the paper easier. Once symbol meanings are known, it becomes quite easy to understand and appreciate the concepts and specifications described in the yellow paper.

Useful symbols

Symbol	Meaning	Symbol	Meaning
≡	Is defined as	≤	Less than or equal to
=	Is equal to	σ	Sigma, World state
≠	Is not equal to	μ	Mu, Machine state
‖ ... ‖	Length of	ϒ	Upsilon, Ethereum state transition function
∈	Is an element of	∏	Block level state transition function
∉	Is not an element of	.	Sequence concatenation
∀	For all	∃	There exists
∪	Union	∧	Contract creation function
∧	Logical AND	Δ	Increment
:	Such that		
{}	Set		
()	Function of tuple		
[]	Array indexing		
∨	Logical OR		
>	Is greater than		
+	Addition		
−	Subtraction		
Σ	Summation		
{	Describing various cases of if , otherwise		
⌊...⌋	Floor, lowest element		

[...]	Ceiling, highest element		
|...|	No of bytes		
⊕	Exclusive OR		
(a,b)	Real numbers >= a and < b		
∅	Empty set, null		

The Ethereum network

The Ethereum network is a peer-to-peer network where nodes participate in order to maintain the blockchain and contribute to the consensus mechanism. Networks can be divided into three types, based on requirements and usage.

MainNet

MainNet is the current live network of ethereum. The current version of MainNet is homestead.

TestNet

TestNet is also called Ropsten and is the test network for the Ethereum blockchain. This blockchain is used to test smart contracts and DApps before being deployed to the production live blockchain. Moreover, being a test network, it allows experimentation and research.

Private net(s)

As the name suggests, this is the private network that can be created by generating a new genesis block. This is usually the case in distributed ledger networks, where a private group of entities start their own blockchain and use it as a permissioned blockchain.

More discussion on how to connect to test net and how to set up private nets will be discussed in the next chapter.

Supporting protocols

There are various supporting protocols that are in development in order to support the complete decentralized ecosystem. This includes whisper and Swarm protocols. In addition to the contracts layer, which is the core blockchain layer, there are additional layers that need to be decentralized in order to achieve a complete decentralized ecosystem. This includes decentralized storage and decentralized messaging. Whisper, being developed for ethereum, is a decentralized messaging protocol, whereas Swarm is a decentralized storage protocol. Both of these technologies are being developed currently and have been envisaged to provide the basis for a fully decentralized web. In the following section, both technologies are discussed in detail.

Whisper

Whisper provides decentralized peer-to-peer messaging capabilities to the ethereum network. In essence, whisper is a communication protocol that nodes use in order to communicate with each other. The data and routing of messages are encrypted within whisper communications. Moreover, it is designed to be used for smaller data transfers and in scenarios where real-time communication is not required. Whisper is also designed to provide a communication layer that cannot be traced and provides "dark communication" between parties. Blockchain can be used for communication, but that is expensive and consensus is not really required for messages exchanged between nodes. Therefore, whisper can be used as a protocol that allows

Whisper is already available with geth and can be enabled using the `--shh` option while running the geth ethereum client.

Swarm

Swarm is being developed as a distributed file storage platform. It is a decentralized, distributed, and peer-to-peer storage network. Files in this network are addressed by the hash of their content. This is in contrast to the traditional centralized services, where storage is available at a central location only. This is developed as a native base layer service for the Ethereum web 3.0 stack. Swarm is integrated with DevP2P, which is the multiprotocol network layer of Ethereum. Swarm is envisaged to provide a **DDOS (Distributed Denial of service)**-resistant and fault-tolerant distributed storage layer for Ethereum Web 3.0. Both whisper and Swarm are under development and, even though Proof of Concept and alpha code has been released for Swarm, there is no stable production version available yet.

The following figure gives a high level overview of how Swarm and whisper fit together and work with blockchain:

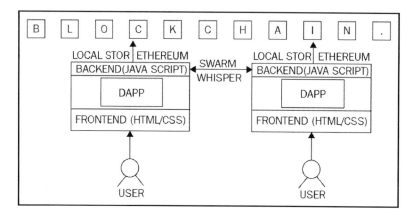

Diagrams shows blockchain, whisper and Swarm

Applications developed on Ethereum

There are various implementations of DAOs and smart contracts in Ethereum, most notably, *the DAO*, which was recently hacked and required a hard fork in order for funds to be recovered. The DAO was created to serve as a decentralized platform to collect and distribute investments.

Augur is another DAPP that has been implemented on Ethereum, which is a decentralized prediction market. Various other decentralized applications are listed on http://dapps.et hercasts.com/.

Scalability and security issues

Scalability in any blockchain is a fundamental issue. Security is also of paramount importance. Issues such as privacy and confidentiality have caused some adaptability issues, especially in the financial sector. However, a great deal of research is being conducted in these areas. A more detailed discussion regarding all blockchain-related issues will be carried out in Chapter 12, *Scalability and other challenges.*

Summary

This chapter started with a discussion on the history of Ethereum, the motivation behind Ethereum development, and Ethereum clients. Then, you were introduced to the core concepts of the Ethereum blockchain, such as state machine model, world and machine state, accounts, and types of accounts. Moreover, a detailed introduction to the core components of the **Ethereum virtual machine** (**EVM**) was also presented. Other concepts such as blocks, block structure, gas, and messages were also introduced and discussed in detail. The later sections of the chapter introduced the practical installation and management of ethereum clients. Two most popular clients, geth and parity, were discussed. Further development-specific discussion on these clients will be carried out in the next chapter, where development using Ethereum is discussed. Finally, supporting protocols and topics related to challenges faced by Ethereum were presented. Ethereum is under continuous development and new improvements are being made by a dedicated community of developers regularly. Ethereum improvement proposals, available at `https://github.com/ethereum/EIPs`, are also an indication of the magnitude of research and keen interest by the community in this technology. Moreover, a recently launched initiative, **Enterprise Ethereum Alliance** (**EAA**) is aiming to develop enterprise grade Ethereum platform which will be capable of meeting enterprise level business requirements. With research being carried out on topics such as scalability, optimization, throughput, capacity, and security, it is envisaged that over time, Ethereum will evolve into a more robust, user-friendly, and stable blockchain ecosystem.

8

Ethereum Development

This chapter introduces the concepts, techniques, and tools related to Ethereum development. Several examples will be introduced in this chapter to complement the theoretical concepts provided in earlier chapters. This chapter will mainly cover the setup of the development environment and how to create smart contracts using Ethereum blockchain. Detailed walkthrough examples will be provided that will help you understand how Ethereum and other supporting tools can be used to develop and deploy smart contracts on the blockchain.

Setting up a development environment

The first task is to set up a development environment. The upcoming section introduces the ethereum setup for Test Net and Private Net. Test Net is called Ropsten and is used by developers or users as a test platform to test smart contracts and other blockchain-related proposals. The Private Net option in Ethereum allows the creation of an independent private network that can be used as a distributed ledger between participating entities and for the development and testing of smart contracts. While there are other clients available for Ethereum, such as Parity, which was discussed in the previous chapter, geth is the leading client for Ethereum and the common tool of choice, as such this chapter will use `geth` in the examples.

Test Net (Ropsten)

The Ethereum Go client, `geth`, can be connected to the test network using the following command:

```
$ geth --TestNet
```

A sample output is shown in the following screenshot. The screenshot shows the type of the network chosen and various other pieces of information regarding the blockchain download.

A blockchain explorer for test net is located at `https://testnet.etherscan.io/` and can be used to trace transactions and blocks on the Ethereum test network.

```
imran@drequinox-OP7010:~$ geth --testnet
I1204 16:03:32.759308 cmd/utils/flags.go:613] WARNING: No etherbase set and no accounts found as default
I1204 16:03:32.759415 ethdb/database.go:83] Allotted 128MB cache and 1024 file handles to /home/imran/.ethereum/testnet/geth/chaindata
I1204 16:03:32.807292 ethdb/database.go:176] closed db:/home/imran/.ethereum/testnet/geth/chaindata
I1204 16:03:32.807589 node/node.go:175] instance: Geth/v1.5.2-stable-c8695209/linux/go1.7.3
I1204 16:03:32.807603 ethdb/database.go:83] Allotted 128MB cache and 1024 file handles to /home/imran/.ethereum/testnet/geth/chaindata
I1204 16:03:32.814016 eth/backend.go:280] Successfully wrote custom genesis block: 0cd786a2425d16f152c658316c423e6ce1181e15c3295826d7c99
04cba9ce303
I1204 16:03:32.814076 eth/db_upgrade.go:346] upgrading db log bloom bins
I1204 16:03:32.814112 eth/db_upgrade.go:354] upgrade completed in 36.513µs
I1204 16:03:32.814128 eth/backend.go:193] Protocol Versions: [63 62], Network Id: 2
I1204 16:03:32.814363 core/blockchain.go:214] Last header: #0 [0cd786a2...] TD=131072
I1204 16:03:32.814375 core/blockchain.go:215] Last block: #0 [0cd786a2...] TD=131072
I1204 16:03:32.814382 core/blockchain.go:216] Fast block: #0 [0cd786a2...] TD=131072
I1204 16:03:32.814840 p2p/server.go:336] Starting Server
I1204 16:03:37.983847 p2p/discover/udp.go:217] Listening, enode://fa838ec3fee8a26d75755b55f7cbdd80efacc4a98b5291acd5a23aea5465b794c84aff
e7be633524d2895768a2122a25e87cf97bd369895ace9f48f868eaef18@[::]:30303
I1204 16:03:37.983966 p2p/server.go:604] Listening on [::]:30303
I1204 16:03:37.984963 node/node.go:340] IPC endpoint opened: /home/imran/.ethereum/testnet/geth.ipc
I1204 16:04:17.984160 eth/downloader/downloader.go:326] Block synchronisation started
```

Output of the geth command connecting to Ethereum test net

Setting up a Private Net

Private Net allows the creation of an entirely new blockchain. This is different from Test Net or Main Net in the sense that it uses its on-genesis block and Network ID. In order to create Private Net, three components are needed:

1. Network ID.
2. Genesis file.
3. Data directory to store blockchain data. Even though data directory is not strictly required to be mentioned, if there is more than one blockchain already active on the system, then data directory should be specified so that a separate directory is used for the new blockchain.

Private Net allows the creation of an entirely new blockchain. This is different from Test Net or Main Net in the sense that it uses its own unique genesis block and Network ID. On Main Net, geth knows about peers by default and connects automatically, but on Private Net, geth needs to be configured by specifying appropriate flags and configuration in order for it to be able to be discoverable by other peers or to discover other peers.

In addition to the previously mentioned three components, it is desirable that you disable **node discovery** so that other nodes on the Internet cannot discover your private network and is truly private. If other networks happen to have the same genesis file and Network ID, they may connect to your Private Net. The chance of having the same Network ID and genesis block is very low, but, nevertheless, disabling node discovery is good practice, and is recommended.

In the following section, all these parameters are discussed in detail with a practical example.

Network ID

Network ID can be any positive number except 1 and 3, which are already in use by Ethereum Main Net and Test Net (Ropsten), respectively. Network ID 786 has been chosen for the example private network discussed later in this section.

The genesis file

The genesis file contains necessary fields required for a custom genesis block. This is the first block in the network and does not point to any previous block. The Ethereum protocol performs rigorous checking in order to ensure that no other node on the Internet can participate in the consensus mechanism, unless they have the same genesis block.

A custom genesis file that will be used later in the example is shown here:

```
{
   "nonce": "0x0000000000000042",
     "timestamp": "0x0",
"parentHash":"0x00000000000000000000000000000000000000000000000000000000000
00000",
     "extraData": "0x0",
     "gasLimit": "0x4c4b40",
     "difficulty": "0x400",
"mixhash":"0x00000000000000000000000000000000000000000000000000000000000000
00",
     "coinbase": "0x0000000000000000000000000000000000000000",
     "alloc": { }
```

```
}
```

This file can be saved in a text file with the JSON extension; for example, `privategenesis.json`. Optionally, ether can be preallocated by specifying beneficiary addresses and the amount of Wei in `alloc`, but it is usually not necessary as, being on the private network, ether can be mined very quickly.

Data directory

This is the directory where the blockchain data for the private Ethereum network will be saved. For example, in the following example, it is `~/.ethereum/privatenet`.

In the geth client, a number of parameters are specified in order to launch, further fine-tune the configuration, and launch the private network. These flags are listed here.

Flags and their meaning

- `--nodiscover`: This flag ensures that the node is not automatically discoverable if it happens to have the same genesis file and Network ID.
- `--maxpeers`: This flag is used to specify the number of peers allowed to be connected to the private net. If it is set to 0, then no one will be able to connect, which might be desirable in a few scenarios, such as private testing.
- `--rpc`: This is used to enable the RPC interface in geth.
- `--rpcapi`: This flag takes a list of APIs to be allowed as a parameter. For example, `eth,web3` will enable the web3 and eth interface over RPC.
- `--rpcport`: This sets up the TCP RPC port; for example: 9999.
- `--rpccorsdomain`: This flag specifies the URL that is allowed to connect to the private geth node and perform RPC operations.
- `--port`: This specifies the TCP port that will be used to listen to the incoming connections from other peers.
- `--identity`: This flag is a string that specifies the name of a private node.

Static nodes

If there is a need to connect to a specific set of peers, then these nodes can be added to a file where the `chaindata` and `keystore` files are saved, for example, in the `~/.ethereum/privatenet` directory. The filename should be `static-nodes.json`. This can be valuable in a private network. An example of the json file is shown as follows:

```
[
"enode://
44352ede5b9e792e437c1c0431c1578ce3676a87e1f588434aff1299d30325c233c8d426fc5
7a25380481c8a36fb3be2787375e932fb4885885f6452f6efa77f@xxx.xxx.xxx.xxx:TCP_P
ORT"
]
```

Here, `xxx` is the public IP address and `TCP_PORT` can be any valid and available TCP port on the system. The long hex string is the node ID.

Starting up the private network

The initial command to start the private network is shown as follows:

```
$ geth --datadir ~/.ethereum/privatenet init
./privether/privategenesis.json
```

This will produce an output similar to what is shown in the following screenshot:

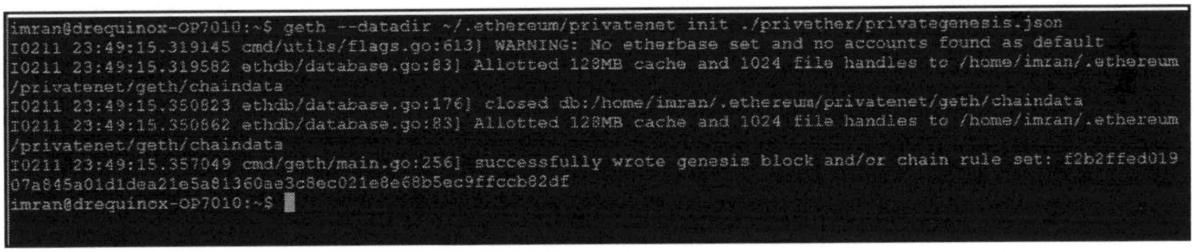

Private network initialization

This output indicates that a genesis block has been created successfully. In order for `geth` to start, the following command can be issued:

```
$ geth --datadir .ethereum/privatenet/ --networkid 786
```

This will produce the following output:

```
imran@drequinox-OP7010:~$ geth --datadir .ethereum/privatenet/ --networkid 786
I0211 23:52:02.322730 cmd/utils/flags.go:613] WARNING: No etherbase set and no accounts found as default
I0211 23:52:02.322814 ethdb/database.go:83] Allotted 128MB cache and 1024 file handles to /home/imran/.ethereu
/privatenet/geth/chaindata
I0211 23:52:02.378525 ethdb/database.go:176] closed db:/home/imran/.ethereum/privatenet/geth/chaindata
I0211 23:52:02.378825 node/node.go:175] instance: Geth/v1.5.2-stable-c8695209/linux/go1.7.3
I0211 23:52:02.378838 ethdb/database.go:83] Allotted 128MB cache and 1024 file handles to /home/imran/.ethereu
/privatenet/geth/chaindata
I0211 23:52:02.388823 eth/db_upgrade.go:346] upgrading db log bloom bins
I0211 23:52:02.388906 eth/db_upgrade.go:354] upgrade completed in 85.497µs
I0211 23:52:02.388930 eth/backend.go:193] Protocol Versions: [63 62], Network Id: 786
I0211 23:52:02.389234 core/blockchain.go:214] Last header: #0 [f2b2ffed…] TD=512
I0211 23:52:02.389251 core/blockchain.go:215] Last block: #0 [f2b2ffed…] TD=512
I0211 23:52:02.389264 core/blockchain.go:216] Fast block: #0 [f2b2ffed…] TD=512
I0211 23:52:02.389750 p2p/server.go:336] Starting Server
I0211 23:52:07.553857 p2p/discover/udp.go:217] Listening, enode://9efe46a58bc3f3d7c8d2ab0e18244c9f72bccdee9300
9751810deab32b8cd8465a0ac3685ea48871ec797f9f534912b2d1b983da25993b27397ecc1abdd5467@[::]:30303
I0211 23:52:07.554074 p2p/server.go:604] Listening on [::]:30303
I0211 23:52:07.555359 node/node.go:340] IPC endpoint opened: /home/imran/.ethereum/privatenet/geth.ipc
```

Starting geth for a private network

Now `geth` can be attached via IPC to the running geth client on a private network using the following command. This will allow you to interact with the running `geth` session on the private network:

```
$ geth attach ipc:.ethereum/privatenet/geth.ipc
```

As shown here, this will open the interactive JavaScript console for the running Private Net session:

```
imran@drequinox-OP7010:~$ geth attach ipc:.ethereum/privatenet/geth.ipc
Welcome to the Geth JavaScript console!

instance: Geth/v1.5.2-stable-c8695209/linux/go1.7.3
 modules: admin:1.0 debug:1.0 eth:1.0 miner:1.0 net:1.0 personal:1.0 rpc:1.0 txpool:1.0 web3:1.0

>
```

Starting geth to attach with Private Net 786

You may have noticed that a warning message appears when `geth` starts up.

WARNING: No etherbase set and no accounts found as default

This message appears because there are no accounts currently available in the new test network and no account is set as etherbase to receive mining rewards. This issue can be addressed by creating a new account and setting that account as etherbase. This will also be required when mining is carried out on the test network. This is shown in the following commands. Note that these commands are entered in the geth JavaScript console, as shown in the preceding figure.

The following command creates a new account. In this context, the account will be created on the Private Network ID 786:

```
> personal.newAccount("Password123")
"0x76f11b383dbc3becf8c5d9309219878caae265c3"
```

Once the account is created, the next step is to set it as an Etherbase/coinbase account so that the mining reward goes to this account. This can be achieved using the following command:

```
> miner.setEtherbase(personal.listAccounts[0])
true
```

Currently, the etherbase account has no balance, as can be seen using the following command:

```
> eth.getBalance(eth.coinbase).toNumber();
0
```

Finally, mining can start by simply issuing the following command. This command takes one parameter that is a number of threads. In the following example, two threads will be allocated to the mining process by specifying 2 as an argument to the start function:

```
> miner.start(2)
true
```

After mining starts, the first DAG generation is carried out and output similar to the following is produced:

```
I0211 23:58:50.380089 eth/backend.go:479] Automatic pregeneration of ethash DAG ON (ethash dir: /home/imran/.ethash)
I0211 23:58:50.380097 miner/miner.go:136] Starting mining operation (CPU=2 TOT=3)
I0211 23:58:50.380138 eth/backend.go:486] checking DAG (ethash dir: /home/imran/.ethash)
I0211 23:58:50.380257 miner/worker.go:542] commit new work on block 1 with 0 txs & 0 uncles. Took 139.49µs
I0211 23:58:50.380292 vendor/github.com/ethereum/ethash/ethash.go:259] Generating DAG for epoch 0 (size 1073739904) (0000000000000000000000000000000000000000000000000000000000000000)
I0211 23:58:51.166755 vendor/github.com/ethereum/ethash/ethash.go:276] Done generating DAG for epoch 0, it took 786.458657ms
```

DAG generation

Once DAG generation is finished and mining starts, `geth` will produce output similar to that shown in the following screenshot. It can be clearly seen that blocks are being mined successfully with the `Mined 5 blocks . . .` message.

I1204 22:38:02.373804 miner/worker.go:438] ⚒ Mined 5 blocks back: block #487
I1204 22:38:02.373908 miner/worker.go:542] commit new work on block 493 with 0 txs & 0 uncles. Took 86.005µs
I1204 22:38:02.637297 miner/worker.go:344] ⚒ Mined block (#493 / 9a95245e). Wait 5 blocks for confirmation
I1204 22:38:02.637415 miner/worker.go:542] commit new work on block 494 with 0 txs & 0 uncles. Took 91.009µs
I1204 22:38:02.637436 miner/worker.go:438] ⚒ Mined 5 blocks back: block #488
I1204 22:38:02.639064 miner/worker.go:542] commit new work on block 494 with 0 txs & 0 uncles. Took 1.609044ms
I1204 22:38:03.538525 miner/worker.go:344] ⚒ Mined block (#494 / cb89cccd). Wait 5 blocks for confirmation
I1204 22:38:03.538719 miner/worker.go:542] commit new work on block 495 with 0 txs & 0 uncles. Took 158.751µs
I1204 22:38:03.538745 miner/worker.go:438] ⚒ Mined 5 blocks back: block #489
I1204 22:38:03.538860 miner/worker.go:542] commit new work on block 495 with 0 txs & 0 uncles. Took 95.822µs
I1204 22:38:03.548923 miner/worker.go:344] ⚒ Mined block (#495 / 539d8079). Wait 5 blocks for confirmation
I1204 22:38:03.549064 miner/worker.go:542] commit new work on block 496 with 0 txs & 0 uncles. Took 120.447µs
I1204 22:38:03.549082 miner/worker.go:438] ⚒ Mined 5 blocks back: block #490
I1204 22:38:03.549159 miner/worker.go:542] commit new work on block 496 with 0 txs & 0 uncles. Took 64.047µs

Mining output

Mining can be stopped using the following command:

```
> miner.stop
true
```

In the JavaScript console, the current balance of total ether can be queried, as shown here. After mining, a significant amount can be seen in the following example. Mining is extremely fast as it is a private network and in the genesis file, the network difficulty has also been set quite low:

```
> eth.getBalance(eth.coinbase).toNumber();
2.72484375e+21
```

If two spaces and two tabs are pressed in a sequence, a complete of list of the available objects will be displayed. This is shown in the following screenshot:

Array	Math	TypeError	constructor	hasOwnProperty	parseFloat	toString
BigNumber	NaN	URIError	debug	inspect	parseInt	txpool
Boolean	Number	Web3	decodeURI	isFinite	personal	undefined
Date	Object	_setInterval	decodeURIComponent	isNaN	propertyIsEnumerable	unescape
Error	RangeError	_setTimeout	encodeURI	isPrototypeOf	require	valueOf
EvalError	ReferenceError	admin	encodeURIComponent	jeth	rpc	web3
Function	RegExp	clearInterval	escape	loadScript	setInterval	
Infinity	String	clearTimeout	eth	miner	setTimeout	
JSON	SyntaxError	console	eval	net	toLocaleString	

Available objects

Furthermore, when a command is typed, it can be autocompleted by pressing tab twice. If two tabs are pressed, then the list of available methods is also displayed. This is shown in the following screenshot:

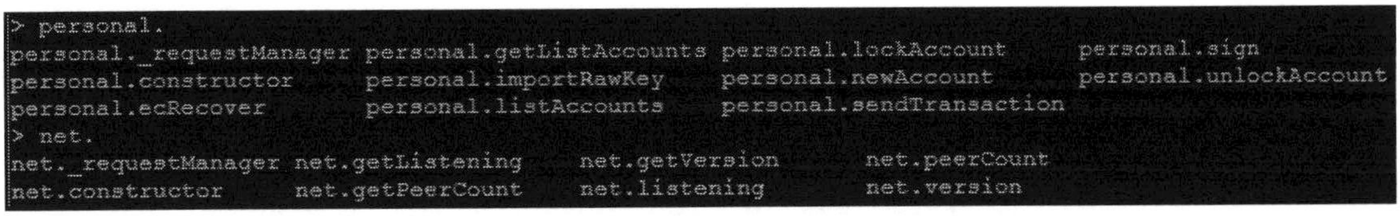

```
> personal.
personal._requestManager   personal.getListAccounts   personal.lockAccount       personal.sign
personal.constructor       personal.importRawKey       personal.newAccount        personal.unlockAccount
personal.ecRecover         personal.listAccounts       personal.sendTransaction
> net.
net._requestManager   net.getListening    net.getVersion    net.peerCount
net.constructor       net.getPeerCount    net.listening     net.version
```

Available methods

In addition to the previously mentioned command, in order to get a list of available methods, after typing any command,; (semicolon) is entered. An example is shown in the next screenshot, which shows a list of all the methods available for `net`:

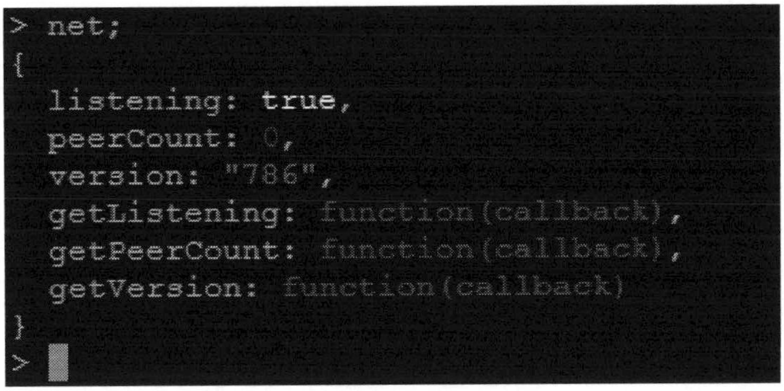

```
> net;
{
    listening: true,
    peerCount: 0,
    version: "786",
    getListening: function(callback),
    getPeerCount: function(callback),
    getVersion: function(callback)
}
>
```

List of methods

There are a few other commands that can be used to query the private network. Some examples are shown as follows:

- Get the current gas price:

```
> eth.gasPrice
20000000000
```

- Get the latest block number:

```
> eth.blockNumber
587
```

Debug can come in handy when debugging issues. A sample command is shown here; however, there are many methods available. The following method will return the RLP of block 0:

- **Encode using RLP:**

```
> debug.getBlockRlp(0)
"f901f7f901f2a00000000000000000000000000000000000000000000000000000
0000000000000000a01dcc4de8dec75d7aab85b567b6ccd41ad312451b948a
7413f0a142fd40d4934794000000000000000000000000000000000000000000
a056e81f171bcc55a6ff8345e692c0f86e5b48e01b996cadc001622fb5e363
b421a056e81f171bcc55a6ff8345e692c0f86e5b48e01b996cadc001622fb5
e363b421a056e81f171bcc55a6ff8345e692c0f86e5b48e01b996cadc00162
2fb5e363b421b90100000000000000000000000000000000000000000000000000
00000000000000000000000000000000000000000000000000000000000000
00000000000000000000000000000000000000000000000000000000000000
00000000000000000000000000000000000000000000000000000000000000
00000000000000000000000000000000000000000000000000000000000000
00000000000000000000000000000000000000000000000000000000000000
00000000000000000000000000000000000000000000000000000000000000
00000000000000000000000000000000000000000000000000000000000000
00000000000000000000000000000082020080834c4b40808000a00000
00000000000000000000000000000000000000000000000000000000000088
0000000000000042c0c0"
```

- **Unlock the account before sending transactions:**

```
> personal.unlockAccount
("0x76f11b383dbc3becf8c5d9309219878caae265c3")
Unlock account 0x76f11b383dbc3becf8c5d9309219878caae265c3
Passphrase:
```

- **Send transactions:**

```
> eth.sendTransaction({from:
"0x76f11b383dbc3becf8c5d9309219878caae265c3", to:
"0xcce6450413ac80f9ee8bd97ca02b92c065d77abc", value: 1000})
```

Another way is to use listAccounts[] method, this can be done as shown below:

```
> eth.sendTransaction({from: personal.listAccounts[0], to:
personal.listAccounts[1], value: 1000})
```

- Get a list of compilers. Note that if no output is shown, it means that no solidity compiler is installed; solidity compiler installation details are provided later in the chapter:

```
> web3.eth.getCompilers()
["Solidity"]
```

Running Mist on Private Net

It is possible to run Mist on Private Net by issuing the following command. This binary is usually available in the `home` folder after the installation of `/opt/Ethereum`:

```
$ ./Ethereum\ Wallet --rpc ~/.ethereum/privatenet/geth.ipc
```

This will allow a connection to the running Private Net `geth` session, and it provides all features, such as wallet, account management, and contract deployment on Private Net via Mist.

Running Ethereum Wallet to connect to Private Net

Once Ethereum is launched, it will show the interface shown here, indicating clearly that it's running in the **PRIVATE-NET** mode.

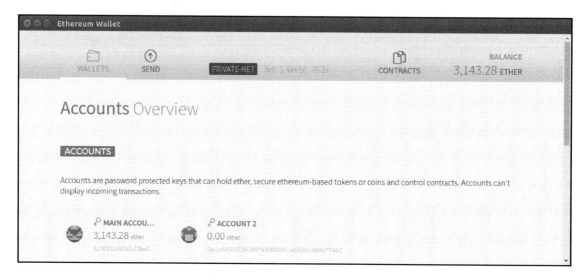

Mist on Private Net

Mist can also run over the network using RPC. This is useful if `geth` is running on a different node and Mist on another. This can be achieved by running Mist with the flag shown here:

```
--rpc http://127.0.0.1:8545
```

Deploying contracts using Mist

It is very easy to deploy new contracts using Mist. Mist provides an interface where contracts can be written in solidity and then deployed on the network.

In the exercise, a simple contract that can perform various simple arithmetic calculations on the input parameter will be used. Steps on how to use Mist to deploy this contract are shown here. As solidity has not been introduced yet, the aim here is to allow users to experience the contract deployment and interaction process. More information on coding and solidity will be provided later in the chapter, after which it will become easy to understand the code shown. Those of you who are already familiar with JavaScript or any other similar language will find the code almost self-explanatory.

The example contract source code is shown as follows:

```
pragma solidity ^0.4.0;
contract SimpleContract2
{
  uint x;
  uint z;
  function addition(uint x) returns (uint y)
{
  z=x+5;
  y=z;
}
function difference(uint x) returns (uint y)
{
  z=x-5;
  y=z;
}
function division(uint x) returns (uint y)
{
 z=x/5;
 y=z;
}

function currValue() constant returns (uint)
{
 return z;
}
}
```

This code can simply be copied into Mist under the contracts section, as shown here. On the left-hand side, the source code can be copied; once verified and when no syntax errors are detected, the option to deploy the contract will appear in the drop-down menu on the right-hand side where it says **SELLECT CONTRACT TO DEPLOY**. Simply select the contract and press the **Deploy** button at the bottom of the screen.

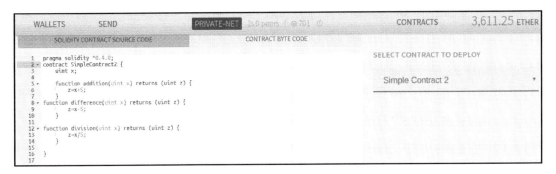

Mist browser contract deployment

Mist will ask for the password of the account and will show a window similar to the one in the following screenshot:

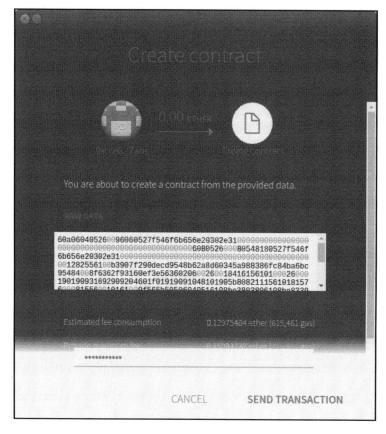

Create a contract using Mist

Enter the password and click on **SEND TRANSACTION** to deploy the contract.

Once deployed and mined successfully, it will appear in the list of transactions in Mist, as shown here:

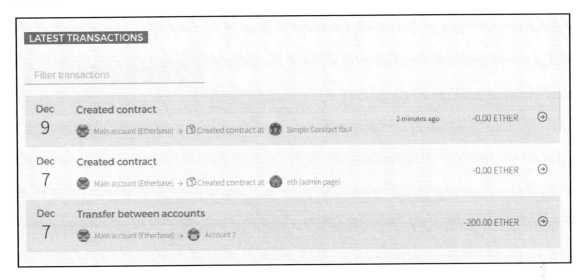

List of transactions after creation in Mist

Once the contract is available, it can be interacted with using the execute transaction and calling available functions via Mist.

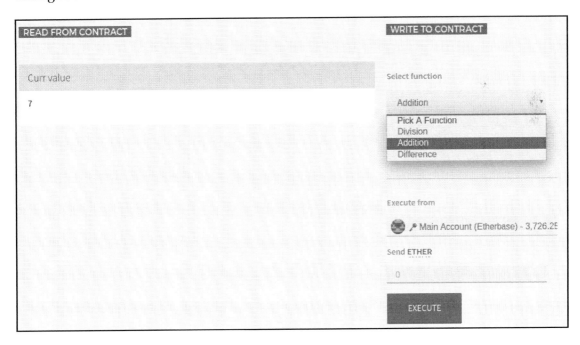

Interaction with the contract using read and write options in Mist

In the preceding screenshot, the **READ FROM CONTRACT** and **WRITE TO CONTRACT** options are available. Also, the function that has been exposed by the contract can be seen on the right-hand side. Once the required function is selected, the appropriate value is entered for the function and the account (execute from) is selected; press execute in order to execute the transaction, which will result in calling the selected function of the contract.

This process is shown in the following screenshot:

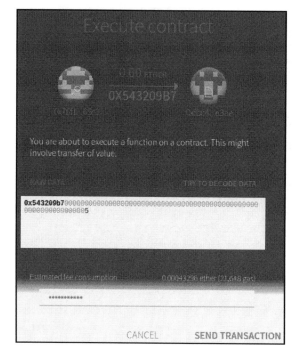

Contract execution in Mist

As shown in the screenshot, enter the appropriate password for the account and then press **SEND TRANSACTION** to send the transaction to the contract.

Development tools and clients

There are a number of tools available for Ethereum development. The following diagram shows the taxonomy of various development tools, clients, IDEs, and development frameworks for Ethereum:

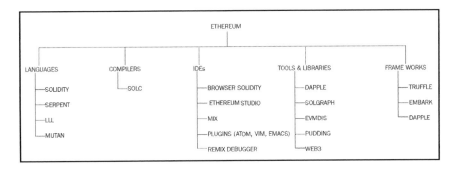

Taxonomy of Ethereum ecosystem components

In this chapter, the main focus will be on `geth`, browser solidity, solidity, solc, and truffle. Rest of the elements will be discussed briefly.

Languages

Contracts can be programmed in a variety of languages. There are four languages that can be used in order to write contracts:

- **Mutan**: This is a Go-style language, which was deprecated in early 2015 and is no longer used.
- **LLL**: This is a Lisp-like language, hence the name LLL. This is also not used anymore.
- **Serpent**: This is a simple and clean Python-like language. It is actively used for contract development.
- **Solidity**: This language has now become almost a standard for contract writing for Ethereum. This language is the focus of this chapter and is discussed in detail in later sections.

Compilers

Compilers are used to convert high-level contract source code into the format that the Ethereum execution environment understands. The solidity compiler is the most common one in use and is discussed here.

Solc

The solidity compiler converts from a high-level solidity language into **Ethereum Virtual Machine (EVM)** bytecode so that it can be executed on the blockchain by EVM.

The solidity compiler on a Linux Ubuntu operating system can be installed using the following commands:

```
$ sudo apt-get install solc
```

If PPAs are not already installed, those can be installed by running the following command:

```
sudo add-apt-repository ppa:ethereum/ethereum
sudo apt-get update
```

In order to verify the existing version of the solidity compiler and verify that it is installed, the following command can be used:

```
$ solc --version
solc, the solidity compiler commandline interface
Version: 0.4.6+commit.2dabbdf0.Linux.g++
```

Solc supports a variety of functions. A few examples are shown as follows:

- Display contract in a binary format.

Solidity compiler binary output

- Estimate gas:

```
imran@drequinox-OP7010:~$ solc --gas contract1.sol
======= SimpleContract =======
Gas estimation:
construction:
   97 + 54600 = 54697
external:
   division(uint256):    230
   addition(uint256):    231
   difference(uint256):  253
```

```
internal:
```

Note that contrat1.sol is shown as an example only; the file can contain any smart contract solidity code. The code of the file is not shown here.

Solc is used internally by web3 from the geth console in order to compile the contract. The syntax is shown here, and contractsourcecode is the solidity source code:

```
web3.eth.compile.solidity(contractsourcecode)
```

This is discussed in detail later in the chapter when you will be introduced to contract development.

Integrated Development Environments (IDEs)

There are various IDEs available for solidity development. Most of the IDEs are available online and are presented via web interfaces. Browser solidity is most commonly used for smaller contracts and is discussed here.

Browser solidity

Browser solidity is the web-based environment for the development and testing of contracts using solidity. It does not run on a live blockchain; in fact, it is a simulated environment in which contracts can be deployed, tested, and debugged. It is available at https://ethereum.github.io/browser-solidity. An example interface is shown as follows:

Browser solidity

On the left-hand side, there is a code editor with syntax highlighting and code formatting, and on the right-hand side, there are a number of tools available that can be used to deploy, debug, test, and interact with the contract. Various features, such as transaction interaction, options to connect to JavaScript VM, configuration of execution environment, debugger, formal verification, and static analysis, are available. They can be configured to connect to execution environments such as JavaScript VM, injected Web3–where Mist or a similar environment has provided the execution environment–or Web3 provider, which allows connection to the locally running Ethereum client (for example, `geth`) via IPC or RPC over HTTP (web3 provider endpoint).

Remix

After the Mix IDE was discontinued in August 2016, the Remix project was started. Remix is a browser-based IDE that is under heavy development currently and only the debugger part of it is available as of now. This debugger is very powerful and can be used to perform detailed level tracing and analysis of the EVM byte code. In the following section, installation and usage examples of Remix are presented.

Installation

Remix is available at `https://github.com/ethereum/remix`. The first step is to clone the GitHub repository:

```
$ git clone https://github.com/ethereum/remix
Cloning into 'remix'...
remote: Counting objects: 2185, done.
remote: Compressing objects: 100% (213/213), done.
remote: Total 2185 (delta 124), reused 0 (delta 0), pack-reused 1971
Receiving objects: 100% (2185/2185), 1.12 MiB | 443.00 KiB/s, done.
Resolving deltas: 100% (1438/1438), done.
Checking connectivity... done.
```

After the preceding steps are completed successfully, execute the following command:

```
cd remix
npm install
npm run build
```

At this point, either `npm run start_node` can be run, or `geth` can be started up using the appropriate flags. Once `geth` is up and running, a simple web server can be run in order to serve the remix web page.

Now `geth` can be started up with the following command:

```
$ geth --datadir .ethereum/privatenet/ --networkid 786 --rpc --rpcapi
'web3,eth,debug' --rpcport 8001 --rpccorsdomain 'http://localhost:7777'
```

Notice the `--rpcapi` flag; it is required in order to allow `web3`, `eth`, `debug` over RPC.

If `npm run start_node` is run, the following message may appear:

```
$ npm run start_node
> ethereum-remix@0.0.2-alpha.0.0.9 start_node /home/imran/remix
> ./runNode.sh
both eth and geth has been found in your system
restart the command with the desired client:
npm run start_eth
or
npm run start_geth
```

Assuming `geth` is required, use the following command:

```
$ npm run start_geth
```

If `geth` was opted to be run, then a simple web server is required to browse to the remix web page. This can be achieved simply by issuing a Python command, as follows. This should be run from the `remix` directory.

```
imran@drequinox-OP7010:~/remix$ python -m SimpleHTTPServer 7777
Serving HTTP on 0.0.0.0 port 7777 ...
```

Python quick web server

Once the command is successful and the web server is running, remix can be browsed using the `http://localhost:7777` URL, as shown in the following screenshot:

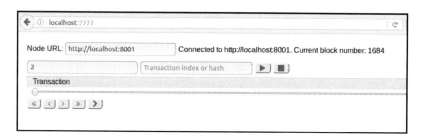

Web browser showing remix running and served via TCP 7777

Remix is also available as part of browser solidity (browser solidity has been discussed separately earlier). It can be connected to the local Private Net by providing the web3 provider endpoint. This is shown as follows:

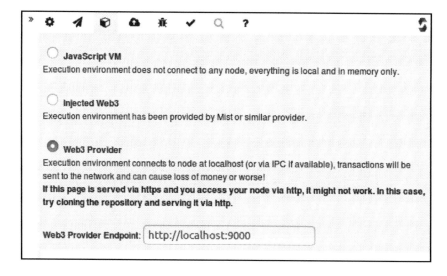

The **Web3 Provider** option on browser solidity to connect to the local `geth` node is as follows:

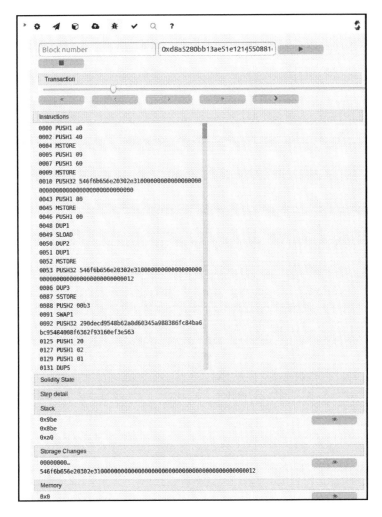

Remix Debugger in browser solidity

Tools and libraries

There are various tools and libraries available for Ethereum. The most common ones are discussed here.

Node.js version 7

As Node js is required for most of the tools and libraries, it can be installed using the following commands:

```
curl -sL https://deb.nodesource.com/setup_7.x | sudo -E bash -
sudo apt-get install -y nodejs
```

Local Ethereum block explorer

Local Ethereum block explorer is a useful tool that can be used to explore the local blockchain. This can be installed by following these steps:

On a Linux Ubuntu machine, run the following command in order to install the local Ethereum block explorer:

```
$ git clone https://github.com/etherparty/explorer
```

This will show output similar to the following:

```
Cloning into 'explorer'...
remote: Counting objects: 253, done.
remote: Total 253 (delta 0), reused 0 (delta 0), pack-reused 253
Receiving objects: 100% (253/253), 51.20 KiB | 0 bytes/s, done.
Resolving deltas: 100% (130/130), done.
Checking connectivity... done.
```

The next step is to change the directory to the explorer and run the following commands:

```
imran@drequinox-OP7010:~$ cd explorer/
imran@drequinox-OP7010:~/explorer$ npm start
> EthereumExplorer@0.1.0 prestart /home/imran/explorer
> npm install
```

Once the installation is finished, output similar to the following will be shown, where the HTTP server for Ethereum explorer starts up:

```
> EthereumExplorer@0.1.0 start /home/imran/explorer
> http-server ./app -a localhost -p 8000 -c-1

Starting up http-server, serving ./app on port: 8000
Hit CTRL-C to stop the server
```

Ethereum explorer HTTP server

Once the web server is up, `geth` should be started up using the following command:

```
geth --datadir .ethereum/privatenet/ --networkid 786 --rpc --rpccorsdomain
'http://localhost:8000'
```

After a successful start up of `geth`, navigate to the localhost on TCP `port 8000`, as shown here, in order to access the local Ethereum block explorer.

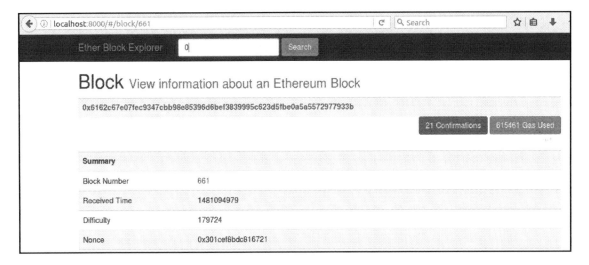

Block explorer

Alternatively, the web server can be started up using Python or any other appropriate provider. In Python, a quick web server can started, as shown in the following code:

```
imran@drequinox-OP7010:~/explorer/app$ python -m SimpleHTTPServer 9900
Serving HTTP on 0.0.0.0 port 9900 ...
```

The `geth` client will need to be started up with appropriate parameters. If not, an error like that shown in the following screenshot can occur:

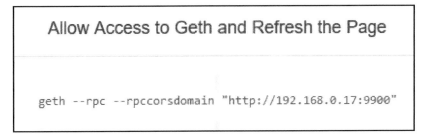

Error message Ethereum local block explorer

Restart `geth` to allow `rpccorsdomain`:

```
geth --datadir .ethereum/PrivateNet/ --networkid 786 --rpc --rpccorsdomain
'http://192.168.0.17:9900'
```

EthereumJS

At times, it is not possible to test on the Test Net and Main Net is obviously not a place to test the contracts. Private Net can be time consuming to set up at times. EthereumJS testrpc comes in handy when quick testing is required and no proper test net is available. It uses EthereumJS to simulate the Ethereum `geth` client behavior and allows for faster development testing. Testrpc is available via npm as a node package.

Before installing testrpc, Node.js should already have been installed and the npm package manager should also be available.

Testrpc can be installed using this command:

```
npm install -g ethereumjs-testrpc
```

In order to start testrpc, simply issue this command and keep it running in the background and open another terminal to work on contracts.

```
$testrpc
```

Contract development and deployment

There are various steps that need to be taken in order to develop and deploy the contracts. Broadly, these can be divided into four steps: writing, testing, verification, and deployment. After deployment, the next step is to create the user interface and present it to the end users via a web server.

The writing step is concerned with writing the contract source code in solidity. This can be done in any text editor. There are various plugins and add-ons available for Vim in Linux, Atom, and other editors that provide syntax highlighting and formatting for solidity source code.

Testing is usually performed by automated means. Later in the chapter, you will be introduced to truffle, which uses the Mocha framework to test contracts. However, manual testing can be performed as well. Once the contract is verified, working, and tested on a simulated environment (for example, EthereumJS testrpc) or on Private Net, it can be deployed to Ropsten Test Net and finally to live blockchain (Homestead).

In the next section, you will be introduced to language solidity. This is a brief introduction to solidity, which should provide the base knowledge required in order to write the contracts. The syntax is very similar to C and JavaScript, and it is quite easy to program.

Introducing solidity

Solidity is a domain-specific language of choice for programming contracts in Ethereum. There are, however, other languages, such as serpent, Mutan, and LLL but solidity is the most popular at the time of writing this. Its syntax is closer to JavaScript and C. Solidity has evolved into a mature language over the last few years and is quite easy to use, but it still has a long way to go before it can become advanced and feature-rich like other well-established languages. Nevertheless, this is the most widely used language available for programming contracts currently.

It is a statically typed language, which means that variable type checking in solidity is carried out at compile time. Each variable, either state or local, must be specified with a type at compile time. This is beneficial in the sense that any validation and checking is completed at compile time and certain types of bugs, such as interpretation of data types, can be caught earlier in the development cycle instead of at run time, which could be costly, especially in the case of the blockchain/smart contracts paradigm. Other features of the language include inheritance, libraries, and the ability to define composite data types.

Solidity is also a called contract-oriented language. In solidity, contracts are equivalent to the concept of classes in other object-oriented programming languages.

Types

Solidity has two categories of data types: value types and reference types.

Value types

These are explained in detail here.

Boolean

This data type has two possible values, true or false, for example:

```
bool v = true;
```

This statement assigns the value `true` to `v`.

Integers

This data type represents integers. A table is shown here, which shows various keywords used to declare integer data types.

Keyword	Types	Details
int	Signed integer	int8 to int256, which means that keywords are available from int8 up to int256 in increments of 8, for example, int8, int16, int24.
uint	Unsigned integer	uint8 to uint256

For example, in this code, note that uint is an alias for uint256:

```
uint256 x;
uint y;
int256 z;
```

These types can also be declared with the constant keyword, which means that no storage slot will be reserved by the compiler for these variables. In this case, each occurrence will be replaced with the actual value:

```
uint constant z=10+10;
```

State variables are declared outside the body of a function, and they remain available throughout the contract depending on the accessibility assigned to them and as long as the contract persists.

Address

This data type holds a 160-bit long (20 byte) value. This type has several members that can be used to interact with and query the contracts. These members are described here:

Balance

The balance member returns the balance of the address in Wei.

Send

This member is used to send an amount of ether to an address (Ethereum's 160-bit address) and returns true or false depending on the result of the transaction, for example, the following:

```
address to = 0x6414cc08d148dce9ebf5a2d0b7c220ed2d3203da;
address from = this;
if (to.balance < 10 && from.balance > 50) to.send(20);
```

Call functions

The `call`, `callcode`, and `delegatecall` are provided in order to interact with functions that do not have **Application Binary Interface (ABI)**. These functions should be used with caution as they are not safe to use due to the impact on type safety and security of the contracts.

Array value types (fixed size and dynamically sized byte arrays)

Solidity has fixed size and dynamically sized byte arrays. Fixed size keywords range from `bytes1` to `bytes32`, whereas dynamically sized keywords include bytes and strings. `bytes` are used for raw byte data and string is used for strings encoded in UTF-8. As these arrays are returned by the value, calling them will incur gas cost. `length` is a member of array value types and returns the length of the byte array.

An example of a static (fixed size) array is as follows:

```
bytes32[10] bankAccounts;
```

An example of a dynamically sized array is as follows:

```
bytes32[] trades;
```

Get `length` of trades:

```
trades.length;
```

Literals

These are used to represent a fixed value.

Integer literals

Integer literals are a sequence of decimal numbers in the range of 0-9. An example is shown as follows:

```
uint8 x = 2;
```

String literals

String literals specify a set of characters written with double or single quotes. An example is shown as follows:

```
'packt'
"packt"
```

Hexadecimal literals

Hexadecimal literals are prefixed with the keyword hex and specified within double or single quotation marks. An example is shown as follows:

```
(hex'AABBCC');
```

Enums

This allows the creation of user-defined types. An example is shown as follows:

```
enum Order{Filled, Placed, Expired };
Order private ord;
ord=Order.Filled;
```

Explicit conversion to and from all integer types is allowed with enums.

Function types

There are two function types: internal and external functions.

Internal functions

These can be used only within the context of the current contract.

External functions

External functions can be called via external function calls.

A function in solidity can be marked as a constant. Constant functions cannot change anything in the contract; they only return values when they are invoked and do not cost any gas. This is the practical implementation of the concept of *call* as discussed in the previous chapter.

The syntax to declare a function is shown as follows:

```
function <nameofthefunction> (<parameter types> <name of the variable>)
{internal|external} [constant] [payable] [returns (<return types> <name of
the variable>)]
```

Reference types

As the name suggests, these types are passed by reference and are discussed in the following section.

Arrays

Arrays represent a contiguous set of elements of the same size and type laid out at a memory location. The concept is the same as any other programming language. Arrays have two members named `length` and `push`:

```
uint[] OrderIds;
```

Structs

These constructs can be used to group a set of dissimilar data types under a logical group. These can be used to define new types, as shown in the following example:

```
Struct Trade
{
uint tradeid;
uint quantity;
uint price;
string trader;
}
```

Data location

Data location specifies where a particular complex data type will be stored. Depending on the default or annotation specified, the location can be storage or memory. This is applicable to arrays and structs and can be specified using the **storage** or **memory** keywords. As copying between memory and storage can be quite expensive, specifying a location can be helpful to control the gas expenditure at times. **Calldata** is another memory location that is used to store function arguments. Parameters of external functions use **calldata** memory. By default, parameters of functions are stored in **memory**, whereas all other local variables make use of **storage**. State variables, on the other hand, are required to use **storage**.

Mappings

Mappings are used for a key to value mapping. This is a way to associate a value with a key. All values in this map are already initialized with all zeroes, for example, the following:

```
mapping (address => uint) offers;
```

This example shows that `offers` is declared as a mapping. Another example makes this clearer:

```
mapping (string => uint) bids;
bids["packt"] = 10;
```

This is basically a dictionary or a hash table where string values are mapped to integer values. The mapping named `bids` has a `packt` string value mapped to value `10`.

Global variables

Solidity provides a number of global variables that are always available in the global namespace. These variables provide information about blocks and transactions. Additionally, cryptographic functions and address-related variables are available as well.

A subset of available functions and variables is shown as follows:

```
keccak256(...) returns (bytes32)
```

This function is used to compute the `keccak256` hash of the argument provided to the function:

```
ecrecover(bytes32 hash, uint8 v, bytes32 r, bytes32 s) returns (address)
```

This function returns the associated address of the public key from the elliptic curve signature:

```
block.number
```

This returns the current block number.

Control structures

Control structures available in solidity are `if - else`, `do`, `while`, `for`, `break`, `continue`, `return`. They work in a manner similar to how they work in C-language or JavaScript.

Events

Events in solidity can be used to log certain events in EVM logs. These are quite useful when external interfaces are required to be notified of any change or event in the contract. These logs are stored on the blockchain in transaction logs. Logs cannot be accessed from the contracts but are used as a mechanism to notify change of state or the occurrence of an event (meeting a condition) in the contract.

In a simple example here, the `valueEvent` event will return true if the x parameter passed to `function Matcher` is equal to or greater than `10`:

```
contract valueChecker {
    uint8 price=10;
    event valueEvent(bool returnValue);
    function Matcher(uint8 x) returns (bool)
    {
        if (x>=price)
        {
            valueEvent(true);
            return true;
        }
    }
}
```

Inheritance

Inheritance is supported in solidity. The `is` keyword is used to derive a contract from another contract. In the following example, `valueChecker2` is derived from the `valueChecker` contract. The derived contract has access to all nonprivate members of the parent contract:

```
contract valueChecker
{
 uint8 price=10;
 event valueEvent(bool returnValue);
 function Matcher(uint8 x) returns (bool)
 {
  if (x>=price)
  {
   valueEvent(true);
   return true;
  }
 }
}
contract valueChecker2 is valueChecker
{
```

```
function Matcher2() returns (uint)
{
 return price + 10;
}
}
```

In the preceding example, if `uint8 price = 10` is changed to `uint8 private price = 10`, then it will not be accessible by the `valuechecker2` contract. This is because now the member is declared as private, it is not allowed to be accessed by any other contract.

Libraries

Libraries are deployed only once at a specific address and their code is called via CALLCODE/DELEGATECALL Opcode of the EVM. The key idea behind libraries is code reusability. They are similar to contracts and act as base contracts to the calling contracts. A library can be declared as shown in the following example:

```
library Addition
{
 function Add(uint x,uint y) returns (uint z)
  {
    return x + y;
  }
}
```

This library can then be called in the contract, as shown here. First, it needs to be imported and it can be used anywhere in the code. A simple example is shown as follows:

```
Import "Addition.sol"
function Addtwovalues() returns(uint)
{
 return Addition.Add(100,100);
}
```

There are a few limitations with libraries; for example, they cannot have state variables and cannot inherit or be inherited. Moreover, they cannot receive Ether either; this is in contrast to contracts that can receive Ether.

Functions

Functions in solidity are modules of code that are associated with a contract. Functions are declared with a name, optional parameters, access modifier, optional constant keyword, and optional return type. This is shown in the following example:

```
function orderMatcher(uint x) private constant returns(bool returnvalue)
```

In the preceding example, `function` is the keyword used to declare the function. `orderMatcher` is the function name, `uint x` is an optional parameter, `private` is the **access modifier/specifier** that controls access to the function from external contracts, `constant` is an optional keyword used to specify that this function does not change anything in the contract but is used only to retrieve values from the contract instead, and `returns (bool returnvalue)` is the optional return type of the function.

- **How to define a function**: The syntax of defining a function is shown as follows:

```
function <name of the function>(<parameters>) <visibility
specifier> returns (<return data type> <name of the variable>)
{
 <function body>
}
```

- **Function signature**: Functions in solidity are identified by its signature, which is the first four bytes of the keccak-256 hash of its full signature string. This is also visible in browser solidity, as shown in the following screenshot. **D99c89cb** is the first four bytes of 32 byte keccak-256 hash of the function named **Matcher**.

Function hash as shown in browser solidity

In this example function, **Matcher** has the signature hash of **d99c89cb**. This information is useful in order to build interfaces.

- **Input parameters of a function**: Input parameters of a function are declared in the form of <data type> <parameter name>. This example clarifies the concept where `uint x` and `uint y` are input parameters of the `checkValues` function:

```
contract myContract
{
 function checkValues(uint x, uint y)
 {
 }
}
```

- **Output parameters of a function**: Output parameters of a function are declared in the form of <data type> <parameter name>. This example shows a simple function returning a uint value:

```
contract myContract
{
  Function getValue() returns (uint z)
  {
    z=x+y;
  }
}
```

A function can return multiple values. In the preceding example function, getValue only returns one value, but a function can return up to 14 values of different data types. The names of the unused return parameters can be omitted optionally.

- **Internal function calls**: Functions within the context of the current contract can be called internally in a direct manner. These calls are made to call the functions that exist within the same contract. These calls result in simple JUMP calls at the EVM byte code level.
- **External function calls**: External function calls are made via message calls from a contract to another contract. In this case, all function parameters are copied to the memory. If a call to an internal function is made using the this keyword, it is also considered an external call. The this variable is a pointer that refers to the current contract. It is explicitly convertible to an address and all members for a contract are inherited from the address.
- **Fall back functions**: This is an unnamed function in a contract with no arguments and return data. This function executes every time ether is received. It is required to be implemented within a contract if the contract is intended to receive ether; otherwise, an exception will be thrown and ether will be returned. This function also executes if no other function signatures match in the contract. If the contract is expected to receive ether, then the fall back function should be declared with the payable**modifier**. The payable is required; otherwise, this function will not be able to receive any ether. This function can be called using the address.call() method as, for example, in the following:

```
function ()
{
  throw;
}
```

In this case, if the `fallback` function is called according to the conditions described earlier; it will call throw, which will roll back the state to what it was before making the call. It can also be some other construct than throw; for example, it can log an event that can be used as an alert to feed back the outcome of the call to the calling application.

- **Modifier functions**: These functions are used to change the behavior of a function and can be called before other functions. Usually, they are used to check some conditions or verification before executing the function. _(underscore) is used in the modifier functions that will be replaced with the actual body of the function when the modifier is called. Basically, it symbolizes the function that needs to be *guarded*. This concept is similar to guard functions in other languages.
- **Constructor function**: This is an optional function that has the same name as the contract and is executed once a contract is created. Constructor functions cannot be called later on by users, and there is only one constructor allowed in a contract. This implies that no overloading functionality is available.
- **Function visibility specifiers (access modifiers)**: Functions can be defined with four access specifiers as follows:
  - **External**: These functions are accessible from other contracts and transactions. They cannot be called internally unless the `this` keyword is used.
  - **Public**: By default, functions are public. They can be called either internally or using messages.
  - **Internal**: Internal functions are visible to other derived contracts from the parent contract.
  - **Private**: Private functions are only visible to the same contract they are declared in.
- **Other important keywords/functions throw**: `throw` is used to stop execution. As a result, all state changes are reverted. In this case, no gas is returned to the transaction originator because all the remaining gas is consumed.

Layout of a solidity source code file

Version pragma

In order to address compatibility issues that may arise from future versions of the solidity compiler version, pragma can be used to specify the version of the compatible compiler as, for example, in the following:

```
pragma solidity ^0.5.0
```

This will ensure that the source file does not compile with versions smaller than 0.5.0 and versions starting from 0.6.0.

Import

Import in solidity allows the importing of symbols from the existing solidity files into the current global scope. This is similar to import statements available in JavaScript, as for example, in the following:

```
Import "module-name";
```

Comments

Comments can be added in the solidity source code file in a manner similar to C-language. Multiple line comments are enclosed in /* and */, whereas single line comments start with //.

An example solidity program is as follows, showing the use of pragma, import, and comments:

```
1   pragma solidity ^0.4.0; //specify compiler version
2   /*
3   This is a simple value checker contract
4   that checks the value provided and returns boolean value
5   based on the condition expression evaluation
6   */
7   import "dev.oraclize.it/api.sol";
8   contract valueChecker {
9       uint  price=10;
10          // This is price variable decared and initialized with value 10.
11      event valueEvent(bool returnValue);
12      function  Matcher (uint8 x) returns (bool)
13      {
14          if (x>=price)
15          {
16              valueEvent(true);
17              return true;
18          }
19      }
20  }
```

Sample solidity program as shown in browser solidity

This completes a brief introduction to the solidity language. The language is very rich and under constant improvement. Detailed documentation and coding guidelines are available online.

Introducing Web3

Web3 is a JavaScript library that can be used to communicate with an Ethereum node via RPC communication. Web3 works by exposing methods that have been enabled over RPC. This allows the development of user interfaces that make use of the web3 library in order to interact with the contracts deployed over the blockchain.

In order to expose the methods via `geth`, the following command can be used:

```
$ geth --datadir .ethereum/privatenet/ --networkid 786 --rpc --rpcapi
'web3,eth,debug' --rpcport 8001 --rpccorsdomain 'http://localhost:7777'
```

Note the `--rpcapi` flag that allows the `web3`, `eth` and `debug` methods.

This is a powerful library and can be explored further by attaching a `geth` instance. Later in the section, you will be introduced to the concepts and techniques of making use of web3 via JavaScript/HTML frontends.

The `geth` instance can be attached using the following command:

```
$ geth attach ipc:.ethereum/privatenet/geth.ipc
```

Once the `geth` JavaScript console is running, web3 can be queried, for example:

web3 via geth

A simple contract can be deployed using `geth` and interacted with using web3 via the command-line interface that `geth` provides (console or attach). The following are the steps to achieve that. As an example, the following source code will be used:

```solidity
pragma solidity ^0.4.0;
contract valueChecker {
    uint   price=10;
    event valueEvent(bool returnValue);
    function  Matcher (uint8 x) returns (bool)
    {
        if (x>=price)
        {
            valueEvent(true);
            return true;
        }
    }
}
```

Now open the `geth` console that has been opened previously and follow these steps:

1. Declare a variable named `simplecontractsource` and assign the program code to it:

```
> var simplecontractsource = "pragma solidity ^0.4.0; contract
valueChecker { uint price=10;event valueEvent(bool returnValue);
function Matcher (uint8 x) returns (bool) { if (x>=price)
{valueEvent(true); return true; } } }"
```

This will display the following output:

undefined

Note that the source code is required to be in a single line, which means that there should be no line breaks. This can be achieved in Linux using the following command:

```
$ tr --delete '\n' < valuechecker.sol > valuecheckersingleline.sol
```

In the preceding example, `valuechecker.sol` is the file that has the new line `\n` character, and `valuecheckersingleline.sol` is the output file produced after removing the new line character from the file. The code can then be copied and pasted from the file into the `geth` JavaScript console.

2. Now verify that the solidity compiler is available, and if it's not available, then refer to the section in the chapter where solidity installation is explained:

```
> eth.getCompilers()
["Solidity"]
```

3. Create a variable and assign and compile the code using solidity:

```
> var
simplecontractcompiled=eth.compile.solidity(simplecontractsource)
undefined
```

4. Enter `simplecontractcompiled`; it will display output similar to the following. as `simplecontractcompiled` has been assigned the data from preceding step 3.

```
> simplecontractcompiled
{
  valueChecker: {
    code: "0x6060604052600a6000553461000057b60878061001c6000396000f3606060405260e060020a60003
50463f9d55e218114601c575b6000565b3460005760029600435603d565b604080519115158252519081900360020019
0f35b6000805460ff8316106081576040805160018152905290517f3eb1a229ff7995457774a4bd31ef7b13b6f4491ad1e
bb8961af120b8b4b6239c9181900360200190a16060015b5b91905056",
    info: {
      abiDefinition: [{...}, {...}],
      compilerOptions: "--combined-json bin,abi,userdoc,devdoc --add-std --optimize",
      compilerVersion: "0.4.6",
      developerDoc: {
        methods: {}
      },
      language: "Solidity",
      languageVersion: "0.4.6",
      source: "pragma solidity ^0.4.0; contract valueChecker { uint price=10; event valueEvent
(bool returnValue); function Matcher (uint8 x) returns (bool) { if (x>=price) { valueEvent(tru
e); return true; } } }",
      userDoc: {
        methods: {}
      }
    }
  }
}
```

simplecontractcompiled output

5. Create a variable to interact with the contract:

```
>var simplecontractinteractor=eth.contract
(simplecontractcompiled.valueChecker.info.abiDefinition);
undefined
```

6. Check the **ABI (Application Binary Interface)**:

```
> simplecontractinteractor.abi
[{
    constant: false,
    inputs: [{
        name: "x",
        type: "uint8"
    }],
    name: "Matcher",
    outputs: [{
        name: "",
        type: "bool"
    }],
    payable: false,
    type: "function"
}, {
    anonymous: false,
    inputs: [{
        indexed: false,
        name: "returnValue",
        type: "bool"
    }],
    name: "valueEvent",
    type: "event"
}]
```

7. Check the code of `valueChecker` in the hexadecimal format:

```
> simplecontractcompiled.valueChecker.code
```

This will return the following output. It can be slightly different for you:

```
"0x6060604052600a60005534610000575b60878061001c6000396000f36060604
05260e060020a6000350463f9d55e218114601c575b6000565b3460005760296004
35603d565b6040805191151582525190819003602001905b6000805460ff83161
06081576040805160018152900517f3eb1a229ff7995457774a4bd31ef7b13b6f449
1ad1ebb8961af120b8b4b6239c9181900360200190a15060015b5b91905056"
```

8. Now enter the following piece of code; note that the data field contains the code for `simplecontractcompiled`:

```
>var simplecontractTransaction = simplecontractinteractor.new({
    from: eth.coinbase,
    data: simplecontractcompiled.valueChecker.code,
    gas: 2000000
},
    function(err, contract) {
```

```
    if (err) {
      console.error(err);
    } else {
      console.log(contract);
      console.log(contract.address);
    }
});
```

Assume that it returns an error message:

```
Error: account is locked
Undefined
```

If so, then unlock the account using the following commands.

First, list the accounts using the following command to get the account IDs:

```
> personal.listAccounts
["0x76f11b383dbc3becf8c5d9309219878caae265c3",
"0xcce6450413ac80f9ee8bd97ca02b92c065d77abc"]
```

Enter the following command with the account to be unlocked, as shown here:

```
> personal.unlockAccount
("0x76f11b383dbc3becf8c5d9309219878caae265c3")
Unlock account 0x76f11b383dbc3becf8c5d9309219878caae265c3
```

Enter the password of the account:

```
Passphrase:
true
```

After unlocking the account, enter the preceding code again; say, an error message appears:

```
> Error: The contract code couldn't be stored, please check your
gas amount.
```

In this case, try to increase the gas. If too great a gas value is entered, then an error message will appear, as follows:

```
Error: Exceeds block gas limit
undefined
```

9. Once the account is successfully unlocked, start the miner so that the contract can be mined (it is not necessary to unlock the account to start mining. Account unlocking is necessary to mine the contract and create it on the blockchain):

```
> miner.start()
true
```

When the contract is created correctly, it will show output similar to this:

```
[object Object]
undefined
undefined
> [object Object]
0x94a1107f2585f0ab931c71f2f8f02e9f5ab888c0
```

This shows the address of the newly created contract after the contract has been mined.

10. In order to make interaction with the contract easier, the address of the account can be assigned to a variable:

```
> var simplecontractaddress=
"0x94a1107f2585f0ab931c71f2f8f02e9f5ab888c0"
Undefined
```

11. There are a number of methods that are now exposed, and the contract can be further queried now, for example:

```
> var deployedaddress=eth.getCode(simplecontractaddress);
undefined
> deployedaddress
"0x606060405260e060020a6000350463f9d55e218114601c575b6000565b346000
576029600435603d565b604080519115158252519081900360200190f35b6000805
460ff831610608157604080516001815290517f3eb1a229ff7995457774a4bd31ef
7b13b6f4491ad1ebb8961af120b8b4b6239c9181900360200190a15060015b5b919
05056"
> eth.getBalance(simplecontractaddress)
0
```

12. After this, an object can be created named `simplecontractinstance`, which will be used to call methods:

```
simplecontractinstance = web3.eth.contract(simplecontractcompiled
.valueChecker.info.abiDefinition).at(simplecontractaddress);
```

13. There are various methods that have been exposed now, and a list can be seen as follows:

```
> simplecontractinstance.Matcher.
simplecontractinstance.Matcher.apply
simplecontractinstance.Matcher.constructor
simplecontractinstance.Matcher.request

simplecontractinstance.Matcher.arguments
simplecontractinstance.Matcher.estimateGas
simplecontractinstance.Matcher.sendTransaction

simplecontractinstance.Matcher.bind
simplecontractinstance.Matcher.getData
simplecontractinstance.Matcher.toString

simplecontractinstance.Matcher.call
simplecontractinstance.Matcher.length
simplecontractinstance.Matcher.uint8

simplecontractinstance.Matcher.caller
simplecontractinstance.Matcher.prototype
```

14. The contract can be further queried as shown here. In the following example, the `Matcher` function is called with the arguments. Remember that in the code, there is a condition that checks that, if the value is equal to or greater than 10, then the function returns `true`; otherwise, it returns `false`. This can be seen as follows:

```
> simplecontractinstance.Matcher.call(12)
true
> simplecontractinstance.Matcher.call(9)
false
> simplecontractinstance.Matcher.call(0)
false
> simplecontractinstance.Matcher.call(12)
true
```

POST requests

It is possible to interact with `geth` via jsonrpc over HTTP. For this purpose, curl can be used. Some examples are shown here in order to familiarize you with the POST request and show how to make post requests using curl. Curl is available at `https://curl.haxx.se/`.

Before using the JsonRPC interface over HTTP, `geth` should be started up with appropriate switches, as shown here:

```
--rpcapi web3
```

This switch will enable the `web3` interface over HTTP.

The Linux command curl can be used for the purpose of communicating over HTTP, as shown here in a few examples.

- **Retrieve the list of accounts**: For example, in order to retrieve the list of accounts using the `personal_listAccounts` method, the following command can be used:

```
$ curl --request POST --data
'{"jsonrpc":"2.0","method":"personal_listAccounts","params":
[],"id":4}' localhost:8001
```

This will return the output, a JSON object with the list of accounts:

```
{"jsonrpc":"2.0","id":4,"result":
["0x76f11b383dbc3becf8c5d9309219878caae265c3","0xcce6450413ac80f9
ee8bd97ca02b92c065d77abc"]}
```

In the preceding `curl` command, the `--request` is used to specify the request command, POST is the request, and `--data` is used specify the parameters and values and, finally, `localhost:8001` is where the HTTP endpoint from `geth` is opened.

The HTML and JavaScript frontend

It is desirable to interact with the contracts in a user-friendly manner via a web page. It is possible to interact with the contracts using the web3.js library from HTML/JS/CSS-based web pages. The HTML content can be served using any HTTP web server, whereas web3.js can connect via local **RPC** to the running Ethereum client (`geth`) and provide an interface to the contracts on the blockchain. This architecture can be visualized in the following diagram:

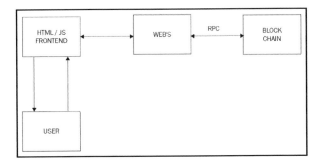

web3.js, frontend, and blockchain interaction architecture

If web3.js is not already installed, use these steps; otherwise, move to the next step.

Installing web3.js

Web3 can be installed via npm by simply issuing the following command:

```
$ npm install web3
```

It can also be directly downloaded from https://github.com/ethereum/web3.js.

web3.min.js, downloaded via npm, can be referred in the HTML files. This can be found under node_modules, for example, /home/drequinox/netstats/node_modules/web3/dist/web3.min.js. The file can optionally be copied into the directory where the main application is and can be used from there. Once the file is successfully referred in HTML or JS, web3 needs to be initialized by providing an HTTP provider. This is usually the link to the localhost HTTP endpoint exposed by the running geth client. This can be achieved using the following code:

```
web3.setProvider(new web3.providers.HttpProvider('http://localhost:8001'));
```

Once the provider is set, further interaction with the contracts and blockchain can be done using the web3 object and its available methods.

The web3 object can be created using the following code:

```
if (typeof web3 !== 'undefined')
{
  web3 = new Web3(web3.currentProvider);
}
else
{
  web3 = new Web3(new
```

```
      Web3.providers.HttpProvider("http://localhost:8001"));
}
```

Example

In the following section, an example will be presented that will make use of web3.js to allow interaction with the contracts via a web page served over a simple HTTP web server. This can be achieved by following these steps:

1. First, create a directory named /simplecontract/app in the home directory.
2. Then, create a file named simplecontractcompiled.js, as shown here:

```
simplecontractcompiled={
valueChecker: {
code:
"0x6060604052600a60005534610000575b60878061001c6000396000f360606040
5260e060020a6000350463f9d55e218114601c575b6000565b34600057602960043
5603d565b604080519115158252519081900360200190f35b6000805460ff83161
0608157604080516001815290517f3eb1a229ff7995457774a4bd31ef7b13b6f449
1ad1ebb8961af120b8b4b6239c9181900360200190a15060015b5b91905056",
info:
{
abiDefinition:
[{
constant: false,
inputs:
[{
name: "x",
type: "uint8"
}],
name: "Matcher",
outputs:
[{
name: "",
type: "bool"
}],
payable: false,
type: "function"
},
{
anonymous: false,
inputs:
[{
indexed: false,
name: "returnValue",
type: "bool"
}],
```

```
name: "valueEvent",
type: "event"
}],
compilerOptions: "--combined-json bin,abi,userdoc,devdoc --add-
std --optimize",compilerVersion: "0.4.6",
developerDoc:
{
methods: {}
},
language: "Solidity",
languageVersion: "0.4.6",
source: "pragma solidity ^0.4.0; contract valueChecker { uint
price=10; event valueEvent(bool returnValue);
function Matcher (uint8 x) returns (bool) { if (x>=price) {
valueEvent(true); return true; } } }",
userDoc: {
methods: {}
}
}
}
}
```

This file contains various elements. The most important is **ABI (Application Binary Interface)**, which can be queried using geth, as shown earlier in step 6 during the contract deployment process.

3. Create a file named simplecontract.js, as shown here:

```
if (typeof web3 !== 'undefined')
{
web3 = new Web3(web3.currentProvider);
}
else
{
 web3 = new Web3(new
 Web3.providers.HttpProvider("http://localhost:8001"));
}
console.log("Coinbase: " + web3.eth.coinbase);
var simplecontractaddress = "0x94a1107f2585f0ab931c71f2f8f02e9
                            f5ab888c0";
 simplecontractinstance =
 web3.eth.contract(simplecontractcompiled.valueChecker
 .info.abiDefinition).at(simplecontractaddress);
 var code = web3.eth.getCode(simplecontractaddress);
 console.log("Contract balance: " +
 web3.eth.getBalance(simplecontractaddress));
 console.log("simple contract code" + code);
 function callMatchertrue()
```

```
{
    var txn = simplecontractinstance.Matcher.call(12);{
};
console.log("return value: " + txn);
}
function callMatcherfalse()
{
var txn = simplecontractinstance.Matcher.call(1);{
};
console.log("return value: " + txn);
}
```

This file is the main JavaScript file that contains the code to create a web3 object. It also provides methods that are used to interact with the contract on the blockchain. An explanation of the code is given here.

Creating a web3 object

```
if (typeof web3 !== 'undefined')
{
  web3 = new Web3(web3.currentProvider);
}
 else
{
  web3 = new Web3(new Web3.providers.HttpProvider("http://localhost:
        8001"));
}
```

This code first checks whether there is already an available provider; if yes, then it will set the provider to the current provider. Otherwise, it sets the web3 provider to `localhost:8001`; this is where the local instance of `geth` is running.

Checking availability by calling any web3 method

```
console.log("Coinbase: " + web3.eth.coinbase);
```

This line of code simply uses `console.log` to print the coinbase by calling the `web3.eth.coinbase` method. Once this call is successful, it means that the web3 object has been created correctly and `HttpProvider` is available. Any other call can be used to verify the availability, but as a simple example, `web3.eth.coinbase` has been used in the preceding example.

Assigning contract address to a variable

```
var simplecontractaddress = "0x94a1107f2585f0ab931c71f2f8f02e9f5ab888c0
        ";
```

This statement will assign the value of the address of the contract deployed on the blockchain. After successful execution of the statement variable, `simplecontractaddress` will contain the address of the contract. This is the address of the contract created in step 9 in the preceding example when the contract is deployed. Simply use that address in the code here.

Creating the main contract object

```
simplecontractinstance = web3.eth.contract(simplecontractcompiled
                                   .valueChecker.info.abiDefinition)
                         .at(simplecontractaddress);
```

This piece of code will create an object that will be used later in the code to interact with the contract on the blockchain. `simplecontractinstance` will expose functions of the contract. `web3.eth.contract` takes the ABI array as an argument. This can be passed using `simplecontractcompiled.valueChecker.info.abiDefinition`. Finally, `.at` takes the address of the contract as an argument.

Getting the code of the contract address (optional)

This is shown as an example here and is entirely optional:

```
var code = web3.eth.getCode(simplecontractaddress);
console.log("simple contract code" + code);
```

The preceding statements are used to query the code of the contract. This is a simple `web3.eth.getCode` call that takes the address of the contract on the blockchain as an argument. Finally, `console.log` is used to print the code of the contract by printing the code variable.

Contract balance

console.log("Contract balance:" +web3.eth.getBalance(simplecontractaddress));The preceding code will call `web3.eth.getBalance` and take the contract address as an argument and will print the balance of the contract, which is 0 at the moment.

Contract functions

Once the `web3` object is correctly created and `simplecontractinstance` is created, calls to the contract functions can be made easily as shown in the following example:

```
function callMatchertrue()
{
 var txn = simplecontractinstance.Matcher.call(12);{
};
```

```
console.log("return value: " + txn);
}

function callMatcherfalse()
{
var txn = simplecontractinstance.Matcher.call(1);{
};
console.log("return value: " + txn);
}
```

Calls can be made using `simplecontractinstance.Matcher.call` and then by passing the value for the argument. Recall the function matcher in solidity code:

```
function  Matcher (uint8 x) returns (bool)
```

It takes one argument x of type `uint8` and returns a Boolean value, either true or false.

Accordingly, the call is made to the contract, as shown here:

```
var txn = simplecontractinstance.Matcher.call(12);
```

In the preceding example, `console.log` is used to print the value returned by the function call. Once the result of the call is available in the `txn` variable, it can be used anywhere throughout the program, for example, as a parameter for another JavaScript function.

Finally, the HTML file named `index.html` is created with the following code:

```
<html>
<head>
    <title>SimpleContract Interactor</title>
    <script src="./web3.min.js"></script>
    <script src="./simplecontractcompiled.js"></script>
    <script src="./simplecontract.js"></script>
</head>
<body>
    <button onclick="callMatchertrue()">callTrue</button>
    <button onclick="callMatcherfalse()">callFalse</button>
</body>
</html>
```

It is recommended that an appropriate web server be running in order to serve the HTML content (`index.html` as an example). Alternatively, the file can browsed from the filesystem but that can cause some issues with larger projects; as good practice, always use a web server. A quick web server in Python can be started using the following command. This server will serve the HTML content from the same directory that it has been run from. Python is not necessary; it can even be an Apache server or any other web container.

```
imran@drequinox-OP7010:~/simplecontract/app$ python -m SimpleHTTPServer 7777
Serving HTTP on 0.0.0.0 port 7777 ...
```

Simple web server in Python

Now any browser can be used to view the web page served over TCP port 7777. This is shown in the following example. It should be noted that the output shown here is in the browser's console window. The browser's console must be enabled in order to see the output.

Interaction with the contract

As the values are hardcoded in the code for simplicity, two buttons have been created in index.html. Both of these buttons call functions with hardcoded values. This is just to demonstrate that parameters are being passed to the contract via web3 and values are being returned accordingly.

There are two functions being called behind the preceding buttons. The `callMatchertrue()` method has a hardcoded value of 12, which is sent to the contract using this:

```
simplecontractinstance.Matcher.call(12)
```

The return value is printed in the console using the following code, which first invokes the `Matcher` function and then assigns the value to the `txn` variable to be printed later in the console:

```
simplecontractinstance.Matcher.call(1)
function callMatchertrue()
{
  var txn = simplecontractinstance.Matcher.call(12);{
};
console.log("return value: " + txn);
}
```

Similarly, the `callMatcherfalse()` function works by passing a hardcoded value of 1 to the contract using this:

```
simplecontractinstance.Matcher.call(1)
```

The return value is printed accordingly:

```
console.log("return value: " + txn);
function callMatcherfalse()
{
 var txn = simplecontractinstance.Matcher.call(1);{
};
console.log("return value: " + txn);
}
```

This example demonstrates how the web3 library can be used to interact with the contracts on the blockchain.

Development frameworks

There are various development frameworks now available for Ethereum. As seen in the examples discussed earlier, it can be quite time consuming to deploy the contract via the usual manual means. This is where truffle and similar frameworks such as embark can be used to make the process simpler and quicker. The most widely used framework is called truffle. In the next section, you will be introduced to the truffle framework.

Truffle

Truffle is a development environment that makes it easier and simpler to test and deploy Ethereum contracts. Truffle provides contract compilation and linking along with an automated testing framework using Mocha and Chai. It also makes it easier to deploy the contracts to any PrivateNet, public, or Test Net Ethereum blockchain. Also, asset pipeline is provided, which makes it easier for all JavaScript files to be processed, making them ready for use by a browser.

Installation

Before installation, it is assumed that the node is available, which can be queried as shown here. If the node is not available, then the installation of the node is required first in order to install truffle:

```
drequinox@drequinox-OP7010:~/testdapp$ nodejs --version
```

```
v7.2.1
drequinox@drequinox-OP7010:~/testdapp$ node --version
v7.2.1
```

The installation of truffle is very simple and can be done using the following command via `npm`:

```
$ sudo npm install -g truffle
```

This will take a while; once it is installed, `truffle` can be used to display help and make sure that it is installed correctly.

```
drequinox@drequinox-OP7010:~/testdapp$ truffle
Truffle v2.1.1 - a development framework for Ethereum

Usage: truffle [command] [options]

Commands:
  build            => Build development version of app
  compile          => Compile contracts
  console          => Run a console with deployed contracts instantiated and available (REPL)
  create:contract  => Create a basic contract
  create:migration => Create a new migration marked with the current timestamp
  create:test      => Create a basic test
  exec             => Execute a JS file within truffle environment
  init             => Initialize new Ethereum project, including example contracts and tests
  list             => List all available tasks
  migrate          => Run migrations
  networks         => Show addresses for deployed contracts on each network
  serve            => Serve app on localhost and rebuild changes as needed
  test             => Run tests
  version          => Show version number and exit
  watch            => Watch filesystem for changes and rebuild the project automatically
```

Truffle help

Alternatively, the repository is available at `https://github.com/ConsenSys/truffle`, which can be cloned locally to install truffle. Git can be used to clone the repository using the following command:

```
https://github.com/ConsenSys/truffle.git
```

Initializing truffle

Truffle can be initialized by running the following command. First, create a directory for the project, for example:

```
mkdir testdapp
```

Then, change to `testdapp` and run the following command:

```
~/testdapp$ truffle init
```

Once the command is successful, it will create the directory structure shown here. This can be viewed using the `tree` command in Linux:

```
drequinox@drequinox-OP7010:~/testdapp$ tree
```

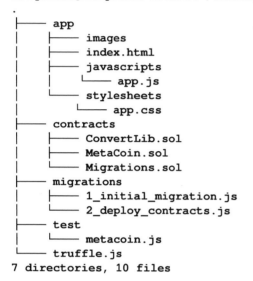

```
├──── app
│     ├──── images
│     ├──── index.html
│     ├──── javascripts
│     │     └──── app.js
│     └──── stylesheets
│           └──── app.css
├──── contracts
│     ├──── ConvertLib.sol
│     ├──── MetaCoin.sol
│     └──── Migrations.sol
├──── migrations
│     ├──── 1_initial_migration.js
│     └──── 2_deploy_contracts.js
├──── test
│     └──── metacoin.js
└──── truffle.js
7 directories, 10 files
```

This command creates four main directories, named `app`, `contracts`, `migrations`, and `test`. As seen in the preceding example, a total of 7 directories and 10 files have been created. In the following section, an explanation of all these files and directories will be presented.

- App: This directory contains all application files including HTML files, images, style sheets and JavaScript files. This folder contains further subdirectories, `images`, `javascripts`, and `stylesheets` that contain relevant application files.
- Contracts: This directory contains solidity contract source code files. This is where truffle will look for solidity contract files during migration.
- Migration: This directory has all the deployment scripts.
- Test: As the name suggests, this directory contains relevant test files for applications and contracts.

Finally, truffle configuration is stored in the `truffle.js` file, which is created in the root folder of the project from where `truffle init` was run. When `truffle init` is run, it will create a sample project named MetaCoin. As an example, you will first be introduced to how to use various commands in truffle in order to test and deploy MetaCoin. Later, further examples will be shown on how to use truffle for custom projects.

Compilation using truffle

Both libraries and contracts can be compiled using truffle. It is expected that the name of the contract file will be the same as the contract name within the file. For example, from the sample MetaCoin project created earlier, the file named `MetaCoin.sol` under the `contracts` directory has the same name as the MetaCoin contract in the file. This applies to library files too and it is case-sensitive.

- Filename:

```
MetaCoin.sol
```

- Contract name within the file:

```
contract MetaCoin {
        mapping (address => uint) balances;
```

Compilation can be run as shown here:

```
~/testdapp$ truffle compile
Compiling ConvertLib.sol...
Compiling MetaCoin.sol...
Compiling Migrations.sol...
Writing artifacts to ./build/contracts
~/testdapp$
```

Once the compilation is finished successfully, all objects will be written in to the `build` directory. The output directory looks like what is shown here:

```
~/testdapp$ tree build/
build/
└── contracts
    ├── ConvertLib.sol.js
    ├── MetaCoin.sol.js
    └── Migrations.sol.js
1 directory, 3 files
```

As shown in the preceding example, the `build` directory is created automatically with the `contracts` subdirectory, which contains three JavaScript files.

Migration

This is the process by which truffle deploys contracts to the blockchain. This process relies on the files available under the `migrations` directory.

The process works as shown here:

```
~/testdapp$ cd migrations/
~/testdapp/migrations$ ls -ltr
-rw-rw-r-- 1 drequinox drequinox 124 Dec 12 12:57 2_deploy_contracts.js
-rw-rw-r-- 1 drequinox drequinox  72 Dec 12 12:57 1_initial_migration.js
~/testdapp/migrations$ cat 2_deploy_contracts.js
module.exports = function(deployer)
{
 deployer.deploy(ConvertLib);
 deployer.autolink();
 deployer.deploy(MetaCoin);
};
drequinox@drequinox-OP7010:~/testdapp/migrations$ cat
1_initial_migration.js
module.exports = function(deployer)
{
 deployer.deploy(Migrations);
};
```

As shown in the preceding output, there are two files that contain the code that specifies which contracts are required to be deployed.

The filenames follow a convention where they are required to be prefixed by a number. This prefix is required in order to keep a record of all migrations. The suffix in the filename can be any descriptive name. First, it is important to change the truffle.js file in order to point to the appropriate network. The truffle.js file contains valuable information about the build and rpc for the application. In this case, geth is already running and it can simply be pointed to use the available client:

```
module.exports = {
  build: {
    "index.html": "index.html",
    "app.js": [
      "javascripts/app.js"
    ],
    "app.css": [
      "stylesheets/app.css"
    ],
    "images/": "images/"
  },
  rpc: {
    host: "localhost",
    port: 8001
  }
};
```

In the preceding file, `rpc` needs to be changed to point to the appropriate network. Once `rpc` is changed (in the example, `geth` is running on port 8001 as opposed to usual 8545), truffle migration can be run using the following command. It is also important that mining be running on the Ethereum node to which `rpc` has been pointed; otherwise, the contract will not be mined.

The contract can be deployed using the command shown here:

```
~/testdapp$ truffle migrate
```

It might show an error message, as shown here. If this occurs, then it means that the account that truffle is using to deploy a contract to the blockchain is locked and is required to be unlocked:

```
Running migration: 1_initial_migration.js
  Deploying Migrations...
Error encountered, bailing. Network state unknown. Review successful
transactions manually.
Error: account is locked
    at Object.InvalidResponse
(/usr/lib/node_modules/truffle/node_modules/ether-
pudding/node_modules/web3/lib/web3/errors.js:35:16)
    at /usr/lib/node_modules/truffle/node_modules/ether-
pudding/node_modules/web3/lib/web3/requestmanager.js:86:36
    at exports.XMLHttpRequest.request.onreadystatechange
(/usr/lib/node_modules/truffle/node_modules/web3/lib/web3/httpprovider.js:1
14:13)
    at exports.XMLHttpRequest.dispatchEvent
(/usr/lib/node_modules/truffle/node_modules/xmlhttprequest/lib/XMLHttpReque
st.js:591:25)
    at setState
(/usr/lib/node_modules/truffle/node_modules/xmlhttprequest/lib/XMLHttpReque
st.js:610:14)
    at IncomingMessage.<anonymous>
(/usr/lib/node_modules/truffle/node_modules/xmlhttprequest/lib/XMLHttpReque
st.js:447:13)
    at emitNone (events.js:91:20)
    at IncomingMessage.emit (events.js:185:7)
    at endReadableNT (_stream_readable.js:974:12)
    at _combinedTickCallback (internal/process/next_tick.js:74:11)
    at process._tickDomainCallback (internal/process/next_tick.js:122:9)
```

The account can be unlocked by using the following commands in the `geth` JavaScript console.

First, list the accounts to see all accounts and then select the account that needs to be unlocked. Truffle assumes the coinbase account by default. Select the appropriate account, as follows:

```
> personal.listAccounts
["0x76f11b383dbc3becf8c5d9309219878caae265c3",
"0xcce6450413ac80f9ee8bd97ca02b92c065d77abc"]
```

The account can be unlocked using following command:

```
> personal.unlockAccount("0x76f11b383dbc3becf8c5d9309219878caae265c3")
Unlock account 0x76f11b383dbc3becf8c5d9309219878caae265c3
Passphrase:
true
```

Once the account is unlocked, migration can be run again using the following command:

```
~/testdapp$ truffle migrate
```

It will show output similar to that shown here. It should be noted that mining must be started for the migration to finish. Migration will perform various steps by finding the files available in the `migrations` directory. As shown in the example, `1_initial_migration.js` and `2_deploy_contracts.js` have been used to provide migration steps and requirements to truffle:

```
Running migration: 1_initial_migration.js
  Deploying Migrations...
  Migrations: 0xf444cce0cee00cab4d04bcfc0005626b8b02add8
Saving successful migration to network...
Saving artifacts...
Running migration: 2_deploy_contracts.js
  Deploying ConvertLib...
  ConvertLib: 0x2ba8a4a75a6b845bf482923cff29ecc98cd68d90
  Linking ConvertLib to MetaCoin
  Deploying MetaCoin...
  MetaCoin: 0x0be9c5de978fa927b93a5c4faab31312cea5704a
Saving successful migration to network...
Saving artifacts...
~/testdapp$
```

Once the command is completed successfully, it will return a command prompt displaying the message `saving artefacts`.

Deployment can be verified using a few commands shown here via the `geth` JavaScript console:

```
> eth.getBalance("0x0be9c5de978fa927b93a5c4faab31312cea5704a")
0
> eth.getCode("0x0be9c5de978fa927b93a5c4faab31312cea5704a")
"0x606060405260e060020a60003504637bd703e8811461003457806390b98a111461005657
8063f8b2cb4f1461007d575b610000565b3461000057610044600435610b98a111461005657
1825251908190036020019f35b3461000057610069600435602435610119565b6040805191
1515825251908190036020019f35b346100005761004460043561b1565b6040805191825
251908190036020019f35b6000732ba8a4a75a6b845bf482923cff29ecc98cd68d906396e4
ee3d6100c4846101b1565b6002600060405160200152604051836e060020a0281526004018
0838152602001828152602001925050506020604051803038186803b156100005760325a03
f4156100005750506040515191505b919050565b600160a060020a033316600090815260
08190526040812054829010156101425750600006101ab565b600160a060020a033381166000
81815260208181526040808320808548890039055938716808352918490208054870190558
1868152935191937fddf252ad1be2c89b69c2b068fc378daa952ba7f163c4a11628f55a4df5
23b3ef929081900390910190a35060015b92915050565b600160a060020a038116600090815
26020819052604090205455b91905056"
```

Note that the address of the newly deployed contract has been taken from the truffle migrate command output shown earlier. (MetaCoin: `0x0be9c5de978fa927b93a5c4faab31312cea5704a`)

- **Interaction with the contract**: Truffle also provides a console (command-line interface) that allows interaction with the contracts. All deployed contracts are already instantiated and ready to use in the console. This is an REPL-based interface that means Read, Evaluate, and Print Loop. Similarly, in the geth client (via attach or console), REPL is used via exposing **JSRE (JavaScript runtime environment)**. The console can be accessed by issuing the following command:

  ```
  ~/testdapp$ truffle console
  ```

  This will open a command-line interface, as shown here:

Truffle console

Once the console is available, various methods can be run in order to query the contract. A list of methods can be displayed by typing the following command and tab-completing:

```
drequinox@drequinox-OP7010:~/testdapp$ truffle console
truffle(default)> MetaCoin.
MetaCoin.__defineGetter__      MetaCoin.__defineSetter__      MetaCoin.__lookupGetter__      MetaCoin.__lookupSetter__
MetaCoin.__proto__             MetaCoin.constructor           MetaCoin.hasOwnProperty        MetaCoin.isPrototypeOf
MetaCoin.propertyIsEnumerable  MetaCoin.toLocaleString        MetaCoin.toString              MetaCoin.valueOf

MetaCoin.apply                 MetaCoin.arguments             MetaCoin.bind                  MetaCoin.call
MetaCoin.caller                MetaCoin.length                MetaCoin.name

MetaCoin.abi                   MetaCoin.address              MetaCoin.all_networks          MetaCoin.at
MetaCoin.binary                MetaCoin.checkNetwork         MetaCoin.class_defaults        MetaCoin.contract_name
MetaCoin.currentProvider       MetaCoin.defaults            MetaCoin.deployed              MetaCoin.events
MetaCoin.extend                MetaCoin.generated_with       MetaCoin.link                  MetaCoin.links
MetaCoin.network_id            MetaCoin.networks             MetaCoin.new                   MetaCoin.next_gen
MetaCoin.prototype             MetaCoin.setNetwork           MetaCoin.setProvider           MetaCoin.unlinked_binary
MetaCoin.updated_at            MetaCoin.web3
```

Exposed methods

Other methods can also be called in order to interact with the contract; for example, in order to retrieve the address of the contract, the following method can be called in the truffle console:

```
truffle(default)> MetaCoin.deployed().address
'0x0be9c5de978fa927b93a5c4faab31312cea5704a'
truffle(default)>
```

- **Query the balance of the contract**:

```
truffle(default)>
MetaCoin.deployed().getBalance.call(web3.eth.accounts[0])
{ [String: '8750'] s: 1, e: 3, c: [ 8750 ] }
```

The output returns a string with the value 8750.

- **Transfer the balance**:

```
truffle(default)>
MetaCoin.deployed().sendCoin("0xcce6450413ac80f9ee8bd97ca02b92c
065d77abc",50, {from:"0x76f11b383dbc3becf8c5d9309219878caae265c
3"})
'0xb8969149fcfb54ec9beac31af1fc86c386f9aa42cb13d2eb9bf946993198
6e0f'
```

This will return the hash of the transaction and, when successful, it will result in increasing the balance of the target by 50. The target account is the argument passed in the sendCoin function.

- **Balance of the target account**: It can be retrieved using the following command:

```
truffle(default)>
MetaCoin.deployed().getBalance.call(web3.eth.accounts[1])
{ [String: '1250'] s: 1, e: 3, c: [ 1250 ] }
truffle(default)>
```

In order to exit from the truffle console, the `.exit` command is used.

Testing using truffle

Testing is a powerful feature of truffle and can be invoked by running the following command:

```
~/testdapp$ truffle test
```

This will read the tests from `test` directory and perform tests accordingly. The testing framework used by truffle is called Mocha, and it uses an assertion framework named Chai.

A sample test run is shown as follows. This test only runs two tests. In the original file, there are three tests, but for simplicity, only two are used here. Also, the test may fail on most of the systems; therefore, it has been removed from the file for simplicity. A failed test case will be discussed later. Also, it should be noted that mining should be running for the tests to run.

Truffle test output showing two successful tests

These two tests are based on the file produced by truffle init. In the following file, only one test is shown for simplification, when truffle creates three tests for the default MetaCoin project. Tests can be removed from the file by editing the `metacoin.js` file in a text editor:

```
contract('MetaCoin', function(accounts)
{
  it("should put 10000 MetaCoin in the first account",
  function()
  {
   var meta = MetaCoin.deployed();
   return meta.getBalance.call(accounts[0]).then(function(balance)
   {
    assert.equal(balance.valueOf(), 10000, "10000 wasn't in the first
    account");
   });
  });
});
```

All test files are required to be present in the `tests` directory under the `project` directory. Tests are specified within `it` blocks.

```
drequinox@drequinox-OP7010:~/testdapp$ truffle test


  Contract: MetaCoin
    ✓ should put 10000 MetaCoin in the first account



  1 passing (1m)

drequinox@drequinox-OP7010:~/testdapp$
```

Test based on the file shown earlier with only one test

In the preceding test case, when the contract is, it should have a balance of 10000 in it. This test basically tests whether the balance of 10000 is available after deploying the contract or not. In order to explain the concept, the error can be simulated, for example, if the `metacoin.js` file is by changing the assertion:

```
assert.equal(balance.valueOf(), 10000, "10000 wasn't in the first
account");
```

to

```
assert.equal(balance.valueOf(), 1000, "10000 wasn't in the first account");
```

This will induce an artificial assertion failure because in assert, the expected amount is 1000, whereas, when the contract is deployed, it has a balance of 10,000. When the test is run, the following output is shown indicating that the tests have failed. This change is made for demonstration purposes only in order to allow you to see that tests can fail and, if so, what type of outputs are produced.

```
drequinox@drequinox-OP7010:~/testdapp$ truffle test


  Contract: MetaCoin
    1) should put 10000 MetaCoin in the first account
    > No events were emitted


  0 passing (49s)
  1 failing

  1) Contract: MetaCoin should put 10000 MetaCoin in the first account:
     AssertionError: 10000 wasn't in the first account: expected '10000' to equal 1000
      at test/metacoin.js:6:14
      at process._tickDomainCallback (internal/process/next_tick.js:129:7)
```

Truffle test failing output

The `truffle test` command takes few optional parameters, especially `--verbose-rpc`, which can be very helpful in understanding the RPC communication between the Ethereum client and truffle.

At times during test execution, an error message like the one shown here can appear:

```
Error: timeout of 120000ms exceeded. Ensure the done() callback is being
called in this test.
```

This error occurs when either the Ethereum node is not mining, or deploying the contracts is taking longer than 2 minutes. This is why timeout occurs; therefore, it is important that tests are run through a mining node if on PrivateNet. Also on Ropsten, it can sometimes take longer than 2 minutes. Alternatively, `ethereumjs-testrpc` can be used, which is commonly used with truffle and provides fast simulated Ethereum RPC client.

Build

Build in truffle is used to bootstrap the frontend for browsers. It works by importing compiled contracts and relevant deployed contract and Ethereum client configurations. All objects, after building, are saved in the `./build` directory. All build configurations are present in the `truffle.js` file, which guides truffle on what to build. By default, this file comes only with `build:` and `rpc:` configurations.

Build can be started by issuing the following command:

```
~/testdapp$ truffle build
```

Once the build is completed, the `build` directory will be created if doesn't exist already and a tree structure similar to the one shown here will be created. This is created based on the `truffle.js` file:

```
build/
├────── app.css
├────── app.js
├────── contracts
│        ├────── ConvertLib.sol.js
│        ├────── MetaCoin.sol.js
│        └────── Migrations.sol.js
├────── images
└────── index.html
```

Once the build is completed successfully, all frontend files will be ready. This can then be viewed in the browser using truffle's `serve` command. The `serve` command creates a web server in order to present the HTML content. The command can be run as shown here.

Note that the command is run with the `-p` flag to specify port TCP 7777. This is required as `geth`, in the example provided previously, is running with the `--rpccorsdomain` `'http://localhost:7777'` option. This means that only the content served over TCP 7777 is allowed. By default, `serve` runs on port 8080, which might be in use by some other process on the system as TCP 8080 is a very common port to be used for web applications.

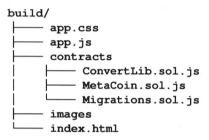

```
drequinox@drequinox-OP7010:~/testdapp$ truffle serve -p 7777
Serving app on port 7777...
Rebuilding...
Completed without errors on Mon Dec 12 2016 22:18:50 GMT+0000 (GMT)
```

Truffle serve

Once the truffle server is up and running on an appropriate port, the content can be browsed using a browser and pointing to URL `http://localhost:7777`.

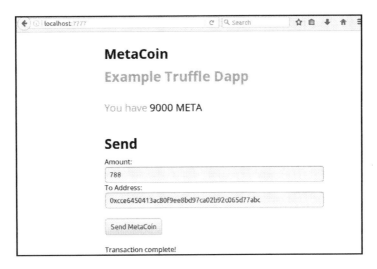

Example MetaCoin frontend

Another example

An example is shown here, where a simple contract in solidity is created with migrations and tests. The contract is very simple and performs only addition:

1. Create a directory named `simpleTest`:

   ```
   $ mkdir simpleTest
   ```

2. Initialize truffle:

   ```
   $ truffle init
   ```

3. Remove files from directories. This is required in order to remove the default MetaCoin project files create by truffle.

   ```
   rm -r test/* contracts/* migrations/*
   ```

4. Place the two files `Addition.sol` and `Migrations.sol` in the contracts directory:

```
Addition.sol:

pragma solidity ^0.4.2;
contract Addition
{
 uint8 x;
```

```
    function addx(uint8 y, uint8 z )
    {
     x = y + z;
    }
function retrievex() constant returns (uint8)
{
 return x;
}
}
Migrations.sol:
pragma solidity ^0.4.2;
contract Migrations
{
  address public owner;
  uint public last_completed_migration;
  modifier restricted()
  {
     if (msg.sender == owner) _;
  }
  function Migrations()
  {
   owner = msg.sender;
  }
  function setCompleted(uint completed) restricted
  {
     last_completed_migration = completed;
  }
  function upgrade(address new_address) restricted
  {
   Migrations upgraded = Migrations(new_address);
   upgraded.setCompleted(last_completed_migration);
  }
 }
```

5. Place the `Addition.js` file in the `test` directory:

```
contract('Addition', function(accounts)
{
it(" 100 + 100 = 200 ", function()
{
var AddContract = Addition.deployed();
AddContract.addx(100, 100,{from:accounts[0],gas:1000000})
.then(function(a)
{
return AddContract.retrievex.call().then(function(Result)
{
assert.equal(Result, 200, "100 + 100 = 200 is expected");
});
```

```
});
});
});
```

6. In the `migrations` folder, place two files:

   `1_initial_migration.js`:

   ```
   module.exports = function(deployer)
   {
    deployer.deploy(Migrations);
   };
   ```

   `2_deploy_contracts.js`:

   ```
   module.exports = function(deployer)
   {
    deployer.deploy(Addition);
    deployer.autolink();
   };
   ```

7. Once all the files are in place, compile all contracts using truffle compile. Optionally, use the `--compile-all` flag in order to recompile the contracts even if they have already been compiled. This is required only if the contracts need to be recompiled:

   ```
   ~/simpleTest$ truffle compile
   Compiling Addition.sol...
   Compiling Migrations.sol...
   Writing artifacts to ./build/contracts
   ```

8. Migrate to the Ethereum test network using truffle migrate. This will deploy the contract on the network. Note that, at this point, `truffle.js` will need to be updated again with port 8001 to point to the Private Net:

   ```
   ~/simpleTest$ truffle migrate
   Running migration: 2_deploy_contracts.js
     Deploying Addition...
     Addition: 0x73934227a1ce7fc44152b7451626759a00b0275c
   Saving successful migration to network...
   Saving artifacts...
   ```

   Finally, tests can be performed using the following command. These tests are based on the `Addition.js` file shown earlier:

   ```
   ~/simpleTest$ truffle test
   ```

This command will first deploy the contract on the Ethereum network (PrivateNet in this example).

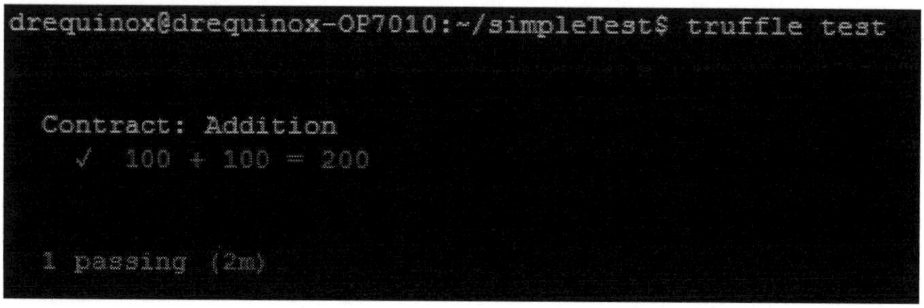

```
drequinox@drequinox-OP7010:~/simpleTest$ truffle test


  Contract: Addition
    ✓  100 + 100 = 200



  1 passing (2m)
```

Sample output showing successful truffle test

9. In order to interact with the contract, the following methods can be used. As the Addition contract is already instantiated and available in the truffle console, it becomes quite easy to interact with the contract using various methods.

For example, in order to retrieve the address of the deployed contract, the following method can be called:

```
truffle(default)> Addition.address
'0x73934227a1ce7fc44152b7451626759a00b0275c'
```

To call the functions from within the contract, the deployed method is used with contract functions. An example is shown here, in which the addx function is called and two parameters are passed:

```
truffle(default)> Addition.deployed().addx(100,100)
    '0xae6f51782c1bcf04ec34dd54ee31da626dc138993ea813bc6c3c1fe0790b130e'
truffle(default)>
'0xb9f8633fbd626466ee2c2f24952a5fca3134f4e7d08f39a4d26ac2689e22b653'
```

Call the retrievex function from the contract:

```
truffle(default)> Addition.deployed().retrievex()
{ [String: '200'] s: 1, e: 2, c: [ 200 ] }
```

Example project: Proof of Idea

The idea behind this program is to provide a service to notarize a document. This can then be used as proof that, at a certain time in the past, the claimant has had access to a certain piece of information. This can be very useful for patent documents. For example, if someone has come up with an idea, he or she can then create a hash of that document and save it on the blockchain. Due to the immutable nature of blockchain, it can serve as permanent proof that a certain idea (documents) existed at a certain time. There are many ways in which this can be achieved, but the key idea is the same and it works on the principle that hash functions provide a digest of the text or document and are unique.

This can be achieved in several ways; the key idea is to create a hash of the document or text string and save it on the blockchain. Once the text is hashed and saved, further requests to save that same text can be disallowed by comparing the hash of the document with the already stored hash.

For this example, browser solidity, truffle, and TestNet (already running Network ID 786, created earlier) will be used. First, the code for the contract will be written. This can be done using any appropriate text editor or integrated development environment. Browser solidity can also be used as that too provides a simulated environment for the test. This example will provide you with the opportunity to learn how a contract project can be developed from an idea into a solidity contract source code and finally to deployment.

Let's look at the code line by line:

```
pragma solidity ^0.4.0;
```

This statement ensures that the minimum compiler version is 0.4.0 and the maximum version cannot be greater than 0.4.9. This ensures compatibility between programs:

```
contract PatentIdea {
```

This statement is the start of the contract with name `PatentIdea`:

```
mapping (bytes32 => bool) private hashes;
```

Next, a mapping is defined, which maps byte32 to Boolean, and this is basically a `hashmap` (dictionary) of bytes32 mapping to the Boolean value:

```
bool alreadyStored;
```

This is a variable declared with the `alreadyStored` name, which is a Boolean type and can have a true or false value. This variable is used to hold the return value from the `SaveIdeaHash` function:

```
event ideahashed(bool);
```

An event is declared as well, which will be used to capture the failure or success of the hashing function (SaveIdeaHash). When the event is triggered, it will return a true or false Boolean value.

A function named saveHash is declared, which takes the hash variable of type bytes32 as parameters and saves it in the hash map. This will result in a change of the state of the contract. Note that the function accessibility is changed to private as it is only required internally in the contract and does not need to be exposed publicly:

```
function saveHash(bytes32 hash) private
{
hashes[hash] = true;
}
```

Another function, saveIdeaHash, is declared, and it takes the variable idea of type string and returns a Boolean (true or false) depending on the outcome of the function:

```
function SaveIdeaHash(string idea) returns (bool)
{
var hashedIdea = HashtheIdea(idea);
if (alreadyHashed(HashtheIdea(idea)))
{
 alreadyStored=true;
 ideahashed(false);
 return alreadyStored;
}
saveHash(hashedIdea);
ideahashed(true);
}
```

This function has a variable declared hashedIdea, which is assigned a value after calling the HashtheIdea function described later. Note that this function can also return a value if saved, but it is not shown here for simplicity.

The next function is the alreadyHashed function, which is declared to take the variable named hash of type bytes32 and returns a Boolean (either true or false) after checking the hash in the hash map. This is again declared as a constant and accessibility is set to private:

```
function alreadyHashed(bytes32 hash) constant private returns(bool)
{
 return hashes[hash];
}
}
```

The next function is `isAlreadyHashed`, which checks whether the idea is already hashed. This takes the input parameter idea of type string, also declared as a constant, which means that it cannot change the state of the contract and returns either true or false based on the outcome of the execution of the function named `alreadyHashed`. This function then calls the `alreadyHashed` function described earlier to check from the hashes map whether the hash is already stored there. This would mean that the same string (`idea`) has already been hashed and stored (patented):

```
function isAlreadyHashed(string idea) constant  returns (bool)
{
 var hashedIdea = HashtheIdea(idea);
 return alreadyHashed(hashedIdea);
}
```

Finally, the `HashtheIdea` function is shown here, which takes the `idea` variable of type string and is of `constant` type, which means that it cannot change the state of the contract. It is also declared as `private` as there is no need to expose this function publicly because it is used only internally in the contract. This function returns the bytes32 type value:

```
function HashtheIdea(string idea) constant private returns (bytes32) {
 return sha3(idea);
}
```

This function calls solidity's built-in function `sha3` and passes a string to it in a variable idea. This function returns the sha3 hash of the string. The `sha3` function is an alias for the `keccak256()` function available in solidity, which computes the Keccak-256 hash of the string passed to it. Note that this is not NIST standard SHA-3; instead, it is Keccak-256, which is the original proposal to NIST for the SHA-3 standard competition. It was later modified slightly and standardized as the SHA-3 standard by NIST. The actual SHA-3 standard hash function will return a different hash compared to Keccak-256 (Ethereum's `sha3` function).

The complete contract source code is shown as follows:

```
pragma solidity ^0.4.0;
contract PatentIdea
{
  mapping (bytes32 => bool) private hashes;
  bool alreadyStored;
  event ideahashed(bool);
  function saveHash(bytes32 hash) private
  {
    hashes[hash] = true;
  }
  function SaveIdeaHash(string idea) returns (bool)
```

```
{
  var hashedIdea = HashtheIdea(idea);
  if (alreadyHashed(HashtheIdea(idea)))
  {
      alreadyStored=true;
      ideahashed(false);
      return alreadyStored;
  }
      saveHash(hashedIdea);
      ideahashed(true);
  }
function alreadyHashed(bytes32 hash) constant private returns(bool)
{
  return hashes[hash];
}
function isAlreadyHashed(string idea) constant  returns (bool)
{
  var hashedIdea = HashtheIdea(idea);
  return alreadyHashed(hashedIdea);
}
  function HashtheIdea(string idea) constant private returns (bytes32)
  {
  return sha3(idea);
  }
}
```

This source code can be simulated in browser solidity in order to verify that it is working correctly. Some examples are shown here.

Once the contract source code is typed and syntax verification is complete, on the right-hand side panel, a screen similar to the following one will be shown.

This code can be improved in many ways. For example, the date can also be stored in a mapping with the document hash and can be returned when queried. It can be expanded by adding structures and more information related to the patent, but this example was intended to be simple and easy to understand; therefore, too much complexity was avoided. Further enhancements to this code are left to you as an exercise.

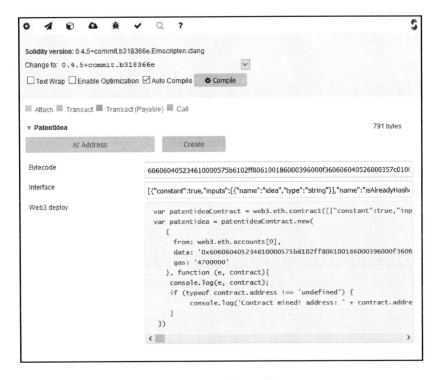

Create contract using browser solidity

After clicking on **Create**, two functions from the contract will be exposed, as shown in the following screenshot:

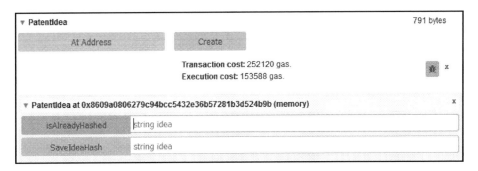

Relevant costs and exposes two methods

Functions can now be invoked as shown in the following example:

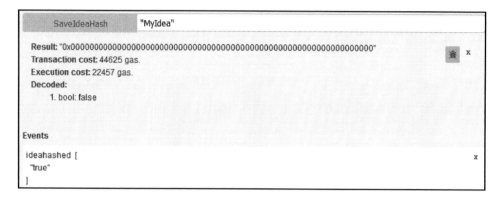

Invoking the SaveIdeaHash function

Similarly, `isAlreadyHashed` can be called.

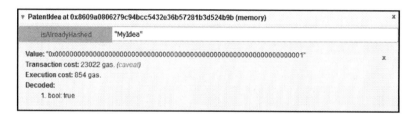

Execute function isAlreadyHashed

If the same string is passed to the function again, it will not be saved, as shown in the following screenshot:

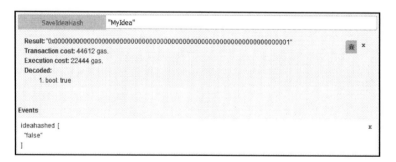

Execute function SaveIdeaHash

Also, note that the event has returned false, indicating that the hash could not be saved and the function returned true, further indicating that the same hash is already saved.

Once the contract is written and simulated in browser solidity, the next step is to use truffle to initialize a new project and deploy and test it on the PrivateNet (ID 786), already created in earlier sections.

The first step is to create a separate directory for the project:

```
~$ mkdir ideapatent
~$ cd ideapatent/
```

The next step is to initialize truffle and create a new project:

```
~/ideapatent$ truffle init
```

Once the sample project is created, remove the sample contracts:

```
~/ideapatent/contracts$ rm MetaCoin.sol ConvertLib.sol
```

Under the contracts folder, create a file named PatentIdea.sol and put the source code in the file shown earlier.

Edit truffle.js to point to the localhost HTTP endpoint:

```
rpc:
  {
    host: "localhost",
    port: 8001
  }
```

Under the ~/ideapatent/migrations folder, edit the 2_deploy_contracts.js file so that it looks like the following:

```
module.exports = function(deployer)
{
  deployer.deploy(PatentIdea);
  deployer.autolink();
};
```

This file is changed in order to specify the name of the contract to be deployed. Take note of deployer.deploy(PatentIdea);.

Next, run the compilation using truffle, as shown here:

```
~/ideapatent$ truffle compile
Compiling Migrations.sol...
Compiling PatentIdea.sol...
Writing artifacts to ./build/contracts
```

Ensure that mining is running the background and deploy to the network, as shown here:

```
~/ideapatent$ truffle migrate
Running migration: 1_initial_migration.js
  Deploying Migrations...
  Migrations: 0x34d63de23de9c9b48251cec94fff427b94976109
Saving successful migration to network...
Saving artifacts...
Running migration: 2_deploy_contracts.js
  Deploying PatentIdea...
  PatentIdea: 0x515fd6a5dbc1eb609dc1700f73be040d9db50d4b
Saving successful migration to network...
Saving artifacts...
```

Once the contract is deployed, it can be interacted with using the truffle console.

Start the truffle console by issuing this command:

```
~/ideapatent$ truffle console
```

Once the console is up and running, functions from the deployed contract can be called as shown here.

For example, register a new idea:

```
truffle(default)> PatentIdea.deployed().SaveIdeaHash("MyIdea")
'0x8644dc66f1173a9103034e17b761f8871ab10ef2a7d19bec9c7eb7164272b8a3'
```

Check whether MyIdea is hashed:

```
truffle(default)> PatentIdea.deployed().isAlreadyHashed("MyIdea")
true
```

Check whether another idea is hashed or not:

```
truffle(default)> PatentIdea.deployed().isAlreadyHashed("MyOtherIdea")
false
truffle(default)>
```

This example demonstrated how a contract can be created from scratch, simulated, and deployed on the private net. In order to deploy this on TestNet (Ropsten) or live blockchain, a similar exercise can be performed. Simply point to the appropriate RPC and use truffle migrate to deploy on the blockchain of your choice.

In the next section, various advanced concepts will be discussed.

Oracles

As discussed in `Chapter 6`, *Smart Contracts*, Oracles are real-world data feeds into smart contracts. There are various services available in order to provide Oracles for smart contracts. A rather prominent one is Oraclize, which is available at `http://www.oraclize.it/`. This is especially useful if the smart contract needs, for example, live prices from a third-party source or any other real-life data, such as weather conditions in a particular city. There are many use cases where oracles can provide a trusted data feed to smart contracts in order to enable them to make decisions according to real-life events. Oraclize makes it easier for smart contracts to access the Internet in order to get the required data.

In order to utilize Oraclize on Ethereum, a transaction needs to be sent to the Oraclize contract along with the appropriate payment and the query. As a result, Oraclize will retrieve the results based on the query provided in the request transaction and send it back to the contract address. Once the transaction is sent back to the contract, the call-back method or fall back function will be called.

At a practical level in solidity, first, the Oraclize library needs to be imported and then all methods that have been inherited from it can be used. Currently, oraclize is available to be used only on the PrivateNet (Ropsten) and Live Main Net Ethereum blockchain.

Oraclize processing can be visualized as shown in the following diagram:

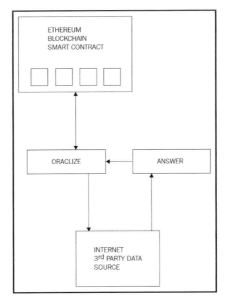

Oraclize data flow

The skeleton structure of a solidity contract using oraclize looks like the one shown here. Note that import works only on the development environment provided on the Web by oraclize; usually, this file needs to be imported manually:

```
import "dev.oraclize.it/api.sol";
contract MyOracleContract is usingOraclize
{
  function MyOracleContract(){
}
```

A sample request looks like what is shown in the following example:

```
oraclize_query("URL", "api.somewebsite.net/price?stock=XYZ");
```

Oraclize can also make use of the TLS notary in order to ensure that the feed is secure and provably honest.

Deployment on decentralized storage using IPFS

As discussed in Chapter 1, *Blockchain 101,* in order to fully benefit from decentralized platforms, it is desirable that you decentralize the storage and communication layer. Traditionally, the web content is served via centralized servers, but that part can also be decentralized using distributed file systems.

The HTML content shown in the earlier examples can be stored on a distributed and decentralized IPFS network in order to achieve enhanced decentralization.

IPFS is available at https://ipfs.io/.

Installing IPFS

IPFS can be installed by following this process:

1. Download the IPFS package using the following command:

   ```
   $ curl https://dist.ipfs.io/go-ipfs/v0.4.4/go-
   ipfs_v0.4.4_linux-amd64.tar.gz -O
   ```

2. Decompress the gz file:

   ```
   $ tar xvfz go-ipfs_v0.4.4_linux-amd64.tar.gz
   ```

3. Move the ipfs file to an appropriate folder in order to make it available in the path:

   ```
   $ mv go-ipfs/ipfs /usr/local/bin/ipfs
   ```

4. Initialize the IPFS node:

```
imran@drequinox-OP7010:~$ ipfs init
initializing ipfs node at /home/imran/.ipfs
generating 2048-bit RSA keypair...done
peer identity: Qmbc726pLS9nUQjUbeJUxcCfXAGaXPD41jAszXniChJz62
to get started, enter:
        ipfs cat
/ipfs/QmYwAPJzv5CZsnA625s3Xf2nemtYgPpHdWEz79ojWnPbdG/readme
```

5. Enter the following command to ensure that **IPFS** has been successfully installed:

Successful IPFS installation

6. Start the IPFS daemon:

```
imran@drequinox-OP7010:~$ ipfs daemon
Initializing daemon...
Swarm listening on /ip4/127.0.0.1/tcp/4001
Swarm listening on /ip4/192.168.0.17/tcp/4001
Swarm listening on /ip4/86.15.44.209/tcp/4001
Swarm listening on /ip4/86.15.44.209/tcp/41608
Swarm listening on /ip6/::1/tcp/4001
API server listening on /ip4/127.0.0.1/tcp/5001
Gateway (readonly) server listening on /ip4/127.0.0.1/tcp/8080
Daemon is ready
```

7. Copy files onto IPFS using the following command:

```
~/sampleproject/build$ ipfs add --recursive --progress .
added QmVdYdY1uycf32e8NhMVEWSufMyvcj17w3DkUt6BgeAtx7
build/app.css
added QmSypieNFeiUx6Sq7moAVCsgQhSY3Bh9ziwXJAxqSG5Pcp
build/app.js
added QmaJWMjD767GvuwuaLpt5tck9dTVCZPJa9sDcr8vdcJ8pY
build/contracts/ConvertLib.sol.js
```

```
added QmQdz9eG2Qd5kwaU86kWebDGPqXBWj1Dmv9MN4BRzt2srf
build/contracts/MetaCoin.sol.js
added QmWpvBjXTP4HutEsYUh3JLDi8VYp73SKNJi4aX1T6jwcmG
build/contracts/Migrations.sol.js
added QmQs7j6NpA1NMueTXKyswLaHKq3XDUCRay3VrC392Q4JDK
build/index.html
added QmPvWzyTEfLQnozDTfgdAAF4W9BUb2cDq5KUUrpHrukseA
build/contracts
added QmUNLLsPACCz1vLxQVkXqqLX5R1X345qqfHbsf67hvA3Nn
build/images
added QmSxpucr6J9rX3XQ3MBG8cVzLCrQFFKmMkTmpcNpjbtf3j build
```

8. Now it can be accessed in the browser as follows:

Browser accessing web pages via IPFS

 Note that the URL is pointing to the IPFS filesystem.

9. Finally, in order to make the changes permanent, the following command can be used:

```
/build$ ipfs pin add QmSxpucr6J9rX3XQ3MBG8cVzLCrQFFKmMkTmpcNpjbtf3j
pinned QmSxpucr6J9rX3XQ3MBG8cVzLCrQFFKmMkTmpcNpjbtf3j recursively
```

The preceding example demonstrated how IPFS can be used to provide decentralized storage for the web part (user interface) of smart contracts.

IPFS can be used with blockchains in another way. As storage is a big issue for blockchains, it is desirable that you are able to save large amounts of data somewhere else and place the links to that data in the blockchain transaction. This way, there will be no need to store large amounts of data on the blockchain and bloat it as a result. IPFS can be used to achieve exactly that by placing the data on IPFS and then storing the IPFS links in blockchain transactions to reference the stored data.

Ethereum's own swarm protocol is also under heavy development and works on similar principles. However, Swarm is currently under development and IPFS is more developed comparatively and seems a better choice at the moment. IPFS works very well and may well become the platform of choice for the decentralized storage of deployments. Swarm allows users to run a light client by storing all the blockchain data on it. This is available with the current version of `geth`, and a detailed guide is available at `https://swarm-guide.readthedocs.io/en/latest/introduction.html`. As this is under heavy development, only a light introduction has been given for this technology as it is likely to evolve very quickly.

For decentralized communication in Ethereum, the Whisper protocol provides the decentralized communication layer. This will serve as an identity-based messaging layer for Ethereum. Both swarm and whisper are envisaged to be enabling technologies for Web 3.0.

Permissioned distributed ledgers

The concept of permissioned distributed ledgers is fundamentally different to a public blockchain. The key idea behind distributed ledgers is that they are permissioned as opposed to an open public blockchain. DLTs do not perform any mining as all the participants are already vetted and known to the network and there is no requirement for mining to secure the network. There is also no concept of digital currency on private permissioned distributed ledgers because the aim of the permissioned blockchain is different from a public blockchain. In a public blockchain, access is open to everyone and requires some form of incentive and network effect in order to grow; on the contrary, in permissioned DLTs, there are no such requirements. It is possible to build permissioned DLTs using Ethereum in private consortium settings, especially to work within existing financial systems. The key benefit of distributed ledger systems is that they are much faster, governable, and possibly interoperable with the existing financial systems.

Summary

This chapter provided detailed and in-depth practical examples on how to set up an Ethereum development environment and create smart contracts. This chapter started with an introduction to various methods that can be used to create Private Ethereum networks for testing and development purposes. After this, an introduction to the solidity language was presented in order to enable you to understand the language fundamentals and syntax. Practical deployment techniques using technologies and tools such as `geth` and web3 were discussed in detail. Moreover, detailed step-by-step examples of smart contract development and deployments were presented. Additionally, development frameworks were discussed with practical examples so that you can experience the smart contract development life cycle of the Ethereum blockchain. This is a lengthy chapter and by following exercises closely, you will gain an in-depth understanding of contract development, testing, and deployment on Ethereum. Finally, various concepts and tools related to decentralized storage, decentralized communication, and oracles were discussed. As Ethereum and related technologies and frameworks are under constant and fast development, it is envisaged that more advanced tools and techniques will evolve over time; however, the fundamentals discussed in this chapter are likely to remain the same. Also, it is not possible to discuss each and every tool and framework available for Ethereum in this chapter, but all tools and techniques discussed are in mainstream use and should provide a solid basis for you to make a transition to a more advanced level. There are a few topics that have not been discussed on purpose in this chapter, such as smart contract security, formal verification of smart contracts, blockchain as a service on cloud, and specific use cases for smart contracts for various industries. All these concepts will be discussed in later chapters. I hope you enjoyed reading this chapter as much as I enjoyed writing it.

9
Hyperledger

Hyperledger is not a blockchain, but it is a project that was initiated by Linux foundation in December 2015 to advance blockchain technology. This project is a collaborative effort by its members to build an open source distributed ledger framework that can be used to develop and implement cross-industry blockchain applications and systems. The key focus is to build and run platforms that support global business transactions. The project also focuses on improving the reliability and performance of blockchain systems.

Projects under Hyperledger undergo various stages of development, starting from **proposal** to **incubation** and graduating to an **active** state. Projects can also be **deprecated** or in **End of Life** state where they are no longer actively developed. In order for a project to be able to move into incubation stage, it must have a fully working code base along with an active community of developers.

Projects

Currently, there are six projects under the Hyperledger umbrella: Fabric, Iroha, Sawtooth lake, blockchain explorer, Fabric chaintool, and Fabric SDK Py. Corda is the most recent addition that is expected to be added to the Hyperledger project. The Hyperledger project currently has 100 members and is very active with more than 120 contributors, with regular meet-ups and talks being organized around the globe.

A brief introduction of all these projects follows, after which we will provide more details around the design, architecture, and implementation of Fabric and Sawtooth lake.

Fabric

Fabric is a blockchain project that was proposed by IBM and **DAH (Digital Asset Holdings)**. This is intended to provide a foundation for the development of blockchain solutions and is based on pluggable architecture where various components, such as consensus algorithm, can be plugged into the system as required. It is available at `https://github.com/hyperledger/fabric`.

Sawtooth lake

Sawtooth lake is a blockchain project proposed by Intel in April 2016 with some key innovations focusing on **decoupling** of ledgers from transactions, flexible usage across multiple business areas using *transaction families*, and **pluggable consensus**. Decoupling can be explained more precisely by saying that the *transactions* are decoupled from the *consensus layer* by making use of a new concept called *Transaction families*. Instead of transactions being individually coupled with the ledger, transaction families are used, which allows for more flexibility, rich semantics and unrestricted design of business logic. Transactions follow the patterns and structures defined in the transaction families. Intel has also introduced a novel consensus algorithm abbreviated as PoET, proof of elapsed time, which makes use of **Intel Software Guard Extensions (Intel's SGX)** architecture's **trusted execution environment (TEE)** in order to provide a safe and random leader election process. It also supports permissioned and permission-less setups. This project is available at `https://github.com/hyperledger/sawtooth-core`.

Iroha

Iroha was proposed by Soramitsu, Hitachi, NTT Data, and Colu in September 2016. Iroha is aiming to build a library of reusable components that users can choose to run on their Hyperledger-based distributed ledgers. Iroha's main goal is to complement other Hyperledger projects by providing reusable components written in C++ with an emphasis on mobile development. This project has also proposed a novel consensus algorithm called Sumeragi, which is a chain based Byzantine fault tolerant consensus algorithm. Iroha is available at `https://github.com/hyperledger/iroha`. Various libraries have been proposed and are being worked on by Iroha, including but not limited to a digital signature library (ed25519), an SHA-3 hashing library, a transaction serialization library, a P2P library, an API server library, an iOS library, an Android library, and a JavaScript library.

Blockchain explorer

This project aims to build a blockchain explorer for Hyperledger that can be used to view and query the transactions, blocks, and associated data from the blockchain. It also provides network information and the ability to interact with chain code.

Currently there are two other projects that are in incubation: Fabric chaintool, and Fabric SDK Py. These projects are aimed at supporting Hyperledger Fabric.

Fabric chaintool

Hyperledger chaincode compiler is being developed to support Fabric chaincode development. The aim is to build a tool that reads in a high-level Google protocol buffer structure and produces a chaincode. Additionally, it packages the chaincode so that it can be deployed directly. It is envisaged that this tool will help developers in various stages of development, such as compiling, testing, packaging, and deployment. It is available at `https://github.com/hyperledger/fabric-chaintool`.

Fabric SDK Py

The aim of this project is to build a python based SDK library that can be used to interact with the blockchain (Fabric). It is available at `https://github.com/hyperledger/fabric-sdk-py`.

Corda

Corda is the latest project that has been contributed by R3 to the Hyperledger project. It was open sourced on November 30, 2016. Corda is heavily oriented towards the financial services industry and has been developed in collaboration with major banks and organizations in the financial industry. At the time of writing it is not yet in incubation under the Hyperledger project. Technically, Corda is not a blockchain but has key features similar to those of a blockchain, such as consensus, validity, uniqueness, immutability, and authentication.

In the following sections of this chapter, Fabric (IBM) and Sawtooth lake (Intel) and Corda (R3) will be discussed in more detail.

Hyperledger as a protocol

Hyperledger is aiming to build a new blockchain platform that is driven by industry use cases. As there have been number of contributions made to the Hyperledger project by the community, Hyperledger blockchain platform is evolving into a protocol for business transactions. Hyperledger is also evolving into a specification that can be used as a reference to build blockchain platforms as compared to earlier blockchain solutions that address only a specific type of industry or requirement. In the following section, a reference architecture is presented that has been published by the Hyperledger project. As this work is under continuous and rigorous development some changes are expected in this, but core services are expected to remain unchanged.

Reference architecture

Hyperledger has published a white paper with reference architecture that can serve as a guideline to build permissioned distributed ledgers. The reference architecture consists of two main components: Hyperledger services and Hyperledger APIs, SDKs, and CLI. Hyperledger services provide various services such as identity services, policy services, blockchain services, and smart contract services. On the other hand, Hyperledger APIs, SDKs, and CLIs provide an interface into blockchain services via appropriate application programming interfaces, software development kits, or command line interfaces. Moreover, an event stream, which is basically a gRPC channel, runs across all services. It can receive and send events. Events are either pre-defined or custom. Validating peers or chaincode can emit events to which external application can respond or listen to.

The reference architecture that has been published in the Hyperledger white paper at the time of writing is shown in the following diagram. Hyperledger is a rapidly changing and evolving project, and the architecture shown here is expected to change somewhat.

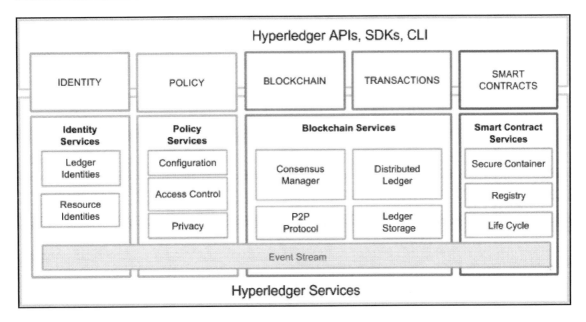

Hyperledger architecture, as proposed in the latest draft V2.0.0 of Hyperledger white paper. (Source: Hyperledger white paper)

Requirements

There are certain requirements of a blockchain service. The reference architecture is driven by the needs and requirements raised by the participants of the Hyperledger project and after studying the industry use cases. There are several categories of requirements that have been deduced from the study of industrial use cases and are discussed in the following sections.

Modular approach

The main requirement of Hyperledger is a modular structure. It is expected that, as a cross-industry fabric (blockchain), it will be used in many business scenarios. As such, functions related to storage, policy, chaincode, access control, consensus and many other blockchain services should be pluggable. The modules should be plug and play and users should be able to easily remove and add a different module that meets the requirements of the business.

For example, if a business blockchain needs to be run only between already trusted parties and performs very basic business operations, then perhaps there is no need to have advanced cryptographic support for confidentiality and privacy, and therefore users should be able to remove that functionality (module) or replace that with a more appropriate module that suits their needs. Similarly, if users need to run a cross-industry blockchain, then confidentiality and privacy can be of paramount importance. In this case, users should be able to plug an advanced cryptographic and access control mechanism (module) into the blockchain (fabric).

Privacy and confidentiality

Privacy and confidentiality of transactions and contracts is of utmost importance in a business blockchain. As such, Hyperledger's vision is to provide a wide range of cryptographic protocols and algorithms and it is expected that users will be able to choose appropriate modules according to their business requirements. The fabric should be able to handle complex cryptographic algorithms without compromising performance.

Identity

In order to provide privacy and confidentiality services, a flexible PKI model that can be used to handle the access control functionality is also required. The strength and type of cryptographic mechanisms is also expected to vary according to the needs and requirements of the users. In certain scenarios it might be required for a user to hide their identity, and as such the Hyperledger is expected to provide this functionality.

Auditability

Auditability is another requirement of a Hyperledger Fabric. It is expected that an immutable audit trail of all identities, related operations and any changes is kept.

Interoperability

Currently there are many blockchain solutions available, but they cannot communicate with each other and this can be a limiting factor in the growth of a blockchain based global business ecosystem. It is envisaged that many blockchain networks will operate in the business world for specific needs, but it is important that they are able to communicate with each other. There should be a common set of standards that all blockchains can follow in order to allow communication between different ledgers. It is expected that a protocol will be developed that will allow the exchange of information between many Fabrics.

Portability

The portability requirement is concerned with the ability to run across multiple platforms and environments without the need to change anything at code level. Hyperledger is envisaged to be portable, not only at infrastructure level but also at code, libraries, and API levels so that it can support uniform development across various implementations of Hyperledger.

Fabric

In order to understand various projects under incubation in Hyperledger project, it is important to understand the foundations of Hyperledger first. A few terminologies that are specific to Hyperledger needs some clarification before readers are introduced to more in-depth material. First there is the concept of Fabric.

Fabric can be defined as a collection of components providing a foundation layer that can be used to deliver a blockchain network. There are various types and capabilities of a fabric network, but all fabrics share common attributes such as immutability and are consensus driven. Some fabrics can provide modular approach towards building blockchain networks. In this case the blockchain network can have multiple pluggable modules to perform various function on the network. For example, consensus algorithms can be a pluggable module in a blockchain network where, depending on the requirements of the network, an appropriate consensus algorithm can be chosen and *plugged* into the network. The modules can be based on some particular specification of the fabric and can include APIs, access control, and various other components. Fabrics can also be designed either to be private or public and can allow the creation of multiple business networks. As an example, bitcoin is an application that runs on top of its fabric (blockchain network). As discussed earlier, blockchain can either be permissioned or permission-less and the same is true for fabric in Hyperledger terminology.

Fabric is also the name given to the code contribution made by IBM to the Hyperledger foundation and is formally called Hyperledger Fabric. IBM also offers blockchain as a service (IBM Blockchain) via its Bluemix cloud service.

Hyperledger Fabric

Fabric is the contribution originally made by IBM to the Hyperledger project. The aim of this contribution is to enable a modular, open and flexible approach towards building blockchain networks. Various functions in the fabric are pluggable, and it also allows use of any language to develop smart contracts. This is possible because it is based on container technology which can host any language. Chaincode (smart contract) is sandboxed into a secure container which includes a secure operating system, chaincode language, runtime environment and SDKs for Go, Java, and Node.js. Other languages can be supported too if required. Smart contracts are called chaincode in the Fabric. This is a very powerful feature compared to domain specific languages in Ethereum, or the very limited scripted language in bitcoin. It is a permissioned network that aims to address issues such as scalability, privacy, and confidentiality. The key idea behind this is modular technology, which would allow for flexibility in design and implementation. This can then result in achieving scalability, privacy and other desired attributes. Transactions in fabric are private, confidential and anonymous for general users, but they can still be traced and linked to the users by authorized auditors. As a permissioned network, all participants are required to be registered with the membership services in order to access the blockchain network. This ledger also provided auditability functionality in order to meet the regulatory and compliance needs.

Fabric architecture

The Fabric is logically organized into three main categories based on the type of service provided. These include membership services, blockchain services, and chaincode services. In the following section, all these categories and associated components are discussed in detail. The current stable version of Hyperledger Fabric is v0.6, however the latest version v1.0 is available but is not yet stable. In version 1.0, many architectural changes have been made, and in later sections of this chapter some changes that have been made in version 1.0 will also be discussed.

Membership services

These services are used to provide access control capability for the users of the fabric network. The following list shows the functions that membership services perform:

1. User identity validation.
2. User registration.
3. Assign appropriate permissions to the users depending on their roles.

Membership services makes use of **Public Key Infrastructure (PKI)** in order to support identity management and authorization operations. Membership services are made up of various components:

- **Registration authority (RA)**: A service that authenticates the users and assesses the identity of the fabric participants for issuance of certificates.
- **Enrolment certificate authority**: **Enrolment certificates (Ecerts)** are long term certificates issued by ECA to registered participants in order to provide identification to the entities participating on the network.
- **Transaction certificate authority**: In order to send transactions on the networks, participants are required to hold a transaction certificate. TCA is responsible for issuing transaction certificates to holders of Enrolment certificates and is derived from Ecerts.
- **TLS certificate authority**: In order to secure the network level communication between nodes on the Fabric, TLS certificates are used. TLS certificate authority issues TLS certificates in order to ensure security of the messages being passed between various systems on the blockchain network.

Blockchain services

Blockchain services are at the core of the Hyperledger Fabric. Components within this category are as follows.

Consensus manager

Consensus manager is responsible for providing the interface to the consensus algorithm. This serves as an adapter that receives the transaction from other Hyperledger entities and executes them under criteria according to the type of algorithm chosen. Consensus is pluggable and currently there are three types of consensus algorithm available in Fabric, namely the batch PBFT protocol, SIEVE algorithm, and NOOPS.

Distributed ledger

Blockchain and world state are two main elements of the distributed ledger. Blockchain is simply a linked list of blocks (as introduced in earlier chapters) and world ledger is a key-value database. This database is used by smart contracts to store relevant states during execution by the transactions. The blockchain consists of blocks that contain transactions. These transactions contain chaincode, which runs transactions that can result in updating the world state. Each node saves the world state on disk in RocksDB. The following diagram shows a typical block in the Hyperledger Fabric with the relevant fields:

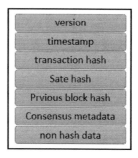

Block structure

The fields shown in the preceding diagram are as follows:

- **Version:** Used for keeping track of changes in the protocol.
- **Timestamp:** Timestamp in UTC epoch time, updated by block proposer.
- **Transaction hash:** This field contains the Merkle root hash of the transactions in the block.
- **State hash:** This is the Merkle root hash of the world state.
- **Previous hash:** This is the previous block's hash, which is calculated after serializing the block message and then creating the message digest by applying the SHA3 SHAKE256 algorithm.
- **Consensus metadata:** This is an optional field that can be used by the consensus protocol to provide some relevant information about the consensus.
- **Non-Hash data:** This is some metadata that is stored with the block but is not hashed. This feature makes it possible to have different data on different peers. It also provides the ability to discard data without any impact on the blockchain.

Peer to Peer protocol

P2P protocol in the Hyperledger Fabric is built using **google RPC (gRPC)**. It uses protocol buffers to define the structure of the messages.

Messages are passed between nodes in order to perform various functions. There are four main types of messages in Hyperledger Fabric: Discovery, transaction, synchronization and consensus. Discovery messages are exchanged between nodes when starting up in order to discover other peers on the network.

Transaction messages can be divided into two types: Deployment transactions and Invocation transactions. The former is used to deploy new chaincode to the ledger, and the latter is used to call functions from the smart contract. Transactions can be public, confidential, and confidential chaincode transactions. Public transactions are open and available to all participants. Confidential transactions are allowed to be queried only by transaction owners and participants. Confidential chaincode transactions have encrypted chaincode and can only be decrypted by validating nodes. Validating nodes run consensus, validate the transactions and maintain the blockchain. Non-validating nodes on the other hand, provide transaction verification, stream server, and REST services. They also act as a proxy between the transactors and the validating nodes. Synchronization messages are used by peers to keep the blockchain updated and in synch with other nodes. Consensus messages are used in consensus management and broadcasting payloads to validating peers. These are generated internally by the consensus framework.

Ledger storage

In order to save the state of the ledger, RocksDB is used, and it is stored at each peer. RocksDB is a high performance database available at `http://rocksdb.org/`.

Chaincode services

These services allow the creation of secure containers that are used to execute the chaincode. Components in this category are as follows:

- **Secure container:** Chaincode is deployed in Docker containers that provide a locked down sandboxed environment for smart contract execution. Currently Golang is supported as the main smart contract language, but any other main stream language can be added and enabled if required.

- **Secure registry:** This provides a record of all images containing smart contracts.

Events

Events on the blockchain can be triggered by validator nodes and smart contracts. External applications can listen to these events and react to them if required via event adapters. They are similar to the concept of events introduced in solidity in the last chapter.

APIs and CLIs

An application programming interface provides an interface into the fabric by exposing various REST APIs. Additionally, command line interfaces that provide a subset of REST APIs and allow for quick testing and limited interaction with the blockchain are also available.

Components of the Fabric

There are various components that can be part of the blockchain. These components include but are not limited to the ledger, chaincode, consensus mechanism, access control, events, system monitoring and management, wallets and system integration components.

Peers or nodes

There are two main types of peers that can be run on a fabric network: Validating and non-validating. Simply put, a validating node runs consensus, creates and validates a transaction, and contributes towards updating the ledger and maintaining the chaincode.

A non-validating peer does not execute transactions and only constructs transactions that are then forwarded to validating nodes.

Both nodes manage and maintain user certificates that have been issued by membership services.

Applications on blockchain

A typical application on Fabric is simply composed of a user interface, usually written in JavaScript/HTML, that interacts with the backend chaincode (smart contract) stored on the ledger via an API layer.

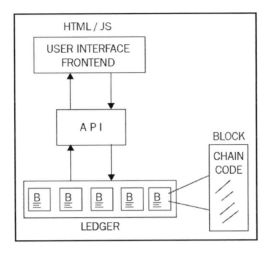

Typical blockchain application

Hyperledger provides various APIs and command line interfaces to enable interaction with the ledger. These APIs include interfaces for identity, transactions, chaincode, ledger, network, storage, and events.

Chaincode implementation

Chaincode is usually written in Golang or Java. Chaincode can be public, confidential or access controlled. These codes serve as a smart contract that users can interact with via APIs. Users can call functions in the chaincode that result in a state change, and consequently updates the ledger. There are also functions that are only used to query the ledger and do not result in any state change.

Chaincode implementation is performed by first creating the chaincode shim interface in the code. It can either be in Java or Golang code. The following four functions are required in order to implement the chaincode:

- `Init()`: This function is invoked when chaincode is deployed onto the ledger. This initializes the chaincode and results in making a state change, which accordingly updates the ledger.

- `Invoke()`: This function is used when contracts are executed. It takes a function name as parameters along with an array of arguments. This function results in a state change and writes to the ledger.

- `Query()`: This function is used to query the current state of a deployed chaincode. This function does not make any changes to the ledger.

- `Main()`: This function is executed when a peer deploys its own copy of the chaincode. The chaincode is registered with the peer using this function.

The following diagram illustrates the general overview of Hyperledger Fabric:

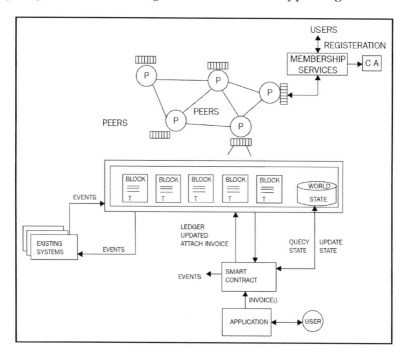

High-level overview of Hyperledger Fabric

Application model

Any blockchain application for Hyperledger Fabric follows MVC-B architecture. This is based on the popular MVC design pattern. Components in this model are Model, View, Control, and Blockchain:

- **View logic**: This is concerned with the user interface. It can be a desktop, web application or mobile frontend.
- **Control logic**: This is the orchestrator between user interface, data model, and APIs.
- **Data model**: This model is used to manage the off-chain data.
- **Blockchain logic**: This is used to manage the blockchain via the controller and the data model via transactions.

Due to the fact that Hyperledger current release v0.6 is under heavy refactoring to build V1.0, no practical exercises have been introduced in this section.

It is expected that by the time this book is published, the information regarding practical setup of Hyperledger fabric will be outdated already. As such, readers are encouraged to keep an eye on the updates at `https://hyperledgerfabric.readthedocs.io/en/latest/`.

Moreover, the IBM Bluemix service offers sample applications for blockchain under its blockchain as a service offering. It is available at `https://console.ng.bluemix.net/docs/services/blockchain/ibmblockchain_tutorials.html`. This service allows users to create their own blockchain networks in an easy to use environment.

Sawtooth lake

Sawtooth lake can run in both permissioned and non-permissioned modes. It is a distributed ledger that proposes two novel concepts: The first is the introduction of a new consensus algorithm called **Proof of Elapsed Time (PoET)**; and the second is the idea of transaction families. A brief description of these novel proposals is given in the following section.

PoET

PoET is a novel consensus algorithm that allows a node to be selected randomly based on the time that the node has waited before proposing a block. This is in contrast to other leader election and lottery based proof of work algorithms, where an enormous amount of electricity and computer resources are used in order be elected as a block proposer, for example in the case of bitcoin. PoET is a type of Proof of Work algorithm but, instead of spending computer resources, it uses a trusted computing model to provide a mechanism to fulfill Proof of Work requirements. PoET makes use of Intel's SGX architecture to provide a trusted execution environment to ensure randomness and cryptographic security of the process. It should be noted that the current implementation of Sawtooth lake does not require real hardware SGX based TEE, as it is simulated for experimental purposes only and as such should not be used in production environments.

Transaction families

A traditional smart contract paradigm provides a solution that is based on a general purpose instruction set for all domains. For example, in the case of Ethereum, a set of opcodes has been developed for the **Ethereum virtual machine (EVM)** that can be used to build smart contracts to address any type of requirements for any industry. Whilst this model has its merits, it is becoming clear that this approach is not very secure as it provides a single interface into the ledger with a powerful and expressive language, which potentially offers a larger attack surface for malicious code. This complexity and generic virtual machine paradigm has resulted in several vulnerabilities that were found and exploited recently by hackers. A recent example is the DAO hack and further **Denial of Services (DoS)** attacks that exploited limitations in some EVM opcodes. A model shown in the following figure describes the traditional smart contract model, where a generic virtual machine has been used to provide the interface into the blockchain for all domains:

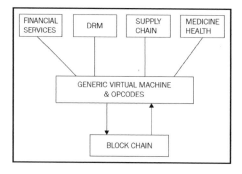

Traditional smart contract paradigm

In order to address this issue, Sawtooth lake has proposed the idea of transaction families. A transaction family is created by decomposing the logic layer into a *set of rules* and a *composition layer* for a specific domain. The key idea is that business logic is composed within *transaction families*, which provides a more secure and powerful way to build smart contracts. Transaction families contain the domain-specific rules and another layer that allows for creating transactions for that domain. Another way of looking at it is that transaction families are a combination of a data model and a transaction language that implements a logic layer for a specific domain. The data model represents the current state of the blockchain (ledger) whereas the transaction language modifies the state of the ledger. It is expected that users will build their own transaction families according to their business requirements.

The following diagram represents this model, where each specific domain, like financial services, **digital rights management (DRM)**, supply chain, and the health industry, has its own logic layer comprised of operations and services specific to that domain. This makes the logic layer both restrictive and powerful at the same time. Transaction families ensure that operations related to only the required domain are present in the control logic, thus removing the possibility of executing needless, arbitrary and potentially harmful operations.

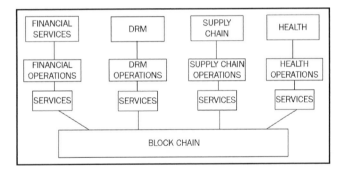

Sawtooth (transaction families) smart contract paradigm

Intel has provided three transaction families with Sawtooth: Endpoint registry, Integerkey, and MarketPlace.

1. **Endpoint registry** is used for registering ledger services.
2. **Integerkey** is used for testing deployed ledgers.
3. **MarketPlace** is used for selling, buying and trading operations and services.

`Sawtooth_bond` has been developed as a proof of concept to demonstrate a bond trading platform. It is available at `https://github.com/hyperledger/sawtooth-core/tre e/master/extensions/bond`.

Consensus in Sawtooth

Sawtooth has two types of consensus mechanisms based on the choice of network. PoET, as discussed previously, is a trusted executed environment based lottery function that elects a leader randomly based on the time a node has waited for block proposal. There is another consensus type called quorum voting, which is an adaptation of consensus protocols built by Ripple and Stellar. This consensus algorithm allows instant transaction finality, which is usually desirable in permissioned networks.

Development environment

In this section, a quick introduction is given on how to set up a development environment for Sawtooth lake. There are few pre-requisites that are required in order to set up the development environment. Examples in this section assume a running Ubuntu system and the following:

1. `vagrant`, at least version 1.9.0, available at `https://www.vagrantup.com/downlo ads.html`.
2. Virtual box, at least 5.0.10 r104061, available at `https://www.virtualbox.org/wi ki/Downloads`.

Once both of the above pre-requisites are downloaded and installed successfully, the next step is to clone the repository.

```
$ git clone https://github.com/IntelLedger/sawtooth-core.git
```

This will produce an output similar to the one shown in the following screenshot:

```
drequinox@drequinox-OP7010:~/project$ git clone https://github.com/IntelLedger/sawtooth-core.git
Cloning into 'sawtooth-core'...
remote: Counting objects: 12527, done.
remote: Compressing objects: 100% (964/964), done.
remote: Total 12527 (delta 452), reused 0 (delta 0), pack-reused 11515
Receiving objects: 100% (12527/12527), 9.26 MiB | 1.76 MiB/s, done.
Resolving deltas: 100% (8131/8131), done.
Checking connectivity... done.
```

GitHub Sawtooth clone

Once Sawtooth is cloned correctly, the next step is to start up the environment. First, run the following command to change the directory to the correct location and then start the `vagrant` box:

```
$ cd sawtooth-core/tools
$ vagrant up
```

This will produce an output similar to the following screenshot:

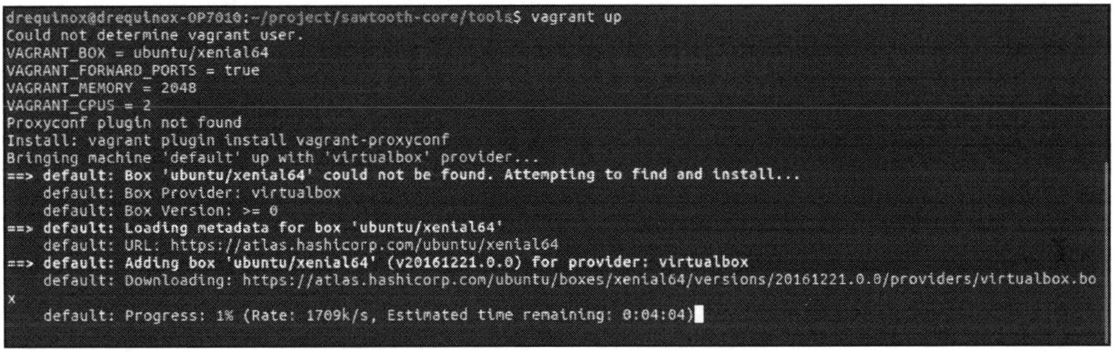

```
drequinox@drequinox-OP7010:~/project/sawtooth-core/tools$ vagrant up
Could not determine vagrant user.
VAGRANT_BOX = ubuntu/xenial64
VAGRANT_FORWARD_PORTS = true
VAGRANT_MEMORY = 2048
VAGRANT_CPUS = 2
Proxyconf plugin not found
Install: vagrant plugin install vagrant-proxyconf
Bringing machine 'default' up with 'virtualbox' provider...
==> default: Box 'ubuntu/xenial64' could not be found. Attempting to find and install...
    default: Box Provider: virtualbox
    default: Box Version: >= 0
==> default: Loading metadata for box 'ubuntu/xenial64'
    default: URL: https://atlas.hashicorp.com/ubuntu/xenial64
==> default: Adding box 'ubuntu/xenial64' (v20161221.0.0) for provider: virtualbox
    default: Downloading: https://atlas.hashicorp.com/ubuntu/boxes/xenial64/versions/20161221.0.0/providers/virtualbox.bo
x
    default: Progress: 1% (Rate: 1709k/s, Estimated time remaining: 0:04:04)
```

Vagrant up command

If at any point Vagrant needs to be stopped, the following command can be used:

```
$ vagrant halt
```

Or

```
$ vagrant destroy
```

Halt will stop the `vagrant` machine, whereas `destroy` will stop and delete `vagrant` machines.

Finally, the transaction validator can be started by using the following commands. First `ssh` into the `vagrant` Sawtooth box.

```
$ vagrant ssh
```

When the `vagrant` prompt is available, run the following commands.

First build the `sawtooth` lake core using following command:

```
$ /project/sawtooth-core/bin/build_all
```

When the build has completed successfully, in order to run transaction validator issue the following commands:

```
$ /project/sawtooth-core/docs/source/tutorial/genesis.sh
```

This will create the genesis block and clear any existing data files and keys. This should show an output similar to the following screenshot:

```
ubuntu@ubuntu-xenial:/project/sawtooth-core$ /project/sawtooth-core/docs/source/tutorial/genesis.sh
writing file: /home/ubuntu/sawtooth/keys/base000.wif
writing file: /home/ubuntu/sawtooth/keys/base000.addr
```

Genesis block and keys generation

The next step is to run the transaction validator, and change the directory as shown follows:

```
$ cd /project/saw-toothcore
```

Run the transaction validator:

```
$ ./bin/txnvalidator -v -F ledger.transaction.integer_key --config
/home/ubuntu/sawtooth/v0.json
```

```
ubuntu@ubuntu-xenial:/project/sawtooth-core$ ./bin/txnvalidator -v -F ledger.transaction.integer_key --config /home/ubuntu/sawto
oth/v0.json
[22:08:22 INFO    validator_cli] validator started with arguments: ['./bin/txnvalidator', '-v', '-F', 'ledger.transaction.intege
r_key', '--config', '/home/ubuntu/sawtooth/v0.json']
[22:08:22 INFO    validator_cli] read signing key from /home/ubuntu/sawtooth/keys/base000.wif
[22:08:24 WARNING validator_cli] validator pid is 10937
[22:08:24 INFO    gossip_core] listening on IPv4Address(UDP, '0.0.0.0', 33713)
[22:08:24 INFO    global_store_manager] create blockstore from file /home/ubuntu/sawtooth/data/base000_state.dbm with flag c
[22:08:24 INFO    validator] set administration node to None
[22:08:24 INFO    validator] starting ledger base000 with id 1K5RNedZ at network address ('127.0.0.1', 33713)
[22:08:24 INFO    web_api] listen for HTTP requests on {ip='localhost', port=8800)
[22:08:24 INFO    validator_cli] adding transaction family: ledger.transaction.integer_key
[22:08:24 INFO    journal_core] restore ledger state from persistence
[22:08:24 INFO    global_store_manager] add block 60af3ec894fa1cb0 to the queue for loading
[22:08:24 INFO    global_store_manager] load block 60af3ec894fa1cb0 from storage
[22:08:24 INFO    journal_core] commit head: 60af3ec894fa1cb0
[22:08:26 INFO    validator] ledger connections using RandomWalk topology
[22:08:26 INFO    random_walk] initiate random walk topology update
[22:08:29 INFO    validator] ledger initialization complete
[22:08:29 INFO    journal_core] process initial transactions and blocks
[22:08:29 INFO    validator] register endpoint 1K5RNedZ with name base000
[22:08:29 INFO    journal_core] build transaction block to extend 60af3ec8 with 1 transactions
[22:08:29 INFO    wait_timer] wait timer created; TIMER, 5.00, 33.69, HE2DQNJWGI2DCNJQ
```

Running transaction validator

The validator node can be stopped by pressing *Ctrl + C*. Once the validator is up and running, various clients can be started up in another terminal window to communicate with the transaction validator and submit transactions.

For example, in the following screenshot the market client is started up to communicate with the transaction validator. Note that keys under `/keys/mkt.wif` are created by using the following command:

```
./bin/sawtooth keygen --key-dir validator/keys mkt
```

This demonstration is just a basic example derived from Sawtooth lake documentation. However, development using Sawtooth lake is quite an involved process and a full chapter could be dedicated to that.

```
ubuntu@ubuntu-xenial:/project/sawtooth-core$ ./bin/mktclient --name market --keyfile validator/keys/mkt.wif
//UNKNOWN> help

Documented commands (type help <topic>):
========================================
EOF        dump          exit       liability   selloffer   tokenstore
account    echo          help       map         session     waitforcommit
asset      exchange      holding    offers      sleep
assettype  exchangeoffer holdings   participant state

Miscellaneous help topics:
==========================
symbols   names

//UNKNOWN> participant reg --name market --description "the market"
transaction ff652e63dadeaf32 submitted
//market>
```

mktclient for marketplace transaction family

Sawtooth lake is also under continuous development and therefore it is recommended that readers keep an eye on documentation available at `http://intelledger.github.io/` in order to keep up with the latest developments.

Corda

Corda is not a blockchain. Traditional blockchain solutions, as discussed before, have the concept of transactions that are bundled together in a block and each block is linked back cryptographically to its parent block, which provides an immutable record of transactions. This is not the case with Corda: Corda has been designed entirely from scratch with a new model for providing all blockchain benefits, but without a traditional blockchain. It has been developed purely for the financial industry to solve issues arising from the fact that each organization manages their own ledgers and thus have their own view of *truth*, which leads to contradictions and operational risk. Moreover, data is also duplicated at each organization which results in an increased cost of managing individual infrastructures and complexity. These are the types of problems within the financial industry that Corda aims to resolve by building a decentralized database platform.

Corda source code is available at `https://github.com/corda/corda`. It is written in a language called Kotlin, which is a statically typed language targeting the **Java Virtual Machine (JVM)**.

Architecture

The main components of the Corda platform include state objects, contract code, legal prose, transactions, consensus, and flows.

State objects

State objects represent the smallest unit of data that represent a financial agreement. They are created or deleted as a result of a transaction execution. They refer to **contract code** and **legal prose.** Legal prose is optional and provides legal binding to the contract. However, contract code is mandatory in order to manage the state of the object. It is required in order to provide a state transition mechanism for the node according to the business logic defined in the contract code. State objects contain a data structure that represent the current state of the object. For example, in the following diagram, a state object represents the current state of the object. In this case, it is a simple mock agreement between **Party A** and **Party B** where **Party ABC** has paid **Party XYZ 1,000 GBP**. This represents the current state of the object; however the referred contract code can change the state via transactions. State objects can be thought of as a state machine, which are consumed by transactions in order to create updated state objects.

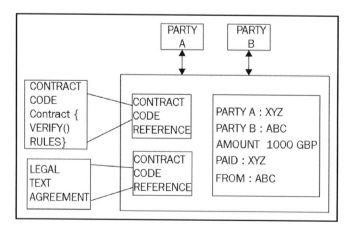

An example state object

Transactions

Transactions are used to perform transitions between different states. For example, the state object shown in the preceding diagram is created as a result of a transaction. Corda uses a bitcoin-style UTXO based model for its transaction processing. The concept of state transition by transactions is same as in bitcoin. Similar to bitcoin, transactions can have none, single or multiple inputs, and single or multiple outputs. All transactions are digitally signed. Moreover, Corda has no concept of mining because it does not use blocks to arrange transactions in a blockchain. Instead, notary services are used in order to provide temporal ordering of transactions. In Corda, new transaction types can be developed using JVM bytecode, which makes it very flexible and powerful.

Consensus

The consensus model in Corda is quite simple and is based on notary services that are discussed in a later section. The general idea is that the transactions are evaluated for their uniqueness by the notary service and, if they are unique, they are signed as valid. There can be single or multiple clustered notary services running on a Corda network. Various consensus algorithms like PBFT or Raft can be used by notaries to reach consensus.

There are two main concepts regarding consensus in Corda: Consensus over state validity, and consensus over state uniqueness. The first concept is concerned with the validation of the transaction, ensuring that all required signatures are available and states are appropriate. The second concept is a means to detect double–spend attack and ensures that a transaction has not been already been spent and is unique.

Flows

Flows in Corda are a novel idea that allow the development of decentralized workflows. All communication on the Corda network is handled by these flows. These are transaction-building protocols that can be used to define any financial flow of any complexity using code. Flows run as an asynchronous state machine and they interact with other nodes and users. During the execution, they can be suspended or resumed as required.

Components

The Corda network has multiple components. All these components are described in the next section.

Nodes

Nodes in a Corda network operated under a trust-less model and run by different organizations. Nodes run as part of an authenticated peer-to-peer network. Nodes communicate directly with each other using the **Advanced Message Queuing Protocol (AMQP)**, which is an approved international standard (ISO/IEC 19464) and ensures that messages across different nodes are transferred safely and securely. AMQP works over **Transport Layer Security (TLS)** in Corda, thus ensuring privacy and integrity of data communicated between nodes.

Nodes also make use of a local relational database for storage. Messages on the network are encoded in a compact binary format. They are delivered and managed by using the **Apache Artemis message broker (Active MQ)**. A node can serve as a network map service, notary, Oracle, or a regular node. The following diagram shows a high-level view of two nodes communicating with each other:

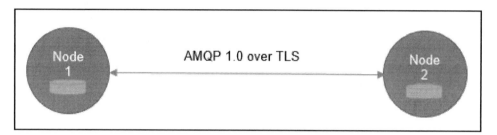

Two nodes communicating in a Corda network

In the preceding diagram, **Node 1** is communicating with **Node 2** over a TLS communication channel using the AMQP protocol, and the nodes have a local relational database for storage.

Permissioning service

A Permissioning service is used to provision TLS certificates for security. In order to participate on the network, participants are required to have a signed identity issued by a root certificate authority. Identities are required to be unique on the network and the Permissioning service is used to sign these identities. The naming convention used to recognise participants is based on the X.500 standard. This ensures the uniqueness of the name.

Network map service

This service is used to provide a network map in the form of a document of all nodes on the network. This service publishes IP addresses, identity certificates and a list of services offered by nodes. All nodes announce their presence by registering to this service when they first start up, and when a connection request is received by a node, the presence of the requesting node is checked on the network map first. Put another way, this service resolves the identities of the participants to physical nodes.

Notary service

In a traditional blockchain, mining is used to ascertain the order of blocks that contain transactions. In Corda, notary services are used to provide transaction ordering and timestamping services. There can be multiple notaries in a network and they are identified by composite public keys. Notaries can use different consensus algorithms like BFT or Raft depending on the requirements of the applications. Notary services sign the transactions to indicate validity and finality of the transaction which is then persisted to the database.

Notaries can be run in a load-balanced configuration in order to spread the load across the nodes for performance reasons; and, in order to reduce latency, the nodes are recommended to be run physically closer to the transaction participants.

Oracle service

Oracle services either sign a transaction containing a fact, if it is true, or can themselves provide factual data. They allow real world feed into the distributed ledgers.

Transactions

Transactions in a Corda network are never transmitted globally, but in a semi-private network. They are shared only between a subset of participants who are related to the transaction. This is in contrast to traditional blockchain solutions like Ethereum and bitcoin, where all transactions are broadcasted to the entire network globally. Transactions are digitally signed and either consume state(s) or create new state(s).

Transactions on a Corda network are composed of the following elements:

- **Input references**: This is a reference to the states the transaction is going to consume and use as an input.

- **Output states**: These are new states created by the transaction.

- **Attachments**: This is a list of hashes of attached zip files. Zip files can contain code and other relevant documentation related to the transaction. Files themselves are not made part of the transaction, instead, they are transferred and stored separately.

- **Commands**: A command represents the information about the intended operation of the transaction as a parameter to the contract. Each command has a list of public keys which represents all parties that are required to sign a transaction.

- **Signatures**: This represents the signature required by the transaction. The total number of signatures required is directly proportional to the number of public keys for commands.

- **Type**: There are two types of transactions namely, Normal or Notary changing. Notary changing transactions are used for reassigning a notary for a state.

- **Timestamp**: This field represents a bracket of time during which the transaction has taken place. These are verified and enforced by notary services. Also, it is expected that if strict timings are required, which is desirable in many financial services scenarios, notaries should be synched with an atomic clock.

- **Summaries**: This is a text description that describes the operations of the transaction.

Vaults

Vaults run on a node and are akin to the concept of wallets in bitcoin. As the transactions are not globally broadcast, each node will have only that part of data in their vaults that is considered relevant to them. Vaults store their data in a standard relational database and as such can be queried by using standard SQL. Vaults can contain both on ledger and off ledger data, meaning that it can also have some part of data that is not on ledger.

CorDapp

The core model of Corda consists of state objects, transactions and transaction protocols, which when combined with contract code, APIs, wallet plugins, and user interface components results in constructing a **Corda distributed application (CorDapp)**.

Smart contracts in Corda are written using Kotlin or Java. The code is targeted for JVM. JVM has been modified slightly in order to achieve deterministic results of execution of JVM bytecode. There are three main components in a Corda smart contract as follows:

1. Executable code that defines the validation logic to validate changes to the state objects.
2. State objects represent the current state of a contract and either can be consumed by a transaction or produced (created) by a transaction.
3. Commands are used to describe the operational and verification data that defines how a transaction can be verified.

Development environment

The development environment for Corda can be set up easily using the following steps.

Required software includes the following:

1. JDK 8 which is available at `http://www.oracle.com/technetwork/java/javase/downloads/index.html`.
2. IntelliJ IDEA community edition which is free and available at `https://www.jetbrains.com/idea/download`.
3. H2 database platform independent zip, and is available at `http://www.h2database.com/html/download.html`.
4. Git, available at `https://git-scm.com/downloads`.
5. Kotlin language, which is available for IntelliJ, and more information can be found at `https://kotlinlang.org/`.
6. Gradle is another component that is used to build Corda.

Once all these tools are installed, smart contract development can be started. CorDapps can be developed by utilizing an example template available at `https://github.com/corda/cordapp-template`. Detailed documentation on how to develop contract code is available at `https://docs.corda.net/`.

Corda can be cloned locally from GitHub using the following command:

```
$ git clone https://github.com/corda/corda.git
```

When the cloning is successful, you should see output similar to the following:

```
Cloning into 'corda'...
remote: Counting objects: 74695, done.
remote: Compressing objects: 100% (67/67), done.
remote: Total 74695 (delta 17), reused 0 (delta 0), pack-reused 74591
Receiving objects: 100% (74695/74695), 51.27 MiB | 1.72 MiB/s, done.
Resolving deltas: 100% (42863/42863), done.
Checking connectivity... done.
```

Once the repository is cloned, it can be opened in IntelliJ for further development. There are multiple samples available in the repository, such as a bank of Corda, interest rate swaps, demo, and traders demo. Readers can find them under the `/samples` directory under `corda` and they can be explored using IntelliJ IDEA IDE.

Summary

In this chapter, we've provided an introduction to the Hyperledger project. Firstly, the core ideas behind the Hyperledger project were discussed and a brief introduction to all projects under incubation in Hyperledger was provided. Three main Hyperledger projects were discussed in detail, namely Hyperledger fabric, Sawtooth lake and Corda. All these projects are currently under heavy development and changes are expected in the next releases. Because of this, no in-depth practical exercises were given. However, the core concepts of all the projects mentioned above are expected to remain unchanged or changed only very slightly. Readers are encouraged to visit the relevant links provided within the chapter in order see the latest updates. It is obvious that a lot is going on in this space and projects like Hyperledger from the Linux foundation are playing a key role in the advancement of blockchain technology. Each of the projects discussed in this chapter has novel approaches towards solving the issues faced in various industries, and any current limitations within the blockchain technology are also being addressed, such as scalability and privacy. It is expected that more projects will soon be proposed to the Hyperledger project, and it is envisaged that with this collaborative and open effort blockchain technology will advance tremendously and will benefit the community as a whole.

10
Alternative Blockchains

This chapter is intended to provide an introduction to alternative blockchain solutions. With the success of bitcoin and subsequent realization of the potential of blockchain technology, a Cambrian explosion started that resulted in the development of various blockchain protocols, applications, and platforms. Some projects did not gain much traction, but many have succeeded in creating a solid place in this space.

In this chapter, readers will be introduced to alternative blockchains and platforms that either are new blockchains on their own or complement other existing blockchains. These new platforms are based on the idea of providing SDKs and tools to make development and deployment of blockchain solutions easier. The success of Ethereum and bitcoin has resulted in various projects that spawned into existence by leveraging the underlying technologies and concepts introduced by them. These new projects add value by addressing the limitations in the current blockchains or enhancing the existing solutions by providing an additional layer of user-friendly tools on top of them.

In the first section of this chapter, an introduction to new blockchain solutions will be given, and later sections will cover various platforms and development kits that complement existing blockchains. For example, BlockApps STRATO is an Ethereum-compliant platform for the development of blockchain applications, and Kadena is a new private blockchain with novel ideas such as Scalable BFT. Various concepts such as sidechains, drivechains, and pegging have also been introduced for the first time with this growth of blockchain technologies. This chapter will cover all these technologies and related concepts in detail. Of course, it's not possible to cover all alternative chains (altchains) and platforms, but all those platforms have been included in this chapter that are related to blockchains, covered in the previous chapters, or are expected to gain traction in the near future.

Blockchains

This section will give an introduction to new blockchain solutions. First, a new blockchain named Kadena is discussed in the following section.

Kadena

Kadena is a recently-introduced private blockchain that has successfully addressed scalability and privacy issues in blockchain systems. A new Turing incomplete language called Pact has also been introduced with Kadena that allows the development of smart contracts. A key innovation in Kadena is its Scalable BFT consensus algorithm, which has the potential to scale to thousands of nodes without performance degradation. Scalable BFT is based on the original Raft algorithm and is a successor of Tangaroa and Juno. Tangaroa, which is a name given to an implementation of Raft with fault tolerance (a BFT Raft), was developed to address the availability and safety issues that arose from the behavior of byzantine nodes in the Raft algorithm, and Juno was a fork of Tangaroa that was developed by *JPMorgan*. Consensus algorithms are discussed in `Chapter 1`, *Blockchain 101* in more detail. Both of these proposals have a fundamental limitation – they cannot scale while maintaining a high level of high performance. As such, Juno could not gain much traction. Private blockchains have the more desirable property of maintaining high performance as the number of nodes increase, but the aforementioned proposals lack this feature. Kadena solves this issue with its proprietary Scalable BFT algorithm, which is expected to scale up to thousands of nodes without any performance degradation.

Moreover, confidentiality is another important aspect of Kadena that enables privacy of transactions on the blockchain. This is achieved by using a combination of key rotation, symmetric on-chain encryption, incremental hashing, and Double Ratchet protocol.

Key rotation is used as a standard mechanism to ensure security of the private blockchain. It is used as a best practice to thwart any attacks if the keys have been compromised, by periodically changing the encryption keys. There is a native support for key rotation in Pact smart contract language.

Symmetric on chain encryption allows encryption of transaction data on the blockchain. These transactions can be automatically decrypted by the participants of a particular private transaction. Double Ratchet protocol is used to provide key management and encryption functions.

Scalable BFT consensus protocol ensures that adequate replication and consensus has been achieved before smart contract execution. Consensus is achieved by following the process described below:

1. First, a new transaction is signed by the user and broadcasted over the blockchain network, which is picked up by a leader node that adds it to its immutable log. At this point, an incremental hash is also calculated for the log. Incremental hash is a type of hash function that basically allows computation of hash messages in the scenario where, if a previous original message which is already hashed is slightly changed, then the new hash message is computed from the already existing hash. This scheme is quicker and less resource intensive compared to a conventional hash function where an altogether new hash message is required to be generated even if the original message has only changed very slightly.

2. Once the transaction is written to the log by the leader node, it signs the replication and incremental hash and broadcasts it to other nodes.

3. Other nodes, after receiving the transaction, verify the signature of the leader node, add the transaction into their own logs, and broadcast their own calculated incremental hashes (quorum proofs) to other nodes. Finally, the transaction is committed into the ledger permanently after an adequate number of proofs are received from other nodes.

A simplified version of this process is shown in the following diagram, where the **leader** node is recording the new transactions and then replicating them to the **follower** nodes:

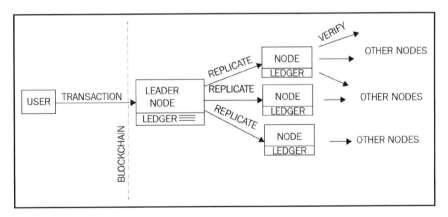

Consensus mechanism in Kadena

Once the consensus is achieved, smart contract execution can start and takes a number of steps, as follows:

1. First, the signature of the message is verified.
2. Pact smart contract layer takes over.
3. Pact code is compiled.
4. The transaction is initiated and executes any business logic embedded within smart contract. In case of any failures, an immediate rollback is initiated that reverts that state back to what it was before the execution started.
5. Finally, the transaction completes and relevant logs are updated.

Pact has been open sourced by Kadena and is available for download at `http://kadena.io/pact/downloads.html`. This can be downloaded as a standalone binary that provides a REPL for Pact language. An example is shown below where Pact is run by issuing the command `./pact` in Linux console:

Pact REPL, showing sample commands and error output

Smart contract in Pact is generally composed of three sections: keysets, modules, and tables. First, **keyset** defines relevant authorization schemes for tables and modules. Second, **module** defines which is the smart contract code encompassing the business logic in the form of **functions** and **Pacts**. Pacts within modules are composed of multiple steps and are executed sequentially.

Pact can be used in several execution modes. These modes include **contract definition**, **transaction execution,** and **querying**. Contract definition mode allows a contract to be created on the blockchain via a single transaction message. Transaction execution mode entails the execution of modules of smart contract code that represent business logic. Querying is concerned with simply probing the contract for data and is executed locally on the nodes for performance reasons.

Pact uses LISP-like syntax and represents in the code exactly what will be executed on the blockchain as it is stored on the blockchain in human-readable format. This is in contrast to Ethereum's EVM, which compiles into byte code for execution, which makes it difficult to verify what code is in execution on the blockchain. Moreover, it is Turing incomplete, supports immutable variables, and does not allow null values, which improves overall safety of the transaction code execution.

It is not possible to cover the complete syntax and functions of Pact in this chapter, however, a small example is shown below that shows the general structure of a smart contract written in Pact. This example shows a simple addition module that defines a function named `addition` that takes three parameters. When the code is executed it adds all three values and displays the result.

The following example has been developed using the online Pact compiler available at `http://kadena.io/try-pact/`:

```
1  (begin-tx) 'testTransaction ;Begin transaction with optional NAME.
2  ;Set transaction  data in JSON format or pact types
3  (env-data { "keyset": { "keys": ["admin"] , "pred": "keys-any" } })
4  ;Define keyset as NAME with KEYSET
5  (define-keyset 'admin-keyset (read-keyset "keyset"))
6  ;Set transaction signature KEYS.
7  (env-keys "admin")
8  ;define module using syntax (module NAME KEYSET [DOCSTRING] DEFS...)
9  (module additionModule 'admin-keyset
10    ;define function that takes three arguments x y z
11    (defun addition (x y z) (+ x (+ y z)))
12  )
13 (commit-tx) ;Commit transaction.
14 ;use the function addition
15 (use 'additionModule)
16 ;run the function addition
17 (format "Result : {}" (addition 100 200 300))
```

Sample Pact code

When the code is run, it produces the output shown as follows:

```
Begin Tx 1
testTransaction
Setting transaction data
Keyset defined
Setting transaction keys
Loaded module "additionModule"
Commit Tx 1
Using "additionModule"
Result : 600
```

Output of the code

As shown in the preceding example, the execution output matches exactly with the code layout and structure, which allows for greater transparency and limits the possibility of malicious code execution.

Kadena is a new class of private blockchains introducing the novel concept of **pervasive determinism** where, in addition to standard public/private key-based data origin security, an additional layer of fully deterministic consensus is also provided. It provides cryptographic security at all layers of the blockchain including transactions and consensus layer.

 Relevant documentation and source code for Pact can be found here: https://github.com/kadena-io/pact.

Ripple

Introduced in 2012, Ripple is a currency exchange and real-time gross settlement system. In Ripple, the payments are settled without any waiting as opposed to traditional settlement networks, where it can take days for settlement. It has a native currency called **Ripples (XRP)**. It also supports non-XRP payments. This system is considered similar to an old traditional money transfer mechanism known as *Hawala*. This system works by making use of agents who take the money and a password from the sender, then contact the payee's agent and instruct them to release funds to the person who can provide the password. The payee then contacts the local agent, tells them the password and collects the funds. An analogy to the agent is Gateway in Ripple. This is just a very simple analogy, the actual protocol is rather complex but principally it is the same.

The Ripple network is composed of various nodes that can perform different functions based on their type. First, **user nodes**: these use in payment transactions and can pay or receive payments. Second, **validator nodes**: these participate in the consensus mechanism. Each server maintains a set of unique nodes, which it needs to query while achieving consensus. Nodes in the **unique node List (UNL)** are trusted by the server involved in the consensus mechanism and will accept votes only from this list of unique nodes. Ripple is sometimes not considered truly decentralized as there are network operators and regulators involved. However it can be considered decentralized due to the fact that anyone can become part of the network by running a validator node. Moreover, the consensus process is also decentralized because any changes proposed to made on the ledger have to be decided by following a scheme of super majority voting. However this is a hot topic amongst researchers and enthusiasts and there are arguments against and in favor of each school of thought.

Ripple maintains a global distributed ledger of all transactions that is governed by a novel low-latency consensus algorithm called **Ripple Protocol Consensus Algorithm (RPCA)**. The consensus process works by achieving an agreement on the state of an open ledger containing transactions by seeking verification and acceptance from validating servers in an iterative manner until an adequate number of votes are achieved. Once enough votes are received (super majority, initially 50% and gradually increasing with each iteration up to at least 80%) the changes are validated and the ledger is closed. At this point, an alert is sent to the whole network indicating that the ledger is closed.

In summary, the consensus protocol is a three-phase process. First, the **collection phase**, where validating nodes gather all transactions broadcasted on the network by account owners and validate them. Transactions, once accepted, are called candidate transactions and can be accepted or rejected based on the validation criteria. Then the **consensus** process starts, and after achieving it the ledger is **closed**. This process runs asynchronously every few seconds in rounds and, as result, the ledger is opened and closed (updated) accordingly.

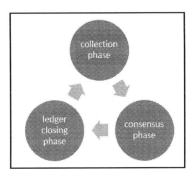

Ripple consensus protocol phases

In a Ripple network there are a number of components that work together in order to achieve consensus and form a payment network. These components are discussed individually below:

- **Server**: This component serves as a participant in the consensus protocol. Ripple server software is required in order to be able to participate in consensus protocol.
- **Ledger**: This is a main record of balances of all accounts on the network. A ledger contains various elements such as ledger number, account settings, transactions, timestamp, and a flag that indicates validity of the ledger.
- **Last closed ledger**: A ledger is closed once consensus is achieved by validating nodes.

- **Open ledger**: This is a ledger that has not been validated yet and no consensus has been reached about its state. Each node has its own open ledger, which contains proposed transactions.
- **Unique node list**: This is a list of unique trusted nodes that a validating server uses in order to seek votes and subsequent consensus.
- **Proposer**: As the name suggests, this component proposes new transactions to be included in the consensus process. It is usually a subset of nodes (UNL defined above) that can propose transactions to the validating server.

Transactions

Transactions are created by network users in order to update the ledger. A transaction is expected to be digitally signed and valid in order for it to be considered as a candidate in the consensus process. Each transaction costs a small amount of XRP, which serves as a protection mechanism against denial of service attacks caused by spamming. There are different types of transaction in the Ripple network. A single field within the Ripple transaction data structure called `TransactionType` is used to represent the type of the transaction. Transactions are executed by using a four step process. First, transactions are prepared whereby an unsigned transaction is created by following the standards. Second step is signing, where the transaction is digitally signed to authorize it. After this, the actual submission to the network occurs via the connected server. Finally, the verification is performed to ensure that the transaction is validated successfully.

Roughly, the transactions can be categorized into three types, namely Payments related, Order related, and Account and security related. All these types are described in the following section.

Payments related

There are several fields in this category that result in certain actions. All these fields are described as follows:

1. `Payment`: This transaction is most commonly used and allows one user to send funds to another.
2. `PaymentChannelClaim`: This is used to claim **Ripples (XRP)** from a payment channel. A payment channel is a mechanism that allows recurring and unidirectional payments between parties. This can also be used to set the expiration time of the payment channel.
3. `PaymentChannelCreate`: This transaction creates a new payment channel and adds XRP to it in *drops*. A single drop is equivalent to 0.000001 of an XRP.

4. `PaymentChannelFund`: This transaction is used to add more funds to an existing channel. Similar to `PaymentChannelClaim` transaction, this can also be used to modify the expiration time of the payment channel.

Order related

This type of transaction includes following two fields:

1. `OfferCreate`: This transaction represents a limit order, which represents an intent for exchange of currency. It results in creating an Offer node in the consensus ledger if it cannot be completely fulfilled.
2. `OfferCancel`: This is used to remove a previously created offer node from the consensus ledger, indicating withdrawal of the order.

Account and security related

This type of transaction include the fields listed as follows. Each field is responsible for performing a certain function.

1. `AccountSet`: This transaction is used to modify the attributes of an account in the Ripple consensus ledger.
2. `SetRegularKey`: This is used to change or set the transaction signing key for an account. An account is identified using a base-58 Ripple address derived from the account's master public key.
3. `SignerListSet`: This can be used to create a set of signers for use in multi-signature transactions.
4. `TrustSet`: This is used to create or modify a trust line between accounts.

A transaction in Ripple is composed of various fields that are common to all transaction types. These fields are listed as follows with description:

1. `Account` , address of the initiator of the transaction.
2. `AccountTxnID` , this is an optional field which contains the hash of another transaction.
3. `Fee`, Amount of XRP.
4. `Flags`, optional flags for the transaction.
5. `LastLedgerSequence`, highest sequence number of the ledger in which the transaction can appear.
6. `Memos`, optional arbitrary information.

7. Sequence, a number incremented by 1 with each transaction.

8. SigningPubKey, public key.

9. Signers, represent signers in a multisig transaction.

10. SourceTag, represents either sender or reason of the transaction.

11. TransactionType, type of the transaction.

12. TxnSignature, verification signature for the transaction.

Various developer's APIs are available with Ripple in order to enable external entities to connect to the Ripple network. Two key components, **Interledger** protocol and **Ripple connect**, work in harmony in order to enable distributed, secure, scalable, and interoperable payments network.

Interledger protocol has been specifically developed to enable interoperability between two different ledgers. It can be used to connect ledgers and blockchains from various different organizations including, but not limited to, payment networks, financial institutions, clearing houses, and exchanges.

Interledger is a simple protocol that is composed of four layers: Application, Transport, Interledger, and Ledger. Each layer is responsible for performing various functions under certain protocols. These functions and protocols are described in the following section.

Application layer

Protocols running on this layer govern the key attributes of a payment transaction. Examples of application layer protocols include **Simple Payment Setup protocol (SPSP)** and **Open Web payment scheme (OWPS)**. SPSP is an Interledger protocol that allows secure payment across different ledgers by creating *Connectors* between them. OWPS is another scheme that allows consumer payments across different networks. Once the protocols on this layer have run successfully, protocols from the transport layer will be invoked in order to start the payment process.

Transport layer

This layer is responsible for managing payment transactions. Protocols such as **Optimistic Transport protocol (OTP)**, **Universal Transport protocol (UTP)** and **Atomic Transport protocol (ATP)** are available currently for this layer. OTP is the simplest protocol, which manages payment transfers without any escrow protection, whereas UTP provides escrow protection. ATP is the most advanced protocol, which not only provides an escrowed transfer mechanism but in addition makes use of trusted notaries to further secure the payment transactions.

Interledger layer

This layer provides interoperability and routing services. This layer contains protocols such as **Interledger protocol (ILP)**, **Interledger quoting protocol (ILQP)**, and **Interledger control protocol (ILCP)**. ILP packet provides the final target of the transaction in a transfer. ILQP is used in making quote requests by the senders before the actual transfer. ILCP is used to exchange data related to routing information and payment errors between connectors on the payment network.

Ledger layer

This layer contains protocols that enable communication and execution of payment transactions between connectors. *Connectors* are basically objects that implement the protocol for forwarding payments between different ledgers. It can support various protocols such as Simple Ledger protocol, various blockchain protocols, legacy protocols, and different proprietary protocols.

Ripple connect consists of various Plug and Play modules that allow connectivity between ledgers by using the ILP. It enables the exchange of required data between parties before the transaction, visibility, fee management, delivery confirmation, and secure communication using Transport layer security. A third-party application can connect to the Ripple network via various connectors.

Overall, Ripple is a solution that is targeted for financial industry and makes real-time payments possible without any settlement risk. As this is a very feature-rich platform, covering all aspects of it are not possible in this chapter. Ripple and very rich documentation for the platform are available at `https://ripple.com/`.

Stellar

Stellar is a payment network based on blockchain technology and a novel consensus model called **Federated Byzantine Agreement (FBA)**. FBA works by creating quorums of trusted parties. **Stellar Consensus Protocol (SCP)** is an implementation of FBA.

Key issues identified in the Stellar whitepaper are the cost and complexity of current financial infrastructure. This limitation warrants the need for a global financial network that addresses these issues without compromising the integrity and security of the financial transaction. This requirement has resulted in the invention of **Stellar Consensus Protocol (SCP)** which is a provably safe consensus mechanism.

It has four main properties: *decentralized control,* which allows participation by anyone without any central party; *low latency,* which addresses the much desired requirement of fast transaction processing; *flexible trust,* which allows users to choose which parties they trust for a specific purpose, and finally, *asymptotic security,* which makes use of digital signatures and hash functions for providing the required level of security on the network.

The Stellar network allows transfer and representation of the value of an asset by its native digital currency, called Lumens, abbreviated as XLM. Lumens are consumed when a transaction is broadcasted on the network, which also serves as a deterrent against **Denial of Service (DOS)** attacks.

At its core, the Stellar network maintains a distributed ledger that records every transaction and is replicated on each Stellar server. The consensus is achieved by verifying transactions between servers and updating the ledger with updates. The Stellar ledger can also act as a distributed exchange order book by allowing users to store their offers to buy or sell currencies.

There are various tools, SDKs, and software that make up the Stellar network. The core software is available at `https://github.com/stellar/stellar-core`.

Rootstock

Before discussing Rootstock in detail, it's important to define and introduce some concepts that are fundamental to the design of Rootstock. These concepts include sidechains, drivechains, and two-way pegging. The concept of the sidechain was originally developed by Blockstream.

Two way pegging is a mechanism by which value (coins) can transfer between one blockchain to another and vice versa. There is no real transfer of coin between chains. The idea revolves around the concept of locking the same amount and value of coins in a bitcoin blockchain (main chain) and unlocking the equivalent amount of tokens in the secondary chain.

, sidechains can be defined as described in the following section. Bearing this definition in mind, sidechains can be defined as described in the following section.

Sidechain

This is a blockchain that runs in parallel with a main blockchain and allows transfer of value between them. This means that tokens from one blockchain can be used in the sidechain and vice versa. This is also called a pegged sidechain because it supports two-way pegged assets.

Drivechain

This is a relatively new concept, where control on unlocking the locked bitcoins (in mainchain) is given to the miners who can vote when to unlock them. This is in contrast to sidechains, where consensus is validated though Simple payment verification mechanism in order to transfer the coins back to the mainchain.

Rootstock is a smart contract platform which has a two-way peg into bitcoin blockchain. The core idea is to increase the scalability and performance of the bitcoin system and enable it to work with smart contracts. Rootstock runs a Turing complete deterministic virtual machine called **Rootstock Virtual Machine** (**RVM**). It is also compatible with the Ethereum virtual machine and allows solidity-compiled contracts to run on Rootstock. Smart contracts can also run under the time-a tested security of bitcoin blockchain. The Rootstock blockchain works by merge mining with bitcoins. This allows RSK blockchain to achieve the same security level as bitcoin. This is especially true for preventing double spends and achieving settlement finality. It allows scalability, up to 100 transactions per second.

RSK has recently released a test network called Turmeric. It is available at `http://www.rsk.co/`.

Quorum

This is a blockchain solution built by enhancing the existing Ethereum blockchain. There are several enhancements such as transaction privacy and a new consensus mechanism that has been introduced in Quorum. Quorum has introduced a new consensus model known as QuorumChain, which is based on a majority voting and time based mechanism. Another feature called Constellation is also introduced which is a general purpose mechanism for submitting information and allows encrypted communication between peers. Furthermore, permissioning at node level is governed by smart contracts. It also provides a higher level of performance compared to public Ethereum blockchains.

Several components make up the Quorum blockchain ecosystem. These are listed in the following section.

Transaction manager

This component enables access to encrypted transaction data. It also manages local storage and communication with other Transaction managers on the network.

Crypto Enclave

As the name suggests, this component is responsible for providing cryptographic services to ensure transaction privacy. It is also responsible for performing key management functions.

QuorumChain

This is the key innovation in Quorum. It is a Byzantine Fault-tolerant consensus mechanism which allows verification and circulation of votes via transactions on the blockchain network. In this scheme, a smart contract is used to manage the consensus process and nodes can be given voting rights to vote on which new block should be accepted. Once an appropriate number of votes is received by the voters, the block is considered valid. Nodes can have two roles, namely *Voter* or *Maker*. The *Voter* node is allowed to vote, whereas the *Maker* node is the one that creates a new block. A node can have either rights, none or only one.

Network manager

This component provides an access control layer for the permissioned network.

A node in the quorum network can take several roles, for example, a Maker node that is allowed to create new blocks. Transaction privacy is provided using cryptography and the concept that certain transactions are meant to be viewable only by their relevant participants. This idea is similar to Corda's idea of private transactions that was discussed in the last chapter. As it allows both public and private transactions on the blockchain, the state database has been divided into two databases representing private and public transactions. As such, there are two separate Patricia-Merkle trees that represent the private and public state of the network. A private contract state hash is used to provide consensus evidence in private transactions between transacting parties.

Transaction in a quorum network consists of various elements such as the recipient, the digital signature of the sender, which is used to identify the transaction originator, optional ether amount, the optional list of participants that are allowed to see the transaction, and a field that contains a hash in case of private transactions.

A transaction goes through several steps before it can reach its destination. These steps are described as follows in detail:

1. User applications (DAPPs) send the transaction to the quorum node via an API exposed by the blockchain network. This also contains the recipient address and transaction data.

2. The API then encrypts the payload and applies any other necessary cryptographic algorithm in order to ensure privacy of the transaction, and is sent to the Transaction manager. The hash of the encrypted payload is also calculated at this step.

3. After receiving the transaction, the Transaction manager validates the signature of the transaction sender and stores the message.

4. The hash of the previously encrypted payload is sent to the Quorum node.

5. Once the Quorum node starts to validate a block that contains the private transaction, it requests more relevant data from the Transaction manager.

6. Once this request is received by the Transaction manager, it sends the encrypted payload and relevant symmetric keys to the requestor quorum node.

7. Once the Quorum node has all the data, it decrypts the payload and sends it to the EVM for execution. This is how Quorum achieves privacy with symmetric encryption on the blockchain, while it is able to use native Ethereum protocol and EVM for message transfer and execution respectively.

8. A similar concept, but quite different in a few aspects, has been proposed before in the form of **Hydrachain**, which is based on Ethereum blockchain and allows creation of permissioned distributed ledgers.

Quorum is available for download at `https://github.com/jpmorganchase/quorum`.

Tezos

Tezos is a generic self-amending cryptographic ledger, which means that it not only allows decentralized consensus on the state of the blockchain but also allows consensus on how the protocol and nodes are evolved over time. Tezos has been developed to address limitations in bitcoin protocol such as issues arising from hard forks, cost, and mining power centralization due to Proof of Work, limited scripting ability, and security issues. It has been developed in a purely functional language called OCaml.

The architecture of Tezos distributed ledger is divided into three layers: the network layer, consensus layer, and transaction layer. This decomposition allows protocol to be evolved in a decentralized fashion. For this purpose, a generic network shell is implemented in Tezos that is responsible for maintaining the blockchain, which is represented by a combination of consensus and transaction layer. This shell provides an interface layer between the network and the protocol. A concept of seed protocol has also been introduced, which is used as a mechanism to allow stakeholders on the network to approve any changes to the protocol. Tezos blockchain starts from a seed protocol compared to a traditional blockchain that starts from a genesis block.

This seed protocol is responsible for defining procedures for amendments in the blockchain and even the amendment protocol itself. The reward mechanism in Tezos is based on a **Proof of Stake (PoS)** algorithm, therefore there is no mining requirement.

Contract script language has been developed in Tezos for writing smart contracts, which is a stack-based Turing complete language. Smart contracts in Tezos are formally verifiable, which allows the code to be mathematically proven for its correctness.

Tezos code is available at `https://github.com/tezos/tezos`.

Storj

Existing models for cloud-based storage are all centralized solutions, which may or may not be as secure as users expect them to be. There is a need to have a cloud storage system that is secure, highly available, and above all decentralized. Storj aims to provide blockchain based, decentralized, and distributed storage. It is a cloud shared by the community instead of a central organization. It allows execution of storage contracts between nodes that act as autonomous agents. These agents (nodes) execute various functions such as data transfer, validation, and perform data integrity checks. The core concept is based on **Distributed Hash Tables (DHT)** -Kademlia, however this protocol has been enhanced by adding new message types and functionalities in Storj. It also implements a peer to peer **publish/subscribe (pub/sub)** mechanism known as Quasar, which ensures that messages successfully reach the nodes that are interested in storage contracts. This is achieved via a bloom filter-based storage contract parameters selection mechanism called **topics**.

Storj stores files in an encrypted format spread across the network. Before the file is stored on the network, it is encrypted using AES-256-CTR symmetric encryption and is then stored piece by piece in a distributed manner on the network. This process of dissecting the file into pieces is called **sharding** and results in increased availability, security, performance, and privacy of the network. Also if a node fails the shard is still available because by default a single shard is stored at three different locations on the network.

It maintains a blockchain, which serves as a shared ledger and implements standard security features such as public/private key cryptography and hash functions similar to any other blockchain. As the system is based on hard drive sharing between peers, anyone can contribute by sharing their extra space on the drive and get paid with Storj's own cryptocurrency called **Storjcoinx (SJCX)**. SJCX was developed as a *counterparty* asset and makes use of bitcoin blockchain for transactions.

Storj code is available at `https://github.com/Storj/`.

Maidsafe

This is another distributed storage system similar to Storj. Users are paid in Safecoin for their storage space contribution to the network. This mechanism of payment is governed by *proof of resource*, which ensures that the disk space committed by a user to the network is available, if not then the payment of Safecoin will drop accordingly. The files are encrypted and divided into small portions before being transmitted on to the network for storage. Another concept of **opportunistic caching** has been introduced with Maidsafe, which is a mechanism to create copies of frequently accessed data physically closer to where the access requests are coming from, which results in high performance of the network. Another novel feature of the SAFE network is that it automatically removes any duplicate data on the network, thus resulting in reduced storage requirements. Moreover, the concept of **churning** has also been introduced, which basically means that data is constantly moved across the network so that the data cannot be targeted by malicious adversaries. It also keeps multiple copies of data across the network to provide redundancy in case a node goes offline or fails.

BigChainDB

This is a scalable blockchain database. It is not strictly a blockchain itself, but complements blockchain technology by providing a decentralized database. At its core it's a distributed database but with the added attributes of a blockchain such as decentralization, immutability, and handling of digital assets. It also allows usage of NoSQL for querying the database. It is intended to provide a database in a decentralized ecosystem where not only processing is decentralized (blockchain) or the file system is decentralized (for example, IPFS) but the database is also decentralized. This makes the whole decentralized application ecosystem decentralized. This is available at `https://www.bigchaindb.com/`.

Multichain

Multichain has been developed as a platform for the development and deployment of private blockchains. It is based on bitcoin code and addresses security, scalability, and privacy issues. It is a highly configurable blockchain platform that allows users to set different blockchain parameters. It supports control and privacy via a granular Permissioning layer. Installation of Multichain is very quick and links to installation files are available at `http://www.multichain.com/download-install/`.

Tendermint

Tendermint is a software that provides a Byzantine fault-tolerant consensus mechanism and state machine replication functionality to an application. Its main motivation is to develop a general purpose, secure, and high-performance replicated state machine.

There are two components in Tendermint, which are described in following section.

Tendermint Core

This is a consensus engine that enables secure replication of transactions on each node in the network.

Tendermint Socket Protocol (TMSP)

This is an application interface protocol that allows interfacing with any programming language to process transactions.

Tendermint allows decoupling of the application process and consensus process, which allows any application to benefit from the consensus mechanism.

The Tendermint consensus algorithm is a round-based mechanism where validator nodes propose new blocks in each round. A locking mechanism is used to ensure protection against a scenario where two different blocks are selected for committing at the same height of the blockchain. Each validator node maintains a full local replicated ledger of blocks that contain transactions. Each block contains a header, which consists of the previous block hash, timestamp of the proposal of block, current block height, and merkle root hash of all transactions present in the block.

Tendermint has recently been used in **Cosmos**, which is a network of blockchains that allows interoperability between different chains running on BFT consensus algorithm. Blockchains on this network are called zones. The first zone in Cosmos is called Cosmos hub, which is in fact a public blockchain and is responsible for providing connectivity service to other blockchains. For this purpose, the hub makes use of **Inter Blockchain Communication protocol (IBC)**. IBC protocol supports two types of transactions called *IBCBlockCimmitTx* and *IBCPacketTx*. The first type is used to provide proof of the most recent block hash in a blockchain to any party, whereas the latter type is used to provide data origin authentication. A packet from one blockchain to another is published by first posting a proof to the target chain. The receiving (target) chain checks this proof in order to verify that the sending chain has indeed published the packet. In addition, it has its own native currency called Atom. This scheme addresses scalability and interoperability issues by allowing multiple blockchains to connect to the hub.

Tendermint is available at `https://tendermint.com/`.

Platforms

This section covers various platforms that have been developed to enhance the experience of existing blockchain solutions. First, an Ethereum-compliant solution named BlockApps STRATO will be discussed.

BlockApps

BlockApps is a platform that provides a rich set of tools to build blockchain applications. This platform is written in Haskell and is based on modular architecture. The solution is scalable and makes it easier to deploy smart contracts and blockchain applications. It is available at `http://www.blockapps.net/`.

In the next section, installation and a simple example of deployment will be discussed.

Installation

BlockApps can be installed via npm by using the command shown as follows:

```
$ sudo npm install -g blockapps-bloc
```

`sudo` is optional, if no administrative rights are required. This will produce an output similar to the one shown in the following screenshot:

```
npm WARN deprecated secp256k1-browserify@0.0.0: secp256k1 now inculdes browser compentents
/usr/bin/bloc -> /usr/lib/node_modules/blockapps-bloc/bin/main.js
/usr/lib
└── blockapps-bloc@1.2.2
  ├── bignumber.js@2.4.0
  ├── blockapps-js@3.1.2
  ├── bn.js@4.11.6
  ├── elliptic@6.3.2
  ├── brorand@1.0.6
  ├── hash.js@1.0.3
  └── inherits@2.0.3
```

bloc installation via npm (output truncated)

Once installation is complete, applications can be created by following the steps shown in following section. An example is shown below that shows how to initialize a new application in BlockApps, deploy it on BlockApps TestNet and interact with it.

Application development and deployment using BlockApps

The first step is to initialize the BlockApps application using the following command:

```
$ bloc init
```

It will ask for several parameters: the name of the app, your name, e-mail, API URL (apiUrl), and blockchain profile. This is shown in the following screenshot.

Once the command runs and completes successfully, it will create an application directory with templates and samples. In this instance, a directory named testApp will be created with relevant directories and sample contracts.

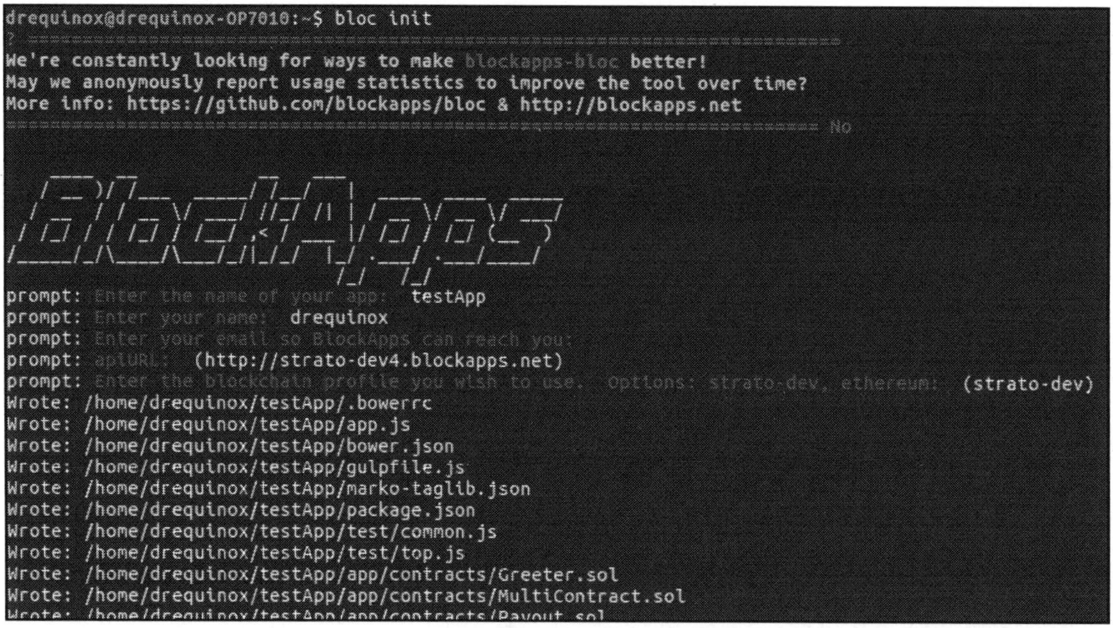

```
drequinox@drequinox-OP7010:~$ bloc init
?
We're constantly looking for ways to make blockapps-bloc better!
May we anonymously report usage statistics to improve the tool over time?
More info: https://github.com/blockapps/bloc & http://blockapps.net
                                                                        No

   /¯¯)/¯¯/ /¯¯/    /¯¯/ /¯¯/¯¯/¯¯/
  /  / /  / <¯ /¯/ /¯/¯/  ./¯/ /¯¯/
 /__/_/__/__/_/_/_/_/_/_/  ./_/ /_/
                        /_/ /_/

prompt: Enter the name of your app:    testApp
prompt: Enter your name:    drequinox
prompt: Enter your email so BlockApps can reach you:
prompt: apiURL:    (http://strato-dev4.blockapps.net)
prompt: Enter the blockchain profile you wish to use.  Options: strato-dev, ethereum:  (strato-dev)
Wrote: /home/drequinox/testApp/.bowerrc
Wrote: /home/drequinox/testApp/app.js
Wrote: /home/drequinox/testApp/bower.json
Wrote: /home/drequinox/testApp/gulpfile.js
Wrote: /home/drequinox/testApp/marko-taglib.json
Wrote: /home/drequinox/testApp/package.json
Wrote: /home/drequinox/testApp/test/common.js
Wrote: /home/drequinox/testApp/test/top.js
Wrote: /home/drequinox/testApp/app/contracts/Greeter.sol
Wrote: /home/drequinox/testApp/app/contracts/MultiContract.sol
Wrote: /home/drequinox/testApp/app/contracts/Payout.sol
```

bloc init

The next step is to install the testApp which can be achieved by running the following command:

```
$ sudo npm install
```

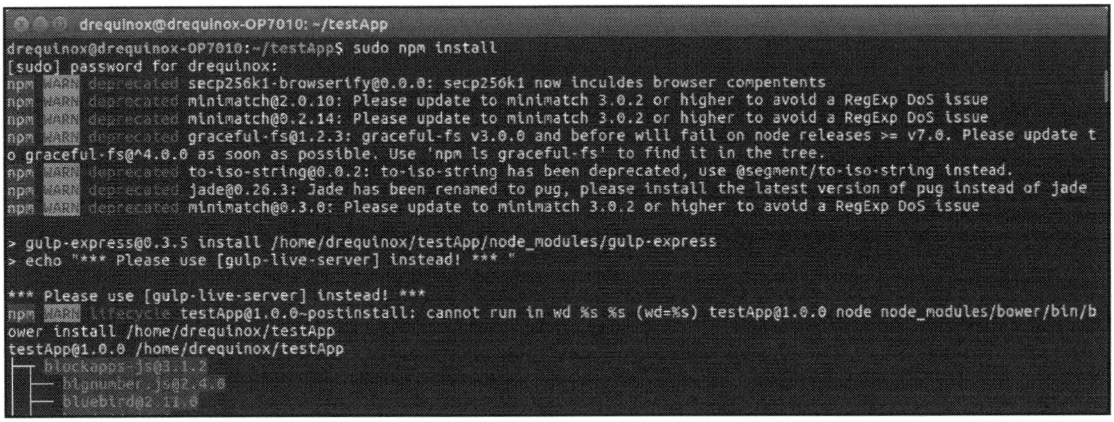

testApp installation

Generation of a new key is required in order to sign the transactions. Keys can be generated by using the following command:

```
$ bloc genkey
```

Once issued, a password will have to be entered in order to protect the key. Once provided, the key will be created and a JSON file will be created. Note that the JSON file name is the actual address of the account on the blockchain. Also, it will display the message transaction mined, indicating success and deployment of the key and transaction (account creation) respectively.

The process is shown in the following screenshot:

Generate key

Now, at this point, the new account can be queried by using curl. Simply pass the address as an argument in the URL and the result will be returned in JSON format.

```
drequinox@drequinox-OP7010:~/testApp$ curl http://strato-dev4.blockapps.net/eth/v1.2/account?add
ress=b16fe63de8fcf9d97f1d787cba37a02309104316
[{"contractRoot":"56e81f171bcc55a6ff8345e692c0f86e5b48e01b996cadc001622fb5e363b421","kind":"Addr
essStateRef","balance":"1000000000000000000000","address":"b16fe63de8fcf9d97f1d787cba37a02309104
316","latestBlockNum":79860,"code":"","nonce":0}]drequinox@drequinox-OP7010:~/testApp$
```

Query the new account using curl

Alternatively, a query can be executed via any web browser as shown in the following screenshot:

BlockApps query via web browser

In the next step, the process to upload the new contract to the test chain will be described. Note that all the contracts are placed in the `./app/contracts` directory under the `testApp` directory. As a sample, `Greeter.sol` contract has been chosen to be deployed to the network. BlockApps provides an easy method to achieve this deployment.

All contracts needs to be placed under the contracts directory in order for the compile command to find them and compile.

```
drequinox@drequinox-OP7010: ~/testApp/app/contracts
drequinox@drequinox-OP7010:~/testApp/app/contracts$ pwd
/home/drequinox/testApp/app/contracts
drequinox@drequinox-OP7010:~/testApp/app/contracts$ ll
total 40
drwxrwxr-x 2 drequinox drequinox 4096 Dec 27 10:24 ./
drwxrwxr-x 8 drequinox drequinox 4096 Dec 27 10:45 ../
-rw-rw-r-- 1 drequinox drequinox  695 Dec 27 10:24 Greeter.sol
-rw-rw-r-- 1 drequinox drequinox  237 Dec 27 10:24 MultiContract.sol
-rw-rw-r-- 1 drequinox drequinox  618 Dec 27 10:24 Payout.sol
-rw-rw-r-- 1 drequinox drequinox  178 Dec 27 10:24 SimpleDataFeed.sol
-rw-rw-r-- 1 drequinox drequinox 1421 Dec 27 10:24 SimpleMultiSig.sol
-rw-rw-r-- 1 drequinox drequinox  181 Dec 27 10:24 SimpleStorage.sol
-rw-rw-r-- 1 drequinox drequinox  998 Dec 27 10:24 Stake.sol
-rw-rw-r-- 1 drequinox drequinox  663 Dec 27 10:24 template.marko
drequinox@drequinox-OP7010:~/testApp/app/contracts$ cat Greeter.sol
contract mortal {
    /* Define variable owner of the type address*/
    address owner;

    /* this function is executed at initialization and sets the owner of the contract */
    function mortal() { owner = msg.sender; }

    /* Function to recover the funds on the contract */
    function kill() { if (msg.sender == owner) suicide(owner); }
}

contract Greeter is mortal {
    /* define variable greeting of the type string */
    string greeting;

    /* this runs when the contract is executed */
    function Greeter(string _greeting) public {
        greeting = _greeting;
    }

    /* main function */
    function greet() constant returns (string) {
        return greeting;
    }
}
drequinox@drequinox-OP7010:~/testApp/app/contracts$ ▮
```

Greeter contract under contracts directory

Contracts can be compiled by using the command shown in the following screenshot. Note that it takes that contract file name as an argument. After successful compilation, all relevant JSON files will be written under `./meta` directory.

```
drequinox@drequinox-OP7010:~/testApp$ bloc compile Greeter
Compiling single contract: Greeter.sol
Compile successful: contract mortal {
    /* Define variable owner of the type address*/
    address owner;

    /* this function is executed at initialization and sets the owner of the contract */
    function mortal() { owner = msg.sender; }

    /* Function to recover the funds on the contract */
    function kill() { if (msg.sender == owner) suicide(owner); }
}

contract Greeter is mortal {
    /* define variable greeting of the type string */
    string greeting;

    /* this runs when the contract is executed */
    function Greeter(string _greeting) public {
        greeting = _greeting;
    }

    /* main function */
    function greet() constant returns (string) {
        return greeting;
    }
}

writing Greeter to app/meta/Greeter/Greeter.json
wrote: app/meta/Greeter/Greeter.json
writing mortal to app/meta/Greeter/mortal.json
wrote: app/meta/Greeter/mortal.json
writing Greeter to app/meta/mortal/Greeter.json
wrote: app/meta/mortal/Greeter.json
writing mortal to app/meta/mortal/mortal.json
wrote: app/meta/mortal/mortal.json
drequinox@drequinox-OP7010:~/testApp$ █
```

Compilation of Greeter contract

Finally, the contract can be uploaded using the following command. This command expects the argument passed to the contract as defined in the contract code. In the example, it expected a text string as shown in the following example screenshot:

```
$ bloc upload Greeter "Hello bloc"
```

```
drequinox@drequinox-OP7010:~/testApp$ bloc upload Greeter "Hello bloc"
address: b16fe63de8fcf9d97f1d787cba37a02309104316
prompt: Enter password to retrieve private key:
upload contract: Greeter
writing: app/meta/Greeter/05ee3af04e903f413402d5438b9de3827b1f4e70.json
writing: app/meta/Greeter/Latest.json
creating metadata for Greeter
drequinox@drequinox-OP7010:~/testApp$
```

Upload of Greeter contract

Note that, in case correct arguments are not passed or missing, an error similar to following screenshot will occur:

```
drequinox@drequinox-OP7010:~/testApp$ bloc upload Greeter
address: b16fe63de8fcf9d97f1d787cba37a02309104316
prompt: Enter password to retrieve private key:
upload contract: Greeter
there was an error: {"errorTags":["Solidity","Solidity"],"message":"function \"Greeter\" arguments must include \"_greeting\""}
creating metadata for Greeter
```

Error in case of wrong or missing arguments

Once the deployment is successful it can be verified that the ether has transferred from the existing contract to the new contract. Note that the balance has dropped. This is shown in the following screenshot:

Deployed contract after installation via web browser

After deployment of the contract, it can be queried using a web browser or any CLI tools such as cURL. The URL
`http://strato-dev4.blockapps.net/eth/v1.2/account?address=05ee3af04e903f413402d`
`5438b9de3827b1f4e70` is required to be passed to the web browser. This is shown in the following screenshot. Note that the code in binary format is also available in the output.

Browse to the deployed contract, with code in binary format

Furthermore, BlockApps has a feature available to run a local HTTP server, which can be started by using the following command:

```
$ bloc start
```

This will start the web browser, and listen on TCP port 8000.

bloc start

After the web server starts, the compiled contracts can be viewed and queried using the local web page available as shown in the following screenshot:

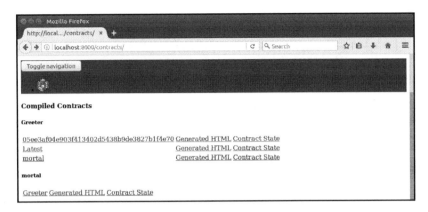

Compiled contracts available via browser

As demonstrated in the preceding example it is easier to build, deploy, and manage contracts using BlockApps. BlockApps aims to provide tools and core infrastructure for blockchain applications, and not just blockchain.

Eris

Eris is not a single blockchain, it is an open modular platform developed by Monax for development of blockchain-based *ecosystem applications*. It offers various frameworks, SDKs, and tools that allow accelerated development and deployment of blockchain applications. The core idea behind the Eris application platform is to enable development and management of *ecosystem applications* with a blockchain backend. It allows integration with multiple blockchains and enables various third party systems to interact with various other systems. This platform makes use of smart contracts written in solidity language. It can interact with blockchains such as Ethereum or bitcoin. The interaction can include connectivity commands, start, stop, disconnection, and creation of new blockchains. Complexity related to setup and interaction with blockchains have been abstracted away in Eris. All commands are standardized for different blockchains, and the same commands can be used across the platform regardless of the blockchain type being targeted.

An ecosystem application can consist the Eris platform, enabling the API gateway to allow legacy applications to connect to key management systems, consensus engines, and application engines. The Eris platform provides various toolkits that are used to provide various services to the developers. These modules are described as follows:

- **Chains**: This allows the creation of and interaction with blockchains.
- **Packages**: This allows the development of smart contracts.
- **Keys**: This is used for key management and signing operations.
- **Files**: This allows working with distributed data management systems. It can be used to interact with file systems such as IPFS and data lakes.
- **Services**: This exposes a set of services that allows the management and integration of ecosystem applications.

Several SDKs has also been developed by Eris that allow the development and management of ecosystem applications. These SDKs contain smart contracts that have been fully tested and address specific needs and requirements of business. For example, a finance SDK, insurance SDK, and logistics SDK. There is also a base SDK that serves as a basic development kit to manage the lifecycle of an ecosystem application.

Monax has developed its own permissioned blockchain client called Eris:db. It is a **Proof of Stake-based (PoS)** blockchain system that allows integration with a number of different blockchain networks. `Eris:db` consist of three components:

- **Consensus**: This is based on the Tendermint consensus mechanism, discussed before.
- **Virtual machine**: Eris uses **Ethereum Virtual Machine (EVM)**, as such it supports solidity compiled contracts.
- **Permissions layer**: Being a permissioned ledger, Eris provides an access control mechanism that can be used to assign specific roles to different entities on the network.
- **Interface**: This provides various commandline tools and RPC interfaces to enable interaction with the backend blockchain network.

The key difference between Ethereum blockchain and Eris:db is that Eris:db makes use of a Practical Byzantine Fault-Tolerance algorithm, which is implemented as a deposit-based Proof of Stake (DPOS system) whereas Ethereum uses **Proof of Work (PoW)**. Moreover, `Eris:db` uses the ECDSA ed22519 curve scheme whereas Ethereum uses the secp256k1 algorithm. Finally, it is permissioned with an access control layer on top whereas Ethereum is a public blockchain.

Eris is a feature-rich application platform that offers a large selection of toolkits and services to develop blockchain-based applications. It is available at `https://monax.io/`.

Summary

This chapter started with the introduction of alternative blockchains and is divided into two main sections discussing blockchains and platforms. Blockchain technology is a very thriving area, as such changes are quite rapid in existing solutions and new relevant technologies or tools are being introduced almost every day. In this chapter, a careful selection of platforms and blockchains was discussed. Several solutions were discussed that complement material covered in previous chapters, for example, BlockApps, which supports Ethereum development. New blockchains such as Kadena, various new protocols such as Ripple, and concepts such as sidechains and drivechains were also discussed. The material covered in this chapter is intended to provide a strong foundation for more in-depth research into areas that readers are interested in. As said before, blockchain is a very fast moving field and there are many other blockchain proposals projects such as **Tauchain**, **Hydrachain**, **Elements**, **credits**, and many more that have not been discussed in this chapter. Readers are encouraged to keep an eye on the developments in this field in order to keep themselves up to date with advancement in this rapidly growing area.

11
Blockchain-Outside of Currencies

Digital currencies were the first ever application of blockchain technology, arguably without realizing its true potential. With the invention of bitcoin the concept of blockchain was introduced for the very first time, but it wasn't until 2013, with the advent of *Blockchain 2.0* that the real benefits of blockchain were realized with its possible application in many different industries. Since then a number of use cases of blockchain technology in different industries, have been proposed including but not limited to finance, the Internet of Things, digital rights management, government, and law. In this chapter, four main industries namely the **Internet of Things (IoT)**, government, health, and finance, have been selected for discussion. Readers will be introduced to all these fields and various related use cases will be presented.

Internet of Things

The Internet of Things or IoT for short has recently gained much traction due to its potential for transforming business applications and everyday life. IoT can be defined as a network of computationally intelligent physical objects that are capable of connecting to the Internet, sensing real-world events or environments, reacting to those events, collecting relevant data, and communicating it over the Internet. This simple definition has huge implications and has led to exciting concepts, such as wearable's, smart homes, smart grids, smart connected cars, and smart cities, that are all based on this basic concept of an IoT device. After dissecting the definition of IoT above, there are four functions that come to light as being performed by an IoT device. These include sensing, reacting, collecting, and communicating. All these functions are performed by using various components on the IoT device.

Sensing is performed by sensors. Reacting or controlling is performed by actuators, collection is a function of various sensors, and communication is performed by chips that provide network connectivity. One thing to note is that all these components are accessible and controllable via the Internet in the IoT. An IoT device on its own is perhaps useful to some extent but if it is part of a larger IoT ecosystem it is more valuable.

A typical IoT can consist of many physical objects connecting with each other and to a centralized cloud server. This is shown in the diagram below:

A typical IoT network: source–IBM

Elements of IoT are spread across multiple layers and various reference architectures exist that can be used to develop IoT systems. Generally, a five layer model can be used to describe IoT, which contains a physical object layer, device layer, network layer, services layer, and application layer. Each layer or level is responsible for various functions and includes various components. These are described in detail below.

Physical object layer

These include any physical real-world objects includes people, animals, cars, trees, fridges, trains, factories, homes, and in fact anything that is required to be monitored and controlled can be connected to the IoT.

Device layer

This layer contains things that make up the IoT such as sensors, transducers, actuators, smart phones, smart devices, and **Radio Frequency Identification tags (RFIDs)**. There can be many categories of sensors such as body sensors, home sensors, and environmental sensors based on the type of work they perform. This is the core of an IoT ecosystem where various sensors are used to sense real-world environments. This includes sensors that can monitor temperature, humidity, liquid flow, chemicals, air, pressure, and much more. Usually, an **Analog to Digital Converter (ADC)** is required on a device in order to turn the real-world analog signal into a digital signal that a microprocessor can understand.

Actuators in this layer provide the means to enable control of external environments, for example, starting a motor or opening a door. These components also require digital to analog converters in order to convert a digital signal into analogue. This is especially relevant when control of a mechanical component is required by the IoT device.

Network layer

This layer is composed of various network devices that are used to provide Internet connectivity between devices and to the cloud or servers that are part of the IoT ecosystem. These devices can include gateways, routers, hubs, and switches. This layer can include two types of communication. First is the horizontal means of communication, which includes radio, Bluetooth, WiFi, Ethernet, LAN, ZigBee, and PAN and can be used to provide a communication between IoT devices. Second, we have communicating to the next layer, which is usually through the Internet and provides communication between machines and people or other upper layers. The first layer can optionally be included in the device layer as it physically is residing on the device layer where devices can communicate with each other at the same layer.

Management layer

This layer provides the management layer for the IoT ecosystem. This includes platforms that enable processing of data gathered from the IoT devices and turn that into meaningful insights. Also, device management, security management, and data flow management are included in this layer. It also manages communication between the device and application layers.

Application layer

This layer includes applications running on top of the IoT network. This can include a number of applications depending on the requirements such as transportation, healthcare, financial, insurance, or supply chain management. This of course is not an exhaustive list by any stretch of the imagination; there is a myriad of IoT applications that can fall into this layer:

Application Layer
Transportation, financial, insurance and many others
Management Layer
Data processing, analytics, security management
Network Layer
LAN, WAN, PAN, Routers
Device Layer
Sensors , Actuators, smart devices
Physical Objects
People, cars, homes etc. etc.

IoT five-layer model

With the availability of cheap sensors, hardware, and bandwidth, IoT has gained popularity in recent years and currently has applications in many different areas including healthcare, insurance, supply chain management, home automation, industrial automation, and infrastructure management. Moreover, advancements in technology such as the availability of IPv6, smaller and powerful processors, and better Internet access have also played a vital role in the popularity of IoT. The benefits of IoT range from cost saving to enabling businesses to make vital decisions and thus improve performance based on the data provided by the IoT devices. Raw data from millions of things (IoT devices) is analyzed and provides meaningful insights that help in making timely and effective business decisions.

The normal IoT model is based on a centralized paradigm where IoT devices usually connect with a cloud infrastructure or central servers in order to report and process the relevant data back. This centralization poses certain possibilities of exploitation including hacking and data theft. Moreover, not having control of personal data on a single, centralized service provider also increases the possibility of security and privacy issues. Whilst there are methods and techniques to build a highly secure IoT ecosystem based on the normal IoT model there are certain much more desirable benefits that blockchain can bring to IoT. A blockchain-based IoT model differs from the traditional IoT network paradigm. According to IBM, blockchain for IoT can help to build trust, reduce costs, and accelerate transactions. Additionally, decentralization, which is at the very core of blockchain technology, can eliminate single points of failure in an IoT network. For example, a central server perhaps is not able to cope with the amount of data that billions of IoT devices (things) are producing at high frequency. Also the peer-to-peer communication model provided by blockchain can help to reduce costs because there is no need to build high-cost centralized data centres or implementation of complex public key infrastructure for security. Devices can communicate with each other directly or via routers.

As an estimate from various researchers and companies, by 2020 there will be roughly 22 billion devices connected to the Internet. With this explosion of billions of devices connecting to the Internet, it is hard to imagine that centralized infrastructures will be able to cope with the high demands of bandwidth, services, and availability without incurring excessive expenditure. Blockchain-based IoT will be able to solve scalability, privacy, and reliability issues in the current IoT model.

Blockchain enables *things* to communicate and transact with each other directly and with the availability of smart contracts negotiation and financial transactions can also occur directly between the devices instead of requiring a middleman, authority, or human intervention. For example, if a room in a hotel is vacant, it can rent itself out, negotiate the rent, and can open the door lock for a human who has paid the right amount of funds. Another example could be that if a washing machine runs out of detergent, it could order it online after finding the best price and value based on the logic programmed in its smart contract.

The above mentioned five-layer IoT model can be adapted to a blockchain-based model by adding a blockchain layer on top of the network layer. This layer will run smart contracts, and provide security, privacy, integrity, autonomy, scalability, and decentralization services to the IoT ecosystem. The management layer in this case can consist of only software related to analytics and processing, and security and control can be moved to the blockchain layer. This can be visualized in the following diagram:

Application Layer
Transportation, financial, insurance and many others
Management Layer
Data processing, analytics
Blockchain Layer
Security, P2P (M2M) autonomous transactions, decentralization, smart contracts
Network Layer
LAN, WAN, PAN, Routers
Device Layer
Sensors , Actuators, smart devices
Physical Objects
People, cars, homes etc. etc.

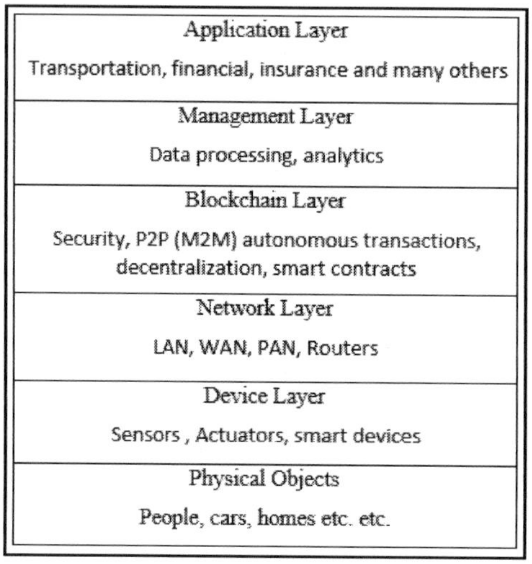

Blockchain-based IoT model

In this model, other layers would perhaps remain the same but an additional blockchain layer will be introduced as a middleware between all participants of the IoT network.

It can also be visualized as a peer-to-peer IoT network after abstracting away all the layers mentioned above. This is shown in the following diagram where all devices are communicating and negotiating with each other without a central command and control entity:

Blockchain-based direct communication model, source–IBM

It can also result in cost saving which is due to easier device management by using a blockchain based decentralised approach. The IoT network can be optimized for performance by using blockchain. In this case there will be no need to store IoT data centrally for millions of devices because storage and processing requirements can be distributed to all IoT devices on the blockchain. This can result in completely removing the need for large data centres for processing and storing the IoT data.

Blockchain-based IoT can also thwart denial of service attacks where hackers can target a centralized server or data centre more easily but with blockchain's distributed and decentralized nature, such attacks are no longer possible. Additionally, if as estimated there will be billions of devices connected to the Internet in the near future, it will become almost impossible to manage security and updates of all those devices from traditional centrally-owned servers. Blockchain can provide a solution to this problem by allowing devices to communicate with each other directly in a secure manner and even request firmware and security updates from each other. On a blockchain network these communications can be recorded immutably and securely which will provide auditability, integrity, and transparency to the system. This is not possible with traditional P2P systems.

In summary, there are clear benefits that can be reaped with the convergence of IoT and blockchain and a lot of research and work in academia and industry are already in progress. There are various projects already proposed providing blockchain-based IoT solutions. For example, IBM Blue Horizon and IBM Bluemix are IoT platforms supporting blockchain IoT platforms. Various start-ups such as Filament have already proposed novel ideas on how to build a decentralised network that enables devices on IoT to transact with each other directly and autonomously driven by smart contracts.

In the following section, a practical example is provided on how to build a simple IoT device and connect it to the Ethereum blockchain. This IoT device is connected to the Ethereum blockchain and is used to open a door (in this case the door lock is represented by an LED) when the appropriate amount of funds are sent by a user on the blockchain. This is a simple example and requires a more rigorously-tested version in order to implement it in production but it demonstrates how an IoT device can be connected, controlled, and responded to in response to certain events on an Ethereum blockchain.

IoT blockchain experiment

This example makes use of a Raspberry device which is a **Single Board Computer (SBC)**. Raspberry Pi is a single-board computer developed as a low cost computer to promote computer education but has also gained much more popularity as a tool of choice for building IoT platforms. A Raspberry Pi 3 model B is shown in the following figure:

Raspberry Pi model B

In the following section, an example will be discussed where a Raspberry Pi will be used as an IoT device connected to the Ethereum blockchain and will perform an action in response to a smart contract invocation.

First, the Raspberry Pi needs to be set up. This can be done by using NOOBS which provides an easy method of installing Raspbian or any other operating system. This can be downloaded and installed from the link `https://www.raspberrypi.org/downloads/noobs/`. Alternatively, only Raspbian can be installed from the link `https://www.raspberrypi.org/downloads/raspbian/`. Another alternative available at `https://github.com/debian-pi/raspbian-ua-netinst` can also be used to install a minimal non-GUI version of Raspbian OS. For the purpose of the example, NOOBS has been used to install Raspbian, as such the rest of the exercise assumes Raspbian is installed on the SD memory card of the Raspberry Pi.

Once the Raspbian operating system is installed, the next step is to download the appropriate `geth` binary for the Raspberry Pi ARM platform. The platform can be confirmed by running the following command in a terminal window in Raspberry Pi Raspbian operating system. The command output shows that which architecture the operating system is running on. In this case it is `armv71`, therefore ARM-compatible binary for `geth` will be downloaded.

Raspberry Pi architecture

The following steps are described in detail:

1. `geth` download:, note that in the example below a specific version is downloaded however other versions are available which can be downloaded from `https://geth.ethereum.org/downloads/`.

   wget https://gethstore.blob.core.windows.net/builds/geth-linux-arm7-1.5.6-2a609af5.tar.gz

2. Unzip and extract into a directory, the directory named `geth-linux-arm7-1.5.6-2a609af5` will be created automatically with that tar command next:

   tar -zxvf geth-linux-arm7-1.5.6-2a609af5.tar

This will create a directory named `geth-linux-arm7-1.5.6-2a609af5` and will extract `geth` binary and related files into that directory. `geth` binary can be copied into `/usr/bin` or the appropriate path on Raspbian to make it available from anywhere in the operating system. When the download is finished, the next step is to create the genesis block.

The same genesis block needs to be used that was created previously in Chapter 8, *Ethereum Development*. The genesis file can be copied from the other node on the network. This is shown in the following screenshot. Alternatively, an entirely new genesis block can be generated. This was discussed in detail in Chapter 8, *Ethereum Development*.

```
pi@raspberrypi:~/geth-linux-arm7-1.5.6-2a609af5 $ cat genesis.json
{
    "nonce": "0x0000000000000042",
    "timestamp": "0x0",
    "parentHash": "0x0000000000000000000000000000000000000000000000000000000000000000",
    "extraData": "0x0",
    "gasLimit": "0x4c4b40",
    "difficulty": "0x200",
    "mixhash": "0x0000000000000000000000000000000000000000000000000000000000000000",
    "coinbase": "0x0000000000000000000000000000000000000000",
    "alloc": {}
}
```

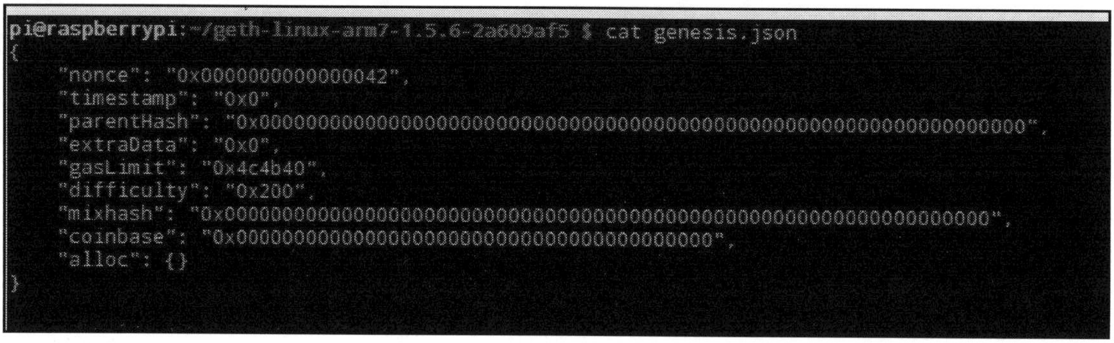

Genesis file

Once the `genesis.json` file is copied onto the Raspberry Pi, the following command can be run in order to generate the genesis block. It is important that exactly the same genesis block is used that was generated previously otherwise the nodes will effectively be running on separate networks:

```
$ ./geth init genesis.json
```

This will show the output similar to the one shown in the following screenshot:

```
pi@raspberrypi:~/geth-linux-arm7-1.5.6-2a609af5 $ ./geth init genesis.json
I0110 23:37:15.714795 cmd/utils/flags.go:612] WARNING: No etherbase set and no accounts found as default
I0110 23:37:15.715283 ethdb/database.go:83] Allotted 128MB cache and 1024 file handles to /home/pi/.ethereum/geth/chaindata
I0110 23:37:15.794383 ethdb/database.go:176] closed db:/home/pi/.ethereum/geth/chaindata
I0110 23:37:15.794723 ethdb/database.go:83] Allotted 128MB cache and 1024 file handles to /home/pi/.ethereum/geth/chaindata
I0110 23:37:15.923300 core/genesis.go:93] Genesis block already in chain. Writing canonical number
I0110 23:37:15.923895 cmd/geth/chaincmd.go:131] successfully wrote genesis block and/or chain rule set: f2b2ffed01907a845a01d1dea21e5a
ec021e8e68b5ec9ffccb82df
```

Initialize genesis file

After genesis block creation, there is a need to add peers to the network. This can be achieved by creating a file named `static-nodes.json`, which contains the enode ID of the peer that geth on the Raspberry Pi will connect to for synching.

```
pi@raspberrypi:~/.ethereum $ cat static-nodes.json
[
"enode://44352ede5b9e792e437c1c0431c1578ce3676a87e1f588434aff1299d30325c233c8d426fc
57a25380481c8a36fb3be2787375e932fb4885885f6452f6efa77f@192.168.0.19:30301"
]
```

static nodes configuration

This information can be obtained from the geth JavaScript console by running the following shown command, this command should be run on the peer to which Raspberry is going to connect:

> **Admin.nodeInfo**

This will show the output similar to the one shown in the following screenshot:

```
> admin.nodeInfo
{
  enode: "enode://44352ede5b9e792e437c1c0431c1578ce3676a87e1f588434aff1299d30325c233c8d426fc57a25380481c8a36fb3
be2787375e932fb4885885f6452f6efa77f@[::]:30301",
  id: "44352ede5b9e792e437c1c0431c1578ce3676a87e1f588434aff1299d30325c233c8d426fc57a25380481c8a36fb3be2787375e9
32fb4885885f6452f6efa77f",
```

geth nodeinfo

After this step, further instructions presented below can be followed in order to connect Raspberry Pi to the other node on the private network. In the example, the Raspberry Pi will be connected to the network ID 786 created in Chapter 8, *Ethereum Development*. The key is to use the same genesis file created previously and different port numbers. Different ports are not a strict requirement however. If the two nodes are running under a private network and access from an environment external to the network is required then a combination of DMZ/router and port forwarding will be used. Therefore it is recommended to use different TCP ports to allow port forwarding to work correctly. The identity switch, which hasn't been introduced previously, in the following command allows for an identifying name to be specified for the node.

First node setup

First, `geth` needs to be started on the first node using the following command:

```
$ geth --datadir .ethereum/privatenet/ --networkid 786 --maxpeers 5 --rpc --rpcapi web3,eth,debug,personal,net --rpcport 9001 --rpccorsdomain "*" --port 30301 --identity "drequinox"
```

```
imran@drequinox-OP7010:~$ geth --datadir .ethereum/privatenet/ --networkid 786 --maxpeers 5 --rpc --rp
capi web3,eth,debug,personal,net --rpcport 9001 --rpccorsdomain "*" --port 30301 --identity "drequinox
"
I0110 23:26:46.032878 ethdb/database.go:83] Allotted 128MB cache and 1024 file handles to /home/imran/
.ethereum/privatenet/geth/chaindata
I0110 23:26:46.072986 ethdb/database.go:176] closed db:/home/imran/.ethereum/privatenet/geth/chaindata
I0110 23:26:46.073243 node/node.go:175] instance: Geth/drequinox/v1.5.2-stable-c8695209/linux/go1.7.3
I0110 23:26:46.073258 ethdb/database.go:83] Allotted 128MB cache and 1024 file handles to /home/imran/
.ethereum/privatenet/geth/chaindata
I0110 23:26:46.082654 eth/backend.go:193] Protocol Versions: [63 62], Network Id: 786
I0110 23:26:46.083188 core/blockchain.go:214] Last header: #7991 [999c534f…] TD=11652654509
I0110 23:26:46.083203 core/blockchain.go:215] Last block: #7991 [999c534f…] TD=11652654509
I0110 23:26:46.083210 core/blockchain.go:216] Fast block: #7991 [999c534f…] TD=11652654509
I0110 23:26:46.083929 p2p/server.go:336] Starting Server
I0110 23:26:48.239776 p2p/discover/udp.go:217] Listening, enode://44352ede5b9e792e437c1c0431c1578ce367
6a87e1f588434aff1299d30325c233c8d426fc57a25380481c8a36fb3be2787375e932fb4885885f6452f6efa77f@[::]:3030
1
I0110 23:26:48.239893 p2p/server.go:604] Listening on [::]:30301
I0110 23:26:48.240913 node/node.go:340] IPC endpoint opened: /home/imran/.ethereum/privatenet/geth.ipc
I0110 23:26:48.241212 node/node.go:410] HTTP endpoint opened: http://localhost:9001
I0110 23:42:58.206205 eth/backend.go:479] Automatic pregeneration of ethash DAG ON (ethash dir: /home/
imran/.ethash)
I0110 23:42:58.206217 miner/miner.go:136] Starting mining operation (CPU=8 TOT=9)
```

geth on first node

Once `geth` is started up it should be kept running and another `geth` instance should be started from the Raspberry Pi node.

Raspberry Pi node setup

On Raspberry Pi, the following command is required to be run in order to start `geth` and sync it with other nodes (in this case only one node). The following is the command:

```
$ ./geth --networkid 786 --maxpeers 5 --rpc --rpcapi
web3,eth,debug,personal,net  --rpccorsdomain "*" --port 30302 --identity
"raspberry"
```

This should produce the output similar to the one shown in the following screenshot. When the output contains the row displaying **Block synchronization started** it means that the node has connected successfully to its peer.

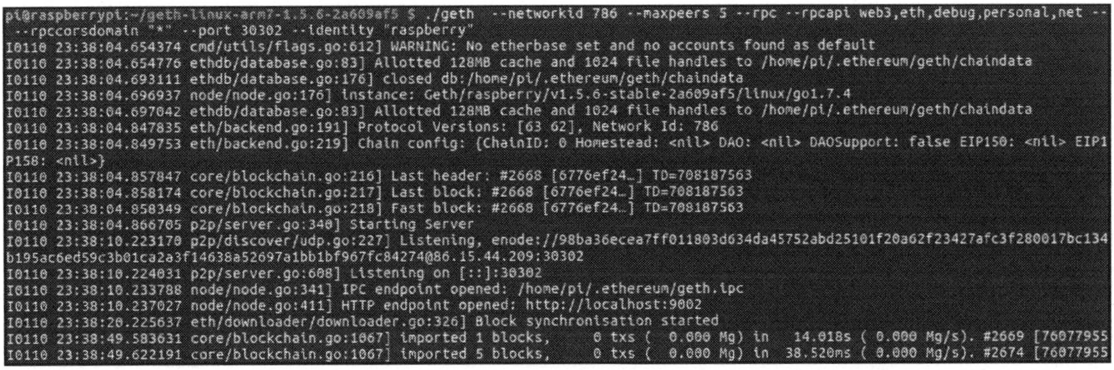

geth on the Raspberry Pi.

This can be further verified by running commands in the `geth` console on both nodes as shown in the following screenshot. `geth` can be attached by simply running the command on the Raspberry Pi:

```
$ geth attach
```

geth console admin peers command running on Raspberry Pi

Similarly `geth` can be attached to by running the command below on the first node:

```
$ geth attach ipc:.ethereum/privatenet/geth.ipc
```

Once the console is available `admin.peers` can be run to reveal the details about other connected nodes as shown in the following screenshot:

```
> admin.peers
[{
    caps: ["eth/62", "eth/63"],
    id: "98ba36ecea7ff011803d634da45752abd25101f20a62f23427afc3f260017bc134833dd5ba400bb195ac6ed59c3b01
ca2a3f14638a52697a1bb1bf967fc84274",
    name: "Geth/raspberry/v1.5.6-stable-2a609af5/linux/go1.7.4",
    network: {
      localAddress: "192.168.0.19:30301",
      remoteAddress: "192.168.0.21:56512"
    },
    protocols: {
      eth: {
        difficulty: 11708306137,
        head: "0x1188f58b4900a1d771d333141ea9400d78400bb8e561494ab436519ae64e1e34",
        version: 63
      }
    }
}]
```

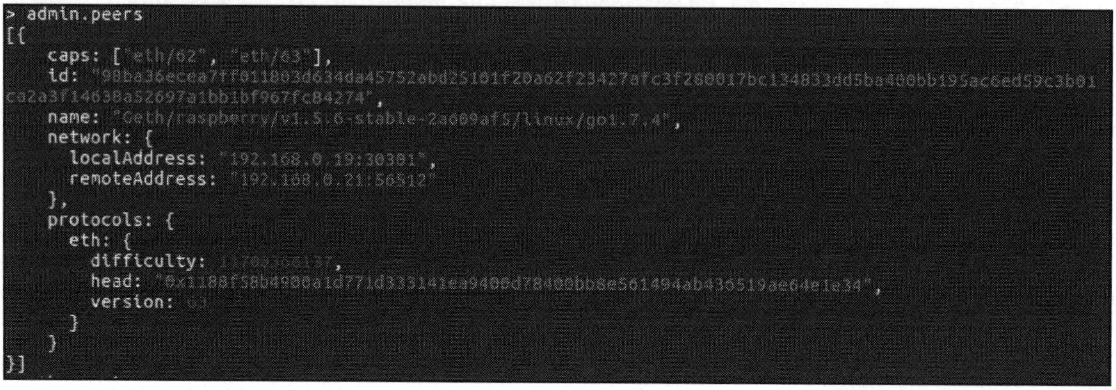

geth console admin peers command running on the other peer

Once both nodes are up-and-running further prerequisites can be installed in order to set up the experiment. Installation of Node.js and the relevant JavaScript libraries is required. The required libraries and dependencies are listed below. First Node.js and npm need to be updated on the Raspberry Pi Raspbian operating system. For this the following steps can be followed:

1. Install latest Node.js on the Raspberry Pi using the following command:

   ```
   $ curl -sL https://deb.nodesource.com/setup_7.x | sudo -E bash
   -
   ```

This should display output similar to the following. The output is quite large therefore only the top part of the output is shown in the following screenshot:

```
pi@raspberrypi:~/testled $ curl -sL https://deb.nodesource.com/setup_7.x | sudo -E bash -
## Installing the NodeSource Node.js v7.x repo...

## Populating apt-get cache...

+ apt-get update
Get:1 http://archive.raspberrypi.org jessie InRelease [22.9 kB]
Get:2 http://mirrordirector.raspbian.org jessie InRelease [14.9 kB]
```

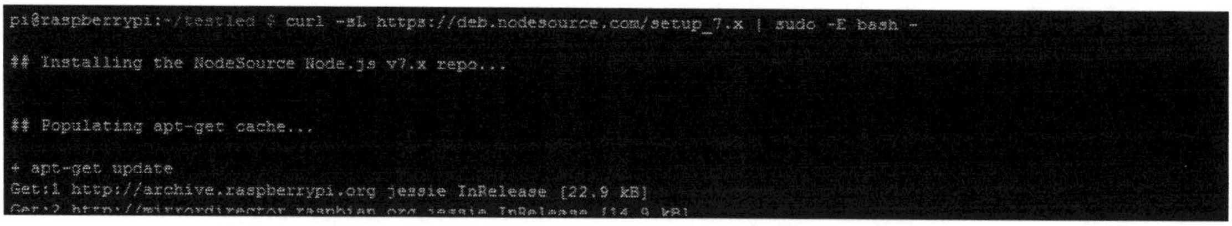

Node.js installation

2. Run the update via `apt-get`:

   ```
   $ sudo apt-get install nodejs
   ```

Verification can be performed by running the following command to ensure that the correct versions of Node.js and npm are installed, as shown in the following screenshot below:

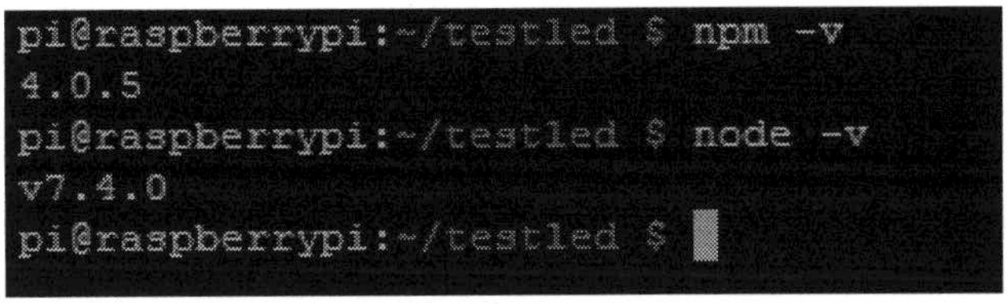

```
pi@raspberrypi:~/testled $ npm -v
4.0.5
pi@raspberrypi:~/testled $ node -v
v7.4.0
pi@raspberrypi:~/testled $
```

npm and node installation verification

It should be noted that these version are not a necessity; any latest version of npm and node will work. The examples in this chapter makes use of npm 4.0.5 and node v7.4.0.

3. Install Ethereum web3 npm, which is required to enable JavaScript code to access the blockchain:

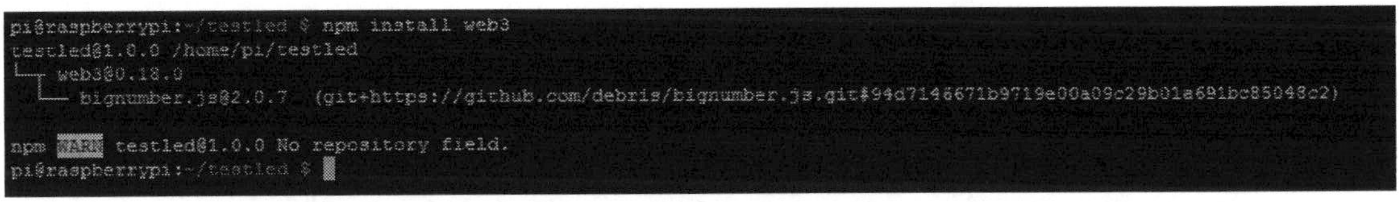

```
pi@raspberrypi:~/testled $ npm install web3
testled@1.0.0 /home/pi/testled
└── web3@0.18.0
    └── bignumber.js@2.0.7  (git+https://github.com/debris/bignumber.js.git#94d7146671b9719e00a09c29b01a691bc85048c2)

npm WARN testled@1.0.0 No repository field.
pi@raspberrypi:~/testled $
```

npm install web3

4. Similarly, npm install onoff can be installed, which is required in order to communicate with the Raspberry Pi and control GPIO:

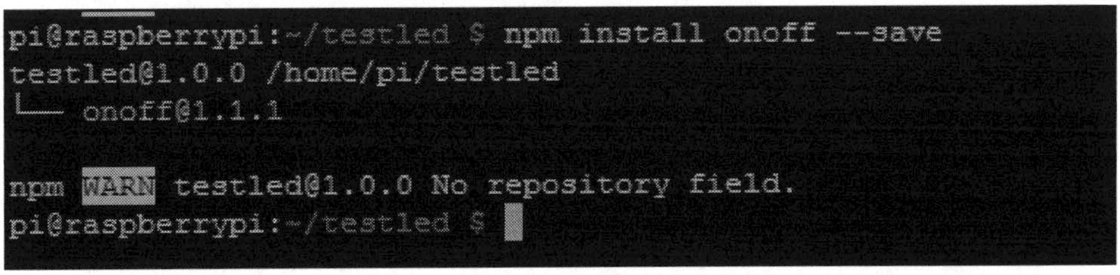

```
pi@raspberrypi:~/testled $ npm install onoff --save
testled@1.0.0 /home/pi/testled
└── onoff@1.1.1

npm WARN testled@1.0.0 No repository field.
pi@raspberrypi:~/testled $
```

onoff installation

When all prerequisites are installed, hardware setup can be performed. For this purpose a simple circuit is built using a breadboard and a few electronic components.

These components are listed as follows:

1. **LED**: The abbreviation of **Light Emitting Diode**, this can be used as visual indication for an event.
2. **Resistor**: A 330 ohm component is required which provides resistance to passing current based on its rating. It is not necessary to understand the theory behind it for this experiment; any standard electronics engineering text covers all these topics in detail.
3. **Breadboard**: This provides a means of building an electronic circuit without requiring soldering.
4. **T-Shaped cobbler**: This is inserted on the breadboard as shown in the figure below and provides a labeled view of all **GPIO (General Purpose I/O)** pins for the Raspberry Pi.
5. **Ribbon cable connector**: This is simply used to provide connectivity between the Raspberry Pi and the breadboard via GPIO. All these components are shown in the following image:

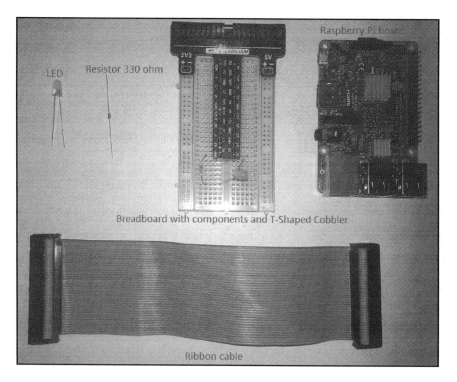

Required components

Circuit

As shown in the following image, the positive leg (long leg) of the LED is connected to pin number 21 of the GPIO and the negative (short leg) is connected to the resistor, which is then connected to the **ground (GND)** pin of the GPIO. Once the connections are set up the ribbon cable can be used to simply connect to the GPIO connector on the Raspberry Pi.

Connections for components on the breadboard

Once the connections are set up correctly and the Raspberry Pi has been updated with the appropriate libraries and geth, the next step is to develop a simple smart contract that expects a value. If the value provided to it is not what it expects it does not trigger an event; otherwise, if the value passed matches the correct value, the event triggers which can be read by the client JavaScript programme running via Node.js. Of course, the solidity contract can be very complex and can also deal with the ether sent to it and if the amount of ether is equal to the required amount then the event can trigger; but in this example the aim is to demonstrate the usage of smart contracts to trigger events that can then be read by JavaScript programmes running on Node.js, which then in turn can trigger actions on IoT devices using various libraries.

The smart contract source code is shown as follows:

```
1   pragma solidity ^0.4.0;
2 ▾ contract simpleIOT {
3       uint  roomrent=10;
4           event roomRented(bool returnValue);
5       function  getRent (uint8 x) returns (bool)
6 ▾     {
7           if (x==roomrent)
8 ▾         {
9               roomRented(true);
10              return true;
11          }
12      }
13  }
```

Solidity code for simple IOT

The solidity online compiler can be used to run and test this contract. The **Application Binary Interface (ABI)** required for interacting with the contract is also available in the **Interface** field as shown in the following screenshot:

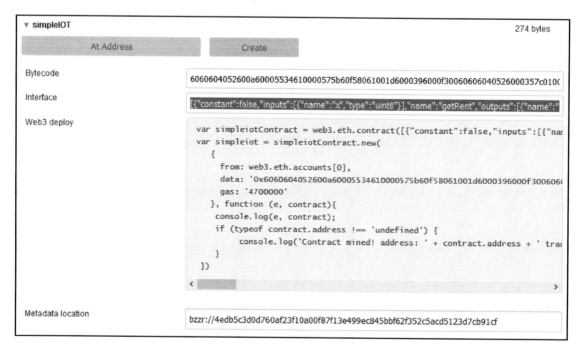

Solidity online compiler

There are two methods by which Raspberry node can connect to the private blockchain via the web3 interface. The first is where the raspberry device is running its own geth and maintains its own ledger but with resource-constrained devices it is not possible to run a full `geth` node, or even a light node in a few circumstances. In that case, the web3 provider can be initialized to connect to the appropriate RPC channel. This will be shown later in the client JavaScript Node.js programme. A comparison of both of these approaches is shown in the following diagram:

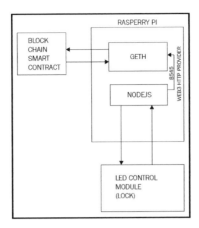

Application architecture of room rent IoT application (IoT device with local ledger)

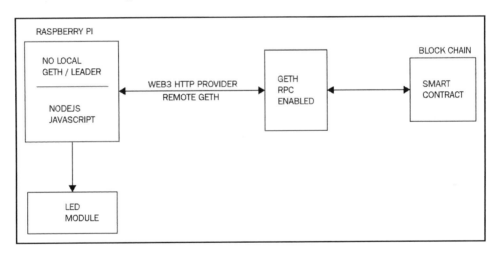

Application architecture of room rent IoT application (IoT device without local ledger)

There are obvious security concerns which arise from exposing RPC interfaces publicly, therefore it is recommended that this option is used only on private networks and if required to be used on public networks appropriate security measures are put in place, such as allowing only the known IP addresses to connect to the geth RPC interface. This can be achieved by a combination of disabling peer discovery mechanisms and HTTP-RPC server listening interfaces. More information about this can be found in geth help. The traditional network security measures such as firewalls, **Transport Layer Security** (**TLS**) and certificates can also be used, but have not been discussed in this example.

Now Truffle can be used to deploy the contract on the private network ID 786 to which at this point the Raspberry Pi is connected. A truffle deploy can be performed simply by using the following shown command; it is assumed that `truffle init` and other preliminaries discussed in Chapter 8, *Ethereum Development* have already been performed:

```
$ truffle migrate
```

It should produce the output similar to the following screenshot:

```
imran@drequinox-OP7010:~/iotcontract$ truffle migrate --reset
Running migration: 1_initial_migration.js
  Deploying Migrations...
  Migrations: 0xdd8a88072aa4ff49b62c25d6f6f2207b731aee76
Saving successful migration to network...
Saving artifacts...
Running migration: 2_deploy_contracts.js
  Deploying simpleIOT...
  simpleIOT: 0x151ce17c28b20ce554e0d944deb30e0447fbf78d
Saving successful migration to network...
Saving artifacts...
```

Truffle deploy

Once the contract is deployed correctly, JavaScript code can be developed that will connect to the blockchain via web3, listen for the events from the smart contract in the blockchain, and turn the LED on via the Raspberry Pi. The JavaScript code is shown as follows:

```
var Web3 = require('web3');
if (typeof web3 !== 'undefined')
{
  web3 = new Web3(web3.currentProvider);
}
else
{
  web3 = new Web3(new
  Web3.providers.HttpProvider("http://localhost:9002"));
}
var Gpio = require('onoff').Gpio;
var led = new Gpio(21,'out');
var coinbase = web3.eth.coinbase;
var ABIString = '[{"constant":false,"inputs":
[{"name":"x","type":"uint8"}],"name":"getRent","outputs":[{"name":"","type"
:"bool"}],"payable":false,"type":"function"},{"anonymous":false,"inputs":[{
"indexed":false,"name":"returnValue","type":"bool"}],"name":"roomRented","t
ype":"event"}]';
var ABI = JSON.parse(ABIString);
var ContractAddress = '0x151ce17c28b20ce554e0d944deb30e0447fbf78d';
web3.eth.defaultAccount = web3.eth.accounts[0];
```

```
var simpleiot = web3.eth.contract(ABI).at(ContractAddress);
var event = simpleiot.roomRented( {}, function(error, result) {
if (!error)
{
led.writeSync(1);
}
});
```

Note that in the example above the contract address
0x151ce17c28b20ce554e0d944deb30e0447fbf78d is specific to the deployment and it
will be different when readers run this example. Simply change the address in the file to
what the readers see after deploying the contract. This JavaScript code can be placed in a file
on the Raspberry PI, for example, index.js. It can be run by using the following
command:

```
$ sudo nodejs index.js
```

This will start the programme, which will run on Node.js and listen for events from the
smart contract. Once the program is running correctly, the smart contract can be invoked by
using the Truffle console as shown in the following screenshot.

In this case the .getRent function is called with parameter 10, which is the expected value.

```
imran@drequinox-OP7010:~/iotcontract$ truffle console
truffle(default)> simpleIOT.deployed().getRent(10)
'0x7e8b33f5354a73e2874ef29b26ea89d5811f23978778a9c05e11d5b19cd0fd40'
```

Interaction with the contract

After the contract is mined, `roomRented` will be triggered, which will turn the LED on. In this example it is a simple LED but it can be any physical device such as a room lock that can be controlled via an actuator. If all works well, the LED will be turned on as a result of the smart contract function invocation as shown in the following image:

Raspberry Pi with LED control

As demonstrated in the preceding example, a private network of IoT devices can be built that runs a geth client on each of the nodes and can listen for events from smart contracts and trigger an action accordingly. The example shown is simple on purpose but demonstrates the underlying principles of an Ethereum network that can be built using IoT devices along with smart contract-driven control of the physical devices.

In the next section, other applications of the blockchain technology in government, finance, and health will be discussed.

Government

There are various applications of blockchain being researched currently that can support government functions and take the current model of e-government to the next level. First, in this section some background for e-government will be provided and then a few use cases such as e-voting, homeland security (border control), and electronic IDs (citizen ID cards) will be discussed.

E-government or electronic government is a paradigm where information and communication technology is used to deliver public services to citizens. The concept is not new and has been implemented in various countries around the world but with blockchain a new avenue of exploration has opened up. Many governments are researching the possibility of using blockchain technology for managing and delivering public services. Transparency, auditability, and integrity are attributes of blockchain that can go a long way in effectively managing various government functions.

Border control

Automated border control systems have been in use for decades now in order to thwart illegal entry into countries and prevent terrorism and human trafficking.

Machine-readable travel documents and specifically biometric passports have paved the way for automated border control; however current systems are limited to a certain extent and blockchain technology can provide solutions. A **Machine-readable Travel Document (MRTD)** standard is defined in document ICAO 9303 by the **International Civil Aviation Organization (ICAO)** and has been implemented by many countries around the world.

Each passport contains various security and identity attributes that can be used to identify the owner of the passport and also circumvent attempts at tampering with the passports. These include biometric features such as retina scan, finger prints, facial recognition, and standard ICAO specified features including **Machine Readable Zone (MRZ)** and other text attributes that are visible on the first page of the passport.

One key issue with current border control systems is centralization whereby the systems are controlled by a single entity and the fact that data is not readily shared between law enforcement agencies. This makes it difficult to track suspected individuals. Another issue is related to the immediate implementation of blacklisting of a travel document, for example, when there is an immediate need to track and control suspected travel documents. Currently, there is no mechanism available to immediately blacklist or revoke a suspected passport.

Blockchain can provide a solution to this problem by maintaining a blacklist in a smart contract which can be updated as required and any changes will be immediately visible to all agencies and border control points thus enabling immediate control over the movement of a suspected travel document. It could be argued that traditional mechanisms like PKIs and P2P networks can also be used for this purpose but they do not provide the benefits that a blockchain can provide. With blockchain the whole system can be simplified without the requirement of complex networks and PKI setups which will also result in cost reduction. Moreover blockchain based systems will provide cryptographically guaranteed immutability which helps with auditing and discourages any fraudulent activity.

The full database of all travel documents perhaps cannot be stored on the blockchain currently due to scalability issues but a backend distributed database such as BigChainDB, IPFS, or Swarm can be used for that purpose. In this case, a hash of the travel document with the biometric ID of an individual can be stored in a simple smart contract and a hash of the document can then be used to refer to the detailed data available on the distributed file system such as IPFS. This way, when a travel document is blacklisted anywhere on the network, that information will be available immediately with the cryptographic guarantee of its authenticity and integrity throughout the distributed ledger. This functionality can also provide effective support in anti-terrorism activities, thus playing a vital role in the homeland security function of a government.

A simple contract in solidity can have an array defined for storing identities and associated biometric records. This array can be used to store the identifying information about a passport. The identity can be a hash of **Machine readable zone** (**MRZ**) of the passport or travel document concatenated with the biometric record from the RFID chip. A simple boolean field can be used to identify blacklisted passports. Once this initial check passes, further detailed biometric verification can be performed by traditional systems and eventually when a decision is made regarding the entry of the passport holder that decision can be propagated back to the blockchain, thus enabling all participants on the network to immediately share the outcome of the decision.

A high-level approach to building a blockchain-based border control system can be visualized as shown in the following figure. In this scenario, the passport is presented for scanning to an RFID and page scanner which reads the data page and extracts machine-readable information along with a hash of the biometric data stored in the RFID chip. At this stage, a live photo and retina scan of the passport holder is also taken. This information is then passed on to the blockchain where a smart contract is responsible for verifying the legitimacy of the travel document by first checking its own list of blacklisted passports and then requesting more data from the backend IPFS database for comparison. Note that the biometric data such as photo or retina scan is not stored on the blockchain, instead only a reference to this data in the backend (IPFS or BigChainDB) is stored in the blockchain.

If the data from the presented passport matches with what is held in the IPFS as files or in BigChainDB and also passes the smart contract logical check then the border gate can be opened.

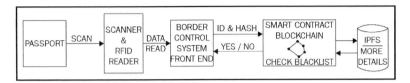

Automated border control using blockchain

After verification this information is propagated throughout the blockchain and is instantly available to all participants on the border control blockchain. These participants can be a worldwide consortium of homeland security departments of various nations.

Voting

Voting in any government is a key function and allows citizens to participate in the democratic election process. Whilst voting has evolved over time into a much more mature and secure process, it still has limitations that need to be addressed in order to achieve a desired level of maturity. Usually, the limitations in current voting systems revolve around fraud, weaknesses in operational processes, and especially transparency. Over the years, secure voting mechanisms have been built which make use of specialized voting machines that promised security and privacy but they still had vulnerabilities that could be exploited in order to subvert the security mechanisms of those machines. This can lead to serious implications for the whole voting process and can result in mistrust in the government by the public.

Blockchain-based voting systems can resolve these issues by introducing end-to-end security and transparency in the process. Security is provided in the form of integrity and authenticity of votes by using public key cryptography which comes as standard in a blockchain. Moreover, immutability guaranteed by blockchain ensures that votes cast once cannot be cast again. This can be achieved through a combination of biometric features and a smart contract maintaining a list of votes already cast. For example a smart contract can maintain a list of already casted votes with the biometric ID (for example a fingerprint) and can use that to detect and prevent double casting. Secondly, zero knowledge proofs can also be used on the blockchain to protect voters' privacy on the blockchain.

Citizen identification (ID cards)

Electronic IDs or national ID cards are issued by various countries around the world at present. These cards are secure and possess many security features that thwart duplication or tampering attempts. However, with the advent of blockchain technology there are several improvements that can be made to this process.

Digital identity is not only limited to just government-issued ID cards, it is a concept that is applicable in online social networks and forums too. There can be multiple identities used for different purposes. A blockchain-based online digital identity allows control over personal information sharing. Users can see who used their data and for what purpose and can control access to it. This is not possible with the current infrastructures which are centrally controlled. The key benefit is that a single identity issued by the government can be used easily and in a transparent manner for multiple services via a single government blockchain. In this case, the blockchain serves as a platform where government is providing various services such as pensions, taxation, or benefits and a single ID is being used for accessing all these services. Blockchain in this case provides an immutable record of every change and transaction made by a digital ID, thus ensuring integrity and transparency of the system. Also citizens can notarize birth certificates, marriages, deeds, and many other documents on the blockchain tied with their digital ID as a proof of existence.

Currently, there are successful implementations of identity schemes in various countries that work well and there is an argument that perhaps blockchain is not really required in identity management systems. Although, there are several benefits such as privacy and control over the usage of identity information but due to the current immaturity of blockchain technology perhaps it is not ready for use in real-world identity systems. However, research is being carried out by various governments to explore the usage of blockchain for identity management.

Moreover, laws such as the right to be forgotten can be quite difficult to incorporate in to blockchain due to its immutable nature.

Miscellaneous

Other government functions where blockchain technology can be implemented in order to improve cost and efficiency include collection of taxes, benefits management and disbursement, land ownership record management, life event registration (marriages, births), motor vehicle registration, and licenses. This is not an exhaustive list and over time many functions and processes of a government can be adapted to a blockchain-based model. The key benefits of blockchain such as immutability, transparency and decentralization can help to bring improvements to most of the traditional government systems.

Health

The health industry has been identified as another major industry that can benefit by adapting blockchain technology. Blockchain provides an immutable, auditable, and transparent system that traditional P2P networks cannot. In addition blockchain provides a cost-effective, simpler infrastructure as compared to traditional complex PKI networks. In healthcare, major issues such as privacy compromises, data breaches, high costs, and fraud can arise from lack of interoperability, overly complex processes, transparency, auditability, and control. Another burning issue is counterfeit medicines; especially in developing countries, this is a major cause of concern.

With the adaptability of blockchain in the health sector, several benefits can be realized, ranging from cost saving, increased trust, faster processing of claims, high availability, no operational errors due to complexity in the operational procedures, and preventing the distribution of counterfeit medicines.

From another angle, blockchains that are providing a digital currency as an incentive for mining can be used to provide processing power to solve scientific problems that can help to find cures for certain diseases. Examples include FoldingCoin, which rewards its miners with FLDC tokens for sharing their computer's processing power for solving scientific problems that require particularly large calculations. FoldingCoin is available at `http://foldingcoin.net/`. Another similar project is called CureCoin which is available at `https://www.curecoin.net/`. It is yet to be seen that how successful these projects will be in achieving their goals but the idea is very promising.

Finance

Blockchain has many applications in the finance industry. Blockchain in finance is the hottest topic in the industry currently and major banks and financial organizations are researching to find ways to adapt blockchain technology especially due to its highly-desired potential to cost-save.

Insurance

In the insurance industry, blockchain technology can help to stop fraudulent claims, increase the speed of claim processing, and enable transparency. Imagine a shared ledger between all insurers that can provide a quick and efficient mechanism for handling inter-company claims. Also with the convergence of IoT and blockchain, an ecosystem of smart devices can be imagined where all these things are able to negotiate and manage their own insurance policies controlled by smart contracts on the blockchain.

Blockchain can reduce the overall cost and effort required to process claims. Claims can be automatically verified and paid via smart contracts and the associated identity of the insurance policy holder. For example a smart contract with the help of Oracles and possibly IoT can make sure that when the accident occurred, it can record related telemetry data and based on this information can release payment. It can also withhold payment if the smart contract after evaluating conditions of payment concludes that payment should not be released. For example in a scenario where the vehicle was not repaired by an authorized workshop or was used outside a designated area and so on and so forth. There can be many conditions that a smart contract can evaluate to process claims and choice of these rules depend on the insurer, but the general idea is that smart contracts in combination with IoT and Oracles can automate the entire vehicle insurance industry.

Several start-ups such as Dynamis have proposed smart contract-based peer-to-peer insurance platforms that run on Ethereum blockchain. This is initially proposed to be used for unemployment insurance and does not require underwriters in the model. It is available at http://dynamisapp.com/.

Post trade settlement

This is the most sought-after application of blockchain technology. Currently, many financial institutions are exploring the possibility of using blockchain technology to simplify, automate, and speed up the costly and time-consuming post-trade settlement process.

In order to understand the problem better, the trade lifecycle is described briefly. A trade lifecycle contains three steps: execution, clearing, and settlement. Execution is concerned with the commitment of trading between two parties and can be entered into the system via front office order management terminals or exchanges. Clearing is the next step whereby the trade is matched between the seller and buyer based on certain attributes such as price and quantity. At this stage, accounts that are involved in payment are also identified. Finally, settlement is where eventually the security is exchanged for payment between the buyer and seller.

In the traditional trade lifecycle model, a central clearing house is required in order to facilitate trading between parties which bears the credit risk of both parties. The current scheme is somewhat complicated, whereby a seller and buyer have to take a complex route in order to trade with each other. This comprises of various firms, brokers, clearing houses, and custodians but with blockchain a single distributed ledger with appropriate smart contracts can simplify this whole process and can enable buyers and sellers to talk directly to each other.

Particularly, the post trade settlement process takes two to three days and has dependency on central clearing houses and reconciliation systems. With the shared ledger approach, all participants on the blockchain can immediately see a single version of truth regarding the state of the trade. Moreover, peer-to-peer settlement is possible, which results in the reduction of complexity, cost, risk, and the time it takes to settle the trade. Finally, intermediaries can be totally eliminated by making use of appropriate smart contracts on the blockchain.

Financial crime prevention

Know your customer (KYC) and **Anti Money laundering** (AML) are the key enablers for the prevention of financial crime. In the case of KYC, currently each institution maintains their own copy of customer data and performs verification via centralized data providers. This can be a time-consuming process and can result in delays in on-boarding a new client. Blockchain can provide a solution to this problem by securely sharing a distributed ledger between all financial institutions that contains verified and accurate identities of customers. This distributed ledger can only be updated by consensus between the participants thus providing transparency and auditability. This can not only reduce costs but also enable meeting regulatory and compliance requirements in a better and consistent manner.

In the case of AML, due to the immutable, shared, and transparent nature of blockchain, regulators can easily be granted access to a private blockchain where they can fetch data for relevant regulatory reporting. This will also result in reducing complexity and costs related to the current regulatory reporting paradigm where data is fetched from various legacy and disparate systems and aggregated and formatted together for reporting purposes. Blockchain can provide a single shared view of all financial transactions in the system that are cryptographically secure, authentic, and auditable, thus reducing the costs and complexity associated with the currently employed regulatory reporting methods.

Media

Key issues in the media industry revolve around content distribution, rights management, and royalty payments to artists. For example, digital music can be copied many times without any restriction and any attempts to apply copy protection have been hacked in some way or other. There is no control over the distribution of the content that a musician or song writer produces; it can be copied as many times as needed without any restriction and consequently has an impact on the royalty payments. Also, payments are not always guaranteed and are based on traditional airtime figures. All these issues revolving around copy protection and royalty payments can be resolved by connecting consumers, artists, and all players in the industry, allowing transparency and control over the process. Blockchain can provide a network where digital music is cryptographically guaranteed to be owned only by the consumers who pay for it. This payment mechanism is controlled by a smart contract instead of a centralized media agency or authority. The payments will be automatically made based on the logic embedded within the smart contract and number of 'downloads'. Moreover, illegal copying of digital music files can be stopped altogether because everything is recorded and owned immutably in a transparent manner on blockchain. A music file for example can be stored with owner information and timestamp which can be traced throughout the blockchain network. Furthermore, the consumers who own a legal copy of some content are cryptographically tied to the content they have and it cannot be moved to another owner unless permissioned by the owner. Copyrights and transfers can be managed easily via blockchain once all digital content is immutably recorded on the blockchain. Smart contracts can then control the distribution and payment to all concerned parties.

Summary

There are many applications of blockchain technology and as discussed in the chapter they can be implemented in various industries to bring about multiple benefits to existing solutions. In this chapter, five main industries that can benefit from blockchain have been discussed. First IoT was discussed, which is another revolutionary technology on its own; and by combining it with the blockchain several fundamental limitations can be addressed, which brings about tremendous benefits to the IoT industry. More focus has been given to IoT as it is the biggest and most ready candidate for adapting blockchain technology. Already, practical use cases and platforms have emerged in the form of **Platform as a Service (PaaS)** for blockchain-based IoT such as the IBM Watson IoT blockchain. IBM Blue Horizon is also now available for experimentation, which is a decentralized blockchain-based IoT network. Second, applications in the government sector were discussed whereby various government processes such as homeland security, identification cards, and benefit disbursements can be made transparent, secure, and more robust. Furthermore, issues in the finance sector were discussed with possible solutions that blockchain technology can provide. Although the finance sector is exploring the possibilities of using blockchain with high energy and enthusiasm, it is still far away from production-ready blockchain-based systems. Finally, some aspects of the health sector and music industry were also discussed. All these use cases and many more in the industry stand on pillars provided by core attributes of blockchain technology such as decentralization, transparency, reliability, and security. However, certain challenges need to be addressed before blockchain technology can be adapted fully; these will be discussed in the next chapter.

12
Scalability and Other Challenges

This chapter aims to provide an introduction to various challenges that need to be addressed before blockchains can become mainstream technology. Even though various use cases and proof of concept systems have been developed and the technology works well for many of the scenarios, there still is a need to address some fundamental limitations that are present in blockchains in order to make this technology more adaptable.

At the top of the list of these issues comes scalability and then privacy. Both of these are important limitations to address, especially as blockchains are envisioned to be used in privacy-demanding industries too. There are specific requirements around confidentiality of transactions in finance, law and health, whereas scalability is generally a concern where blockchains do not meet the adequate performance levels expected by the users. These two issues are becoming inhibiting factors toward blockchain technology's wider acceptance. A review of currently proposed and ongoing research in these two specific areas will be presented in this chapter. In addition to privacy and security, other challenges include regulation, integration, adaptability, and security in general. Although, in bitcoin blockchain security is provably bulletproof and has stood the test of time, there still are some caveats that may allow security to be compromised to an extent in some subtle scenarios. Also, there are some reasonable security concerns in other blockchains, such as Ethereum, regarding smart contracts, denial of service attacks, and large attack surface. All of these will be discussed in detail in the following sections.

Scalability

This problem has been a focus of intense debate, rigorous research, and media attention for the last few years. This is the single most important problem that could mean the difference between wider adaptability of blockchains or limited private use only by consortiums. As a result of substantial research in this area, many solutions have been proposed, which are discussed in the following section.

From a theoretical perspective, the general approach toward tackling the scalability issue generally revolves around protocol-level enhancements. For example, a commonly mentioned solution to bitcoin scalability is to increase its block size. Other proposals include off-chain solutions that offload certain processing to off-chain networks, for example, off-chain state networks. Based on the solutions mentioned above, generally, the proposals can be divided into two categories: on-chain solutions that are based on the idea of changing fundamental protocols on which the blockchain operates, and off-chain solutions that make use of network and processing resources off-chain in order to enhance the blockchain.

Another approach to addressing limitations in blockchains has been recently proposed by *Miller* and others in their position paper *On Scaling Decentralized Blockchains*. In this paper, it is shown that a blockchain can be divided into various abstract layers called **planes**. Each plane is responsible for performing specific functions. These include the network plane, consensus plane, storage plane, view plane, and side plane. This abstraction allows bottlenecks and limitations to be addressed at each plane individually and in a structured manner. A brief overview of each layer is given below with some references to the bitcoin system.

First the network plane is discussed. A key function of the network plane is transaction propagation. It has been identified in the above-mentioned paper that in bitcoin, this plane underutilizes the network bandwidth due to the way transaction validation is performed by a node before propagation and duplication of transaction propagation, first in the transaction broadcast phase, and then after mining in a block. It should be noted that this issue was addressed by **BIP 152 (Compact Block Relay)**.

The second layer is called the consensus plane. This layer is responsible for mining and achieving consensus. Bottlenecks in this layer revolve around limitations in Proof of Work algorithms whereby increasing consensus speed and bandwidth results in compromising security of the network due to an increase in the number of forks.

The storage plane is the third layer, which stores the ledger. Issues in this layer revolve around the need for each node to keep a copy of the entire ledger, which leads to certain inefficiencies, such as increased bandwidth and storage requirements. Bitcoin has a method available called pruning, which allows a node to operate without the need to download the full blockchain. This functionality has resulted in major improvements from a storage point of view.

Next on the list is the view plane, which proposes an optimization which is based on the proposal that bitcoin miners do not need the full blockchain to operate, and a view can be constructed out of the complete ledger as a representation of the entire state of the system, which is sufficient for miners to function. Implementation of views will eliminate the need for mining nodes to store the full blockchain.

Finally, the side plane has been proposed by the authors of the above-mentioned research paper. This plane represents the idea of off-chain transactions whereby the concept of payment or transaction channels is used to offload the processing of transactions between participants, but is still backed by the main bitcoin blockchain.

The above-mentioned model can be used to describe limitations and improvements in current blockchain designs in a structured manner. Also, there are several general strategies that have been proposed over the last few years which can address the limitations in current blockchain designs such as Ethereum and bitcoin. These approaches are also characterized and discussed individually in the following section.

Block size increase

This is the most debated proposal for increasing blockchain performance (transaction processing throughput). Currently, bitcoin can process only about three to seven transactions per second, which is a major inhibiting factor in adapting the bitcoin blockchain for processing micro-transactions. Block size in bitcoin is hardcoded to be 1 MB, but if block size is increased, it can hold more transactions and can result in faster confirmation time. There are several **Bitcoin Improvement Proposals (BIPs)** made in favor of block size increase. These include BIP 100, BIP 101, BIP 102, BIP 103, and BIP 109. In Ethereum, the block size is not limited by hardcoding; instead, it is controlled by gas limit. In theory, there is no limit on the size of a block in Ethereum because it's dependent on the amount of gas, which can increase over time. This is possible because miners are allowed to increase the gas limit for subsequent blocks if the limit has been reached in the previous block.

Block interval reduction

Another proposal is to reduce the time between each block generation. The time between blocks can be decreased to achieve faster finalization of blocks but may result in less security due to the increased number of forks. Ethereum has achieved a block time of approximately 14 seconds and, at times, it can increase. This is a significant improvement from the bitcoin blockchain, which takes 10 minutes to generate a new block. In Ethereum, the issue of high orphaned blocks resulting from smaller times between blocks is mitigated by using the **Greedy Heaviest Observed Subtree (GHOST)** protocol whereby orphaned blocks (uncles) are also included in determining the valid chain. Once Ethereum moves to Proof of Stake, this will become irrelevant as no mining will be required and almost immediate finality of transactions can be achieved.

Invertible Bloom lookup tables

This is another approach that has been proposed to reduce the amount of data required to be transferred between bitcoin nodes. **Invertible Bloom lookup tables (IBLTs)** were originally proposed by *Gavin Andresen,* and the key attraction in this approach is that it does not result in a hard fork of bitcoin if implemented. The key idea is based on the fact that there is no need to transfer all transactions between nodes; instead, only those that are not already available in the transaction pool of the synching node are transferred. This allows quicker transaction pool synchronization between nodes, thus increasing the overall scalability and speed of the bitcoin network.

Sharding

Sharding is not a new technique and has been used in distributed databases for scalability such as MongoDB and MySQL. The key idea behind sharding is to split up the tasks into multiple chunks that are then processed by multiple nodes. This results in improved throughput and reduced storage requirements. In blockchains, a similar scheme is employed whereby the state of the network is partitioned into multiple shards. The state usually includes balances, code, nonce, and storage. Shards are loosely coupled partitions of a blockchain that run on the same network. There are a few challenges related to inter-shard communication and consensus on the history of each shard. This is an open area for research.

State channels

This is another approach proposed for speeding up the transaction on a blockchain network. The basic idea is to use side channels for state updating and processing transactions off the main chain; once the state is finalized, it is written back to the main chain, thus offloading the time-consuming operations from the main blockchain. State channels work by performing the following three steps:

1. First, a part of the blockchain state is locked under a smart contract, ensuring the agreement and business logic between participants.
2. Now off-chain transaction processing and interaction is started between the participants that update the state only between themselves for now. In this step, almost any number of transactions can be performed without requiring the blockchain and this is what makes the process fast and a best candidate for solving blockchain scalability issues. However, it could be argued that this is not a real on-blockchain solution such as, for example, sharding, but the end result is a faster, lighter, and robust network which can prove very useful in micropayment networks, IoT networks, and many other applications.
3. Once the final state is achieved, the state channel is closed and the final state is written back to the main blockchain. At this stage, the locked part of the blockchain is also unlocked.

This technique has been used in the bitcoin lightning network and Ethereum's Raiden.

Private blockchain

Private blockchains are inherently fast because no real decentralization is required and participants on the network do not need to mine; instead, they can only validate transactions. This can be considered as a workaround to the scalability issue in public blockchains; however, this is not the solution to the scalability problem. Also, it should be noted that private blockchains are only suitable in specific areas and setups.

Proof of Stake

Instead of using Proof of Work, Proof of Stake algorithm based blockchains are fundamentally faster.

Sidechains

Sidechains can improve scalability indirectly by allowing many sidechains to run along with the main blockchain while allowing usage of perhaps comparatively less secure and faster sidechains to perform transactions but still pegged with the main blockchain. The core idea of sidechains is called a two-way peg, which allows transfer of coins from a parent chain to a side chain and vice versa.

Subchains

This is a relatively new technique recently proposed by *Peter R. Rizun* which is based on the idea of weak blocks that are created in layers until a strong block is found. Weak blocks can be defined as those blocks that have not been able to be mined by meeting the standard network difficulty criteria but have done enough work to meet another weaker difficulty target. Miners can build subchains by layering weak blocks on top of each other, unless a block is found that meets the standard difficulty target. At this point, the subchain is closed and becomes the strong block. Advantages of this approach include reduced waiting time for the first verification of a transaction. This technique also results in a reduced chance of orphaning blocks and speeds up transaction processing. This is also an indirect way of addressing the scalability issue. Subchains do not require any soft fork or hard fork to implement but need acceptance by the community.

Tree chains

There are also other proposals to increase bitcoin scalability, such as tree chains that change the blockchain layout from a linearly sequential model to a tree. This tree is basically a binary tree which descends from the main bitcoin chain. This approach is similar to sidechain implementation, eliminating the need for major protocol change or block size increase. It allows improved transaction throughput. In this scheme, the blockchains themselves are fragmented and distributed across the network in order to achieve scalability. Moreover, mining is not required to validate the blocks on the tree chains; instead, users can independently verify the block header. However, this idea is not ready for production yet and further research is required in order to make it practical.

In addition to the above-mentioned general techniques, some bitcoin-specific improvements have also been proposed by *Christian Decker* in his book *On the Scalability and Security of Bitcoin*. This proposal is based on the idea of speeding up propagation time as the current information propagation mechanism results in blockchain forks. These techniques include minimization of verification, pipelining of block propagation, and connectivity increase. These changes do not require fundamental protocol-level changes; instead, these changes can be implemented independently in the bitcoin node software. With regards to verification minimization, it has been noted that the block verification process is contributing toward propagation delay. The reason behind this is that a node takes a long time to verify uniqueness of the block and transactions within the block. It has been suggested that a node can send the inventory message as soon as the initial Proof of Work and block validation checks are completed. This way, propagation can be improved by just performing the first *difficulty check* and not waiting for transaction validation to finish. In addition to the above proposal, pipelining of block propagation has also been suggested, which is based on the idea of anticipating the availability of a block. In this scheme, the availability of a block is already announced without waiting for actual block availability, thus reducing the round-trip time between nodes. Finally, the problem of long distances between transaction originator and nodes also contributes toward the slowdown of block propagation. It has been shown in the research conducted by *Christian Decker* that connectivity increase can reduce propagation delay of blocks and transactions. This is possible because, if at any one time the bitcoin node is connected to many other nodes, it will result in reducing the distance between nodes and can speed up information propagation on the network.

An elegant solution to scalability issues will most likely be a combination of some or all of the above-mentioned general approaches. A number of initiatives taken in order to address scalability and security issues in blockchains are now almost ready for implementation. For example, bitcoin segregated witness is a proposal that can help massively with scalability and only needs a soft fork in order for it to be implemented. The key idea behind so called *segwit* is to separate signature data from the transactions, which resolves the transaction malleability issue and allows block size increase.

Another proposal, Bitcoin NG, which is based on the idea of micro blocks and leader election, has gained some attention recently. The core idea is to split blocks into two types, namely leader blocks (also called key blocks) and micro blocks. Leader blocks are responsible for Proof of Work whereas micro blocks contain actual transactions. Micro blocks do not require any Proof of Work and are generated by the elected leader every block-generation cycle. This block-generation cycle is initiated by a leader block. The only requirement is to sign the micro blocks with the elected leader's private key. The micro blocks can be generated at a very high speed by the elected leader (miner), thus resulting in increased performance and transaction speed.

On the other hand, recently, an Ethereum mauve paper written by *Vitalik Buterin* has been presented at Ethereum Devcon 2 in Shanghai; it describes the vision of a scalable Ethereum. The mauve proposal is based on a combination of sharding and implementation of Proof of Stake algorithm. Certain goals such as efficiency gain via Proof of Stake, maximally fast block time, economic finality, scalability, cross-shard communication, and censorship resistance have been identified in the paper.

Privacy

Privacy of transactions is a much desired property of blockchains. However, due to its very nature, especially in public blockchains, everything is transparent, thus inhibiting its usage in various industries where privacy is of paramount importance, such as finance, health, and many others. There are different proposals made to address the privacy issue and some progress has already been made. Several techniques, such as indistinguishability obfuscation, usage of homomorphic encryption, zero knowledge proofs, and ring signatures. All these techniques have their merits and demerits and are discussed in the following sections.

Indistinguishability obfuscation

This cryptographic technique may serve as a silver bullet to all privacy and confidentiality issues in blockchains but the technology is not yet ready for production deployments. **Indistinguishability obfuscation (IO)** allows for code obfuscation, which is a very ripe research topic in cryptography and, if applied to blockchains, can serve as an unbreakable obfuscation mechanism that will turn smart contracts into a black box. The key idea behind IO is what's called by researchers a *multilinear jigsaw puzzle*, which basically obfuscates program code by mixing it with random elements, and if the program is run as intended, it will produce expected output but any other way of executing would render the program look random and garbage. This idea was first proposed by *Sahai* and others in their research paper *Candidate Indistinguishability Obfuscation and Functional Encryption for All Circuits.*

Homomorphic encryption

This type of encryption allows operations to be performed on encrypted data. Imagine a scenario where the data is sent to a cloud server for processing. The server processes it and returns the output without knowing anything about the data that it has processed. This is also an area ripe for research and fully homomorphic encryption that allows all operations on encrypted data is still not fully deployable in production; however, major progress in this field has already been made. Once implemented on blockchains, it can allow processing on cipher text which will allow privacy and confidentiality of transactions inherently. For example, the data stored on the blockchain can be encrypted using homomorphic encryption and computations can be performed on that data without the need for decryption, thus providing privacy service on blockchains. This concept has also been implemented in a project named *Enigma* by MIT's Media Lab. Enigma is a peer-to-peer network which allows multiple parties to perform computations on encrypted data without revealing anything about the data.

Zero knowledge proofs

Zero knowledge proofs have recently been implemented in Zcash successfully, as seen in previous chapters. More specifically, SNARKs have been implemented in order to ensure privacy on the blockchain. The same idea can be implemented in Ethereum and other blockchains also. Integrating Zcash on Ethereum is already a very active research project being run by the Ethereum R&D team and the Zcash Company.

State channels

Privacy using state channels is also possible, simply due to the fact that all transactions are run off-chain and the main blockchain does not see the transaction at all except the final state output, thus ensuring privacy and confidentiality.

Secure multiparty computation

The concept of secure multiparty computation is not new and is based on the notion that data is split into multiple partitions between participating parties under a secret sharing mechanism which then does the actual processing on the data without the need of the reconstructing data on single machine. The output produced after processing is also shared between the parties.

Usage of hardware to provide confidentiality

Trusted computing platforms can be used to provide a mechanism by which confidentiality of transaction can be achieved on a blockchain, for example, by using Intel **Software Guard Extension (SGX)**, which allows code to be run in a hardware-protected environment called an *enclave*. Once the code runs successfully in the isolated enclave, it can produce a proof called a *quote* that is attestable by Intel's cloud servers. However, it is a concern that trusting Intel will result in some level of centralization and is not in line with the true spirit of blockchain technology. Nevertheless, this solution has its merits and, in reality, many platforms already use Intel chips anyway, therefore trusting Intel may be acceptable in some scenarios.

If this technology is applied on smart contracts then, once a node has executed the smart contract, it can produce the quote as a proof of correct and successful execution and other nodes will only have to verify it. This idea can be further extended by using any **Trusted Execution Environment (TEE)** which can provide the same functionality as an enclave and is available even on mobile devices with **Near Field Communication (NFC)** and a secure element.

Coinjoin

Coinjoin is a technique which is used to anonymize the bitcoin transactions by mixing them interactively. The idea is based on forming a single transaction from multiple entities without causing any change in inputs and outputs. It removes the direct link between senders and receivers, which means that a single address can no longer be associated with transactions, which could lead to identification of the users. Coinjoin needs cooperation between multiple parties that are willing to create a single transaction by mixing payments. Therefore, it should be noted that, if any single participant in the Coinjoin scheme does not keep up with the commitment made to cooperate for creating a single transaction by not signing the transactions as required, then it can result in a denial of service attack. In this protocol, there is no need for a single trusted third party. This concept is different from mixing a service which acts as a trusted third party or intermediary between the bitcoin users and allows shuffling of transactions. This shuffling of transactions results in the prevention of tracing and the linking of payments to a particular user.

Confidential transactions

Confidential transactions make use of Pedersen commitments in order to provide confidentiality. Commitment schemes allow a user to commit to some value while keeping it secret with the capability of revealing it later. Two properties that need to be satisfied in order to design a commitment scheme are *binding* and *hiding*. Binding makes sure that the committer is unable to change the chosen value once committed, whereas the hiding property ensures that any adversary is unable to find the original value to which the committer made commitment. Pedersen commitments also allow addition operations and preserve commutative property on the commitments, which makes it specifically useful for providing confidentiality in bitcoin transactions. In other words, it supports homomorphic encryption of values. Using commitment schemes allows the hiding of payment values in a bitcoin transaction. This concept is already implemented in the Elements Project (`https://e lementsproject.org/`).

MimbleWimble

The MimbleWimble scheme was proposed somewhat mysteriously on the bitcoin IRC channel and since then has gained a lot of popularity. MimbleWimble extends the idea of confidential transactions and Coinjoin, which allows aggregation of transactions without requiring any interactivity. However, it does not support the use of bitcoin scripting language along with various other features of standard Bitcoin protocol. This makes it incompatible with existing Bitcoin protocol. Therefore, it can either be implemented as a sidechain to bitcoin or on its own as an alternative cryptocurrency.

This scheme can address privacy and scalability issues both at once. The blocks created using the MimbleWimble technique do not contain transactions as in traditional bitcoin blockchains; instead, these blocks are composed of three lists: an input list, output list, and something called *excesses* which are lists of signatures and differences between outputs and inputs. The input list is basically references to the old outputs, and the output list contains confidential transactions outputs. These blocks are verifiable by nodes by using signatures, inputs, and outputs to ensure the legitimacy of the block. In contrast to bitcoin, MimbleWimble transaction outputs only contain pubkeys, and the difference between old and new outputs is signed by all participants involved in the transactions.

Security

Even though blockchains are generally secure and make use of asymmetric and symmetric cryptography as required throughout the blockchain network, there still are few caveats that can result in compromising the security of the blockchain.

There are a few examples of transaction malleability, eclipse attacks, and possibility of double spending in bitcoin that, in certain scenarios, have been shown to work by various researchers. Transaction malleability opens up the possibility of double withdrawal or deposit by allowing a hacker to change a transaction's Unique ID before the bitcoin network can confirm it, resulting in a scenario where it would seem that transactions did not occur. BIP 62 is one of the proposals along with segregated witness (segwit) that have suggested solutions to solve this issue. It should be noted that this is a problem only in the case of unconfirmed transactions, that is, scenarios where operational processes rely on unconfirmed transactions. In the case of normal applications that only rely on confirmed transactions, this is not an issue.

Information eclipse attacks in bitcoin can result in double spending. The idea behind eclipse attacks is that the bitcoin node is tricked into connecting only with the attacker node IPs. This opens up the possibility of a 51 % attack by the attacker. This has been addressed to some extent in bitcoin client v0.10.1.

Smart contract security

Recently, a lot of work has been started in smart contract security and, especially, formal verification of smart contracts is being discussed and researched. This was all triggered especially due to the infamous DAO hack. Formal verification is a process of verifying a computer program to ensure that it satisfies certain formal statements. This is now a new concept and there are a number of tools available for other languages that achieve this; for example, Frama-C is available for analyzing C programs. The key idea behind formal verification is to convert the source program into a set of statements that is understandable by the automated provers. For this purpose, Why3 is commonly used, and a formal verifier for solidity also makes use of that. An experimental but operational verifier is available in browser solidity already.

Smart contract security is of paramount importance now, and many other initiatives have also been taken in order to devise methods that can analyze solidity programs and find bugs. A recent and seminal example is Oyente, which is a tool built by researchers and has been introduced in their paper *Making Smart Contracts Smarter*. Several security bugs in smart contracts have been discovered and analyzed in this paper. These include transaction ordering dependence, time stamp dependence, mishandled exceptions such as call stack depth limit exploitation, and re-entrance vulnerability. The transaction ordering dependency bug basically exploits the scenarios where the perceived state of a contract might not be what the state of the contract changes to after execution. This weakness is a type of race condition. It is also called frontloading and is possible due to the fact that the order of transactions within a block can be manipulated. As all transactions first appear in the memory pool, the transactions there can be monitored before they are included in the block. This allows a transaction to be submitted before another transaction, thus leading to controlling the behavior of a smart contract.

Time stamp dependency bugs are possible in scenarios where the time stamp of the block is used as a source of some decision-making within the contract, but time stamps can be manipulated by the miners. Call stack depth limit is another bug that can be exploited due to the fact that the maximum call stack depth of EVM is 1,024 frames. If the stack depth is reached while the contract is executing then, in certain scenarios, the send or call instruction can fail, resulting in non-payment of funds. The call stack depth bug was addressed in the EIP50 hard fork. The re-entrancy bug was exploited in the DAO attack to siphon out millions of dollars into a child DAO. The re-entrancy bug basically means that a function can be called repeatedly before the previous (first) invocation of the functions has completed. This is particularly unsafe in Ether withdrawal functions in solidity smart contracts.

In additional to the above-mentioned bugs, there are several other problems that should be kept in mind while writing contracts. These bugs include that fact that if sending funds to another contract, handle it carefully because send can fail and even if throw is used as a *catch-all* mechanism, it will not work.

Other standard software bugs such as integer overflow and underflow are also quite significant and any use of integer variables should be carefully implemented in solidity. For example, a simple program where `uint8` is used to parse through elements of an array with more than 255 elements can result in an endless loop. This occurs because uint8 is limited to 256 numbers.

In the following sections, two examples of contract verification will be shown using Why3 and Oyente respectively.

Why3 formal verification

Formal verification of solidity code is now available as a feature in the solidity browser. First the code is converted into Why3 language that the verifier can understand. In the example below, a simple solidity code that defines the variable z as maximum limit of uint is shown. When this code runs, it will result in returning 0, because `uint z` will overrun and start again from 0. This can also be verified using Why3, which is shown below:

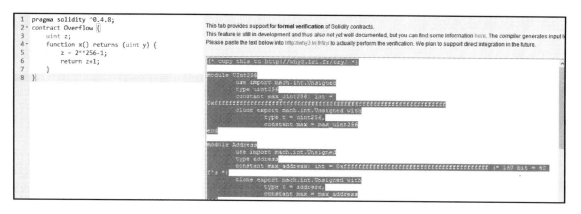

Solidity online compiler with formal verification

Once the solidity is compiled and available in the formal verification tab, it can be copied into the Why3 online IDE available at `http://why3.lri.fr/try/`. The example below shows that it successfully checks and reports integer overflow errors. This tool is under heavy development but is still quite useful. Also, this tool or any other similar tool is not a silver bullet. Even formal verification generally should not be considered a panacea because specifications in the first place should be defined appropriately:

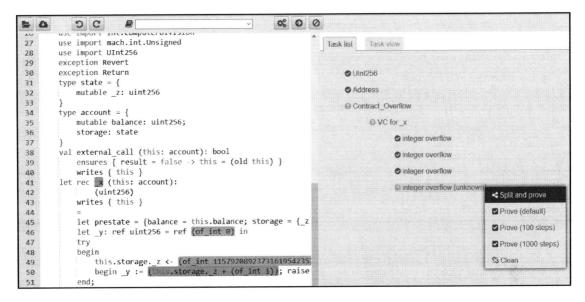

Why3

Oyente tool

Currently, Oyente is available as a Docker image for easy testing and installation. It is available at `https://github.com/ethereum/oyente`, and can be quickly downloaded and tested. In the example below, a simple contract taken from solidity documentation that contains a re-entrancy bug has been tested and it is shown that Oyente successfully analyzes the code and finds the bug:

```
1   pragma solidity ^0.4.0;
2   contract Fund {
3       mapping(address => uint) shares;
4       function withdraw() {
5           if (msg.sender.send(shares[msg.sender]))
6               shares[msg.sender] = 0;
7       }
8   }
```

Contract with re-entrancy bug – source: solidity documentation

This sample code contains a re-entrancy bug which basically means that if a contract is interacting with another contract or transferring ether, it is effectively handing over the control to that other contract. This allows the called contract to call back into the function of the contract from which it has been called without waiting for completion. For example, this bug can allow calling back into the `withdraw` function shown in the preceding example again and again, resulting in getting Ethers multiple times. This is possible because the share value is not set to 0 until the end of the function, which means that any later invocations will be successful, resulting in withdrawing again and again.

An example is shown of Oyente running to analyze the contract shown below and as can be seen in the following output, the analysis has successfully found the re-entrancy bug. The bug is proposed to be handled by a combination of the Checks-Effects-Interactions pattern described in the solidity documentation:

```
root@fa9ef6ac8455: /home/oyente/oyente
(venv)root@fa9ef6ac8455:/home/oyente/oyente# python oyente.py a1.sol
Contract Fund:
Running, please wait...
            ============ Results ===========
            CallStack Attack:       False
THIS IS A CALLLLLLLLLL
{'path_condition': [Iv >= 0, init_Is >= Iv, init_Ia >= 0, If(Id_0/
    269599466671506397946670150870196306736371444225405724811036102249216 ==
    1020253707,
    1,
    0) !=
0, Not(Iv != 0)], 'Is': Is, 'Iv': Iv, 'some_var_1': some_var_1, 'Id_0': Id
_0, 'Ia_store_some_var_1': Ia_store_some_var_1, 'Ia': Ia}

 This is the global state
{'Ia': {'some_var_1': 0}, 'miu_i': 3L, 'balance': {'Ia': init_Ia + Iv, 'Is
': init_Is - Iv}}
{64: 96, 0: Is & 14615016373309029182036848327162830196559325429 75, 32: 0}

CALL params

Is & 14615016373309029182036848327162830196559325429 75

Ia_store_some_var_1


 =>>>>>> New PC: []

Reentrancy_bug? True

Added True
            Concurrency Bug:        False
            Time Dependency:        False
            Reentrancy bug exists:  True
            ====== Analysis Completed ======
(venv)root@fa9ef6ac8455:/home/oyente/oyente# 
```

Oyente tool detecting solidity bugs

Summary

In this chapter, readers have been introduced to the security, confidentiality, and privacy aspects of blockchain technology. Privacy was discussed, which is another major inhibiting factor in adapting public blockchains for various industries. Next, smart contract security, which is a very hot topic currently, was discussed. It is a deep and extensive subject but a brief introduction on various aspects has been given, which should serve as a solid ground for further research in this area. For example, formal verification on its own is a vast area for research. Furthermore, examples of formal verification have also been provided to give readers an idea of what tools are available. It should be noted that the tools mentioned above are under heavy development and lack various desirable features. Also, documentation is quite scarce; therefore, readers are encouraged to keep an eye on developments, especially around formal verification and developments related to the Ethereum mauve paper, as it is going to develop rapidly very soon. The field of blockchain security and especially smart contract security is so ripe now that a whole book can be written on the subject. There are many experts and researchers in academia and the commercial sector exploring this area and soon there will be many automated tools available for the verification of smart contracts.

13
Current Landscape and What's Next

Blockchain technology will change the way we conduct our day-to-day business. It has challenged existing business models and has the promise of great benefits in terms of cost saving, and greater efficiency and transparency. This chapter will explore the latest developments, emerging trends, issues, and future predictions about this technology. Furthermore, some topics related to open research problems and improvements will be discussed in detail in the chapter.

Emerging trends

Blockchain technology is under rapid change and intense development due to deep interest in it by academics and the commercial sector. As the technology is becoming mature, a few trends have started to emerge recently. For example, private blockchains have recently gained quite a lot of attention due to their specific use cases in finance. Also, enterprise blockchains are another new trend that is aiming to develop blockchain solutions that meets enterprise-level efficiency, security, and integration requirements. Some of the trends are listed below and discussed.

Application-specific blockchains (ASBCs)

Currently, an inclination toward ASBCs is noticed, whereby a blockchain or distributed ledger is specifically developed for only one application in mind and is focused on a specific industry, for example, everledger, which is a blockchain that has been developed to be used for providing an immutable tracing history and audit trail for diamonds and other high-value items. This approach thwarts any fraud attempts because everything related to ownership, authenticity, and value of the items is verified and recorded on the blockchain. This is very valuable for insurance and law enforcement agencies.

Enterprise-grade blockchains

As blockchains in their original form are not ready for use at enterprise level due to privacy and scalability issues, a recent trend in developing enterprise-grade blockchains has emerged, whereby various companies have started to provide enterprise-grade blockchain solutions that are ready to be deployed and integrated at enterprise level. Requirements such as testing, documentation, integration, and security are all addressed already in this type of solution and can be implemented with minimal or no change at the enterprise level. This is in contrast to public blockchains, which are unregulated and do not meet specific enterprise-level security requirements. This also implies that enterprise-grade blockchains are usually supposed to be implemented in private configurations; however, public enterprise-grade blockchain implementation is also a possibility. 2016 has been a year when many technology start-ups have started to offer enterprise-grade blockchain solutions such as bloq, tylmez, chain, and many others. This trend continues to grow and 2017 will see more technology initiatives like this.

Private blockchains

With the need for privacy and confidentiality, a major focus is on developing private distributed ledgers that can be used within a group of trusted participants. As public blockchains, due to their open and comparatively less secure nature, are not suitable for industries such as finance, medicine, and law, private blockchains hold the promise to address this limitation and bring end users one step closer to reaping the benefits of blockchains while meeting all security and privacy requirements. Public blockchains are less secure because generally they do not provide privacy and confidentiality services. Private blockchains allow the participants or a subset of participants to be in full control of the system, thus making it desirable for use in finance and other industries where privacy and control are required.

Ethereum can be used in both private and public modes, whereas there are a few projects that have been developed solely as private blockchains, such as Hyperledger and Corda.

Start-ups

In recent years, many technology start-ups have emerged that are working on blockchain projects and are offering solutions specific to this technology. 2016 especially has seen a significant increase in the number of start-ups that are offering blockchain consultancy and solutions.

Strong research interest

Blockchain technology has stimulated intense research interest both in academia and the commercial sector. In recent years, the interest has greatly increased and now major institutions and researchers around the world are exploring this technology. This growth in interest is especially due to the fact that blockchain technology can help to make businesses efficient, reduce costs, and make things transparent. Academic interest is around addressing hard problems in cryptography, consensus mechanisms, performance, and addressing other limitations in blockchains. As blockchain technology comes under the wider umbrella of distributed systems, many researchers from distributed computing research have focused their research on blockchain technology. For example, UCL has a dedicated department, the *UCL Research Centre for Blockchain Technologies*, that focuses on blockchain technology research. Another example is the ETH Zurich distributed computing group that has published seminal research regarding blockchain technology. A recent journal called the Ledger Journal has recently published its first issue of research papers. It is available at `http://www.ledgerjournal.org/ojs/index.php/ledger`. There are now teams and departments dedicated to blockchain research and development in various academic and commercial institutes. Although the above-mentioned initiatives are not an exhaustive list by any stretch of imagination, it is still a solid indication that this is a subject of extreme interest for researchers, and more research and development is expected to be seen in 2017 and beyond. Another organization called **The Initiative for CryptoCurrencies and Contracts (IC3)**, is also conducting research in smart contract and blockchain technologies. IC3 aims to address performance, confidentiality, and safety issues in blockchains and smart contracts and runs multiple projects to address these issues. More information about projects running in IC3 is available online at `http://www.initc3.org/`.

Standardization

Blockchain technology is not yet mature enough to be able to readily integrate with existing systems. Even, as the current technology stands, two blockchain networks cannot easily talk to each other. Standardization will help to improve interoperability, adoptability, and integration aspects of blockchain technology. Some attempts have been made recently to address this and the most notable out of these attempts is the establishment of ISO/TC 307, which is a technical committee with the scope of standardizing blockchain and distributed ledger technology. The aim of the committee revolves around increasing interoperability and data interchange between users, applications, and systems. On the other hand, the recent creation of consortia and open source collaborative efforts such as R3 and Hyperledger has helped with standardization of this technology by sharing ideas, tools, and code with other participants. R3 works with a consortium of more than 80 banks that all have similar goals, which in a way results in standardization. Hyperledger, on the other hand, has a reference architecture that can be used to build blockchain systems and is supported by the Linux foundation and many other participants from the industry. Another example is the chain open standard, which is a protocol developed for financial networks. The chain OS1 standard is already available, which was built in collaboration with major financial institutions around the world. This standard allows faster settlement of transactions and immediate peer-to-peer transaction routing. It aims to address regulatory, security, and privacy requirements in blockchain technologies. OS1 also provides a framework for smart contract development and allows the participant to meet AML and KYC requirements easily.

Smart contract standardization efforts have also started with a seminal paper authored by *Lee* and others, which formally defines the smart contract templates and presents a vision for future research and necessities in smart contract related research and development. This paper is available at `https://arxiv.org/abs/1608.00771v2`. Moreover, some discussion on this topic has been carried out in `Chapter 12`, *Scalability and Other Challenges* and `Chapter 6`, *Smart Contracts*.

All of the above-mentioned efforts are a clear indication that very soon, standards will emerge in the industry that will further make adoption of blockchain technology easier and quicker. Standards will also result in exponential growth of the blockchain industry because availability of standards will eliminate hurdles such as interoperability.

Enhancements

Various enhancements and suggestions to further develop existing blockchains have been made over the last few years. Most of these suggestions have been made in response to security vulnerabilities and to address inherent limitations in blockchain technology. There are certain limitations in blockchain technology, such as scalability, privacy, and interoperability, that are required to be addressed before it can become mainstream like any other technology. Recently, there have been tremendous efforts made toward addressing scalability issues in blockchain technology, which have been discussed in the previous chapter. Also blockchain-specific improvement proposals such as **BIPs (bitcoin improvement proposals)** and **EIPs (Ethereum improvement proposals)** are being made regularly by developers to address various concerns in these systems. Some recent and notable improvement proposals for both of these chains will be discussed later in the chapter. Moreover, recent advancements such as state channels are examples that blockchain technology is improving rapidly and very soon will evolve as a mature and more practical technology.

Real-world implementations

Many proofs of concept have been developed in recent years, especially in 2016, using blockchain technology. A few application-specific implementations emerged, such as everledger for diamond tracking and filament for **Internet of Things (IoT)**, but are still lacking in various areas. Concrete, real-life, end-to-end implementations are not available yet, especially in the finance industry. This seems not too far now as many proofs of concept have already been developed and proved to work; the next stage is to implement these in real-life scenarios. For example, recently, a group of seven banks agreed to build a **Digital Trade Chain (DTC)** that will simplify the trade finance process.

Consortia

2016 has been seen as a year when consortia and shared open source efforts started. This trend is expected to grow and more and more consortia, committees, and open source efforts will emerge soon. A prime example is R3,which has developed Corda with a consortium of the world's largest financial organizations.

Answers to challenges

Already, due to intense research effort and interest from the community in blockchain technology, answers to various challenges have started to emerge. For example, the concept of state channels has been developed as a response to scalability and privacy issues on the blockchain. Using state channels, the bitcoin lightning network and Ethereum's Raiden are already almost ready for implementation. Moreover, various blockchain solutions emerged, such as Kadena, that directly addressed the confidentiality issues in blockchains. Other concepts such as Zcash, Coinjoin, and confidential transactions have also been developed and were discussed in previous chapters. This trend will also continue to grow in years to come and even if almost all fundamental challenges are addressed in blockchain technology, further enhancement and optimization will never stop.

Convergence

Convergence of other technologies with blockchains brings about major benefits. At their core, blockchains provide resilience, security, and transparency, which, when combined with other technologies, results in a very powerful technology that complement each other. For example, the IoT can gain major benefits when implemented via blockchains, such as integrity, decentralization, and scalability. **Artificial intelligence (AI)** is expected to gain benefits from blockchain technology, and in fact, within blockchain technology, AI can be implemented in the form of **Autonomous Agents (AAs)**. More examples and the above-mentioned converging technologies will be discussed in detail in later sections in the chapter.

Education of blockchain technology

Whilst blockchain technology has spurred a great interest among technologists, developers, and scientists throughout almost every industry around the world, there is a lack of formal learning resources and educational material. As this is a new technology, various courses are now being offered by various reputed institutions such as Princeton University that introduce the technology to anyone who wants to learn about this technology. For example, Princeton University has started a cryptocurrency and digital currencies course that is delivered online and is quite popular. Many private organizations are also offering similar online and classroom training courses. More efforts like this will be seen in the near future due to the popularity and acceptance of blockchain technology.

Employment

There is a recent trend emerging in the job market whereby recruiters are now looking for blockchain experts and developers who can program for blockchains. This is especially relevant to the financial industry and recently many start-ups and large organizations have started to hire blockchain specialists. This trend is of course expected to grow as the technology gains more acceptance and maturity. There is also concern about the lack of blockchain developers, which surely will be addressed as the technology progresses and more and more developers either gain experience on a self-learning basis or gain formal training from some training providers.

Crypto-economics

New fields of research are emerging with blockchains, most notably, crypto-economics, which is the study of protocols governing the decentralized digital economy. With the advent of blockchains and cryptocurrencies, research in this area has also grown. Crypto-economics has been defined as a combination of mathematics, cryptography, economics, and game theory by *Vitalik Buterin*.

Research in cryptography

Even though cryptography was an area of keen interest and research for many decades before bitcoin invention, blockchain technology has resulted in renewed interest in this field. With the advent of blockchains and related technologies, there is a significant increase in the interest in cryptography also. Especially in the area of financial cryptography, new research is being carried out and published regularly. Technologies such as zero knowledge proofs, fully homomorphic encryption, and functional encryption are being researched for their use in blockchains. In the form of Zcash, already zero knowledge proofs have been implemented for the first time at a practical level. It can be seen that blockchains and cryptocurrencies have helped with the advancement of cryptography and especially financial cryptography.

New programming languages

There is also an increased interest in the development of programming languages for developing smart contracts. The efforts are more focused on domain-specific languages, for example, solidity for Ethereum and Pact for Kadena. This is just a start and many new languages are likely to be developed as the technology advances.

Hardware research and development

When it was realized in 2010 that current methods are not efficient for mining bitcoins, miners started shifting toward optimizing mining hardware. These initial efforts included usage of **graphical processing units (GPUs)** and then **field-programmable gate arrays (FPGAs)** were used after GPUs reached their limit. Very quickly after that, **application-specific integrated circuits (ASICs)** emerged, which increased the mining power significantly. This trend is expected to grow further as now there is more research in further optimizing ASICs by parallelizing and decreasing the die size. Moreover, GPU programming initiatives are also expected to grow because new cryptocurrencies are emerging quite regularly now and many of them make use of Proof of Work algorithms that can benefit from GPU processing capabilities. For example, recently Zcash has spurred interest in GPU mining rigs and related programming using NVidia CUDA and OpenCL. The aim is to use multiple GPUs in parallel for optimizing mining operations. Also, some research has been in the field of using trusted computing hardware such as Intel's **Software Guard extensions (SGX)** to address security issues on blockchains. Also Intel's SGX has been used in a novel consensus algorithm called **Proof of Elapsed Time (PoET)** which has been discussed in previous chapters. Another project, *the 21 bitcoin computer*, has also been developed, which serves as a platform for developers to learn bitcoin technology and easily develop applications for the bitcoin platform.

The hardware research and development trend is expected to continue and soon many more hardware scenarios will be explored.

Research in formal methods and security

With the realization of security issues and vulnerabilities in smart contract programming languages, there is now keen interest in the formal verification and testing of smart contracts before production deployments. For this, various efforts are already underway, including Why3 for Ethereum's Solidity. Hawk is another example that has been developed to allow smart contract confidentiality.

Alternatives to blockchains

As the blockchain technology advanced in recent years, researchers started to think about the possibility of creating platforms that can provide guarantees and services which a blockchain provides but without the need for a blockchain. This has resulted in development of R3's Corda, which in fact is not really a blockchain because it is not based on the concept of blocks containing transactions; instead, it is based on the concept of a state object that transverses throughout the Corda network according to the requirements and rules of the network participants representing the latest state of the network. Other examples include IOTA, which is an IoT blockchain which makes use of a **Directed Acyclic Graph (DAG)** as a distributed ledger named *Tangle*, instead of conventional blockchain with blocks. This ledger is claimed to have addressed scalability issues along with high-level security which even protects against quantum computing based attacks. It should be noted that bitcoin is also somewhat protected against quantum attacks because the quantum attack can only work on exposed public keys which are only revealed on the blockchain if both send and receive transactions are made. If the public key is not revealed, which is the case in unused addresses or the addresses that may have only used to receive bitcoins, then quantum safety can be guaranteed. In other words, using a different address for each transaction provides protection against quantum attacks. Also, in bitcoin, it is quite easy to change to another quantum signature protocol if required.

Interoperability efforts

Recent realization of limitations around interoperability of blockchains has resulted in development of systems that can work across multiple blockchains. A recent example is Qtum, which is a blockchain that is compatible with both Ethereum and bitcoin blockchains. It makes use of bitcoin's UTXO mechanism for transfer of value and an Ethereum virtual machine for smart contracts. This means that Ethereum projects can be ported onto Qtum without requiring any change.

Blockchain as a service

With the current level of maturity of cloud platforms, many companies have started to provide **Blockchain as a Service (BaaS)**. The most prominent examples are Microsoft's Azure, where Ethereum blockchain is provided as a service, and IBM's bluemix platform, that provides IBM BaaS. This trend is only expected to grow in the next few years and more companies will emerge that provide BaaS. **EgaaS (Electronic Government as a Service)** is another example which is in fact BaaS but provides application-specific blockchains for governance functions. The aim of this project is to organize and control any activity without document circulation and bureaucratic overhead.

Efforts to reduce electricity consumption

It is clearly evident from bitcoin's blockchain that the Proof of Work mechanism is very inefficient. Of course, this computation secures the bitcoin network but there is no other benefit of this computation and it wastes a lot of electrical energy. In order to reduce this waste, now there is more focus on greener options such as Proof of Stake algorithms which do not need enormous resources like bitcoin's Proof of Work algorithm. This trend is expected to grow, especially with Proof of Stake planned for Ethereum.

Improvement proposals

Two major blockchain technologies, namely bitcoin and Ethereum, have a formal mechanism of proposing improvements in the existing protocols. These are called improvement proposals, BIPs and EIPs. Both of these mechanisms have allowed participation from developers and technology enthusiasts around the world and have helped bitcoin and Ethereum evolve into a more mature and secure technology over time. In the sections below, notable improvement proposals for both blockchains are discussed.

BIPs

In this section, some of the latest BIPs will be discussed.

BIP 152

This proposal is an improvement suggestion to introduce compact blocks in the bitcoin network in order to save bandwidth. In its current state, bitcoin protocol is not bandwidth-efficient and this proposal is aiming to address that issue by allowing relaying of compact blocks between nodes. Several changes, such as new data structures and messages, are required in order to implement this proposal. Currently, this proposal is in draft state. It is available on GitHub at `https://github.com/bitcoin/bips/blob/master/bip-0152.medi awiki`.

BIP 151

This improvement proposal has been made to introduce peer-to-peer communication encryption. This proposal has been made in response to various security issues in Bitcoin protocol such as possibility of traffic analysis and manipulation. This proposal will help to thwart the attempts to identify users via source IPs and transaction contents on the bitcoin network. Several new messages to request and enable encryption among participating nodes have been proposed in the BIP. It is available at `https://github.com/bitcoin/bips /blob/master/bip-0151.mediawiki`.

BIP 150

This proposal presents a method for peer authentication. This will allow man-in-the-middle attacks to be addressed and will provide a guarantee that the peers are connecting to a legitimate node. This is available on GitHub at `https://github.com/bitcoin/bips/blob /master/bip-0150.mediawiki`.

BIP 147

This proposal has been made to address dummy stack element malleability. Signature malleability is a known issue and can be performed by any relay node by simply changing the signature associated with a transaction. This is a consensus layer level improvement proposal which will need soft fork to implement. BIP 147 is documented on GitHub at `http s://github.com/bitcoin/bips/blob/master/bip-0147.mediawiki`.

BIP 146

This improvement is made to address the signature encoding malleability issue. This requires a soft fork to be implemented. If implemented, this will resolve the signature malleability issue which is related to a fundamental limitation in the ECDSA signature encoding mechanism. This limitation is inherent in ECDSA. Secondly, due to the fact that if a signature has failed, verification script evaluation will still continue and would allow for any value to be set on the signature. This BIP is a proposal to resolve this issue. It is documented at `https://github.com/bitcoin/bips/blob/master/bip-0146.mediawiki`.

There are many other BIPs made for suggesting improvements in the Bitcoin protocol. In this section, only the five latest proposals have been introduced. There are almost 90 improvement proposals for bitcoin that have been made in recent years and this process continues.

EIPs

Ethereum has its own version of improvement proposals, called EIPs. Several of the recent EIPs are discussed as follows.

EIP 170

This improvement proposal has been made to address certain vulnerabilities that can arise from excessive usage of gas triggered by large contract code size during the preprocessing stage or when the code is read from the disk. The proposal is to limit the contract code size to 23,999 bytes. Further discussion regarding this proposal has resulted in improving this proposal further and has been accepted. This, however, has not been implemented yet.

EIP 150

This improvement proposal was made in response to denial of service attacks on the Ethereum blockchain. It has already been implemented as a hard fork since block 2463000 of the live Ethereum blockchain. This EIP addressed issues arising from transaction spam attacks, for example, repeatedly calling `EXTCODESIZE` Opcode, resulting in slowdown of the validation process of the blockchain. The EIP is to increase the gas cost of several of the opcodes to thwart denial of service attacks resulting from excessive repeated usage of these opcodes.

EIP 161

This proposal has been made to allow the removal of empty accounts from the Ethereum blockchain. This was put in place as response to a denial of service attack on the Ethereum blockchain whereby the attacker(s) created a large number of empty accounts. This was possible due to the low cost of account creation. This is called state trie clearing which will allow removal of empty accounts by making a CALL instruction to the accounts.

EIP 160

This suggestion has been made to increase EXP Opcode cost. The core idea behind this improvement proposal is to make cost of EXP operation proportional to the complexity of the operation. This proposal has helped to thwart denial of service attacks that arose from invoking computationally expensive operations.

EIP 155

This improvement proposal is made to eliminate the possibility of replaying a transaction from a different chain on the main live Ethereum blockchain. For example, if a transaction is made on the Ethereum network then it would be able to be replayed on Ethereum classic network; this EIP addresses this issue. Also, any transactions that have already been made on the test network should not be able to replay on the main live network.

All of the above-mentioned improvements have resulted in a hard fork and were implemented as a response to recent Ethereum denial of service attacks. Improvement proposals are a key mechanism to introduce new enhancement and protocol level bug fixes to Ethereum blockchain. There are about 11 improvement proposals implemented or proposed for Ethereum. All of these are documented on GitHub at `https://github.com/ethereum/EIPs/`.

Other challenges

Apart from security and privacy, discussed in the previous chapter, there are several other hurdles that should be addressed before mainstream adoption of blockchains can be realized. These include regulation, government control, immature technology, integration with existing systems, and implementation costs.

Regulation is considered one of the biggest challenges that need to be addressed. The core issue is that blockchains and especially cryptocurrencies are not recognized as a legal currency by any government. Even though, in some cases, it has been classified as money in the US and Germany, it is still far from being accepted as a normal currency. Moreover, blockchains in their current state are not recognized as a platform that can be used by financial institutions. No financial regulatory body has yet accepted it as a platform that can be authorized to be used. There are, however, various initiatives taken by regulatory authorities around the world to research and propose regulations. Bitcoin in its current state is fully unregulated, even though some attempts have been made by governments to tax the bitcoin. In the UK, under the EU VAT directive, bitcoin transactions are exempt from **Value Added Tax (VAT)** but this may change after Brexit. However, **Capital Gains Tax (CGT)** may still be applicable in some scenarios.

Some regulation attempt is expected very soon from financial regulatory authorities generally regarding blockchain technology, especially after the recent announcement by the **Financial Conduct Authority (FCA)** in the UK that it may approve some companies that are using blockchain.

It is a general concern that the blockchain technology is not really ready for production deployments. Even though the bitcoin blockchain has evolved into a solid blockchain platform and is used in production, it is not suitable for every scenario. This is especially true in the case of sensitive environments such as finance and health. However, it is likely to change very soon as ample efforts discussed previously in the chapter are being made to improve the technology and address any technical limitations such as scalability and privacy. Security is also another general concern which has been highlighted by many researchers and is especially applicable to the finance and health sectors. A recent report by the **European Union Agency for Network and Information Security (ENISA)** has highlighted distributed ledger specific concerns that should be addressed. Some concerns highlighted in the report include smart contract management, key management, anti-money-laundering, and anti-fraud tools. Also, the need for regulation, audit, control, and governance has been highlighted in the report.

Integration with existing legacy systems is also a prime concern. It is not clear how blockchains can be integrated with the existing financial systems.

Hurdles toward adoption are more or less related to regulatory, security, and interoperability. Integration with existing systems can be carried out in several ways.

Dark side

With the key attributes of censorship resistance and decentralization, blockchain technology can help to improve transparency and efficiency in many walks of life but this somewhat unregulated nature of this technology means that it can be used by criminals for illegal activities too. For example, compare a scenario where if some illegal content is published over the Internet it can be immediately shut down by approaching the concerned authorities and website service providers but this is not possible in blockchains. Once something is there on the blockchain, it is almost impossible to revert it back. This means that any inacceptable content, once published on the blockchain, cannot be removed. If the blockchain is used for distributing immoral content then there is no way for anyone to shut it down. This poses a serious challenge and it seems that some regulation and control is beneficial in this scenario, but how can a blockchain be regulated? That is another important question. It may not be prudent to create the regulatory laws first and then see if blockchain technology adapts to that because it might disrupt innovation and progress in this technology. It would be more sensible to let the blockchain technology grow first, just like the Internet and when it reaches a critical mass then governing bodies can call for applying some regulation around the implementation and usage of blockchain technology.

There are various examples where the Dark Web is used in conjunction with bitcoin to perform illegal activities. For example, *SilkRoad*, which was used to sell illegal drugs over the Internet, used bitcoin for payments and the Dark Web using onion URLs which are only visible with *Tor*. Although *SilkRoad* was shut down after months of effort by law enforcement agencies, new similar sites started to emerge. Now other alternatives are available that offer similar services; as such, generally, this type of problem still remains a big concern. Imagine that an illegal website is on IPFS and a blockchain; there is no easy way of shutting it down. It is clear that absence of control and regulation can encourage criminal activity and similar issue like *SilkRoad* will keep arising. Further development in totally anonymous transaction capabilities such as Zcash could provide another layer of protection for criminals but at the same time may be quite useful in various legitimate scenarios. It really depends that who is using the technology; anonymity can be good in many scenarios, for example in the health industry where patient records should be kept private and anonymous, but may not be appropriate if it can also be used by criminals to hide their activities.

One solution might be to introduce intelligent bots or AAs or even contracts that are programmed with regulatory logic embedded within them. They are most likely to be programmed by regulators and law enforcement agencies and *live* on the blockchain as a means to provide governance and control. For example, a blockchain could be designed in such a way that every smart contract has to go through a *controller contract* that scrutinizes the code logic and provides a regulatory mechanism to control the behavior of the smart contract. It may also be possible to get each smart contract's code to be inspected by regulatory authorities and once a smart contract code has a certain level of authenticity attached to it in the form of certificates issued by a regulator, it can be deployed on the blockchain network. This concept of binary signing is akin to the concept of already established concept of code signing where by executables are digitally signed as a means to confirm that the code is bona fide and is not malicious. This idea is more applicable in the context of semi-private or regulated blockchains, where a certain degree of control is required by a regulatory authority, for example, in finance. It means that there is some degree of trust required to be placed in a trusted third party (regulator) which may not be desirable due to deviation from the concept of full decentralization. However, to address this, the blockchain itself can be used to provide a decentralized, transparent, and secure certificate issuance and digital signing mechanism.

Blockchain research

Whilst major innovations have been made in blockchain technology in recent years, the area is still very ripe for further research. Some selected research topics are listed as follows with some information about existing challenges and state of the art. Some ideas are also presented on how to address these issues.

Smart contracts

Major progress has been made in this area in order to define the key requirements of smart contracts and development of templates. However, further research is required in the area of making smart contracts more secure and safe.

Centralization issues

Especially in relation to bitcoin mining centralization, there is a growing concern about how bitcoin can be really decentralized again.

Limitations in cryptographic functions

Cryptography used in the bitcoin blockchain is extremely secure and has stood the test of time. In other blockchains, similar security techniques are used and are also very secure. However, specific security issues such as the possibility of generation and usage of duplicate signature nonces in elliptic curve digital signature schemes (leading to private key recovery attack), collisions in Hash functions, and possibility of quantum attacks that may break the underlying cryptographic algorithms remain an interesting area of research.

Consensus Algorithms

Research in Proof of Stake algorithms or alternatives to Proof of Work is also an important area of research. This is especially relevant due to the fact the current bitcoin network's power consumption is expected to reach almost 14 gigawatts by 2020. It has also been suggested that instead of performing inefficient or single-purpose type of work as is the case with bitcoin's Proof of Work, the network power can be used to solve some mathematical or scientific problems. Also, alternatives such as Proof of Stake algorithms have already gained much traction and are due to be implemented in major blockchains, for example, Ethereum's Casper. However, so far, Proof of Work remains the best option for securing a public blockchain.

Scalability

Detailed discussion has already been carried out on scalability in the last chapter; briefly, it is sufficient to say in this section that while some progress has already been made, still there is a need for more research to enable on-chain scalability and further improve off-chain solutions such as state channels. Some initiatives like block size increase and transaction-only blockchains (without blocks) have been proposed to address scalability issues that increase the capacity of the blockchain itself instead of using side channels. Examples of *without blocks* implementation include IOTA (Tangle). It is a **Directed Acyclic Graph (DAG)** which is used to store transactions as compared to traditional blockchain solutions where a block is used to store transactions. This makes it inherently faster as compared to block-based blockchains such as bitcoin where waiting time between block generations is at least approximately 10 minutes.

Code Obfuscation

As discussed in the last chapter, code obfuscation by using indistinguishability obfuscation can be used as a means to provide confidentiality and privacy in the blockchain. However, this is still not practical and major research effort is required in order to achieve this.

List of notable projects

Following is a list of notable projects in the blockchain space that are currently in progress. In addition to these projects, there is also a myriad of start-ups and companies working in the blockchain space and offering blockchain-related products.

Zcash on Ethereum

A recent project by the Ethereum R&D team is implementation of Zcash on Ethereum. This is an interesting project whereby developers are trying to create a privacy layer for Ethereum using zk-SNARKs already used in Zcash project. With Zcash implementation on Ethereum, the aim is to create a platform that allows applications such as voting where privacy is of paramount importance. It will also allow creation of anonymous tokens on Ethereum that can be used in number of applications.

CollCo

This is a project developed by Deutsche Börse which is based the Hyperledger code base and is used for managing commercial bank cash transfers. **Collateralized Coin (CollCo)** provides a blockchain-based platform that allows real-time transfer of commercial bank money while still relying on traditional capabilities provided by Eurex Clearing CCP. This is major project that can be used to address inefficiencies in the post trade settlement processes.

Cello

As of February 2017, this is the most recent addition to Hyperledger project. The aim of this project is to provide on-demand BaaS which will make deployments and management of multiple blockchains convenient and easy for users. It is envisioned that Cello will support all future and current Hyperledger blockchains, such as Fabric and Sawtooth Lake.

Qtum

This project is based on the idea of combining capabilities of bitcoin and Ethereum blockchains. Qtum makes use of the bitcoin code base but uses Ethereum's EVM for smart contract execution. Ethereum smart contracts can run using bitcoin's **UTXO (unspent transactions**) model. It is available at `https://qtum.org/`.

Bitcoin-NG

This is another proposal for addressing scalability, throughput, and speed issues in the bitcoin blockchain. **Next Generation (NG)** protocol is based on a mechanism of leader election which verifies transactions as soon as they occur, as compared to Bitcoin's protocols, where time between blocks and block size are the key limitations in relation to scalability.

Solidus

This is a new cryptocurrency which provides solution for selfish mining while addressing scaling and performance issues. It also addresses confidentiality issues. It is based on permissionless Byzantine consensus. The protocol in its current state is comparatively complex and is an open area for research.

Hawk

This is a project that is aiming to address privacy issues of smart contracts in blockchains. It is a smart contract system that allows encryption of transactions on the blockchain. Hawk is able to generate a secure protocol for interaction with blockchains automatically without the need for manually programming the cryptographic protocol.

Town-Crier

This is a project that is aiming to provide real-world authentic feed into smart contracts. This system is based on Intel's SGX trusted hardware technology. This is a step further in Oracle design whereby smart contracts can request data from online sources while preserving confidentiality.

SETLCoin

This is a system built by *Goldman Sachs* and is filed for patent under the *Cryptographic currency for Securities settlement* application. As the name suggests, this cryptocurrency *coin* can be used for fast and efficient settlement. The technology makes use of virtual wallets to exchange assets over the network between peers and allows immediate settlement via ownership of SETLCoin.

TEEChan

This is novel idea of using **trusted execution environments (TEEs)** to provide a scalable and efficient solution for scaling the bitcoin blockchain. This is similar to the concept of payment channels whereby off-chain channels are used for faster transfer of transactions. The key attraction in this idea is that it is implementable on bitcoin blockchain without the need for any changes in the bitcoin network because it's an off-the-chain solution. There is, however, a small caveat that this solution does require trusting Intel for remote attestation (verification) as Intel's SGX CPUs are used to provide TEEs. This is not a desirable property in decentralized blockchains; however, it should be noted that the confidentiality of transactions is still preserved even if remote attestation is used as remote attester (Intel) cannot see the contents of the communication between users. This limitation makes it debatable that whether it is a fully decentralized and trustless solution or not.

Falcon

Falcon is a project that helps bitcoin to scale by providing a fast relay network for broadcasting bitcoin blocks over the network. The core idea revolves around a technique to reduce orphan blocks, thus helping with overall scalability of the bitcoin network. The technique used for this purpose has been called application-level cut-through routing.

Bletchley

This project has been introduced by Microsoft, indicating the commitment by Microsoft to blockchain technology. Bletchley allows use of Azure cloud services to build blockchains in a user-friendly manner. A major concept introduced by Bletchley is called *cryptlets*, which can be thought of as an advanced version of Oracles that reside outside the blockchain and can be called by smart contracts using secure channels. These can be written in any language and execute within a secure container.

There are two types of cryptlets: utility cryptlets and contract cryptlets. The first type is used to provide basic services such as encryption and basic data fetching from external sources, whereas the latter is a more intelligent version that is created automatically when a smart contract is created on the chain and resides off the chain but still linked to the on-chain contract. Due to this off-chain existence, there is no need to execute the contract cryptlets on all nodes of the blockchain network, therefore this approach results in increased performance of the blockchain.

Casper

This is the Proof of Stake algorithm for Ethereum in development. Major research has already been conducted in this area and is expected to be implemented in 2017. The nodes become bonded validators in a Casper-based Ethereum network and are required to pay a security deposit in order for them to be able to propose new blocks.

Metropolis

This is the next release of Ethereum for which a lot of work has already been completed. A hard fork will be required to implement this release. A series of EIPs have been released which include all major improvements for this release. Improvements include moving the signature verification and nonce logic into smart contracts, which will provide more flexibility to the developers with regards to choice of security schemes. Another improvement is related to block hash and state root changes which result in protocol simplification and allow parallel transaction processing. Other proposals include big integer support for cryptographic functions (elliptic curve cryptography). All the above improvements, along with various others, are covered under EIP86, EIP98, EIP96, EIP100, EIP101, EIP116, EIP195, EIP140, and EIP 141. There is no release date yet and it's not clear whether all EIPs will be implemented in the new release; however, the main aim of this release is protocol simplification, privacy, and flexibility for developers.

Miscellaneous Tools

Some tools that have not been discussed previously are listed below and introduced briefly in order to make readers aware of the myriad of development options available for blockchains. This list includes platforms, utilities, and tools that can be used for blockchain development.

Solidity extension for Microsoft Visual studio

This extension provides Intellisense, auto completion, and templates for decentralized apps, and works within the familiar Visual Studio IDE, making it easier for developers to familiarize themselves with Ethereum development.

MetaMask

This is a DAPP browser that is similar to Mist from a DAPP browsing point of view but allows users to run Ethereum decentralized applications within the browser without the requirement of running a full Ethereum node. This is available from `https://metamask.io /` and can be installed as a Chrome plugin.

Stratis

This is a blockchain development platform that allows creation of custom private blockchains and works in conjunction with the main Stratis blockchain (Stratis chain) for security reasons. It allows provisioning of major blockchains such as bitcoin, Ethereum, and Lisk easy. Also, it allows development using C# .Net technologies. It is also available via Microsoft Azure as BaaS. This is available at `https://stratisplatform.com/`.

Embark

This is a development framework for Ethereum which allows similar functionality to truffle, discussed in previous chapters. It allows automatic deployment of smart contracts, easier integration with JavaScript, and, especially, easier integration with IPFS. This is very feature-rich framework and many more functionalities are available. It can be installed via npm. This framework is available at GitHub: `https://github.com/iurimatias/embark-fr amework`.

DAPPLE

This is another framework for Ethereum that allows easier development and deployment of smart contracts by taking care of more complex tasks. It can be used for package management, contract building, and deployment scripting. This is also available via npm. It is also available via GitHub at `https://github.com/nexusdev/dapple`.

Meteor

This is a full-stack development framework for single-page applications. It can be used for Ethereum DAPP development. There is a development environment available in meteor and it allows easier and manageable development of complex DAPPs. It is available at `http s://www.meteor.com/` and Ethereum-specific DAPP building information is available at `ht tps://github.com/ethereum/wiki/wiki/Dapp-using-Meteor`.

uPort

This platform is built on Ethereum and provides a decentralized identity management system. This allows users to have full control over their identity and personal information. This is based on the idea of reputation systems enables users to attest each other and build trust. This is available at `https://www.uport.me/`.

INFURA

This project aims to provide enterprise-level Ethereum and IPFS nodes. INFURA consists of Ethereum nodes, IPFS nodes, and a service layer named Ferryman which provides routing and load balancing services.

Convergence with other industries

Convergence of blockchain with IoT has been discussed at length in the last chapter. Briefly, it can be said that due to the authenticity, integrity, privacy, and shared nature of blockchains, IoT networks will benefit greatly from blockchain technology. This can be realized in the form of an IoT network that runs on a blockchain and makes use of a decentralized mesh network for communication in order to facilitate **machine-to-machine (M2M)** communication in real time. All this data which is generated as a result of M2M communication can be used in the machine learning process to augment the functionality of Artificially Intelligent DAOs or simple AAs. AAs can act as *agents* in a **Distributed Artificial Intelligence (DAI)** environment provided by a blockchain and can learn over time using machine learning processes.

AI is a field of computer science that endeavors to build intelligent agents that can make rational decisions based on the scenarios and environment that they observe around them. Machine learning plays a vital role in AI by making use of raw data as a learning resource. A key requirement in AI-based systems is the availability of authentic data that can be used for machine learning and model building. The explosion of data coming out IoT devices, smartphone's, and other data acquisition means that AI and machine learning is becoming more and more powerful. There is, however, a requirement of authenticity of data. Once consumers, producers, and other entities are on a blockchain, the data that is generated as a result of interaction between these entities can be readily used as an input to machine learning engines with a guarantee of authenticity. This is where AI converges with blockchains. It could be argued that if an IoT device is hacked, it can send malformed data to the blockchain. This issue is mitigated because an IoT device is part of the blockchain (as a node) and has all security properties applied to it as a normal node in the blockchain network. These properties include incentivization of good behavior, rejection of malformed transactions, and strict verification of transactions and various other checks that are part of blockchain protocol. Therefore, even if an IoT device is somehow hacked, it would be treated as a Byzantine node by the blockchain network and would not cause any adverse impact on the network.

Moreover, the possibility of combining intelligent Oracles, intelligent smart contracts, and AAs will give rise to **Artificially Intelligent Decentralized Autonomous Organizations (AIDAOs)** that can act on behalf of humans to run entire organizations on their own. This is another side of AI that can become norm in the future. However, more research is required in order to realize this vision.

Also, convergence of blockchain technology with other fields such as 3D printing, virtual reality, augmented reality, and the gaming industry is also envisaged. For example, in a multiplayer online game, blockchain's decentralized approach allows for more transparency and can ensure that no central authority is gaining unfair advantage by manipulating the game rules. All these topics are active areas of research currently and more interest and development is expected in these areas in the near future.

Future

The year 2017 is predicted to be the year when blockchain technology is implemented in real-world production environments and move from the Proof of concept and theoretical stage of previous years. There are few careful predictions being made in the section that are based on the current advancement and speed of progress in the concerned field. All of these predictions are likely to come true between the years 2020 and 2050:

- The IoT will run on multiple blockchains and will give rise to an M2M economy.
- Medical records will be shared securely while preserving the privacy of patients between various private blockchains run by consortia of health providers. It may well be a single private blockchain shared among all service providers.
- Elections will be held via decentralized web applications with a backend of blockchains in a transparent and secure manner.
- Financial institutions will be running many private blockchains to share data between participants and for internal processes.
- Financial institutions will be making use of semi-private blockchains that will provide identity information for anti-money-laundering and know-your-customer functions and will be shared between many or all of the financial institutions around the world.
- Immigration and border control related activities will be recorded on the blockchain and passport control will be conducted via a blockchain shared between all ports of entries and border agencies around the world.
- Research in cryptography and distributed systems will reach new heights and universities and educational establishment will be providing dedicated courses on crypto-economics, cryptocurrencies, and blockchains.
- Artificially Intelligent DAOs (Machina Economicus) will prevail on blockchains that will make rational decisions on behalf of humans.
- A publicly available regulated blockchain will be used on day-to-day basis by citizens to perform their day-to-day activities.
- BaaS will be provided as standard to anyone who wishes to run their business or day-to-day transactions on a blockchain. In fact, it could be envisaged that just like the Internet, blockchains will seamlessly integrate into our daily lives and people will be using them without knowing much about the underlying technology and infrastructure.
- Blockchains will be normally used to provide **DRM (digital rights management)** services for arts and media and can be used to deliver content to the consumers, enabling direct communication between consumer and the producer. This will eliminate the need for any central party to govern the licensing and rights managing of valuable goods.
- Existing cryptocurrencies such as bitcoin will continue to grow in value and with the availability of state channels and scalability efforts, this trend is only expected to grow.
- Cryptocurrency investment will greatly increase and a new crypto-economic society will emerge.
- Bitcoin value will reach tens of thousands of dollars per coin.

- Digital identities will be routinely managed on the blockchain and different government functions such as voting, taxation, and funds disbursement will be conducted via blockchain-enabled platforms.
- Financial institutions and clearing houses will start to introduce blockchain-based solutions for their customers in late 2017 or early 2018.

Summary

Blockchains are going to change the world. The revolution has already started and it is only expected to grow at an exponential scale. This chapter has explored various projects and the current state of blockchain technology. First, a few trends were discussed that are expected to continue as the technology progresses further. There is deep research interest in blockchain technology by many researchers and organizations around the world and some research topics have also been introduced in this chapter. Furthermore, convergence with other fields such as the IoT and AI has also been discussed. Finally, some predictions regarding the growth of blockchain technology have been made. Most of these predictions are likely to come true within the next decade or so, while some may take a longer time. Blockchain technology has the potential to change the world and a few positive signs have already been seen in the form of successful Proof of concept implementations and a growing number of enthusiasts and developers taking interest in this technology. Very soon, blockchains will be intertwined with our lives just as the Internet is now. This chapter is just a modest overview of the vast and tremendous potential of blockchains, and in the near future, exponential growth in this technology is expected.

Index

Made in the USA
San Bernardino, CA
25 July 2017